FOR

# DUMMIES®

**The fun and easy way™ to travel!**

P9-AQY-068

## U.S.A.

### Also available:

America's National Parks For Dummies

Arizona For Dummies

Boston For Dummies

California For Dummies

Chicago For Dummies

Florida For Dummies

Los Angeles & Disneyland For Dummies

New Mexico For Dummies

New Orleans For Dummies

New York City For Dummies

San Francisco For Dummies

Seattle For Dummies

Washington, D.C. For Dummies

RV Vacations For Dummies

Walt Disney World & Orlando For Dummies

## EUROPE

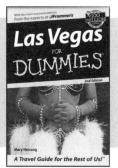

### Also available:

England For Dummies

Europe For Dummies

Ireland For Dummies

London For Dummies

Paris For Dummies

Scotland For Dummies

Spain For Dummies

## OTHER DESTINATIONS

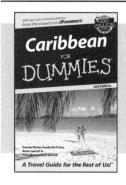
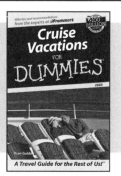

### Also available:

Bahamas For Dummies

Honeymoon Vacations For Dummies

Mexico's Beach Resorts For Dummies

Vancouver & Victoria For Dummies

**Available wherever books are sold.**

**Go to www.dummies.com or call 1-877-762-2974 to order direct.**

WILEY

# Scotland For Dummies,®
# 2nd Edition

Cheat Sheet

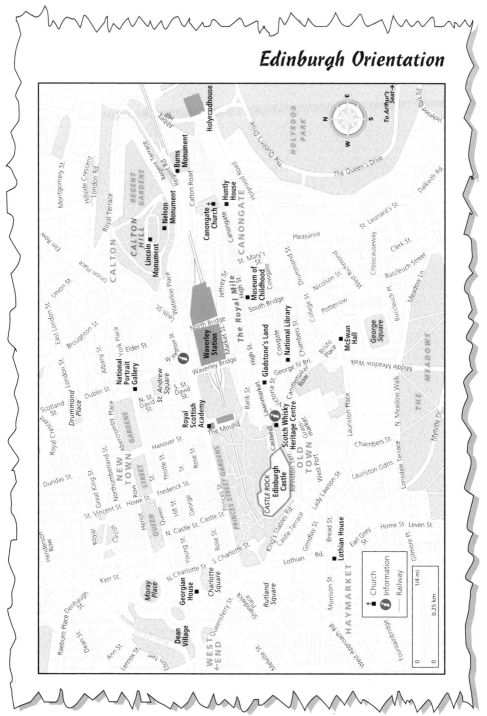

## Edinburgh Orientation

**For Dummies: Bestselling Book Series for Beginners**

# Scotland For Dummies, 2nd Edition

## Glasgow Orientation

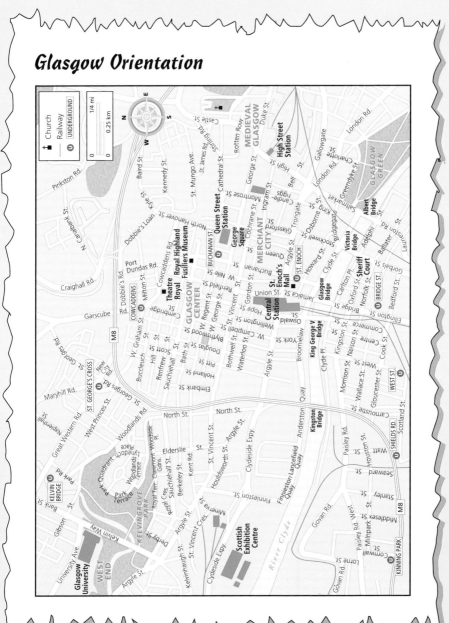

Wiley, the Wiley Publishing logo, For Dummies, the Dummies Man logo, the For Dummies Bestselling Book Series logo and all related trade dress are trademarks or registered trademarks of Wiley Publishing, Inc. All other trademarks are property of their respective owners.

Copyright © 2003 Wiley Publishing, Inc.
All rights reserved.

Item 5477-8.

For more information about Wiley Publishing,
call 1-800-762-2974.

## For Dummies: Bestselling Book Series for Beginners

# Scotland

## FOR

# DUMMIES®

## 2ND EDITION

**by David G. Allan**

**WILEY**

Wiley Publishing, Inc.

**Scotland For Dummies, 2nd Edition**

Published by
**Wiley Publishing, Inc.**
909 Third Avenue
New York, NY 10022
www.wiley.com

Copyright © 2003 by Wiley Publishing, Inc., Indianapolis, Indiana

Published simultaneously in Canada

No part of this publication may be reproduced, stored in a retrieval system, or transmitted in any form or by any means, electronic, mechanical, photocopying, recording, scanning, or otherwise, except as permitted under Sections 107 or 108 of the 1976 United States Copyright Act, without either the prior written permission of the Publisher, or authorization through payment of the appropriate per-copy fee to the Copyright Clearance Center, 222 Rosewood Drive, Danvers, MA 01923, 978-750-8400, fax 978-646-8700. Requests to the Publisher for permission should be addressed to the Legal Department, Wiley Publishing, Inc., 10475 Crosspoint Blvd., Indianapolis, IN 46256, 317-572-3447, fax 317-572-4447, or e-mail permcoordinator@wiley.com

**Trademarks:** Wiley, the Wiley Publishing logo, For Dummies, the Dummies Man logo, A Reference for the Rest of Us!, The Dummies Way, Dummies Daily, The Fun and Easy Way, Dummies.com and related trade dress are trademarks or registered trademarks of Wiley Publishing, Inc., in the United States and other countries, and may not be used without written permission. Frommer's is a trademark or registered trademark of Arthur Frommer. Used under license. All other trademarks are the property of their respective owners. Wiley Publishing, Inc., is not associated with any product or vendor mentioned in this book.

LIMIT OF LIABILITY/DISCLAIMER OF WARRANTY: WHILE THE PUBLISHER AND AUTHOR HAVE USED THEIR BEST EFFORTS IN PREPARING THIS BOOK, THEY MAKE NO REPRESENTATIONS OR WARRANTIES WITH RESPECT TO THE ACCURACY OR COMPLETENESS OF THE CONTENTS OF THIS BOOK AND SPECIFICALLY DISCLAIM ANY IMPLIED WARRANTIES OF MERCHANTABILITY OR FITNESS FOR A PARTICULAR PURPOSE. NO WARRANTY MAY BE CREATED OR EXTENDED BY SALES REPRESENTATIVES OR WRITTEN SALES MATERIALS. THE ADVICE AND STRATEGIES CONTAINED HEREIN MAY NOT BE SUITABLE FOR YOUR SITUATION. YOU SHOULD CONSULT WITH A PROFESSIONAL WHERE APPROPRIATE. NEITHER THE PUBLISHER NOR AUTHOR SHALL BE LIABLE FOR ANY LOSS OF PROFIT OR ANY OTHER COMMERCIAL DAMAGES, INCLUDING BUT NOT LIMITED TO SPECIAL, INCIDENTAL, CONSEQUENTIAL, OR OTHER DAMAGES. PLEASE BE ADVISED THAT TRAVEL INFORMATION IS SUBJECT TO CHANGE AT ANY TIME AND THIS IS ESPECIALLY TRUE OF PRICES. WE THEREFORE SUGGEST THAT YOU WRITE OR CALL AHEAD FOR CONFIRMATION WHEN MAKING YOUR TRAVEL PLANS. THE AUTHORS, EDITORS, AND PUBLISHER CANNOT BE HELD RESPONSIBLE FOR THE EXPERIENCES OF READERS WHILE TRAVELING. YOUR SAFETY IS IMPORTANT TO US, HOWEVER, SO WE ENCOURAGE YOU TO STAY ALERT AND BE AWARE OF YOUR SURROUNDINGS. KEEP A CLOSE EYE ON CAMERAS, PURSES, AND WALLETS, ALL FAVORITE TARGETS OF THIEVES AND PICKPOCKETS.

For general information on our other products and services or to obtain technical support, please contact our Customer Care Department within the U.S. at 800-762-2974, outside the U.S. at 317-572-3993, or fax 317-572-4002.

Wiley also publishes its books in a variety of electronic formats. Some content that appears in print may not be available in electronic books.

Library of Congress Cataloging-in-Publication Data:

Library of Congress Control Number: 2003101838

ISBN: 0-7645-5477-8

ISSN: 1531-7579

Manufactured in the United States of America

10  9  8  7  6  5  4  3  2  1

**WILEY**    is a trademark of Wiley Publishing, Inc.

# About the Author

**David G. Allan** has taken the wanderlust plunge into a one-year trip around the world, from Mongolia to Morocco — including, of course, Scotland. He is also the author of *Ireland For Dummies,* 2nd Edition.

# Dedication

This book is dedicated to Scotland and other countries wrestling with their independence in a post-imperialist world.

# Author's Acknowledgments

I would like to thank my fiancée, Kate Rope, who helped with this update and is the world's best travel companion, and her family, Bill, Priscilla, and brother Robert, who joined me and contributed their insights during the updating of this book. Thanks to Fiona Parrott, my Scottish *consigliere,* and Collin Campbell. The contribution by the excellent editorial team at Frommer's, especially Christine Ryan and Marie Morris, was more than a writer could ask for. And a final thanks to the Scottish Tourist Board, which assisted me greatly while I was in the country.

# Publisher's Acknowledgments

We're proud of this book; please send us your comments through our Dummies online registration form located at www.dummies.com/register/.

Some of the people who helped bring this book to market include the following:

## Editorial

**Editors:** Tere Drenth, Marie Morris, Christine Ryan

**Cartographer:** Roberta Stockwell

**Editorial Manager:** Michelle Hacker

**Editorial Assistant:** Elizabeth Rea

**Senior Photo Editor:** Richard Fox

**Cover Photos:** The Stock Market, © David Ball (front); Tony Stone Images © John Darling (back)

**Cartoons:** Rich Tennant, www.the5thwave.com

## Production

**Project Coordinator:** Erin Smith

**Layout and Graphics:** Seth Conley, Sean Decker, Carrie Foster, Stephanie D. Jumper, Shelley Norris

**Proofreaders:** John Greenough, Andy Hollandbeck, Angel Perez, Charles Spencer TECHBOOKS Production Services

**Indexer:** TECHBOOKS Production Services

---

### Publishing and Editorial for Consumer Dummies

**Diane Graves Steele,** Vice President and Publisher, Consumer Dummies

**Joyce Pepple,** Acquisitions Director, Consumer Dummies

**Kristin A. Cocks,** Product Development Director, Consumer Dummies

**Michael Spring,** Vice President and Publisher, Travel

**Brice Gosnell,** Publishing Director, Travel

**Suzanne Jannetta,** Editorial Director, Travel

### Publishing for Technology Dummies

**Andy Cummings,** Vice President and Publisher, Dummies Technology/General User

### Composition Services

**Gerry Fahey,** Vice President of Production Services

**Debbie Stailey,** Director of Composition Services

# Contents at a Glance

# Maps at a Glance

# Table of Contents

# Introduction

*1*f you reached for *Scotland For Dummies,* 2nd Edition, because it stood out from the pack of Scotland guidebooks, or just because it seemed different, pat yourself on the back — you have smart instincts.

This guide was conceived as a departure from conventional travel guidebooks, many of which emphasize quantity over quality and then layer every page with exhaustive detail. Rather than just throwing out dizzying reams of information for you to sift through until you're too tired to tell Edinburgh from Inverness, *Scotland For Dummies,* 2nd Edition, cuts the wheat from the chaff. I've done the legwork for you, and I want you to benefit from my expertise. Just think of me as that good buddy who returns from a Scotland vacation with the straight poop on what to see and what to pass on.

I know that you work hard to set aside a few precious weeks of vacation time, and money doesn't grow on trees. No matter how much you have, you don't want to waste it. So I'm not afraid to take a stand to help you decide exactly what to include in your Scotland vacation — and, even more importantly, what to bypass.

I walk you through the whole process of putting together your perfect trip, from the ins and outs of laying out a manageable itinerary to choosing the right places to stay to how much time to allot for which attractions and activities. No one right answer exists for everybody, of course. The goal here is to give you the tools you need — *just* what you need, not too much and not too little — to really tell what works for you and what doesn't. I know your time is valuable, so I strive to get right to the point. *Scotland For Dummies,* 2nd Edition, gives you the clearest picture of what you need to know, what choices you have to make, and what your options are, so that you can make informed decisions easily and efficiently.

## About This Book

The honest truth is that some parts of Scotland are far more worthy of your valuable time and hard-earned money than others are. That's why I focus not on covering Scotland comprehensively, but on covering the *best* that Scotland has to offer — so that you have a research tool in hand that answers all of your questions about the country's most terrific destinations, places such as Loch Ness and the Highlands.

Perhaps this is your first Scotland vacation — or maybe you haven't been to Scotland in ages, or you haven't visited a particular region. Maybe you don't want to dedicate your life to trip planning, wasting a whole vacation's worth of time wading through hundreds of dense pages and having to read between the lines — as so many conventional guidebooks require — to try to figure out what the authors actually like and what they felt they had to include. *Scotland For Dummies,* 2nd Edition, directs you to all the worthiest destinations in a lively, straightforward manner with a minimum of fuss and muss. You're not going to have to wade through a big chapter on Arran, say, to get to the Hebridean Islands recommendations you really want. In this book, the best of Scotland awaits you.

# Conventions Used in This Book

I list the hotels and restaurants in this book alphabetically. Attractions generally appear in order of preference, unless otherwise noted. I use the following abbreviations for credit cards in the hotel and restaurant reviews:

**AE** (American Express)

**DC** (Diners Club)

**MC** (MasterCard)

**V** (Visa)

Cost is probably a factor for you when choosing hotels and restaurants. To cut out the hassle of closely reading to find out exact prices, I denote the relative cost of things with dollar signs. The actual prices are there, too, but this way a quick glance lets you know approximately how much something will cost. My scale for restaurants and accommodations ranges from one dollar sign ($) to four ($$$$). Following are two scales that indicate how much the dollar signs mean.

## Dining

| | |
|---|---|
| **$** | £5 ($7.25) or less |
| **$$** | £5–£10 ($7.25–$14.50) |
| **$$$** | £10–£17 ($14.50–$24.65) |
| **$$$$** | £17 ($24.65) or more |

## Accommodations

| | |
|---|---|
| **$** | £50 ($72.50) or less, double |
| **$$** | £50–£100 ($72.50–$145), double |
| **$$$** | £100–£200 ($145–$290), double |
| **$$$$** | £200 ($290) or more, double |

# Foolish Assumptions

As I wrote this book, I made the following assumptions about you and what your needs may be as a traveler:

- ✔ You may be an inexperienced traveler looking for guidance when determining whether to take a trip to Scotland and how to plan for it.

- ✔ You may be an experienced traveler who hasn't had much time to explore Scotland and who wants expert advice when you finally do get a chance to enjoy it.

- ✔ You're not looking for a book that provides all the information available about Scotland or that lists every hotel, restaurant, or attraction. Instead, you're looking for a book that focuses on the places that will give you the best experiences in Scotland.

If you fit any of these criteria, then *Scotland For Dummies,* 2nd Edition, gives you the information you're looking for!

# How This Book Is Organized

*Scotland For Dummies,* 2nd Edition, consists of five parts. The chapters within each part cover specific travel topics or regions in detail. You can read each chapter or part without reading the one that came before it — no need to read about the Orkney Islands if you're staying on the mainland, after all. Following are brief descriptions of what you can find in each part.

## Part 1: Getting Started

This part introduces you to the best of Scotland and touches on every-thing you want to consider before actually getting down to the nitty-gritty of trip planning, including the following:

- ✔ When to go (and when you may want to stay home)

- ✔ Tips on planning your itinerary, plus actual time-tested itineraries that you can use as blueprints for your own vacation

- ✔ How much you can expect your trip to cost, with tips on how to save money

- ✔ Special considerations for families, seniors, travelers with disabilities, students, vegetarians, and gay and lesbian travelers

# Part II: Ironing Out the Details

This part is where I get down to the nuts and bolts of travel planning, including the following helpful information:

- ✔ Planes, trains, and automobiles: How to get to Scotland and how to get around Scotland after you arrive
- ✔ The pros and cons of working with a travel agent versus planning on your own
- ✔ The advantages of all-inclusive travel packages
- ✔ Getting ready to go, from the pluses and minuses of buying travel insurance to making advance dinner reservations to knowing what to pack

# Part III: Edinburgh and Glasgow

If you think of this book as a sandwich, this part and Part IV are the meat, forming the bulk of the book and covering the destinations you want to visit. Each chapter offers specific details and recommendations you need for a given destination, including the following:

- ✔ How much time you need
- ✔ How to get there
- ✔ Where to stay
- ✔ Where to eat
- ✔ What to do after you arrive

Part III covers the country's two major cities, **Edinburgh** and **Glasgow.** Along with Loch Ness (which is discussed in Chapter 16), these cities are the most popular destinations in Scotland. They have the most options for dining, drinking, and accommodations, as well as the most attractions in a concentrated area. I cover just about everything you want to see, from Edinburgh Castle and the Royal Mile to the art galleries and museums of Glasgow.

# Part IV: The Major Regions

This part covers the major regions of Scotland. You have the southern **Borders** region, the eastern coast and the **Kingdom of Fife,** the western **Argyll Region** and the **Hebridean Islands,** and, of course, the legendary **Highlands.**

For a more thorough destination overview of Scotland, including a brief overview of these regions, flip to Chapter 1.

## Part V: The Part of Tens

Every *For Dummies* book has a Part of Tens. If Parts III and IV are the meat of the sandwich, think of these fun chapters, each their own top ten list, as dessert. These quick and handy lists highlight the best golf courses, distilleries, pubs, historic spots, and more.

## Quick Concierge Appendix

This appendix is where I list the details you need for your trip, all in one, handy place. In the Quick Concierge, you have facts about Scotland at your fingertips — from locating local American Express offices to finding the most accurate online weather forecasts — and everything in between. You also get toll-free numbers and Web addresses for all the major airlines and car-rental agencies.

# Icons Used in This Book

You can't miss the icons (little pictures) sprinkled throughout the margins of this book. Think of them as signposts; I use them to highlight special tips, draw your attention to things you don't want to miss, and give you a heads-up on a variety of topics.

This icon gives useful advice on things to do, ways to schedule your time, and any other tips you don't want to miss.

Keep an eye out for this icon, which highlights tourist traps, rip-offs, and time-wasters.

This icon directs you to the attractions, hotels, restaurants, and activities that are especially family-friendly.

This icon draws your attention to money-saving tips and particularly great values.

# *Where to Go from Here*

This travel guide is not necessarily designed to be read from front to back, although you're certainly welcome to pore over every word. Instead, it provides detailed information on loads of topics — from getting your passport to finding the best golf courses — in an organized way. So choose your own adventure and look for the topics or destinations you want to explore by using the Table of Contents or the Index.

As you read through this book and start to formulate your Scotland vacation, remember this: The planning really is half the fun. Don't think of choosing your destinations and solidifying the details as a chore. Make the homebound part of the process a voyage of discovery, and you'll end up with an entire vacation experience that is much more rewarding and enriching — really. Happy planning!

# Part I
# Getting Started

The 5th Wave    By Rich Tennant

"It's the room next door. They suggest
you deflate your souvenir bagpipes before
trying to pack them in your luggage."

# In this part . . .

Any place with a history as storied and rich as Scotland's has much to offer the traveler. But you probably won't come just for the history; you may also come for the country's unique natural beauty, the friendliness of its people, and the old-world stirrings of the soul that Scotland inspires.

In this part, I help you plan your trip to Scotland—soup to nuts—with loads of helpful insider information and advice. I've done all the planning legwork for you, taking you through every aspect of trip preparation. Want to know the best season to visit? Are discounts available for seniors or children? What, for heaven's sake, is haggis? Look no further; the answers are here. You get a budget worksheet, suggested itineraries, money-saving tips, a glossary of common Scottish lingo, and special advice for special situations. You even get a condensed history lesson on the country through the ages. After you've finished planning your trip to Scotland, you'll be ready to enjoy the best that it has to offer.

# Chapter 1

# Discovering the Best of Scotland

## In This Chapter

▶ Finding the region of Scotland that's right for you

▶ Discovering how to eat, drink, and talk like a Scot

▶ Getting the lowdown on the links and fishing holes

▶ Brushing up on Scottish history

. . . . . . . . . . . . . . . . . . . . . . . . . . . . . . . . . . . . . . . . . . . . . . . . . .

**A**sk someone who has been to Scotland what the country is like, and you'll see a wistful, faraway look. That's the magic of a trip to Scotland. With its postcard-perfect scenery, dazzle and vitality, and one of the friendliest populations in the world, it's like a Brigadoon that never fades away. From urban chic to ancient castles, from misty hillsides of heather to legendary golf courses, Scotland is a dream destination.

Do you want to go to the Highlands? To the Hebridean Islands? To Edinburgh and Glasgow? (Answer to all: Yes!) This chapter starts with a region-by-region breakdown of the country, giving you a better idea of what these places have to offer and how long you may want to stay in each spot, given your particular interests and budget. This chapter also runs through Scottish food and drink and what you can expect and look forward to on those fronts. Interested in golf, bagpipes, and Scottish history? Well, you find primers on these important topics here, as well, giving you at least a cocktail-trivia level of knowledge that makes you sound like a Scottish expert!

## Being Everywhere You Want to Be: The Regions of Scotland

Should you fly into Edinburgh or Glasgow? Do you want to see Loch Ness or Loch Lomond? Are the Shetland Islands worth the time and trouble? In this section, I provide a quick primer on the various regions of the island so that you can make informed choices about where to spend your precious vacation time.

For more information, check out Part III, which discusses the two major cities in Scotland: Edinburgh and Glasgow. Part IV tells you all about the rest of Scotland, and the chapters in that part run more or less from south to north, starting with the southernmost region and finishing with the northernmost islands.

## Edinburgh and Glasgow

No question: A trip to Scotland without these cities on your agenda would be sorely lacking. Although only 45 minutes apart, **Edinburgh** and **Glasgow** are vastly different but equally fascinating and culturally rich. Edinburgh (pronounced *Edin*-burra) is older and boasts a striking cityscape — a castle on a hill surrounded by historic sites and tourist-friendly shops and restaurants. Glasgow (pronounced *glass*-go), traditionally a working-class industrial city, has come into its own in the last decade, evolving from a shipbuilding town into a cultural center full of dynamic architecture, dining, and nightlife.

You will most likely fly into one city or the other when you arrive, but I recommend flying into Glasgow — its central location on the island makes it a good starting point from which to drive to Edinburgh and points south or west.

---

### Glossary of place names

Picture this: You're passing through a quaint town with an even quainter name. Wonder what the name means? Use this glossary to mix and match parts of names to get their meaning.

- **ben:** mountain
- **bothy:** hut
- **brae:** hill
- **craig:** rock
- **croft:** small plot of land
- **drum:** ridge
- **dun:** hill fort
- **eilean:** island
- **firth:** estuary
- **gate:** street

- **glen:** valley
- **inche:** meadow
- **inver:** river mouth
- **kirk:** church
- **loch:** lake
- **mor:** great
- **ness:** headland
- **strath:** river valley
- **uig:** shelter
- **wynd:** street, lane

# The Borders

The southernmost region of Scotland is the **Borders,** so named because it borders northern England. I allot a relatively small section of the book (see Chapter 12) to this region. Although the region contains several excellent attractions and accommodations, it is essentially a sprawling landscape, with little in between the sights worth visiting. Home to the national poet Robert Burns and several ancient abbeys commissioned by King David I, the Borders is worth a day or two of exploring, or at least a side trip out of Glasgow.

# Argyll and the islands

The **Argyll** region (yes, like the socks) and the lower islands offer several sights worth visiting (see Chapter 13 for more). On the mainland, you can enjoy a little recreation on bonnie **Loch Lomond** or visit the prehistoric sites in the **Kilmartin** region, the oldest settled area of the country.

If you have time, you can drive the beautiful **Kintyre Peninsula** or visit one of the islands in the region, such as the **Islay,** with its whisky distilleries, or **Arran,** where many Glaswegians spend their holidays. Even if you don't have time to explore the region fully, you would be remiss to skip the entertaining coastal town of **Oban** and the pretty castle of **Inveraray** as you make your way north.

# Fife and the Central Highlands

East of Argyll are the Kingdom of **Fife** and the **Central Highlands** (discussed in more detail in Chapter 14). Close to Glasgow and Edinburgh, this compact area is good for packing in a lot of adventure without driving long distances.

Golfers come from all over the world to make the pilgrimage to the home of golf, **St. Andrews** — a great little East Coast college town that draws not just golf enthusiasts but also students and sightseers. History buffs won't want to miss the town and castle of **Stirling,** home to Robert the Bruce and the battlegrounds of William "Braveheart" Wallace. And while I'm name-dropping, the **Trossachs** area of the Central Highlands is the old stomping grounds of the legendary Rob Roy.

# Tayside and Grampian

North of Fife and east of the Highlands are the **Grampian** and **Tayside** regions (see Chapter 15), which together make up the vast northeast section of the country. From the north coast down, these adjoining regions are full of castles, distilleries, and handsome countryside.

Among the major cities in the area are the oil-made granite city of **Aberdeen,** the theater mecca of **Pitlochry,** and the royal burgh of **Perth.** A well-planned route through the region can be the best way to get from the big cities to the northern Highlands.

## West Highlands

The **West Highlands,** discussed at length in Chapter 16, are a huge tourist draw in large part because of one particularly big, dark body of water: **Loch Ness.** You may not see any monsters (outside of the cartoon and stuffed kind), but the area's castles and distilleries, as well as the unofficial capital of the Highlands, **Inverness,** make this region worth exploring. The craggy Highlands are the soul of Scotland — this is the home of tartan-wearing clans and bagpipes, after all — so after you take the obligatory snapshots of Loch Ness and wine and dine in Inverness, I recommend settling in to fully experience the beauty and heart of this region.

## Hebridean Islands

After the Highlands, you're ready for the islands. The **Hebrideans** (pronounced *heb*-ri-deez) are several large inhabited islands and many smaller ones (see Chapter 17). The **Isle of Skye** is the biggest and arguably the most beautiful (when the weather's clear). If you're going to visit only one island, make it this one — you can even drive to it. Worth the ferry trip are other islands, such as **Mull** and its little sister **Iona,** the birthplace of Christianity in Scotland. Feeling a little more adventurous? Head to the rugged outer islands of **North** and **South Uist** or farther north to the connected islands of **Lewis** and **Harris** — home of the famous tweed.

# Not ready for prime time

This book doesn't cover every part of Scotland. The northernmost area of the mainland, north of the towns of **Ullapool** and **Dornoch,** has too few attractions to justify driving into the mostly rural area. Most of the nearly 800 Scottish islands are uninhabited, and only 60 are larger than 3 square miles. As a whole, three-fourths of Scotland is unsuitable for agriculture, and the majority of the remaining land is rural and unspoiled by modern sprawl. Outside major towns, Scotland is like one large petting zoo. I don't recommend hugging the local wildlife, but expect to have close encounters with sheep and cows, which you'll see rather apathetically blocking traffic on the smaller roads. I certainly don't want to discourage you from going "off the book," but this guide is designed to give you the most bang for your buck. If you want to visit an uninhabited island or spend time in a small village not mentioned here, just visit the nearest Scottish tourist office to get all the supplemental information you need.

## Shetland and Orkney islands

The far northern islands of **Shetland** and **Orkney** are remote and rural (and they're discussed in Chapter 18). Unless you have the time and inclination, they may not be worth the trouble to visit. On the other hand, their very remoteness makes them a welcome reprieve from the tourist trail.

# Having Haddock and Haggis: Scottish Cuisine

The reputation of Scottish food as provincial and rough-edged is fast becoming a myth. In the last decade or so, the country has become home to many culinary expatriates, so your choices extend beyond meat and potatoes. But I highly recommend making an effort to try some local Scottish cuisine during your trip. It may not sound exotic, but much of it is good and hearty. Staples of the country's traditional cuisine include **fish** (usually **haddock**), **potatoes, oatcakes, porridge, turnips,** and local game, like **venison** and **Angus beef.**

Often eaten at your hotel or B&B, one traditional meal you're sure to have and enjoy is a Scottish breakfast. Expect most or all of the following: **coffee** or **tea, cereal** or **muesli, bacon** or **sausage, black pudding, grilled tomatoes and mushrooms, eggs,** and **fried bread** or **potato scones.** A feast this size can often keep your tummy full through the afternoon.

## Of mad cows and Englishmen

By now, you've heard all the talk about **mad cow disease** and may wonder whether ordering steak in Scotland is safe. According to the government, it is. The government no longer issues warnings about diseased beef, and health officials have expressed confidence that the new beef entering the country and cattle raised in the U.K. are safe for consumption.

As for **foot-and-mouth disease** (which affects animals, not people), although much of the Scottish countryside remained free of the disease during the 2001 outbreak, many rural areas and nature preserves closed to visitors. The long-term impact of foot-and-mouth disease on the visitor is uncertain. For up-to-the-minute info, visit the Web sites of the **Scottish Tourist Board** (www.visitscotland.com) or the British government's **News Co-ordination Center** (www.co-ordination. gov.uk).

# Food lingo

Here are a few common local dishes that you may run across on your travels around Scotland:

✓ **black pudding:** blood sausage

✓ **bridie:** meat and potato pie

✓ **clapshot:** mashed turnips and potatoes

✓ **cullen skink:** haddock soup

✓ **haggis:** sheep innards, oatmeal, and spices boiled in the intestines

✓ **Irn-bru:** local orange soft drink

✓ **kippers:** smoked herrings

✓ **neeps:** turnips

✓ **oatcake:** oatmeal biscuit

✓ **ploughman's lunch:** roll, cheese, and salad

✓ **sultanas:** yellow raisins

✓ **tattie:** potato

✓ **toastie:** toasted sandwich

If one food has captured the traveler's imagination, it's **haggis.** You may have heard the old yarn that haggis is a wild animal indigenous to Scotland, but don't believe it. It is a spicy mix of sheep's liver and heart, oatmeal, and spices boiled inside a sheep's paunch. Give it a try at some point during your trip, if only to tell your friends about it when you get back home. You can even get a vegetarian haggis (although purists would call that a contradiction in terms) at a good number of veggie-friendly restaurants.

You may find the cuisine as a whole to be more European than Scottish. The number of Indian, French, and Italian restaurants rivals that of places serving traditional cuisine. In fact, curry take-out shops outnumber fish-and-chips shops (called *chippers*). Throughout this book, I try to recommend both traditional choices and ethnic and European-style dining spots.

And if you're feeling really homesick, you can find American fast-food chains like Burger King and McDonald's in most major cities. Try to resist, however: I can't stress enough how eating at one of these chains makes you miss out on the experience of eating abroad. One local chain that I do recommend, especially for travelers with children, is Littlejohn's (www.littlejohns.co.uk). It operates decent family restaurants not unlike TGI Friday's in the States.

Not a lot of major differences exist between meals or services in Scotland and at home, but you may find portions to be smaller and service to be slower — and don't expect to find ice in your drink.

# Pub Crawling in Scotland

Much of the social life in Scotland centers on the local pub. It's more than a watering hole; it's a gathering place for the community, where the locals go to gossip or join in on a pickup session of music. Even if you're not a big drinker, going out for a pint of lager or a bit of whisky or even just a bite to eat at a Scottish bar or pub can be a memorable part of your trip.

## Join 'em for a pint of beer

From region to region, you'll come across many local microbrews. The most widely available Scottish beers are Tennants and McEwens, and each brand has different types of ales, from light-colored lager to dark ale.

Beers are labeled by shillings (for example, Tennants/80), and they start at 60 shillings. The higher the number, the stronger the beer. Usually a bar serves either Tennants or McEwens but not both, in the same way North American bars serve either Budweiser or Molson. The most popular stout in Scottish bars is Guinness, from neighboring Ireland, and you'll find American beers like Miller as well.

Before you visit a Scottish bar, take a lesson in pub terminology. A *heavy,* for example, is dark ale that's between *lager* (light, golden-colored) and *stout* (strong, dark, sometimes bitter-tasting). The brand of the heavy changes from bar to bar, but because each pub usually has only one to offer, you can simply order a heavy and get a similar drink every time. You have the option of ordering a pint or half-pint. And a popular expression for being nearly drunk is *half cut.*

Remember, pints of beer, especially stouts like Guinness, are commonly served with the beer spilling over the sides. This happens because the bartender spills off a large head to give you more beer than foam, so don't be upset if your pint drips on your shoes.

## *Whisky a go-go!*

Scotch, or Scottish whisky (spelled whiskey when referring to the Irish version), dates to the 1600s, when Irish monks likely introduced it. Barley is the top-produced grain in Scotland, and most of that is produced as "barley juice" — Scotch. Highlanders once drank the stuff for breakfast. Today Scotch is the country's greatest export. Scotland produces more than 2,000 brands, all but about 100 of them blended (different whiskys mixed together); the rest are more expensive single-malt whiskys.

Each of Scotland's six whisky regions has its own characteristic taste. Whisky made in the Hebridean Islands tends to have a peaty, smoky flavor caused by the water traveling through peat in the ground. In the southern region, where there is no peat, the Scotch is a much lighter, milder spirit; its easy-to-drink quality has led lowland whisky to be dubbed "Ladies Whisky" or "Beginner's Whisky." Heather, which adds spiciness, flavors the Highland whiskys. Other factors that affect the taste of whisky and create the subtle differences from one distillery to the next include the size of the still, the water, the cooking time, the kind of yeast, and the type of cask used in maturing.

When ordering whisky, ask for a *dram,* or small shot. The established way to drink the spirit is *neat;* that is, nothing added and nothing done to it. If you want to drink yours with a little water or soda, that's perfectly acceptable, too. Also, if you order a mixed drink (a vodka tonic, for example), don't be surprised if the barkeep hands you a glass with ice and liquor and a bottle of mixer. It's not out of laziness; it's just how it's done.

---

## Know your whisky terminology

A few terms to know during your visit to the local pubs:

- **angel's share:** Percentage of whisky lost in the maturing process as it evaporates and escapes the cask
- **dram:** A small shot of whisky, roughly 50 milliliters (mL) or 1.7 ounces
- **neat:** Whisky served without ice or water
- **nip:** A whisky chaser to a pint of beer
- **Scotch:** Don't call it Scotch while you're in Scotland; whisky will do

## Scotch whisky versus Irish whiskey

Irish whiskey and Scotch whisky have always been in healthy competition; the Irish taught the Scottish how to make the spirit. In 1170, British troops discovered Ireland's best-kept secret and fell in love with *uisce beatha* (pronounced *ish*-ka ba-ha and translated ever so appropriately as "the water of life"). Unable to pronounce the Gaelic, they shortened it to *fuisce* and finally to *whisky*.

In the 20th century, Ireland gained its independence from the British crown, and the countries engaged in an economic war. They stopped buying each other's products completely. With Irish whiskey out of the picture, Scotch jumped in to fill the void. Scotch also gained popularity in the States after American GIs got a taste for it during World War II.

Under Irish law, whiskey must mature in oak casks for no less than 3 years; premier distilleries mature whiskey for 5 to 12 years. Scotch, on the other hand, must be aged in Scotland for as few as 3 years. The Irish distill their whiskey three times before it's ready to drink. American whiskey is usually distilled only once, and Scotch whisky usually twice.

# Harps and Bagpipes: Enjoying Scottish Music

Traditional Scottish music is more than "Scotland the Brave" on bagpipes. The Gaelic-influenced songs and sounds of the Hebridean Islands and Highlands have been around for centuries. The harp (*clarsach*), accordion, and flute are part of the musical tradition as well. You know you're listening to real Scottish music when the lyrics are in Gaelic and your toes are tappin'. The best opportunity to hear the real deal is at a *ceilidh* (pronounced *kay*-lee), a large music and dance gathering. I include some of the bigger ones in Parts III and IV of this book.

Bagpipes are exclusively Scottish and so entrenched in the national identity that they were outlawed after the failed Jacobite uprising in 1746. The bagpipes, often carried into battle by boys too young to be soldiers, were considered weapons by the crown. They're legal today, and you can purchase a set of pipes and even play them while you're in Scotland.

# Visiting the Home of Golf

Scotland is proud to be the birthplace of this international sport. While golf may have originated in mainland Europe, Scotland gets credit for developing the official game. It's been played here for more than 500 years. With more than 400 courses, the country has more courses per capita than any other country. As the old joke goes, Scotland is one large course surrounded by a water hazard.

Scots are very nationalistic about the game, and many play it for most of their walking years, crossing all economic classes. Don't be surprised if your caddies aren't young — the average age of a golf caddy is about 50. And please, *please,* don't play a championship course if you're a beginner. There's no faster way to upset good golfers than to force them to play behind novices who create traffic jams at every hole; it's just good etiquette for newcomers to play at more public-friendly courses.

Golf comes from the Dutch game of *kolf,* played at shorter distances. The word first appeared in the Scottish language in 1457, when an act of Parliament banned it for interfering with archery practice. Mary Queen of Scots played golf, as did her son, James VI.

You can play on many public and private courses (the Great Outdoors tour in Chapter 3 gives suggestions, while Chapter 19 lists the best), but members have priority for tee times. Some courses have dress codes, so always ask before you play. On average, the fees for a public course run you £7–£10 ($10.15–$14.50); for a private course, expect to pay £12–£40 ($17.40–$58.00), with championship courses on the high end. Renting clubs will cost around £5 ($7.25) per round.

 If you plan to play a lot of golf during your trip, you can save a few dollars by getting a weekly or multi-day ticket and renting clubs from a golf shop instead of paying per round.

# Fishing: Where to Catch the Big Ones

Scotland has another world-class outdoor offering: fishing. Rivers and streams abound with trout, salmon, pike, and more. The two most popular catches are probably the **brown trout** (season runs October to March) and **salmon** (between February and October).

Unlike other countries in Europe, Scotland doesn't require a license to fish. You can buy a local permit, which is required for fishing on private land, for about £15 ($21.75) at bait and tackle shops. Local tourism offices have specific information. A great source for regional information is www.where-to-fish.com/2.html. It lists all the major fishing regions and rivers in Scotland.

## Movies to get you in the mood

Here are a few flicks you can check out to introduce yourself to the land, the people, and the brogue before you head off to bonnie ol' Scotland.

✔ *Braveheart* (1995): Mel Gibson stars as the unwilling patriot William Wallace in this Academy Award–winning film. The movie probably did more to stir nation-alistic pride among Scots than all the books ever written on the popular hero.

✔ *Highlander* (1986): This popular adventure-fantasy epic with a cult following is the tale of an immortal 16th-century Scottish warrior who battles his evil enemy through the centuries. Sean Connery has a small role as the Highlander's mentor.

✔ *Local Hero* (1983): This sweetly eclectic Scottish-produced movie about a small town in Scotland facing the big, bad oil guys has a fervent cult following.

✔ *Rob Roy* (1995): Liam Neeson stars as the strong-willed Rob Roy MacGregor, who defeats the evil British landowners in a story of honor and bravery, car-rying on the legend molded by Sir Walter Scott.

✔ *Shallow Grave* (1994): Then-unknown Ewan MacGregor (who later gained fame as young Obi Wan Kenobi in *Star Wars*) stars in this independent film about three Glasgow flatmates who come into some ill-gotten cash and try to outwit each other to keep it for themselves.

✔ *Trainspotting* (1996): From one of the most popular books by a Scottish author (Irvine Welsh), *Trainspotting,* which also stars Ewan MacGregor, is the gritty and often hilarious account of a group of unforgettable drug-addled characters in Edinburgh in the 1980s.

✔ *Whisky Galore* (1949): Residents of a small Scottish isle get an intoxicating windfall when a ship carrying 50,000 cases of whisky crashes off their coast.

To get specific information before you leave concerning the type of fishing you're interested in, contact one of the following organizations: **Scottish Federation of Sea Anglers** (☎ **0131-317-7192;** www.sfsa. freeserve.co.uk), the **Scottish National Anglers Association** (☎ **0131-339-8808;** www.sana.org.uk), **Scottish Federation for Coarse Angling** (☎ **01592-64-2242;** www.sfca.co.uk), or **Salmon and Trout Association** (☎ **0131-225-241;** www.salmon-trout.org).

The one major fishing tour company, **Fishing Scotland,** leads fly, spin, and bait fishing excursions for individuals, small groups, families, and kids. It covers instruction, coaching, all fishing tackle, and *wellie boots* (long rubber shoes that keep you dry while you stand in the stream). The Web site is also a fly-fishing encyclopedia. For information, contact Roy Bridge, Invernesshire, Scotland PH31 4AG (☎ **01397-712-812;** www.Fishing-Scotland.co.uk).

# Braving the Brogue: Decoding Scottish English

Yes, English is spoken in Scotland, but between the occasional odd expression and the thick brogue, it may sound like a foreign language. Often, especially in a loud bar, I've found myself nodding along to a discussion I simply didn't understand.

To compound the confusion, the country has several regional accents. Unless you have a good ear or have spent a lot of time traveling the country, you probably won't detect the difference between a Hebridean islander and a Highlander. There is one city, however, where the brogue is unique and extra-difficult to decipher: Glasgow.

Glaswegians are very friendly to tourists, so don't feel intimidated by their thick brogue. Be patient and ask those you don't understand to repeat themselves. And if someone says to you, "Hi, how'r ye dae'in," reply with, "Aye, canna complain." You just may be mistaken for a local — for a minute, anyway.

To keep you from having to maintain one of those polite but puzzled smiles on your face while talking to locals, review this handy glossary of common terms. You'll be one step ahead and won't miss a beat if someone asks you to "put some tins in the press."

| | | | |
|---|---|---|---|
| **auld** | old | **ken** | know |
| **aye** | yes | **lad** | boy |
| **bairn** | baby | **lassie** | girl |
| **blether** | to talk a lot | **lift** | elevator |
| **bonnet** | car hood | **loch** | lake |
| **bonnie** | pretty | **petrol** | gas |
| **boot** | car trunk | **press** | cabinet |
| **cairn** | stone landmark | **quid, or bob** | pounds, or money |
| **ceilidh** | gathering, usually with music | **take-away** | fast food, to go |
| **cheers** | thanks | **till** | cash register |
| **creche** | day care | **tins** | canned goods |
| **dinnae** | don't | **tolbooth** | town hall or jail |
| **footpath** | sidewalk | **torch** | flashlight |
| **hen** | woman | **wee** | little |
| **hogmanay** | New Year's Eve | **windscreen** | windshield |

> ## Understanding everyday words and phrases
>
> Unlike Ireland, where residents fought to keep the native tongue alive, Scotland absorbed English with relative ease. Over the years, Scottish schools were discouraged from teaching Gaelic, effectively eliminating it from the vernacular. Today, Gaelic survives in just a few remote areas, and only 3% of Scots speak it. Unlike Gaelic, Scots English was never an official vernacular but served, instead, as a native dialect. Still, a handful of important writers, such as poet Robert Burns, wrote in Scots English. Today, English-speaking visitors to Scotland are likely to be flummoxed by the Scots-influenced versions of standard English.

And any time you feel like corralling a local to give you the lowdown on all the handsome Highland cows, know that in this part of the world they're pronounced "coos."

# Don't Know Much about Scotland's History?

Technically, you don't have to know Scotland's history to decide which areas you want to visit or to appreciate what the country has to offer today. But Scotland's history is so fascinating that I include a summary here.

It's often said that history is told through war, and this is especially true of Scotland. The nation has been invaded and seized and fought over for most of its 4,000 years of civilization. The sheer number of fortressed castles and battlegrounds are living testament to centuries of violent warring.

The first settlers, the Celtic-Iberians, came to the area around 2,000 B.C., building astrological standing stones and forts to protect themselves from neighboring tribes. In the fifth century A.D., the Romans were the first invaders to try to take the country, which they called Caledonia. They failed, but about 100 years later, **St. Columba** came over from Ireland and introduced Christianity to the locals. It took hold, erasing the heritage of the pre-Christian Picts, about whom little is known outside the carved rocks they left behind in western Scotland.

The Vikings also wanted a piece of Scotland. Starting in the ninth century, they began a series of raids on the Hebridean Islands that would last for nearly 400 years. Although the Vikings had little interest in taking anything but local game, the Norse occupation left its mark and led to the first unification of Scots under **King Malcolm** in 1018. Until that time, Scotland was a Gaelic-speaking region, but the English influence had been creeping in from the south and had taken over during the reign of the powerful and popular **King David I.** David established royal burghs, or towns, throughout Scotland, creating cities like Edinburgh and Stirling that flourish today. David also created a national system of weights and measures, as well as a code of justice.

Uniting Scotland under one flag proved difficult. A feudal system worked well in the southern Borders area, but in the Highlands the common social structure was the family clan. Geographically, some parts of the country proved too remote to encourage loyalty to the Scottish kings, including the famed 11th-century ruler **Macbeth.** Helped by this lack of unity, Edward I of England invaded Scotland in the 1200s, took the symbolic **Stone of Destiny** (the coronation stone for Scottish monarchs), and put a puppet king in charge of the country. One man, **William Wallace,** led a rebellion against the British that helped open the door to Scotland's independence, which the Scots eventually secured at the Battle of Bannockburn in 1314 under the leadership of **King Robert the Bruce,** Wallace's contemporary.

Another 300 years of war with the British followed. For much of that time, the powerful Stuart line ruled Scotland. The best-known Stuart ruler was **Mary Queen of Scots,** a Catholic in an increasingly Protestant country. Mary made some poor matrimonial choices, and personal scandals led to her imprisonment by church reformers. Following Martin Luther and the Protestant Reformation, Scottish reformers like **John Knox** became increasingly popular. After languishing for years in the Tower of London, Mary finally was executed under order of her cousin, Queen Elizabeth I of England.

Mary's son, **James VI** of Scotland, inherited the throne of England after his childless aunt Elizabeth passed away in 1603. The Protestant James VI of Scotland became James I of England, moving the united monarchy permanently to London. The Scottish parliament was summarily dissolved. Despite the unhappiness of Catholics, many wealthy Scots saw unification with England as good for trade and commerce. Interestingly, the current British royal family descends from James.

With the government even farther away, the Highlands became a hotspot of internal feuding among clans. The **Massacre of Glencoe** in 1692, between the MacDonalds and the Campbells, occurred during this bloody period, and **Rob Roy MacGregor** found fame in his opposition to the British-backed Duke of Montrose. Back in England, the Hanovers began their rule, and Scotland attempted to organize and overthrow the crown. The heir to the Stuart line, **Prince Charles Edward Stuart,** set out for London with a few Highland chiefs in 1745. Bonnie Prince Charlie, as he was known, and his Jacobite troops charged into England but turned around only 125 miles short of London and eventually met defeat at the **Battle of Culloden.** A fugitive, Charlie ultimately escaped to his native France. Despite his failure to capture the throne, Prince Charlie to this day remains a national hero in the Scottish conscience.

After the Jacobite defeat, England was quick to crack down on any symbol of Scottish nationalism. It outlawed **bagpipes** and clan **tartans,** and clan chiefs were given the role of feudal landlords over their property and served the will of the king. In the wake of mass evictions, many Scots left the country. Many traveled to America, where they again faced hostility from the British, who were embroiled in the war for American independence.

Despite their mutual animosity, Scotland and England waged no war throughout the 19th and 20th centuries, sharing a period of rapid industrialization and artistic growth. Glasgow boomed along with its shipbuilding. Edinburgh produced such luminaries as philosopher **David Hume,** poet **Robert Burns,** and novelist **Sir Walter Scott.**

In 1997, the Scot-influenced Labour Party in England passed a referendum to re-establish the **Scottish Parliament.** Although England still has some influence over taxes, the new parliament, which convened in 1999, has final say over all other matters of local and national concern. It took more than 700 years, but the Stone of Destiny and the Scottish crown jewels were finally returned to the people they belong to.

## Great Scots!

Did you know that a whopping 61 percent of American presidents have a Scottish ethnic background? That stock draws from the bloodlines of many heroic and dynamic native Scots. Impress tour guides and fellow travelers by studying this quick-reference guide to big-name Scots throughout history.

✔ **St. Andrew:** The patron saint of Scotland, one of Jesus's apostles, never actually set foot in the country. The Romans crucified St. Andrew in Greece sometime after the Crucifixion, and some of his remains were said to be in the possession of an Irish monk when the monk was shipwrecked in eastern Scotland. That monk set up a mission in present-day St. Andrews. The relics were eventually entombed in St. Andrew's Cathedral, and the town became the religious capital of Scotland and a center for medieval pilgrims who flocked to view the relics. Today, unfortunately, the cathedral is in ruins and the relics lost, most likely destroyed during the Scottish Reformation. In 1969, Pope Paul VI gave relics of St. Andrew to Scotland and they are currently on display in a reliquary in St. Mary's Roman Catholic Cathedral in Edinburgh. The blue Scottish flag contains a white X-shaped cross that represents the one St. Andrew was executed upon.

✔ **St. Columba** (521–597): This Irish missionary founded a monastery on the island of Iona in 563 in an attempt to convert the local Pict heathens. As a result, Catholicism became popular, and Columba is considered Scotland's second patron saint (after St. Andrew). The monk is also noted for giving the first eyewitness account of the Loch Ness Monster.

*(continued)*

*(continued)*

- **Macbeth** (d. 1057): Famous as the murderous Scottish usurper in the Shakespeare play, Macbeth was actually a popular and good king who maintained Scottish independence from England. His son, Malcolm, became a puppet king to the English.

- **William Wallace** (ca. 1270–1305): This hero of Scottish independence reached star-power recognition after the release of Mel Gibson's film *Braveheart.* Wallace's most decisive victory over the British army of Edward I was at the Battle of Stirling Bridge. William Wallace was eventually captured and executed, but his efforts were not in vain — soon after his death, Robert the Bruce re-established Scotland's independence.

- **Robert the Bruce** (1274–1329): Robert was crowned King of Scotland in 1306 and retained power by defeating English King Edward II at the famous **Battle of Bannockburn** in 1314. Legend also tells the story of his lesson in perseverance, learned by watching a spider build a web in the cave in which he was hiding. Robert descended from the first king of Scotland, **David I.**

- **John Knox** (1514?–1572): Considered the father of the Protestant Reformation in Scotland, Knox was the most outspoken critic of the Roman Catholic church and a catalyst for its replacement with the Presbyterian Church of Scotland. He was a contemporary of Mary Queen of Scots, the Catholic queen, and lived to see her downfall.

- **Mary Queen of Scots** (1542–1587): A Catholic in Protestant Scotland, Mary failed to take over the British crown from her cousin Elizabeth I and was later imprisoned and executed. She gave birth to James VI of Scotland, who later became the first king of a united England and Scotland.

- **James VI of Scotland** (1566–1625): Son of Mary Queen of Scots, the Presbyterian-raised James became King of England when Queen Elizabeth I, his aunt, died without an heir. He ruled both countries during his entire reign.

- **Rob Roy MacGregor** (1671–1734): He was a known cattle thief and Jacobite soldier, but a little revisionist history, Hollywood, and Sir Walter Scott have been kind to Rob Roy. He is now considered a Robin Hood–style hero and defender of the Highland way of life.

- **Charles Edward Stuart,** also known as **Bonnie Prince Charlie** (1720–1788): Charlie was the grandson of James VII of Scotland (James II of England) and was exiled by William of Orange. His Jacobite Rebellion of 1745 sought to regain the thrones, but it ended in bloody defeat at **Culloden** a year later. With the help of Isle of Skye resident Flora MacDonald, Charlie escaped to France, where he lived the rest of his life in exile. He is buried in St. Peter's Cathedral in Rome.

- **Flora MacDonald** (1722–1790): A native of the Hebridean Islands, Flora secured her place in Scottish history by helping Bonnie Prince Charlie escape the British crown following his failed rebellion of 1745. She later emigrated to North Carolina and was active in the American War of Independence.

- **Robert Burns** (1759–1796): Scotland's national poet, Burns wrote in both standard English and Scots English. He is perhaps best known for the poem "My Love is Like a Red, Red Rose" and the New Year's Eve staple "Auld Lang Syne."

✔ **Sir Walter Scott** (1771–1832): Arguably Scotland's best writer (J.K. Rowling fans may disagree), Scott did much to create a Scottish cultural identity through literature. He wrote a series of books known as the Waverly novels that include glowing accounts of Rob Roy MacGregor, Ivanhoe, and other Scottish figures.

✔ **Robert Louis Stevenson** (1850–1894): The author of *Kidnapped, Treasure Island,* and *The Strange Case of Dr Jekyll and Mr. Hyde* suffered from poor health while living in his hometown of Edinburgh. He moved to Samoa, where he died.

✔ **Charles Rennie Mackintosh** (1868–1928): Scotland's most famous architect and designer, Mackintosh created a unique style that had a major influence on 20th-century design. His original blend of Art Nouveau and Scottish Celtic traditionalism can be seen throughout Scotland, particularly in Glasgow.

✔ **Sir Arthur Conan Doyle** (1859–1930): The creator of the legendary detective Sherlock Holmes, Doyle graduated from Edinburgh University with a degree in medicine and practiced in Edinburgh.

✔ **Sean Connery** (b. 1930): A vocal supporter of Scottish home rule, Scotland's greatest contribution to film was a milkman and a nude model at an art school in Edinburgh before finding fame as Her Majesty's most famous cinema spy. He may be best known as James Bond, but he won an Oscar for *The Untouchables* and is an accomplished amateur golfer. Sir Sean Connery was knighted in Edinburgh in 2000.

✔ **J.K. Rowling** (b. 1965): The Edinburgh-based author of the wildly popular Harry Potter series, Rowling has become one of the wealthiest writers of her time.

# Chapter 2

# Deciding When to Go

● ● ● ● ● ● ● ● ● ● ● ● ● ● ● ● ● ● ● ● ● ● ● ● ● ● ● ● ● ● ● ● ● ● ● ● ● ●

## In This Chapter

▶ Evaluating when to go, season by season

▶ Anticipating Scotland's weather, come rain or come shine

▶ Planning around a calendar of festivals and events

● ● ● ● ● ● ● ● ● ● ● ● ● ● ● ● ● ● ● ● ● ● ● ● ● ● ● ● ● ● ● ● ● ● ● ● ● ●

*T*he success of a Scotland vacation often depends on when you go. You don't want to spend a lot of time and energy planning your trip just to end up visiting at the wrong time — or worse, stay too long in one place and miss something else worth seeing. Good planning ensures that certain factors, such as bad weather, too many tourists, being stuck in a place for too long, or not giving yourself enough time to see the big attractions, don't distract from a great trip.

In this chapter, I offer advice and insight on when to go so that you can more easily determine the best way to spend your Scotland vacation.

## The Secrets of the Seasons: Deciding the Best Time to Travel

So when is the best time to take a trip to Scotland? Well, in a perfect world you'd be going when situations are ideal — fine weather, low prices, and minimal crowds. More realistically, you'll plan your vacation around your own schedule. No matter when you go, however, each season boasts advantages and certain drawbacks. I this section, I give you the highlights and drawbacks of the four seasons.

### Summer

I start with the obvious. The most popular and arguably the best time to tour Scotland is the summer. For the unsure traveler, this is the best time to go; you'll have lots of company and plenty of leads to follow.

✔ **The upside:** First, and most important, is the weather. It's just plain gorgeous during this time of year. (If you're grumbling about the few extra pounds you'll pay for a hotel room in high season, just think of it as a cover charge for the great weather.) Scotland never swelters — in fact, conditions stay comfortably warm and breezy during the day and drop to that perfect light-sweater temperature at night. This, coupled with the amazing effect the warm weather has on the scenery, is enough reason to go. Don't hold me to this forecast — you'll still get caught in the rain, especially on the islands, in June and July. But countrywide, the precipitation will be bearable, if not pleasant and refreshing.

Summer's the busiest tourist season by far, but crowds aren't always a bad thing when traveling. Shops, streets, and attractions that are teeming with people may actually enhance your trip. The more the merrier — empty pubs don't make for lively fun. Scotland is such a friendly place in general that throwing a ton of people into the mix makes for a spirited atmosphere. Oh, and some of those castles can be pretty doomy and gloomy — it helps to have a few people around to ward off the creeps!

✔ **The downside:** The summer is the high season, so during the months between May and August, visitors can expect to find just as many compatriots as Scots in a pub or park. This massive influx of tourists creates more than foreign solidarity, though. It means, in a nutshell, that every major attraction, hotel, and restaurant is bound to be jampacked. So if you're craving a break from crowds, summer is not the time to go.

Remember, though, that summer travelers are what these services exist for, so you *will* be welcomed with open arms — or, more bluntly, open palms. Most of the people offering travel services make their entire year's income in one season, so they take full advantage of tourists' flush wallets and increase their prices for the summer. No need to take out a second mortgage, though; the jump from off-season prices to high-season prices isn't enough to make you replan your trip. Generally it's a small increase — you'd only notice if you went during another season and benefited from cheaper prices.

For the most part, the weather everywhere is great, except on the islands. Island summers can be quite rainy, making the best time for island travel the months of May and September. The worst thing about summer conditions are the *midges* — little blood-sucking insects invisible to the naked eye that will drive you bonkers as they chow down on your epidermis. The legendary swarming bugs are especially bad in the Highlands during their peak season, July through September. The only precaution — and it's hardly foolproof — is bug spray.

# Fall

This season is probably the most underrated time to visit Scotland. Revealing this well-kept secret may make me unpopular with my Scottish friends, but here goes: I'm a huge advocate of visiting in the fall. The weather is a big draw. The prospect of mild days without too much rain (except out in the islands) and daylight beyond 9 p.m. is great for marathon sightseeing. The countryside in autumn colors is an added bonus.

✔ **The upside:** Beginning around October, the high season ends and prices drop. As I said earlier in this section, the summertime price increase isn't outrageous, but any money saved is a good thing. It's great to know you're getting a prime hotel room for less than it cost just weeks before. Some tours also cost less, and even restaurants offer new menus (translation: same food, lower prices).

There are still plenty of people traveling during the fall. In fact, this season is when many Europeans take vacations, so it's certainly not a desolate place, and you'll still get that feeling of being in a group. And after the bulk of tireless travelers have headed back to their homes, the Scots come back out to play, especially in larger cities. The field is theirs again, so to speak, and they come out of hiding to reclaim their turf. In fact, many Scots have done the same as visitors to Scotland and gone on holiday during the summer months. So in the fall, you're likely to find pubs filled with locals rather than tourists.

✔ **The downside:** Honestly, I don't think there are any downsides to fall travel, weather-wise. A few attractions and tourist offices are open only during the summer, but most are open year-round. (December does get pretty cold, but because of airfare considerations, I've chosen to think of December as part of winter.)

# Winter

Okay, if I didn't love Scotland so much I'd probably tell you to high-tail it down to the warm and sunny Caribbean for your winter vacation. While this may not be the ideal time to go to Scotland, you'll discover a few benefits of visiting in this harsh season.

✔ **The upside:** Some of the rules about the fall apply in winter, too. It's an ideal time for money-minded people to go. Prices are at their lowest all across the country, and you're likely to find the cheapest airfares of the year. Because it's the least popular time to go, you'll find tons of special rates and package deals, and you could be the envy of all your friends when they hear how little your trip is costing.

If you hate crowds of any kind, this, too, is the time for you. From November to March, you'll likely have the run of the country. This quiet time is the best time to fully experience museums, galleries, and permanent attractions. And the landscape is almost as beautiful as during the full swing of summer — winter doesn't take as hard a toll on Scotland's flora as it does in many U.S. states.

✔ **The downside:** The winter weather can get a bit *driech* (Scottish slang for nasty). It's cold and rainy and windy, especially on the islands. The temperature doesn't dip to extreme lows, but the elements are, well, miserable. Lots of attractions close for the season, too, and several are shuttered for a few months a year. Some small hotels and B&Bs take a month or two off, as well. And lots of places have shorter hours during this time. This reduced activity is all because tourism slows to a crawl (like molasses going uphill in — you guessed it — January). Still, you'll find plenty of things to do, but you'll get an abbreviated tour offering fewer highlights than you'd get in the other seasons.

## Spring

Many consider spring to be the perfect time to travel in Scotland. As the snow melts and trickles downstream and the salmon head upstream, smart tourists head for the hills and dales.

✔ **The upside:** Warmer temperatures, lush scenery, and longer days combine to make wonderful conditions for touring the country. The locals have had their time away from tourists and are ready to start the long months of playing host. The countryside is carpeted in spring greenery. On the whole, it's quite a nice time to go.

✔ **The downside:** Almost all the factors involved in going during the summer apply in spring, too. This is the beginning of the high season, so prices go up. Tourists start flooding in (though it's not as crowded as in the summer). The weather's pretty rainy in the spring, but often the rain showers last only part of the day, opening up the sky to sun and, yes, even rainbows.

# Walking on Sunshine, Singing in the Rain: Scotland's Climate

I know what you're thinking: rain, right? All that green doesn't happen in a *dry* place, after all.

Yes, it's rain that makes the grass green and the beautiful heather grow. That said, however, Scotland isn't one of those destinations that boast uniform conditions year-round, and though there's no real dry season, there are *drier* seasons and regions. And *wetter:* The western side of the country is particularly prone to rain, which, when combined with strong winds, becomes horizontal rain — not the most conducive conditions for touring.

# The rain in Spain stays mainly in the plain, but in Scotland it falls everywhere

No matter what time of the year you go, chances are slim that you'll make it back without having had raindrops falling on your head. But that's all part of the Scottish experience! You'd feel cheated if you didn't get a little wet.

More specifically, though, rain falls more heavily and more often during certain times of the year — winter, especially. Also, certain places on Scotland see more rain. The northwestern region of the country, especially the Hebridean Islands, tends to get more rain year-round.

As far as temperature goes, Scotland is reasonably mild year-round (see Table 2-1). Not much risk of frostbite here.

| Table 2-1 | Average Monthly Temperature in Scotland | | | | |
|---|---|---|---|---|---|
| *Month* | *Temp (F)* | *Temp (C)* | *Month* | *Temp (F)* | *Temp (C)* |
| January | 33–42 | 1–6 | July | 52–67 | 12–20 |
| February | 34–43 | 2–7 | August | 51–67 | 11–20 |
| March | 35–48 | 3–8 | September | 47–61 | 8–17 |
| April | 39–52 | 4–12 | October | 42–55 | 6–13 |
| May | 42–58 | 6–14 | November | 35–48 | 3–8 |
| June | 49–63 | 9–18 | December | 34–43 | 2–7 |

# Don't let the sun go down on me

Weather and temperatures aren't the only factors involved in deciding when to go. The amount of daylight varies greatly from season to season. Scotland is at such a high latitude that summer days are really long (the sun sets as late as 10:30 p.m.) while winter days are tragically short (the sun sets as early as 4:30 p.m.). The more daylight there is, the more sights you'll get to see.

TIP

---

## Don't get tangled, get smart: Using the Web

Lots of sites offer information on Scotland: some great, some good, some not so good. I've saved you the trouble and time of surfing around and discovered some of the best Web sites for travelers to Scotland. Here are my picks for the top five. (Remember, though, that things change quickly in mercurial cyberspace, so a site may have been transformed by the time you read this.)

✔ www.geo.ed.ac.uk/scotgaz/scotland.html: A one-stop shop for shopping, recreation, attractions, weather, maps, tours, and much more.

✔ www.cntraveller.co.uk: Condé Nast's site, with general information and good airport information.

✔ www.travelscotland.co.uk/: For news, sports, history, attraction information, clan finder, and Scotland travel chats.

✔ www.geo.ed.ac.uk/scotgaz/scotland.html: This geography site has the best interactive maps around.

✔ www.geo.ed.ac.uk/home/scotland/scotland.html: Get Scottish history, maps, and demographics and search the encyclopedic reference guide. *Warning:* Turn the sound off on your computer first; a headache-inducing soundtrack of Scottish muzak plays nonstop while the site is up.

---

Scotland has one phenomenon that's sure to surprise you: palm trees! Scotland escapes its high latitude's normally cold weather, thanks to the curve of the Gulf Stream, which roars out of the Gulf of Mexico, through the straits of Florida, across the Atlantic, and up past Scotland's west coast. So you really can see palm trees throughout the country. (You can bet it still won't *feel* tropical, though.)

Before you go, get up-to-date weather forecasts on the Internet. The best site on the Web for Scotland weather forecasts is www.cnn.com/WEATHER/newcities/europe.html, with four-day forecasts for 15 cities. While in Scotland you can phone for seven-day weather forecasts at ☎ 0891-65-4612. Then dial 101 for northwestern and western Scotland and 102 for northeastern and eastern Scotland.

# Calendar of Festivals and Events

No matter when you visit Scotland, you're sure to encounter some sort of event or festival — and the Scots take these things seriously, so whatever you find is bound to be a big deal. There are about a zillion of them a year, of all sizes and flavors, but I've sorted through and picked the ones I consider the best.

# January

✔ **The Ba' Games:** January 1; Kirkwall, Orkney. The whole town gets together for this centuries-old New Year's event, pitting two teams against each other in a game that involves getting a large ball into the other team's goal. For information, call ☎ **01856-872-856.**

✔ **Celtic Connections:** Last two weeks in January; Glasgow. The city's annual Celtic music festival grows larger every year. This huge gathering for music or dance, called a *ceilidh,* features international artists as well as workshops and opportunities to play an instrument. For details, call ☎ **0141-353-4137** or 0141-332-6633.

✔ **Up Helly Aa:** Last Tuesday in January; Shetland Islands. Shetlanders really know how to throw a bonfire. This popular festival celebrates the island's traditional Norse roots and concludes with the burning of a replica Viking galley ship. For information, call ☎ **01595-69-3434.**

✔ **Burns Night:** January 25. Celebrated in Ayr, Dumfries, and Edinburgh restaurants, Burns Night is an evening of traditional food and music. Burns suppers, named for Robert Burns and served on the great poet's birthday, usually consist of haggis (see Chapter 1), potatoes, and turnips washed down with whisky. Call ☎ **01292-28-8688** for info about Ayr, ☎ **0131-557-5118** for Edinburgh, and ☎ **01387-253-862** for Dumfries.

# February

✔ **Inverness Music Festival:** Last week in February. This week-long musicfest features classical and traditional music, as well as dancing at venues throughout the city. For information, call ☎ **01463-23-2835.**

# March

✔ **Whuppity Scourie Festival:** First week in March; Lanark. To beat the winter blahs, Lanark sponsors a week of family activities. There is dancing, singing, music, and storytelling. The final day of the festival concludes with a large ceilidh. For details, call ☎ **01555-66-1661.**

✔ **Tobermory Drama Festival:** Last week in March; Tobermory, Isle of Mull. For one week, the Isle of Mull becomes the theatrical capital of Great Britain. Production companies from London, Glasgow, and Edinburgh head west to do a short run of their shows. For more information, call ☎ **01688-30-2182.**

# April

- ✔ **Edinburgh International Science Festival:** Second and third week in April. For two weeks, Scotland hosts the world's largest science festival at various venues throughout Edinburgh. Adults and kids will find the festival's 250 shows, workshops, exhibitions, and lectures lots of fun and quite interesting. For details, call ☎ 0131-530-2001 or visit www.sciencefestival.co.uk.

- ✔ **Melrose Seven:** Mid-month; Melrose. This international rugby event features seven high-octane players on each side. Call ☎ 01343-54-2666 for the scoop.

- ✔ **Shoots and Roots I:** Easter weekend; Edinburgh. This festival of traditional and folk music also features world-renowned jazz, rock, and classical music with folk influences. This is part one of a festival that meets again in November. For information, call ☎ 0131-557-1050.

- ✔ **Spirit of Speyside Whisky Festival:** Last week in April; Speyside. If you're a whisky fan, you'll enjoy days of tastings, distillery visits, music, and other Scotch whisky–themed activities in the Highlands. Get more information by calling ☎ 01343-54-2666 or pointing your browser to www.spiritofspeyside.com.

# May

- ✔ **Pitlochry Festival Theatre:** Mid-May; Pitlochry. The Pitlochry Theatre is the country's premier venue for drama. When the season kicks off in May, the theater and town host a series of events to coincide with the plays' openings, such as traditional music and dancing in the city's Recreation Park. For details, call ☎ 01796-47-2215 or visit www.pitlochry.org.uk/index.php.

- ✔ **Scottish FA Cup Final:** Mid-May; Glasgow. This is the deciding match for Scotland's premier football (read: soccer) tournament. The center of the festivities, merriment, and fanaticism is Hamden Park in Glasgow. For information, call ☎ 0141-204-4400.

- ✔ **Perth Festival of the Arts:** Mid-May. Perth's annual festival of music, art, and drama features local and international artists and is considered one of the best places to see orchestral concerts, opera, and even ballet. Get more info by calling ☎ 01738-47-2706 or visiting www.perthfestival.co.uk.

- ✔ **Highland Walking Week:** Mid-May. This unique event is an opportunity to see some of Scotland's most remote and beautiful scenery. The week is a series of organized walks and evening activities. Call ☎ 01875-32-0127 for information.

✔ **Scottish International Children's Festival:** Last week in May; Edinburgh. This is Britain's largest performing-arts festival for young people. Renowned companies from around the world sponsor shows, workshops, and storytelling. Anyone under 15 will be easily engaged, and parents won't be bored either. For details, call ☎ **0131-225-8050** or surf to www.imaginate.org.uk.

✔ **Dundee Jazz Festival:** Last week in May. The best in modern and old-school jazz culminates in a series of concerts and late-night events. The three main venues are the Dundee Reperatory Theatre, the Westport Bar, and the Dundee Contemporary Arts Centre. For information, call ☎ **01382-22-353.**

# June

✔ **Scotland's Larder Food Festival:** Mid-June; Upper Largo. This huge celebration of Scottish food has no shortage of barbecues, cooking demonstrations, and tastings. Live music and entertainment accompany the food and drink. Call ☎ **01333-36-0414** for details.

✔ **Selkirk Common Riding:** Mid-June; Selkirk. Hundreds of horses parade around town in a magnificent display of horsemanship. The event commemorates a 16th-century battle that left only one survivor to sound the alarm for the city. The main event of the Common is the coronation of one local who represents the lucky soldier. Get details by calling ☎ **01750-20-054.**

✔ **St. Magnus Fest:** Third week in June; Orkney Islands. This excellent music festival showcases new singing and composing talent and mixes up modern and classical sounds to the delight of fans. Music is the main focus, but local arts-and-crafts folks come out, as well. Call ☎ **01856-87-2669** for information.

✔ **Royal Highland Show:** Last week in June; Royal Highland Centre, Ingliston, near Edinburgh. This agriculture and food fair is the highlight of Scotland's country calendar. It's a great opportunity to get up close and personal to pedigree livestock, flowers, show jumping, crafts, and more. For information, call ☎ **0990-803-0444** or visit www.royalhighlandshow.org.

# July

✔ **Glasgow International Jazz Festival:** First weekend in July. Top Scottish and international jazz performers converge for a weekend of concerts that gets the whole city grooving. The main venues are the Old Fruitmarket, the Marriott Hotel, and the Tron Theatre. Call ☎ **0141-552-3552** or click on www.jazzfest.co.uk for information.

✔ **T in the Park:** Second weekend in July; Balado Airfield, Fife, near Kinross. The Woodstock of Scotland, this annual outdoor music show is the biggest and best pop festival in the country. Big acts from the U.S. and U.K. play on five stages accompanied by good food and craft stalls and plenty of camping space. Call ☎ **0141-339-8383** for tickets or 07000-11-3114 for the Festival Information Hotline, or visit www.tinthepark.com.

✔ **Hebridean Celtic Festival:** Mid-July; Stornoway, Isle of Lewis. Celtic music highlights this festival, which also includes historical and genealogical exhibitions and fringe events that show off the cultural and archaeological treasures of the islands. For details, call ☎ **07001-87-8787** or check out www.hebceltfest.com.

✔ **Inverness Tattoo:** Mid-July; Northern Meeting Park, Inverness. For 50 years, the week-long Inverness Tattoo program has rivaled its big brother, the Edinburgh Tattoo. And what exactly is a *tattoo* (besides a permanent skin etching or the sidekick on "Fantasy Island")? A military tattoo is a display of bagpipe bands and army gun and parachuting teams strutting their stuff. Contact Bob Shark (☎ **01463-24-4395**) or visit www.invernessmilitary tattoo.co.uk for more info.

✔ **Edinburgh International Jazz & Blues Festival:** Last week of July and into August. This is the longest-running jazz festival in the U.K. The whole city opens its doors to host the best in jazz and blues performances. Concert halls, theaters, clubs, pubs, and even the streets feature all styles of jazz; artists hail from the four corners of the globe. For more information, call ☎ **0131-667-7776** or 0131-225-2202 or point your browser to www.jazzmusic.co.uk.

## August

✔ **Edinburgh Military Tattoo:** Month of August. This amazing blend of music, ceremony, and theater is one of the highlights of the Edinburgh Festival season. The martial music and displays of pipes, drums, and marching of the Scottish Regiments are set on the esplanade, just outside Edinburgh Castle. Tickets go for £9–£31 ($13–$45). Call ☎ **8707-555-1188** or visit www.edintattoo.co.uk for information.

✔ **Edinburgh Festival:** All month; The Hub, Castlehill, Royal Mile. The largest arts festival in the world, the Festival and its unofficial Fringe counterpart comprise theater, dance, music, and comedy. It's a book, film, music, opera, dance, comedy, and drama festival all rolled into one, with approximately 14,000 events. For festival info, call ☎ **0131-473-2000** or visit www.eif.co.uk; for the scoop on the Fringe, contact the Fringe Office, 180 High St. (☎ **0131-226-5257;** www.edfringe.com).

✔ **World Pipe Championships:** Mid-August; Glasgow Green. The largest bagpipe band gathering takes place every year in Glasgow. Nearly 200 bands from around the world compete for the highest honors in piping. The competition gives the music-playing a sportslike fervor, and the weeklong event includes some Highland game action, as well. Call ☎ **0141-221-5414** for details.

# September

✔ **Ben Nevis Hill Race:** First Saturday in September; Fort William. Not for the faint of heart, this intense race up and down Britain's highest mountain is one footrace you won't find boring to watch. For information, call ☎ **01397-70-3781**.

✔ **Braemar Royal Highland Games & Gathering:** First weekend in September; Braemar. This is one of the largest of the city-sponsored Highland games. The huge gathering of clansmen usually includes a visit from the royal family. Spectators take in piping, dancing, and strength competitions. Call ☎ **01339-75-5377** for details.

# October

✔ **Royal National Mod:** Second week in October; multiple locations. This large, nomadic festival of Gaelic music, culture, and song moves from one city to the next every year. The performing-arts competition and all the good food and crafts that surround the Mod make it worth calling to find out whether the festival may be in a city that's on your itinerary. For information, call ☎ **01369-70-2059**.

# November

✔ **Shoots & Roots II:** Mid-November; Edinburgh. The second part of the folk music jamboree takes place in venues throughout the city. The focus is on more traditional Scottish folk music, and listeners enjoy Gaelic lyrics and music history. For details, call ☎ **0131-557-1050**.

✔ **St. Andrews Night:** November 30; St. Andrews. In celebration of Scotland's patron saint, the namesake town hosts a series of society dinners. It's not difficult to get into one of these dinners if you call ahead, but be prepared for only the most traditional of Scottish cuisine. Call ☎ **01334-47-2021** for more information.

## December

✔ **Hogmanay:** Last week in December; Edinburgh. This four-day winter festival features dozens of indoor and outdoor events (some free) and ends with a New Year's Eve Street Party. A highlight is a torchlight procession down Prince's Street. Hoping to rival Edinburgh, Glasgow also has Hogmanay celebrations that include a party in George's Square. For the scoop on Edinburgh, call ☎ **0131-473-2001** or click on www.edinburghshogmanay.org; visit www.glasgows-hogmanay.co.uk for Glasgow information.

# Chapter 3

# Great Itineraries

● ● ● ● ● ● ● ● ● ● ● ● ● ● ● ● ● ● ● ● ● ● ● ● ● ● ● ● ● ● ● ● ● ● ● ● ● ● ● ● ● ● ● ● ●

## In This Chapter

▶ Mapping out a strategy

▶ Taking off on a whirlwind one-week tour

▶ Rambling along for a couple of weeks

▶ Exploring Scotland with kids

▶ Discovering Scotland's great outdoors

● ● ● ● ● ● ● ● ● ● ● ● ● ● ● ● ● ● ● ● ● ● ● ● ● ● ● ● ● ● ● ● ● ● ● ● ● ● ● ● ● ● ● ● ●

*S*ome people like to travel with absolutely no direction — just get off
the plane and go where the wind takes them. Other people prefer a
little more structure in their travel schedule. Maybe you have your heart
set on specific sights you just have to see, or you're not willing to waste
time on attractions that don't interest you. Whether you prefer your
trips planned with military precision or plotted out by a pro, a trip out
there is right for you. You can hop on someone's magic bus and let a tour
guide show you the sights or customize your own tour that includes
every attraction you're dying to see. In this chapter, I've done the work
for you and have developed four great sample itineraries for you to
follow or use to jump-start your own personalized tour.

For in-depth information on the sights and attractions listed in this
chapter, go to the Index at the back of the book, which will direct you
to the appropriate city and region chapters in Parts III and IV.

## Itinerary Planning for Do-It-Yourselfers

Packages simply don't work for some people. You may cast about and
find that the available package vacations just don't meet your needs —
you have your heart set on staying at a hotel that isn't offered as part
of a package, say, or you want to use frequent-flier miles for your airline tickets, or the activities options just don't seem like great deals.
Or maybe you're just the kind of type-A control freak who'd just rather
handle everything yourself.

Fear not: This doesn't mean that you'll get stuck paying high rates for everything. You can find plenty of ways to put together your own customized trip and save *mucho dinero.* (See Chapter 4 for more on saving money in Scotland.) Planning your own trip, you can see the country one of two ways: the base-camp approach or the nomadic approach.

## Taking the base-camp approach

This is the approach I recommend. Pick two or three cities as your base and make day-trips from them. Stay in lovely towns, such as Glasgow (to explore the South), St. Andrews (for the East), Oban (for the West), Inverness (for the Highlands), or Edinburgh (for, well, Edinburgh). If you have only one week, you have to be selective in what you see and do. Planting yourself in Edinburgh for a couple days, then staying in a northern city such as Inverness for a few more, is a smart way to go — many sights are an easy drive from these two points. By staying a couple nights in the same place, you also save the time and hassle of switching hotels every day and worrying about check-in and check-out times.

Self-catering is one cost-efficient option to consider if you're taking the base-camp approach. *Self-catering* means that you rent a home or apartment with kitchen facilities for a week or two and do all your sightseeing from there. You save money on both accommodations and dining, and many of the cottages and apartments available are just beautiful.

## Using the nomadic approach

The *nomadic approach* (moving from one hotel to another throughout your trip) may take more planning and require you to waste time checking in and out of hotels, but the advantage is that you won't ever see the same thing twice. If you take this approach, you have to decide what to see and what to skip based on your interests and the amount of time you have. If, for example, the islands hold no interest for you, go straight from Glasgow to Fort William. The risk with this approach is spreading yourself too thin: The longer the distance between each day's destination, the less time you'll have to stop and really see attractions before it gets too late.

The nomadic approach is best if you really know what you want to see and don't want to waste time on attractions of lesser interest. Moving daily, however, can eat up sightseeing time. Plus, I believe that every traveler should have a little air in a vacation schedule — not only to sit back and relax but also to allow for those unexpected moments of travel serendipity.

# Mileage chart

Use Table 3-1 to help in planning your Scotland itinerary:

**Table 3-1**

| Aberdeen | Ayr | Carlisle | Dumfries | Edinburgh | Fort William | Glasgow | Inverness | Perth | Stirling | Ullapool |
|---|---|---|---|---|---|---|---|---|---|---|
| 175 | Ayr |  |  |  |  |  |  |  |  |  |
| 221 | 90 | Carlisle |  |  |  |  |  |  |  |  |
| 200 | 61 | 37 | Dumfries |  |  |  |  |  |  |  |
| 125 | 73 | 96 | 80 | Edinburgh |  |  |  |  |  |  |
| 165 | 132 | 179 | 200 | 146 | Fort William |  |  |  |  |  |
| 145 | 33 | 96 | 75 | 42 | 104 | Glasgow |  |  |  |  |
| 105 | 198 | 262 | 235 | 158 | 66 | 166 | Inverness |  |  |  |
| 81 | 94 | 136 | 125 | 44 | 105 | 61 | 112 | Perth |  |  |
| 116 | 63 | 114 | 93 | 36 | 96 | 30 | 142 | 34 | Stirling |  |
| 165 | 268 | 327 | 307 | 220 | 142 | 232 | 61 | 176 | 141 | Ullapool |

## Making a list, checking it twice

The most important thing? *Have fun.* Sit down with this guidebook and a pint of ale and pick out the places you really want see. It's important, however, to be realistic about the amount of time you'll spend in the car or bus, burning up precious daylight hours. You can spend a full (and tiring) day seeing only a few big sights while driving just the distance between Ullapool and Inverness. I suggest getting up and out early (try to have breakfast at 9 a.m. instead of 11 a.m.) to see the sights. Head to the next town late in the day rather than making the trip early and wasting daylight or risking being too tired after you get to town.

Make an *A list* of places you most want to see and a *B list* of sites to see only if you have extra time. Make your A-list items a priority when mapping out your itinerary and fill in the gaps with secondary sights. (And remember, some places that look small and quick on a map — such as the Isle of Mull — can surprise you and take all day.) Just don't try to cram too much into each day. If you're constantly rushing from one place to the next, you'll enjoy none of them. Relax and enjoy yourself — you're on vacation.

# Exploring Scotland in One Week

You have only one week? Yikes. It'll be a busy week, but you can see most of the major highlights if you stick to this compact and comprehensive itinerary — plus, you won't go home dissatisfied. Tired, maybe. But satisfied.

## Day 1: Edinburgh

With only one day in the capital, your best bet is to see **Edinburgh Castle** first, then take the **Guide Friday** bus tour around town and get on and off at top attractions such as the **Royal Mile, Holyrood Palace, Grassmarket, Princes Street,** and **New Town.** Lunch at the **Elephant House,** and stop in at the **Museum of Scotland** and the **Royal Museum.** Choose from a number of great dinner options, such as the **Atrium,** and take the **McEwen's Literary Pub Tour** (at 7:30 p.m.).

## Day 2: Glasgow

Less than an hour away from Edinburgh, Glasgow offers another packed day of sightseeing. Again, your best bet is the bus tour, especially because it takes you out to the **West End** of town, which is a longer walk than you have time for. Get on the bus early enough and you'll have time to get off for big attractions such as the **Glasgow**

Cathedral, **St. Mungo Museum,** the **Necropolis, People's Palace,** the **Huntarian Museum,** and the **Transport Museum.** For a lovely midday break, have a spot of tea and a scone at the **Willow Tea Room.** Do a little shopping, grab dinner at a great place such as **Yes** or **Air Organic,** and finish off the evening with some dancing at the **Riverside Club** and a pub crawl around town.

# Day 3: Fort William

Today is a big nature day. On your way to Fort William, stop and take a boat tour of lovely **Loch Lomond.** Next stop is **Glencoe,** a stunningly beautiful glen full of hikes and history. Also near Fort William is **Ben Nevis,** the tallest mountain in Scotland, which you can climb, ski, or just ogle. If you think you have time, 18 miles east of Fort William is the Jacobite monument **Glenfinnan.** Dinner and off to bed — you'll be tuckered out.

# Day 4: Loch Ness/Inverness

Head north along Scotland's most famous body of water until you reach the village of **Drumnadrochit,** home to two Loch Ness exhibits, and take in nearby **Urquhart Castle** and a tour of the lake (such as the monster-hunting **Loch Ness Cruises** or the more erudite **Loch Ness Shuttle**). Get to Inverness for dinner, have a libation or two, and drop off the pictures you took of the mysterious image in the lake at an overnight photo shop.

# Day 5: Aberdeen

It's a long trek to Aberdeen with plenty to see on the way, so get an early start and stop at the **Culloden Moor Battlefield** site, the ancient **Clava Cairns, Fort George, Cawdor Castle,** and the **Glenfiddich** and **Strathisla distilleries.** You'll get to Aberdeen late, but not too late for a fine dinner at **Silver Darling,** a jig at the **Lemon Tree,** and a pint or two at the **Prince of Wales.**

# Day 6: St. Andrews

Before leaving Aberdeen, take in the **Maritime Museum,** then bid adieu to the Granite City on your way to the golf mecca of Scotland and golfers everywhere. On the way is the town of Dundee, where you can tour the **RRS** *Discovery* and the **HMS** *Unicorn.* In St. Andrews, be sure to visit the ruins of **St. Andrews Cathedral and Castle** and see the famous **Old Course** links. Then enjoy a great dinner at **Balaka, Estaminet,** or the **Vine Leaf,** and maybe a drink at the **Central Bar** or **Chariots.**

## Day 7: Stirling

On your way to Stirling, visit the **Secret Bunker.** After you're in Stirling, tour the **Holy Rude Church, Stirling Castle,** and the winding streets of this fun little royal burgh. Take a wee side trip to the **Bannockburn Battlefield** and the **National Wallace Monument,** for a view that's the best finish to your whirlwind tour of Scotland.

# Seeing Scotland in Two Weeks

In two weeks, you can see all the major regions of Scotland and a fair number of the major attractions. You may be a pilgrim on the tourist trail, but you won't leave feeling you missed a trick.

## Day 1: Edinburgh

When you arrive in town, throw your bags in the hotel room and head straight for **Edinburgh Castle.** If you get in early enough, you should have time for a **Guide Friday** bus tour around the city, dinner, and then the **McEwen's Literary Pub Tour** (which starts at 7:30 p.m.). A good, safe bet for dinner is **Black Bo's.** If you get the castle out the way early enough, you can have lunch at the **Elephant House Coffee Shop** and take in the nearby **Museum of Scotland and the Royal Museum.** After the literary pub tour, you'll still have plenty of time for your own pub crawl (if you're not too beat). The tour begins at the **Beehive** and ends in **Milne's** — but be sure to visit **Bannerman's,** the **White Hare,** and the **Last Drop** in between.

## Day 2: Edinburgh/Glasgow

It's going to be a busy morning, so have an early breakfast and get to those attractions you passed on the bus tour. If you can squeeze in **Holyrood Palace, Arthur's Seat, Princes Street Gardens, Canongate Church,** and **Calton Hill,** plus a little shopping on the **Royal Mile** and **Princes Street,** you've done well. Now hop in the car and get thee to Glasgow, less than an hour away. Unpack, go to **George Square** and take the bus tour there. This time, get off in the **West End.** While you're on the hip collegiate end of town, take in the **Kelvingrove Art Gallery and Museum,** the nearby **Transport Museum,** and the **Huntarian Art Gallery,** which features Whistler and Mackintosh. While you're out on the West End, have dinner at the ultra-popular **Ubiquitous Chip** and then a pint or two at **Halt Bar.**

# Day 3: Glasgow

Lots of sights to see today. **St. Mungo Museum, Glasgow Cathedral,** and the **Necropolis** are all next to each other on **High Street** (where William Wallace once fought a battle). A little farther east are the **People's Palace and Winter Gardens, Glasgow Green,** and on weekends the crazy shopping experience of the **Barras.** Make your way back toward town center and stop at Babbity Bowster for a friendly pint or at the Mackintosh-designed **Willow Tea Room** for a cup of tea. Do some serious shopping on **Sauchiehall** and **Buchanan streets,** and perhaps take in the **Museum of Modern Art.** Of the many great dinner options, two favorites are the nouveau **Air Organic** or the old-school **Rogano.** Sneak in a **ghost tour with Mercat** and then a beer crawl that should include top choices such as the underground **Republic Bier Halle** and **Brunswick Cellar** and the authentic old **Victoria Bar.** If you're up for traditional dancing, go to the **Riverside Club.** If you have the energy for late-night club dancing, head to **Archaos.**

# Day 4: Inveraray

You can sleep in a little this morning, unless there's something in Glasgow you have left to see. On your way to the wee town of Inveraray, take a boat tour on **Loch Lomond.** Your best option for a late lunch or early dinner is the **Loch Fyne Oyster Bar,** on the main road to Inveraray. After you're there, take in **Inveraray Castle** and the **Jail** before settling in at **Minard Castle, Argyll Hotel,** or the **George.**

# Day 5: Oban

On your way to Oban, stop at the excellent **Kilmartin Museum,** which will give you insight into the historic region you're passing through. The ride to Oban is long, so sit back and enjoy the drive. After you arrive in Oban, climb up **McCaig's Tower,** walk around the lovely town and have dinner at the **Gallery Restaurant** and a nightcap at the **Oban Inn.**

# Day 6: Mull and Iona

Try to catch the first ferry to Mull in the morning. When you arrive, take in **Duart** and **Torosay castles,** then head down to Fionnphort, where you catch the ferry to Iona. See the **Abbey** there, and then take another side trip to **Staffa** and **Fingal's Cave.** The scenic drive between Fionnphort and Tobermory is worth the scary cliff roads. If you prefer to spend the evening on Iona, take in **Tobermory** first.

## Day 7: Fort William

Take the ferry from Tobermory and head along the coast until you reach the main road (A830) into Fort William. Along the way, stop at the **Glenfinnan Monument,** but keep on movin' on, because you have to take in historic **Glencoe,** a bevvie at the **Claichaig Inn,** and **Ben Nevis** (no time to hike it, I'm afraid — that takes all day) before dinner. In Fort William, I recommend the gruel at the **Grog and Gruel** and, as a pub choice, the **Ben Nevis Pub.**

## Day 8: Skye

Leave as early as you can and backtrack on A830 all the way to Mallaig to catch the ferry to Skye. Skye's views of the hikeable **Cuillin Hills** make for a pleasurable drive; be sure to stop in at **Armadale Castle, Dunvegan Castle,** and **Talisker Distillery.** Stay in Portree, where you'll have the best food and hotel options, and don't miss the **Skye Scene Highland Ceilidh.**

## Day 9: Inverness

Take the A87 and stop by Skye on your way to Inverness, making sure you see the stunning sight that is **Eilean Donan Castle.** You'll get to Inverness in the late afternoon, time perhaps for a side trip to the **Culloden Moor Battlefield** and nearby ancient **Clava Cairns.** If you have enough time, **Fort George** is 10 miles east of Inverness. Back in Inverness, you'll have plenty of decent dining and hotel options.

## Day 10: Inverness/Loch Ness

Before you pack the car for a full day at Loch Ness, visit **Inverness Castle** and the **Inverness Museum** across the street. Take the A82 along the loch to the small village of Drumnadrochit, home to two exhibits on the lake and monster lore. There are a few excellent tours of the loch, such as the history-minded **Loch Ness Shuttle** and the monster-oriented **Loch Ness Cruises.** Fill out the rest of the day visiting **Urquhart Castle,** on the banks of Ness. You can either head back to Inverness tonight or stay in one of the fine B&B country houses in the area. Either way you'll be well fed and put to bed.

## Day 11: Pitlochry

Between Inverness and Pitlochry, you'll be driving straight through the Highlands and all the valleys of heather and hills that that implies. Slightly out of the way but totally worth a visit is **Cawdor Castle** on the road to Nairn. From Nairn, wind your way south, through **Glenmore**

**Forest Park.** Stop for a quick tour and dram at **Dalwhinnie Distillery,** and a visit to **Blair Castle.** In the little town of Pitlochry, check out the interesting **Fish Ladder and Dam,** and try to see a show at the nationally famous **Pitlochry Theatre.** A great dinner option near the dam is the **Old Armoury.**

## Day 12: Perth

You can sleep in this morning because Perth is rather close. Check out the **Macbeth Experience** on the way. The biggest attraction near Perth is **Scone Palace,** where many Scottish kings were crowned. Check in to the **Parklands Hotel** and stroll around town for some shopping. Visit **St. John's Kirk** before you have dinner at one of the town's top spots, such as **Let's Eat, Number Thirty Three,** or **Tempo.**

## Day 13: St. Andrews

Head east for the coast and don't stop till you reach the splendid ruins of **St. Andrews Cathedral and Castle.** Even nongolfers will want to make the pilgrimage to the **Old Course.** The **St. Andrews University** tour is good; for something completely different, take the small jaunt out of town to the **Secret Bunker** (which I can't tell you about). In town, you'll find no shortage of great eats and watering holes.

## Day 14: Stirling

Head back toward Edinburgh for a final day in the royal town of Stirling. On the way, have lunch at the **Cellar** in Anstruther (the best seafood in the Kingdom) and visit the **Andrew Carnegie Birthplace Museum** in Dunfermline. In Stirling, visit the historic **Holy Rude Church,** tour **Stirling Castle,** and take the back walks to other interesting monuments in town. Nearby are the **Bannockburn Battlefield** and the **National Wallace Monument,** overlooking the stomping grounds of Braveheart. After your last night in Stirling, you'll be in equally convenient distance to both Edinburgh and Glasgow to fly (boo-hoo) home.

# Seeing Scotland with Kids

Traveling with children doesn't have to be a big headache or a battle of patience and wills as you tour stuffy castles and museums. Plenty of attractions and even restaurants and hotels appeal to all ages. If you have little ones in tow, following the itinerary in this section will be the path of least resistance. Also see the section on traveling with children in Chapter 5. Follow the same circuit as the one- and two-week tours (see the two preceding sections of this chapter), adjusting for your schedule and interests.

If you fly into Edinburgh, make sure to visit **Edinburgh Castle.** The CD-guided tour will confuse little kids, and older ones will play around with it too much, but the castle is amazing and fun to explore even without the commentary. Make a side trip to the **Edinburgh Zoo** to see the amazing penguins, and while in town, see the toy-filled **Museum of Childhood** and the walking science project **Dynamic Earth.** The most family-friendly hotel in town is the **Caledonian,** and even if the little ones hate shopping, they won't mind the dress-up and interactive fun of the **Edinburgh Old Town Weaving Co.**

In Glasgow, drop the bags off at the family-friendly **Kelvin Park Lorne** and split up your other sightseeing with kiddie favorites such as the car-, truck-, and train-filled **Museum of Transport** and the fun, hands-on **People's Palace.** You may want to follow it up with a romp around **Glasgow Green.** The family-friendly **Littlejohn's** restaurant will please all ages.

As you make your way up the West Coast, make sure to stop in the town of Oban, where the kids will enjoy a kitschy musical dinner at **McTavish's Kitchen.** On the way there, stop at the **Oban Seal & Marine Centre,** a wonderful nursery and hospital for stray, sick, and injured seal pups. Then take a boat trip across **Loch Lomond.** If you want to make a side trip out to the Hebridean Islands, I recommend taking the ferry from Mallaig, home to **Mallaig Marine World,** to the Isle of Skye. The ferry ride alone is fun, and the slithery **Skye Serpentarium** and cheesy **Aros Experience** appeal particularly to the 13-and-under crowd. The **Sligachan Hotel,** with video games and a playroom, is about as kid-friendly as you can get.

The **Loch Ness** region is loads of fun for children. **Inverness Castle** has an interactive role-playing tour of the underground passages. The cavernous **Loch Ness 2000 Exhibition,** with its lasers and visual effects, is great fun. The sonar-using, monster-hunting "Nessie Hunter" of **Loch Ness Cruises** is the best tour for the young and imaginative. Nearby and delightful for romping around are the ruins of **Urquhart Castle** and **Glenmore** Forest Park. There is another McTavish's Kitchen in Fort William, and the **Polmaily House Hotel,** next to Loch Ness, has a heated indoor pool, movies, a babysitting service, organized children's activities, indoor and outdoor play areas, and family-size suites.

The Tayside, Grampian, and Western Highlands regions are better known for their distilleries and castle tours, not the stuff of children's dreams. But as you make your way through the eastern part of the mainland, try to fit in the **Auchingarrich Wildlife Centre** near Comrie; **J.M. Barrie's Birthplace** (he wrote *Peter Pan*) in Kirriemuir; **Discovery Point,** the home of the adventure ship RRS *Discovery,* in Dundee; and, just north of Edinburgh in North Queensferry, **Deep Sea World,** one of the best aquariums in Europe.

# Chapter 4

# Planning Your Budget

. . . . . . . . . . . . . . . . . . . . . . . . . . . . . . . . . . . . . . . . . . . . .

### In This Chapter

▶ Budgeting for your trip

▶ Reviewing money-saving tips

▶ Shopping Scotland the smart way

▶ Carrying money conveniently and safely

. . . . . . . . . . . . . . . . . . . . . . . . . . . . . . . . . . . . . . . . . . . . .

*A*n important consideration for any vacation is money. How much is this trip going to cost, anyway? If you're like most travelers, you don't want to be tied down to a bare-bones budget that restricts you from seeing the best that Scotland has to offer — but you don't want to throw money away for no good reason, either.

The smart way to travel is to plan your budget in advance. Knowing what things cost ahead of time — and choosing what you can and can't afford — ensures that you won't suffer sticker shock once you're on the road.

In this chapter, I discuss what you should expect to pay for accommodations, dining, and sightseeing and attractions. Plus I give you some invaluable money-saving tips to follow both before you go and after you're there. Use the budget worksheet to plot out your expenses. I also provide some smart shopping tips, because let's face it: You're going to want to bring a little bit o' Scotland back home with you when you leave. And finally, I give you some tips for keeping your money safe when you're touring around Scotland.

## Budgeting for Your Trip

As far as destinations go, Scotland is neither the cheapest nor the most expensive place to visit. Can you do Scotland on $5 a day? Maybe in 1965, but not now. On $50 a day? Sure, if you don't mind hostel bunk beds and convenience-store dinners. Being realistic, you can bet on a figure more like $100 to $150 per person per day — and that doesn't include the rental car and airfare. When the credit card statement greets you a month after you've returned home, you'll know it was worth every penny, but it's best to know what you're getting into before you leave.

## So how much is this trip going to cost?

How much the trip costs depends on how smart a traveler you are. Are you a money manager or the type who has your credit card out of the holster before you can say, "Don't leave home without it"? One week in Scotland can cost you hundreds, even thousands, of dollars. You've made a huge step in the right money-saving direction by having this book in your hand. But know that being on a tight budget doesn't mean sacrificing a memorable vacation or any of the special comforts that Scotland offers.

Base your budget on your specific tastes and length of stay. Do you want only the best rooms in the best hotels in the best locations? It will cost you a little more. Do you plan to play golf every day? Factor that in to your total cost.

Generally speaking, a double room will run about $80; those on the low end will be around $50, and on the high end about $130 to $170. A good per-person allowance for lunch is $10, and for dinner between $15 and $30. Most accommodations include breakfast in the room rate, so you don't have to figure that in your daily costs. Even if you see two or three attractions each day, a fair amount to budget for sights is $15. Transportation costs vary, depending on whether you're busing it or renting a car. Driving — the transportation choice for most tourists — costs $30 to $50 a day, plus an additional $15 for a half-tank of gas — those little rental cars get really good mileage, and frankly, you'd have to drive all day to use up a full tank.

 Remember, though, that I'm providing you with a skeleton budget. Make sure you have access to emergency money. If you golf, add up greens fees and the price of renting clubs (assuming you're not lugging your own). Horseback riding and fishing also make for added costs. Perhaps the most defining factor for having a supply of money available is shopping. Do you plan to buy clothes, jewelry, crystal, and antiques, or just pick up a few postcards, a snow globe, and a couple of cheap souvenirs? A modest piece of crystal can set you back $80; a nice Edinburgh sweatshirt, about $50. So gauge your impulse-buying tendencies and factor that in, as well.

## Looking at a low-end one-week tour budget

Use the one-week tour budget in Table 4-1 to estimate your per-person costs. When figuring for a second person, deduct the cost of the rental car and gas from the total. And if you're traveling with a child and planning to share a hotel room, you may be able to lower the hotel figure by $10 or $15 (an average rate for a third guest in a room). Keep in mind, however, that a lot of places in Scotland charge by the head for accommodations — whether that extra person is a child or an adult.

Airfare, of course, is an average that can change at the whim of the airline industry.

Obviously, you can just extrapolate these figures out if you're going for longer than a week. And bulk any of these figures up, depending on your personal needs and habits.

| Table 4-1 | A Typical Week in Scotland — Per Person |
|-----------|------------------------------------------|
| **Expense** | **Cost** |
| Airfare (round-trip NY–London–Glasgow/Edinburgh) | $700 |
| Rental car | $350 |
| Two to three tanks of gas | $60–$100 |
| Seven nights in hotels ($40 per person average) | $280 |
| Seven lunches (at $10 each average) | $70 |
| Seven dinners (at $22 each average) | $154 |
| Sightseeing admissions ($15 per day) | $105 |
| Souvenirs and miscellaneous ($10 per day) | $70 |
| TOTAL | $1,789–$1,829 |

## Budget worksheet: Knowing that you can afford this trip

Look at the low-end sample budget in the preceding section and think about any areas you expect to spend more. Are you a shopping banshee? Add to the souvenir expense. Do you like to go to the theater (or, for that matter, do you expect to spend a few hours in a pub every night)? Add to the attractions (or incidentals) expense. Are you a real gourmet? You know you'll spend more than $10 on lunch. Be honest with yourself on Table 4-2: It'll make for better planning and a more enjoyable trip.

| Table 4-2 | Your Scotland Budget Worksheet | |
|---|---|---|
| **Expense** | | **Amount** |
| Airfare (multiplied by number of people traveling) | | |
| Car rental (if you expect to rent one) | | |
| Gas (expect to need a tankful, at about $30 per, for every three to four days of driving) | | |
| Lodging (multiplied by the number of nights you'll be in the country) | | |
| Breakfast (your room rate likely includes it) | | |
| Lunch (multiplied by the number of days in the country) | | |
| Dinner (multiplied by the number of days in the country) | | |
| Attractions (admission charges to museums, gardens, tours, theaters, nightclubs, and so on) | | |
| Souvenirs (T-shirts, postcards, and that antique you just gotta have) | | |
| Tips (think 15% of your meal total plus $1 a bag every time a bellhop moves your luggage) | | |
| Incidentals (whisky, snacks, and so on) | | |
| Getting from your hometown to the airport, plus long-term parking (if applicable) | | |
| Grand Total | | |

# Getting the Lowdown on 22 Money-Saving Tips

If worries about money still leave you hesitant to travel, relax. Scotland's not the cheapest European country to visit, but it *is* affordable. And you can cut a lot of corners, as necessary, to make your vacation quite a bargain. Even starving college students can afford to travel to Scotland. It just takes a little insider trading — which I'm here to give you.

Unless you have your heart set on being pampered in five-star hotels, Scotland's smaller lodges and guesthouses fit most travel budgets. A nice perk of most Scottish accommodations is the breakfast that's included in the price of the room. Sometimes the *brekkie* is hearty enough to keep you full until dinner. Also, many attractions are free.

Even if you stick to seeing things that cost nothing, you'll still experience a vast amount of the country. You can find plenty of ways, some little and some big, to cut down on costs.

Here are 22 smart ways to save on your trip to Scotland.

✔ **Go in the off-season.** Traveling between November and April will save you plenty on airfare and accommodations. Christmas week is the exception — it's the main time of year many Scots in other countries come home to visit, and the airlines cash in. (See Chapter 2 for more info on Scotland's seasons.)

✔ **Travel on off days of the week.** Airfares vary depending on the day of the week. Everybody wants to travel on the weekend, so if you can travel on a Tuesday, Wednesday, or Thursday, you may find cheaper flights. When you inquire about airfares, ask whether you can get a cheaper rate by flying on a different day. Also remember that staying over a Saturday night can occasionally cut your airfare by more than half.

✔ **Remember that group rates are a fantastic way to save money.** And you don't necessarily have to be one of a busload to get them. Sometimes a group as small as three people can snag group rates.

✔ **Get the Scottish Explorer ticket.** The *Scottish Explorer* gets you into multiple (and many of the best) sights all around the country. Whether you get the 3-, 7-, or 14-day pass, you'll save loads of money. The individual prices of Edinburgh, Sterling, and Urquhart castles total more than the cost of the one-week ticket. Buy one at the first place you see it for the length of your stay; they're on sale everywhere they can be used. For more information: ☎ 44-131-668-8664; Internet: www.historic-scotland.net.

✔ **Get the ASVA card.** Another multiple-attraction card, the *ASVA card* covers mainly historic sights and museums. Like the Scottish Explorer, it's a bargain. Both will save you pounds unless you plan on skipping attractions for golf and whisky drinking.

✔ **Try a package deal.** Many people believe that planning a trip entirely on their own saves them a lot of money, but this isn't necessarily true. Packages can save not only money but also time. A single phone call to a tourist guide or package tour operator can cover your flight, accommodations, transportation within the country, and sightseeing. Even if you don't want to go with a complete package — if you'd prefer to pay for your plane tickets with frequent-flier miles, say, or you don't like some of the things the package tour operators offer — you can book room-car deals (which include a free rental car) or other special packages directly through many hotels. (See Chapter 7.)

✔ **Always ask about discounts.** Membership in AAA, frequent-flier plans, trade unions, AARP, the military, or other groups often qualifies you for discounted rates on plane tickets, hotel rooms, and (mainly with U.S. companies) car rentals. Some car-rental companies give discounts to employees of companies that have corporate accounts. With valid identification, students, teachers, youths, and seniors may be entitled to discounts. Many attractions have discounted family prices. Ask about everything — you may be pleasantly surprised.

✔ **Book your rental car at weekly rates, when possible.** Weekly rentals are most often offered at a discounted rate.

✔ **Know where to buy petrol.** The United Kingdom has some of the highest gas (called petrol) prices in Europe, Scotland has the highest price in the U.K. outside of London, and the northern part of Scotland is the most expensive of all. One way to ease the burden is to fill your tank in larger towns (the farther south, the better) as you drive through the Highlands. *Remember:* The smaller the town, the higher the price of gas. Also, you may find gas prices lower at petrol stations at large supermarkets.

✔ **Walk.** All cities in the country are easy to walk, even Glasgow and Edinburgh. So avoid the bus and cab fare and hoof it to save a few extra pounds. You may even lose some of those eating-out pounds — and see more sights, to boot.

✔ **Skimp on souvenirs.** As a general rule, souvenirs (and we're talking those especially created for the tourist market) are poorly made and junky. Take pictures, keep a journal, and let your memories suffice. When you get home, you'll wonder what to do with all that "Scottish" stuff anyway.

✔ **Use American Express to exchange money.** Amex offers the best rate and exchanges American Express traveler's checks for free (although you probably have to pay a fee for the traveler's checks when you first get them at home). It charges a flat fee (under $5) to exchange dollars to pounds or pounds to dollars, but that beats the competition, which invariably charges a percentage of the cash exchanged. Make it your last stop before you head to the airport at the end of your trip, as well; there's no joy going home with a pocketful of useless, weighty "souvenir" coins.

✔ **Use libraries for Internet access.** Because of Western tourists' growing use of the Internet, online access is popping up all over Scotland. Most town libraries have access, and they usually don't charge or require you to be a member. This may change in the coming years, but for now, it's a good, cheap option.

✔ **Pick up free, coupon-packed visitor pamphlets and magazines.** Detailed maps, feature articles, dining and shopping directories, and discount and freebie coupons make these pocket-size giveaways a smart pickup. You'll find these types of materials sitting around in tourist board offices and, perhaps, in the lobby of your hotel.

✔ **Skip the fantabulous views.** Rooms with great views are the most expensive in any hotel. And because you probably won't be hanging out in your room all day anyway, why pay the price?

✔ **Get out of town.** In many places, hotels just outside popular tourist areas may be a great bargain and require only a little more driving — and they may even offer free parking. Sure, you may not get all the fancy amenities, and you'll probably have to carry your own bags, but the rooms may be just as comfortable and a whole lot cheaper.

✔ **Ask whether your kids can stay in your room with you for free.** Although many accommodations in Scotland charge by the head, some may allow your little ones to stay free. Even if you have to pay $10 or $15 for a rollaway bed, in the long run you'll save hundreds by not taking two rooms.

✔ **Never make phone calls from a hotel.** The inflated fees that hotels charge for phone calls are scandalous. Walk to the nearest Coin-Phone or Card-Phone for calls in and out of the country. See Chapter 9 for information about using public phones.

✔ **Take rooms that aren't *en-suite*.** Rooms without a bathroom are cheaper. Sharing a bathroom is a small sacrifice when it comes to saving money. And it's not going to detract from your trip. Group hostel rooms are even cheaper. (See Chapter 8.)

✔ **Check out accommodations with kitchens.** By renting apartments or houses for a week or more, you can save money overall on accommodations (especially if you're traveling with a group) and on food, because you can prepare your own meals in the kitchen. By avoiding big-ticket restaurant meals, you'll save a heck of a lot of money, as well as a hefty room-service bill. (See Chapter 8.)

✔ **Have the same meal for less money.** If you enjoy a late lunch at a nice restaurant and have a small dinner or snack later, your wallet and stomach will thank you. Lunch menus often offer the same food as dinner menus, but the prices are much less expensive.

✔ **Look before you tip.** Many restaurants include a service fee or gratuity on the bill, especially if you're with a group. Study your bill: You could be paying a double tip by mistake.

# *Three Corners You Shouldn't Cut*

Even if you're the most budget-conscious traveler, you need to relax every now and again and remember that each destination has certain sights, attractions, and comforts that shouldn't be missed. It's all about deciding what's really important to you and making compromises to enjoy it.

✔ **Don't skimp on sightseeing.** The sights are what you came for. If £8 ($11.60) seems like a lot for the Edinburgh Castle, know that you'll have a lot of explaining to do when the folks back home ask what it was like to visit one of Europe's most historic castles.

✔ **Don't trade money for time.** Maximizing time is essential, so don't wait hours for a cheaper bus when the more expensive one is leaving now. For example, if it costs a little more to fly straight to Glasgow rather than taking a train from London, you'll need to weigh that against the fact that the train can take all day and the plane ride takes an hour. It just may not be worth saving a few bucks when you're losing a few good hours or a day.

✔ **Invest in good shoes.** Whether you like to walk or not, you'll be doing a good bit of it after you get to Scotland. So don't bring a pair of cheap sneaks or straight-from-the-box dress shoes and just figure you'll brave the blisters. Go for comfortable and sturdy. And no Birkenstocks — they're comfy at first, but after ten hours you'll have strap sores that kill!

# *Shopping, Scottish Style*

From local jewelry to whisky to traditional Scottish apparel, you'll find many great souvenirs and uniquely Scottish gifts to bring home with you.

Locally made crafts, such as **pottery, glassware,** and **jewelry,** are big-selling items for visitors. By buying these original works, you support arts and crafts in the country and bring home something unique in the bargain. Caithness glasswork, Mackintosh-inspired home furnishings, and earrings and necklaces made with native gems and stones are among the finds. If you're in the market for furniture, be sure to ask about shipping — some antiques shops have the resources to ship large items to you back home. Most music stores sell traditional instruments, such as bagpipes, harps, and accordions.

Take home a real taste of Scotland by buying local whisky and foods. You can find items, such as shortbread, oatcakes, and tea biscuits, at any grocery, and good Scotch whisky at an off-licence (liquor store). Gourmet shops stock items such as fudge, toffee, chocolate, preserves, and even haggis (see Chapter 1).

Wool and tweed clothing are popular Scottish exports. A sweater (called a *jumper*) is the right thing to wear for cooler temperatures in northern sheep country. Harris tweed (which can be made only on the Isle of Harris) is of the highest quality and worth the price. Tweed jackets, cardigans, cashmere sweaters, scarves, and sheepskin rugs are among the popular wool items.

## How to get the total Highland look

If you want to sport the complete Highland look, you'll have to get yourself a *fillimore* (big blanket in Gaelic) and learn how to wrap it around your waist and up over your shoulder. Locals say it also makes a fine cover for sleeping beneath the stars; we'll just take their word for it. Short of that, you can get a classic kilt in a favorite family *tartan* (the distinctive pattern on the fabric that denotes clan or regional connections). To fill out the classic look, you'll also need a *dirk* (the dagger), belt, and *sporran* (the purse-like pouch).

Interestingly, it is believed that the kilt is actually a version of the Roman tunic. It dates to the fifth century A.D., when Romans invaded Scotland. If you're in the market for a kilt, check out *So You're Going to Wear the Kilt* by J. Charles Thomson (Heraldic Art Press, P.O. Box 7192, Arlington, VA 22207). And you'll want to pick out a tartan. You can view and search tartan patterns before you leave home at www.tartans.scotland.net, or you can pick up a tartan book anywhere in Scotland.

## *Shopping wisely*

Smart shoppers should follow the following guidelines:

- ✔ **Check prices on items you think you may want to buy before you leave home.** This way, you'll know whether you're really getting a bargain by buying them abroad.

- ✔ **Shop in out-of-the-way places.** Main Street shops in smaller towns and main-drag stores in larger cities offer great window-shopping, but be prepared to drop a bigger chunk of change than you would in a less central location. You may find the same item in another shop on a lower-rent street for less.

- ✔ **Shop in street markets.** This is a fun way to do business, especially when you start haggling, which you may. Scottish street hawkers are real characters, and you'll have an experience that's hard to come by at home. The quality of the merchandise is iffier than that at retail shops, but you can get great deals on everything from designer knockoffs to items identical to those discarded by overstocked retail shops.

- ✔ **Shop around.** Prices vary dramatically from shop to shop — and market stall to market stall — and they usually drop as you get farther away from touristy places. Let the store owners know you're comparison shopping, and the price may go down on the spot.

✔ **Forget designer clothing.** Unless you're looking for particularly Scottish clothes, you probably won't find any bargains on European designer clothes that you can't get at home for the same price (or even lower). Just because you're in Europe doesn't mean you'll get great deals on French or Italian clothes hot off the runway.

✔ **Curb your impulses.** Shop selectively and don't buy every trinket you see. Go for the items that truly capture the spirit and culture of Scotland and will hold the best memories. Before you buy it, make sure that the Loch Ness–monster doll or castle key chain is something you really, really want. Also, take into consideration how much you can comfortably fit into your luggage (unless you're planning to mail some things home).

✔ **Make sure any videotapes you purchase are in U.S. format.** European videotapes aren't compatible with U.S. machines. (Luckily, tourist sites that are accustomed to serving Americans offer them in the U.S. format.)

✔ **Don't let yourself be led by the nose.** On most escorted tours, the guide takes or directs you to shops that offer "special prices" to people on your tour. Ninety percent of the time, this means that the tour guide is getting a kickback for bringing in revenue. (Guides are so scandalously underpaid that this often is the only way they can scrape by.) Usually, the store passes the burden along to you by jacking up the price. Although some guides do give honest recommendations, and even some of those kickback arrangements don't adversely affect you, it's impossible to know when a recom-mendation is on the level. Be cynical and comparison shop. If it seems too expensive, it probably is.

✔ **Act like an old shopping hand.** Scrutinize labels, kick the prover-bial tires, and otherwise show that (or look like) you know what you're doing. Shopkeepers who see a savvy customer are less likely to try to pull the wool over your eyes — even when you're trying on sweaters.

✔ **Dress respectably, but not too well.** You want merchants to know you're a potential paying customer and not riffraff, but you don't want to give them the idea that you're loaded — especially in markets, where prices can go up on the spot if you look like you're willing to pay anything.

## Sold! Knowing what to do now

Okay, you've bought it; now what do you do? Here are a few tips on ensuring the fairness of the sale and the safety of your purchase.

✔ **Count your change and check that the receipt is complete and accurate.** Don't be rude about it, but make sure you haven't gotten a rotten shopkeeper who's trying to scam or shortchange you. Even if there's no malice aforethought, cashiers have been known to make mistakes.

> ✔ **Ship breakables home.** It may cost a bit more, but the longer you keep your fragile purchases with you bouncing down the road of your trip, the greater the chances that your crystal vase will end up as crystal shards.

> ✔ **Make a photo record.** Save yourself time and hassle should something go wrong with a purchase to be shipped home by snapping a photo of it before it's wrapped up. This photo makes an excellent proof of purchase when it comes to insurance claims.

# Managing Money When You're on the Road

After you settle on a budget for your trip, you can start figuring out the nuts and bolts of carrying money abroad. How much money do you want to bring along? Do you want to carry cold hard cash, credit cards, traveler's checks, or all three? How can you get more money once you're in Scotland? What's the best way to exchange dollars for pounds? And how can you ensure that your money will be safe and secure while you're vacationing? This section offers just about everything you need to know about money matters in Scotland.

## The local currency: What it's worth to you

The currency in Scotland, the *British pound,* is similar to American currency. Denominations are the same, except that the U.K. has a coin for 2 pence, and the single pound can be a coin or a bill. Sometimes the British pound is referred to as *sterling* (which would differentiate it from pounds printed by the Royal Bank of Scotland) and also as *quid* or *bob.* Smaller denominations are called *pence* and sometimes just *p.* There is no value difference between pounds printed in Scotland and England, and both are accepted throughout Scotland. The only difference between them is that a single pound is a coin in England and a paper bill in Scotland; you'll end up using both.

Generally, things are more expensive in Scotland than they would be in the States and other English-speaking countries. I have found that many items in Scotland cost the same as they do in America in numerical amounts — for instance, if a soda is a dollar in America, it's often a pound in Scotland. But because you only get about 70 pence for every dollar you exchange, things cost about 50 percent more in Scotland. This isn't true of all items, but it gives a general idea of how far your new cash and weighty coins will go.

# What is VAT?

The tax-back scheme in Scotland is great for tourists who spend a good deal of money on books, jewelry, musical instruments, clothes, you name it. But many tourists come to Scotland, spend a good deal of money, and never find out how to get their VAT back or don't bother because they don't fully understand how it works. So that you don't make the same mistake, here's your quick guide to the VAT.

VAT stands for *value-added tax,* and it's a whopping 17.5% tacked on to the price of many goods. The good news is, as a tourist, you are entitled to get it back in stores that are part of the Retail Export Scheme (signs are posted in the window). Show your passport and ask for the VAT form to fill out when you make your purchase. When you leave the U.K., you submit the form to Customs for approval. After Customs has stamped it, mail the form back to the shop with the envelope provided — but you must do it before you leave the country. Your refund will then be mailed to you.

***Note:*** Not all VATs are refundable. For the most part, taxes added to services aren't refundable. Hotels, restaurants, and car rentals, for example, charge VATs that you won't get back.

The exchange rate fluctuates daily (by small amounts). The best source for up-to-date currency exchange information is www.cnn.com/travel/currency. The average rates are something like those shown in Table 4-3:

| Table 4-3 | A Typical Currency Exchange Rate | | |
|---|---|---|---|
| *One Dollar* | *Equals* | *One British Pound* | *Equals* |
| $1 U.S. | £0.71 | £1 | $1.45 U.S. |
| $1 Canadian | £0.45 | £1 | $2.20 Canadian |
| $1 Australian | £0.36 | £1 | $2.75 Australian |
| $1 New Zealand | £0.28 | £1 | $3.61 New Zealand |

You can *exchange money* anywhere you see the **Bureau de Change** sign. You see them at travel agencies, banks, post offices, and tourist information offices. Generally, you'll get the best rates at banks; find out the location of the bank branch nearest you at the local tourist office.

# All about ATMs

The rise of the mighty ATM has made money matters a cinch for modern travelers, but there are still a few things to keep in mind. Yes, you probably can use your ATM cards in Scotland, and the machines work the way they do at home. But don't ask locals where the "ATM" is: They're called *service tills* or *cash machines* in Scotland. Most ATMs can give cash advances against major credit cards, as well.

ATMs are linked to networks that most likely include your bank at home. **Cirrus** (☎ **800-424-7787;** www.mastercard.com/atm/) and **Plus** (www.visa.com/atms) are the two most popular networks; check the back of your ATM card to see which network your bank belongs to. Before you leave home, call the 800 numbers to locate ATMs at your destination.

Be sure to check the daily withdrawal limit with your bank before you set off on your trip.

If you lose your ATM card, contact your bank at home and report it immediately. You don't want your bank account depleted in the event that the card (and, in a worst-case scenario, personal identification number) falls into the wrong hands.

# Using credit cards

Credit cards are invaluable when traveling. They're a safe way to carry money and provide a convenient record of all your expenses. You can also withdraw cash advances from your credit cards at most banks (though you'll start paying hefty interest on the advance the moment you receive the cash, and you won't receive frequent-flier miles on an airline credit card). At most banks, you don't even need to go to a teller; you can get a cash advance at the ATM if you know your personal identification number or PIN. If you've forgotten your PIN or didn't even know you had one, call the phone number on the back of your credit card and ask the bank to send it to you. It usually takes five to seven business days, though some banks will provide the number over the phone if you tell them your mother's maiden name or pass some other security clearance.

Visa, MasterCard, American Express, and Diner's Club are all widely used in Scotland.

# What's up with the euro?

Don't sweat it, yet. The European common currency, the *euro,* has not been legislated in the U.K. as of this writing, which means that the U.K. isn't participating in the euro currency. A major debate is raging, among politicians and the population alike, about whether to phase out the pound. Most agree that it's inevitable in the next few years. You may see euro equivalents calculated on some money transactions, but that's only to get consumers familiar with the new money. And even if the euro is in wide circulation by the time you go to Scotland, it'll be just like exchanging your dollars for pounds now.

Call your credit card companies immediately if cards are **lost or stolen.** Most Scottish merchants are careful about checking the signatures on receipts against the card, but a smart thief will quickly master the fine art of forging your signature. By getting to your credit card company before the thief makes any illegal purchases, you save the hassle of getting those purchases exempted and maybe even help the police find the thief. Make sure your cards really are lost, though, before canceling and reporting them. You'll kick yourself if, after you've gone to the trouble of canceling your cards, you discover them stashed in that secret place where you hid them so that they wouldn't be stolen.

Almost every credit card company has an **emergency toll-free number** that you can call to report a loss or theft. The company may be able to wire you a cash advance off your credit card immediately, and in many places can deliver an emergency credit card in a day or two.

The issuing bank's number is usually on the back of the credit card — but that doesn't help much if the card is stolen. Call toll-free directory assistance (☎ 800-555-1212) before you leave home to get the number.

The phone numbers to report stolen credit cards while you're in Scotland are:

- ✔ Visa (☎ 0800-891-725)
- ✔ MasterCard (☎ 0800-964-767)
- ✔ American Express (☎ 0800-700-700)
- ✔ Diner's Club (☎ 702-797-5532; members can call collect)

If you're an **American Express** card member, bring a single blank personal check and keep it in a separate place from your card. If the card is lost or stolen, you can use that check to draw a cash advance against your account. Just bring it, unsigned, into any Amex office, and it'll be cashed on the spot.

# Traveler's checks: Pros and cons

Traveler's checks are something of an anachronism from the days before ATMs made cash accessible at any time. Many banks, however, impose a fee every time you use an ATM in a different city or at a different bank. If you're withdrawing money every day, you may be better off with traveler's checks — provided that you don't mind showing identification every time you want to cash a check.

You can get traveler's checks at almost any bank in the States and in Canada. **American Express** offers denominations of $10, $20, $50, $100, $500, and $1,000. You'll pay a service charge ranging from 1% to 4%. You can also get American Express traveler's checks over the phone by calling ☎ **800-221-7282;** by using this number, Amex gold and platinum cardholders are exempt from the service charge. Members of **AAA** can obtain checks without a fee at most AAA offices.

**Visa** offers traveler's checks at Citibank locations across the U.S. and Canada, and at several other banks. The service charge is 1.5% to 2%; checks come in denominations of $20, $50, $100, $500, and $1,000. **MasterCard** also offers traveler's checks. Call ☎ **800-223-9920** for a location near you.

Don't use **traveler's checks** to pay for a meal or a room. The exchange rate is worse than at a bank or exchange bureau. Ideally, cash traveler's checks at an American Express office to avoid commission costs and to get a better rate.

Always keep a list of the traveler's checks numbers in a safe and separate place. Keep a record of the serial numbers either in a different pocket from your checks or in your luggage (or both), so that you're ensured a refund if checks are lost or stolen. Also, dual checks are available for traveling couples, and either person can sign for them. If your checks are lost or stolen, call **American Express** toll-free (☎ **0800-700-700** in Scotland) to have the checks replaced. To make a report, you will need to know which checks were unused. The best way to keep track of this is by creating a list of the check numbers and crossing them off as you use them.

# Traveling smart: Crime and safety

Rest easy: You're going to a pretty darn safe place. The occurrence of violent crime and theft is low in Scotland. You're actually safer there than in most major American cities. Scotland has so few guns on the streets that many police don't even carry them. As a tourist, the most important thing you can do is guard yourself against theft. Pickpockets look for people who seem to have the most money on them and know the least about where they are. Standing on a street corner at night with your nose in this book will immediately give you away: Tourist! Money waiting to be taken! Scotland is quite safe, but crime is a fact of modern life. And it's always more prevalent in larger cities.

Scotland recently passed a law to help cut down on tourist-targeted crime. Thieves consider out-of-towners good targets for crime because they can't testify in court if they've left the country. Now, just identifying a suspect's mug shot is enough evidence to arrest someone, so you aren't such a sitting duck. But that doesn't stop the baddies from trying, so here are a few simple precautions that can help safeguard you against crime:

- ✔ **Leave the Tiffany cufflinks at home.** You don't need to bring valuable jewelry or irreplaceable heirlooms with you when you travel. If possible, arrange to store excess cash, traveler's checks, passports, plane tickets, and other valuables in a hotel safe or security box; do not mistake a locked suitcase in your rental car for a secure hiding place. If you carry traveler's checks, keep the list of numbers and denominations and the emergency refund phone number separate from the checks.

- ✔ **Use a handbag or backpack instead of the familiar "I'm a tourist!" camera bag.** Straps that can go around your neck and under your arm make for more secure bags than those that go over just a shoulder. Bags are most likely to be stolen in crowded streets and shops, and while you're having a drink or bite to eat; don't think that lots of people milling around make you safe from theft. Wallets should be kept in a buttoned back pocket. If you don't have a buttoned pocket, put your wallet in a front pocket.

- ✔ **Don't carry more cash than you'll need for that day or evening.** Leave excess money in the hotel safe. While you're out, keep half of your money in your wallet or purse and "hide" the rest in the small, or fifth, pocket of your jeans or pants. This way, if you're mugged or your pocket is picked, you won't be forking over all your cash — and robbers will be none the wiser about the stash in your hiding place.

- ✔ **When visiting a larger city, park your car in a controlled car park and keep the ticket with you.** When parking overnight, ask the receptionist at your hotel about secure car parking. Lock your car even if you're only leaving it for a few minutes. It takes just seconds for a thief to open a car door and steal the bag that contains your copy of *Scotland For Dummies,* 2nd Edition. Then where would you be?

- ✔ **Never leave luggage, valuables, or camera bags in an unattended parked car.** Bring as much as you can into your hotel room for safekeeping, and during the day put as much as you can in the trunk. Luggage on a roof rack is catnip for thieves as well.

✔ **If you're camping, do so only in designated sites.** Setting up camp in public areas and on unapproved sites is dangerous and often illegal.

✔ **Be aware of your surroundings.** If you're lost in a "dodgy" area, don't appear frightened or confused or even look in the guide to orient yourself — this makes you a target. Proceed calmly and assuredly till you come to a shop or public building and ask for assistance.

# Stop, thief! What to do if your wallet is stolen or lost

First of all, don't panic. Whether your valuables are lost or stolen, contact the police by dialing ☎ **999** on any telephone: Your credit-card company or insurer may require a police report, and any lost items can easily be returned to you if they're found.

Except for the cash, everything else is replaceable. Here are a couple of ways to get emergency cash.

✔ **Contact your bank.** Some larger banks will even accept collect calls. You may be able to get cash from your checking account wired as a Moneygram and sent to a travel agent or perhaps your hotel in Scotland. Fees will apply, but at least you won't starve.

✔ **Get a money transfer.** Have a friend back home wire you money through **Western Union.** There are locations in just about every major town in Scotland, located in post offices, hotels, and travel agencies. It takes only minutes to complete the transaction and get your money. Call the toll-free number (☎ **0800-833-833**) for the nearest location and information.

# Chapter 5

# Tips for Travelers with Special Interests

● ● ● ● ● ● ● ● ● ● ● ● ● ● ● ● ● ● ● ● ● ● ● ● ● ● ● ● ● ● ● ● ● ● ● ● ● ● ● ● ● ● ● ● ● ● ●

*In This Chapter*

▶ Traveling with kids

▶ Enjoying the perks of senior travel

▶ Easing the way if you're traveling with a disability

▶ Discovering student-friendly deals

▶ Using resources for gay and lesbian travelers

▶ Searching for the meatless meal

● ● ● ● ● ● ● ● ● ● ● ● ● ● ● ● ● ● ● ● ● ● ● ● ● ● ● ● ● ● ● ● ● ● ● ● ● ● ● ● ● ● ● ● ● ● ●

Scotland's population is a friendly one that welcomes visitors of all stripes. Some aspects of travel can be challenging for people with special needs, however, so this chapter provides valuable travel advice to help make the trip successful for everyone involved.

## Family Planning: Tips on Traveling with Kids

Ah, the family vacation. It's a rite of passage for many households, one that in a split second can dissolve into a *National Lampoon* movie. Fear not, adventurous parents: Taking the family to Scotland can be as pleasant a trip as your own honeymoon. But — and this is a *big* but — you have to lay the groundwork and set up some rules, such as not letting your children play hide-and-seek in Edinburgh Castle!

The first thing you may notice while traveling with children is that you're not alone. Plenty of people make Scotland a family vacation destination each year, with complete success. See Chapter 3 for a terrific itinerary that's all about kids.

## Taking steps before you leave

To help ensure a peaceful trip, take care of a few preliminaries before lift-off. First, even if your children are old enough to pack for themselves, **check what they've packed.** You want to make sure that they have the clothes necessary for any changes in weather conditions (see the section on climate in Chapter 2). You also want to make sure they haven't overpacked: Even if they insist on lugging their own bags throughout Scotland, be prepared to take up the slack. Think of it as lower-back self-preservation.

**Bring a few toys for younger children,** but nothing that can't be replaced at the local Toys 'R Us upon return. Also, you don't want them paying more attention to an action figure than to the attractions, so don't go overboard.

Music tapes and even books on tape are great diversions on long drives. Puzzles and car games work well for those times when the scenery from the back window isn't sufficiently engaging. These, as well as a deck of cards, also work well when children are waiting for food in a restaurant. When the place isn't too fancy, I bide the time waiting for dinner on a small electronic travel chessboard. (Guess you don't actually have to have kids to appreciate this section!)

## Employing kid-friendly strategies

Keep in mind that most attractions, and, occasionally, public transportation, offer **reduced prices for children.** And most attractions, even places that don't seem family oriented, have family group prices (usually for two adults and two or three children). Be sure to ask, and see more money-saving tips in Chapter 4.

**When you book your flight,** let the booking agent know the age of your children. Some airlines offer child-companion fares and even have a special children's menu upon request. Flight attendants are usually happy to warm up baby food, formula, or milk, if you need it.

Car-rental companies provide necessary **car seats,** and all vehicles have rear seatbelts. The law requires that children be buckled when in the front and back seats.

Contact your hotel, guesthouse, or B&B's concierge or manager when you arrive, or better yet, call ahead before you go. Many times, an **extra cot for a child** is just a small additional cost — a welcome exception to the per-person pricing standard in Scotland. Also, hotels, guesthouses, and some B&Bs will have a **babysitter** list at their fingertips, if you and your spouse decide to kick up your heels on your own for an evening.

## Recognizing resources for traveling with kids

For more specific information and advice on traveling with families, contact **Travel with your Children** (☎ 212-206-0688) for an information packet. Six times a year, TWYCH publishes *Family Travel Times*. Subscriptions ($39 a year) include a weekly Wednesday call-in service, during which you can talk to an expert who has traveled the world with her kids. A free publication list and a sample issue are available by calling ☎ 888-822-4388 or visiting www.familytraveltimes.com.

Check out the travel sections in your library and bookstore; you can discover books geared specifically toward traveling with little ones. Most concentrate on the U.S., but two, *Family Travel* (Lanier Publishing International) and *How to Take Great Trips with Your Kids* (The Harvard Common Press), are full of good general advice that applies to traveling anywhere. Another reliable book with a worldwide focus is *Adventuring with Children* (Foghorn Press).

# Advice for Seniors

The worldwide travel market has never been more open to senior citizens. With fantastic discounts for seniors available for almost every single aspect of travel, you have practically no reason not to pack up and get out of the house. Whether you've always wanted to go to Scotland or decided to visit on a lark, there's no time like the present. And best of all, Scotland is a senior-friendly country, with lots of discounted admission prices for attractions and plenty of holiday packages devoted solely to your age group. Note: **OAP,** common on many admission price lists, stands for **old age pensioner,** and can be translated as senior citizen.

When **booking your flight and rental car,** remember to ask about senior discounts. In addition, some hotel chains and rental-car companies offer discounts for being a member of the **AARP** (which used to stand for the American Association of Retired Persons, but is now just "AARP"). Call the AARP (☎ 800-424-3410) for information on Scotland in particular.

Seniors qualify for **discounts throughout Scotland,** typically 10% at attractions and theaters, unless otherwise posted.

American tour operators that specialize in senior travel programs include **CIE Tours** (☎ 800-CIE-TOUR), which gives discounts on select tours for persons over 65, and **Elderhostel** (☎ 877-426-8056, www.elderhostel.org), which offers longer tours out of New York, such as the 17-day "Castles & Gardens of the Highlands of Scotland" for $3,800. Elderhostel offers comprehensive educational programs for anyone over 55 and will send you a free catalog of its tours.

Keep in mind that many senior-targeted tour operators are of the tour-bus variety, with free trips thrown in for those who organize groups of 20 or more. If you're seeking more independent travel, you should probably consult a regular travel agent (see Chapter 6).

The *Mature Traveler,* a monthly newsletter on senior citizen travel, is a valuable resource. It is available by subscription ($29.95 a year); for a free sample, call ☎ **800-460-6676** or send a postcard with your name and address to The Mature Traveler, Box 1543, Wildomar, CA 92595 (Internet: www.thematuretraveler.com).

GEM publishes *The Book of Deals,* a collection of more than 1,000 senior discounts on airlines, lodging, tours, and attractions; it's available for $9.95 by calling ☎ **800-460-6676.** Another helpful publication is *101 Tips for the Mature Traveler,* available from Grand Circle Travel, 347 Congress St., Suite 3A, Boston, MA 02210 (☎ **800-221-2610;** www.gct.com).

# Advice for Travelers with Disabilities

These days, sensitivity to persons with disabilities extends to most of the world's best-loved travel destinations. So, generally speaking, a physical impairment shouldn't slow you down or stop you from traipsing the globe. Specifically, it won't be too difficult to get around Scotland and have a great time.

Scotland has regulations for public areas ensuring accessibility, although these regulations aren't as comprehensive as they are in the United States. Most sidewalks have ramps, and many accommodations are wheelchair accessible. Getting around in cities and towns isn't that hard. I have, however, come across a good number of B&Bs that aren't accessible and attractions that would pose difficulties for tourists with disabilities.

Scotland is an old country, and its attractions prove it. You'll find that not every museum has closed captions for media presentations, and not every castle has an entrance ramp. You want to call ahead at attractions and B&Bs, but you can feel fairly confident that most restaurants and newer hotels will be entirely accessible.

For further assistance, the "Information for Visitors with Disabilities" guide, published by the National Trust of Scotland and available at most tourist offices, lists all the major attractions in Scotland and details the accessibility of each portion of the attraction (for example, the castle may be accessible but the gardens and toilets are not). The publication even details access points and views that are available from a wheelchair.

*A World of Options,* a 658-page book of resources for disabled travelers, covers everything from biking trips to scuba outfitters. It costs $35 and is available from Mobility International USA, P.O. Box 10767, Eugene, OR, 97440 (☎ **541-343-1284,** voice and TTY; www.miusa.org).

Many of the major car-rental companies now offer hand-controlled cars for disabled drivers. Avis can provide such a vehicle at many locations with advance notice; Hertz requires between 24 and 72 hours of advance reservation at most of its locations.

If you or someone in your family is traveling with a disability, you may also want to consider joining a tour that caters specifically to you. One of the best operators is **Flying Wheels Travel,** P.O. Box 382, Owatonna, MN 55060 (☎ **800-535-6790;** fax 507-451-1685). It offers various escorted tours and cruises, as well as private tours in minivans with lifts. Another good company is **FEDCAP Rehabilitation Services,** 211 W. 14th St., New York, NY 10011. Call ☎ **212-727-4200** or fax 212-727-4373 for information about membership and summer tours. **Directions Unlimited** (☎ **800-533-5343**) is a travel agency that specializes in serving mentally challenged travelers.

The **American Foundation for the Blind** (☎ **800-232-5463**) offers specific travel advice for the visually impaired, including information on taking a seeing-eye dog with you as you travel. And you can obtain a copy of *Air Transportation of Handicapped Persons* by writing to Free Advisory Circular No. AC12032, Distribution Unit, U.S. Department of Transportation, Publications Division, M-4332, Washington, DC 20590.

**Accessible Journeys,** 35 W. Sellers Ave., Ridley Park, PA 19078 (☎ **800-846-4537** or 610-521-0339; www.disabilitytravel.com), is an organization that provides guided tours if you're in need of a wheelchair or other assistance.

If you're looking for a **disability-specialist travel agent** or other tips and resources, point your Internet browser to www.access-able.com, which is, hands down, the best source for disabled travelers. You'll also find relay and voice numbers for hotels, airlines, and car-rental companies on this user-friendly site, as well as links to accessible accommodations, attractions, transportation, and tours, local medical resources and equipment repairers, and much more.

A final note if you're sensitive to cigarette smoke. If you have serious problems with smelling other people's smoke, you're bound to be uncomfortable just about everywhere in Scotland, except in your own room. Smoking is allowed all over — from pubs and restaurants to the airport. Many, but not all, restaurants have nonsmoking sections, but after a night in the pubs, your clothes will likely smell of smoke.

# Advice for Students

Having been a starving college student once, I thoroughly respect the plight of the fiscally challenged student traveler. Also, I'm inclined to congratulate you on not shying away from what I think is a rite of passage — traveling when you're young!

The biggest mistake potential travelers make is assuming that globe-trotting is out of their reach — namely, too expensive. Luckily, an entire market is devoted to making travel accessible to the student traveler.

**Council Travel,** under **CIEE (Council on International Educational Exchange),** is a great source for cheap flights, reasonably priced traveler's insurance, and international student and youth identification cards that get you discounts at many attractions in Scotland. You don't need to bring in photos of yourself; they'll take them at the office. You don't even have to be a student to use CIEE, either. They have the same fares available for anyone 25 years and younger, as well as for teachers, as long as you have an ID card to prove it. Call ☎ **800-2-COUNCIL** or visit www. ciee.org for information, flight bookings, and the nearest location to you. The Canadian version of CIEE is **Travel CUTS** (☎ **416-979-2406**).

After you're in the country, Council Travel has a partner organization in Scotland called **USIT,** with offices open year-round in Edinburgh at 53 Forrest Road (☎ **0131-225-6111**), and in Glasgow, at 122 George Street (☎ **0141-553-1818**).

If you lose your ticket or need to change your departure date, these offices can and will happily help you. The CIEE toll-free number for Traveler's Assistance is (☎ **877-370-ISIC**). Outside the United States, you can call collect (☎ **715-342-4104**).

Getting an ID as an international student, teacher, or youth is worth the money. Even if you don't see a sign that says, "Student discounts available," always ask. In some cases, the savings are more than half the regular admission.

If you're looking for a great guide specifically targeted to college-age travelers, pick up Frommer's *Hanging Out in England, Scotland, and Wales* (Wiley Publishing, Inc.), which gives the unvarnished lowdown on inexpensive little hostels and inns, happening nightclubs, and the best cheap eats in every corner of the region ($21.99; www.frommers.com).

# Advice for Gay and Lesbian Travelers

Although it's not considered the most tolerant or open-minded country in Europe, Scotland is not unsafe for gay and lesbian travelers. While Glasgow and Edinburgh are relatively progressive-minded, public displays of affection there may garner disapproving looks, and smaller towns and villages won't have a gay club — you can count on that. In Edinburgh, contact the **Gay and Lesbian Switchboard** (☎ 0131-556-4049) for more information.

**The International Gay & Lesbian Travel Association** (☎ 800-448-8550 or 954-776-2626; fax 954-776-3303; www.iglta.org) links travelers with the appropriate gay-friendly service organization or tour specialist. With approximately 1,200 members, the IGLTA offers quarterly news-letters, marketing mailings, and a membership directory that's updated quarterly. Membership often includes gay or lesbian businesses but is open to individuals for $150 yearly, plus a $100 initial fee for new members. Members are kept informed of gay and gay-friendly hoteliers, tour operators, and airline and cruise line representatives. Contact the IGLTA for a list of its member agencies, who will be tied in to the IGLTA's information resources.

Travel agencies geared to both gay men and lesbians include **Family Abroad** (☎ 800-999-5500 or 212-459-1800) and **Yellowbrick Road** (☎ 800-476-5466); **Above and Beyond Tours** (☎ 800-397-2681) is primarily geared toward gay men.

There are also two good, biannual English-language gay guidebooks, both focused on gay men but including information for lesbians, as well. You can get the *Odysseus* or *Spartacus International Gay Guide* from most gay and lesbian bookstores and often from the large chain stores as well. Or you can order them from **Giovanni's Room** (☎ 215-923-2960) or **A Different Light Bookstore** (☎ 800-343-4002 or 212-989-4850). Both lesbians and gay men may want to pick up a copy of *Gay Travel A to Z* ($16). The **Ferrari Guides** (www.q-net.com) is yet another comprehensive series of gay and lesbian guidebooks.

**Out and About,** 8 W. 19th St. #401, New York, NY 10011 (☎ 800-929-2268 or 212-645-6922), offers guidebooks and a monthly newsletter packed with good information on the global gay and lesbian scene. A year's subscription to the newsletter costs $49. *Our World,* 1104 North Nova Rd., Suite 251, Daytona Beach, FL 32117 (☎ 904-441-5367), is a slick monthly maga-zine promoting and highlighting travel bargains and opportunities. Annual subscription rates are $35 in the United States, $45 outside the U.S.

## Staying safe

Scotland very well could be, in general, a safer place than most for people travel-ing alone — especially women — but be careful not to be lulled into a false sense of security. To read more, I recommend the book *Safety and Security for Women Who Travel,* by Sheila Swan Laufer and Peter Laufer, which caters to the concerns of the female traveler. It's well worth $12.95.

# *Advice for Vegetarians*

Don't have a cow, man! Any place that loves blood pudding and haggis as much Scotland does is enough to scare off even the most fickle vegetarian. The good news is, you will not go hungry on your trip, I promise. It turns out that the Scots are pretty veg-friendly, and you'll find a surprisingly large variety of meatless meals throughout the country. I include some good vegetarian restaurants in this guide, and you can rest assured that most of the restaurants I recommend have at least a couple of veggie selections.

A **traditional Scottish breakfast** is a pretty meaty event, and the cost of a room nearly always includes it. You can still partake of this element of true local culture by asking your host to hold the meat and lavish you with eggs, beans, toast, fried tomatoes, potatoes, and homemade breads and goodies. You can count on a selection of cereals and fruit, too.

Food in stores carries labels marked by a **green leaf icon** and the phrase "suitable for vegetarians." And you may be shocked to know how much fast food is vegetarian! **McDonald's** and **Burger King** have veggie burgers, and the King has a delicious spicy bean burger. Chippers (take-outs) usually offer veggie burgers, too, plus items like a hamburger without the meat (salad burgers). If you're a strict vegetarian, you may want to pass on chips — they're fried in the same oil as everything else.

## Scotland for the Scottish: Digging up your roots

Many visitors come to Scotland to find their ancestors. If you're interested in tracking your family tree while you're in the country, you can do some legwork before you go. If you are a Mackenzie, a McDonald, a Campbell, or a descendant from another large clan, you may have more luck tracing your roots than if you're from a smaller clan. Which begs the question: What exactly is a clan?

A *clan* is essentially a group of people with a common ancestor. Keep in mind, however, that even if you share the last name of a Scottish clan, you aren't necessarily a descendant of an ancient or royal line. Instead, your ancestor may have been loyal to that clan and was rewarded with a gift of land.

Here are some tips on discovering your Scottish roots:

✔ **Begin your research at home.** The most immediate and valuable sources of research are living family members. Details like surnames, occupations, and religious practices are all important clues for a successful search.

✔ **Dig up documents.** Birth, marriage, and death certificates (civil and parochial), census returns, and immigration papers are all valuable. Your parent's marriage certificate lists both sets of grandparents, so bring a copy. In the United States, the **National Archives** has a great service for helping you trace your family back to the port of origin. In Canada, the best launching board for genealogical research is a Web site called Netring (www.geocities.com/genealogy pages).

✔ **Use a professional agency.** You can save time and hassle by utilizing local and professional research agencies in Scotland. Costs can range from the price of copies of certificates to the hourly cost of researchers. Hand over any materials you've dug up on your own and let the **Scottish Roots Ancestral Research Service,** 16 Forth St., Edinburgh, EH1 3LH (☎ **0131-477-8214**; fax: 0131-550-3701; www.scotweb.co.uk/scotroots), do the rest of the work. To begin tracing your ancestral roots and researching your family tree, the **Scottish Family Research** service, P. O. Box 12760, Edinburgh, EH8 7TZ (☎ **0131-659-6249**; fax: 0131-620-1386; www.linnet.co.uk/linnet/tour/scottishfamily research.htm), requires only the birth or marriage or death details of an ancestor in Scotland.

✔ **Do your own detective work in Scotland.** Several local genealogical sources in counties throughout Scotland function more as records storage facilities or archives than as full-service research services. The **Scottish Genealogy Society Library,** 15 Victoria Terrace, Edinburgh, EH1 2JL (☎ **0131-220-3677**; www.scotsgenealogy.com/library.htm), is a large collection of family history material. The **General Register Office for Scotland,** New Register House, 3 West Register St. Edinburgh, EH1 3YT (☎ **0131-334-0380**; www.ori gins.net or www.gro-scotland.gov.uk), has civil registration records, census returns, and pre-1855 Church of Scotland parish registers. The **National Archives of Scotland,** H. M. General Register House, 2 Princes St., Edinburgh EH1 3YY (☎ **0131-535-1314**; fax: 0131-535-1328; www.nas.gov.uk), has wills and testaments, nonconformist church records, church session records, legal and court records, estate records, land records, and maps and plans. The **National Library of Scotland,** George IV Bridge, Edinburgh, EH1 1EW (☎ **0131-226-4531** x2101; fax: 0131-466-2804; www.nls.uk), has an extensive collection of books, manuscripts and maps. **Registers of Scotland,** Lomond House, 9 George Square, Glasgow G2 1DY (☎ **0845-604-0164**; fax 0141-306-4424; www.ros.gov.uk), is an organization that handles the registration of land and property ownership.

# Part II
# Ironing Out the Details

## The 5th Wave
By Rich Tennant

"Welcome to our nonstop flight to Scotland. Will you be sitting among the heather with us sir, or back in the moors?"

## In this part . . .

In Part I, I lay the groundwork for your trip to Scotland, and in this part, I get down to the nitty-gritty. I help you find the smartest value in airfares, whether or not you're teaming up with a travel agent. I also offer advice on the best ways to get around after you're there: how to drive on Scotland's roads, how to find the right accommodations for your needs, and how to manage visas and passports.

Finally, I provide valuable tips on packing, what to do if you get sick in Scotland, whether you should invest in travel insurance, and how to mail packages and phone home from Scotland—all the last-minute details that help make your trip a smooth and safe one.

# Chapter 6

# Getting to Scotland

. . . . . . . . . . . . . . . . . . . . . . . . . . . . . . . . . . . . . . . . . . . . . . . .

*In This Chapter*

▶ Deciding how (and even whether) to use travel agents

▶ Weighing the pros and cons of package tours

▶ Getting the best airfares

▶ Taking the train to Scotland

. . . . . . . . . . . . . . . . . . . . . . . . . . . . . . . . . . . . . . . . . . . . . . . .

*S*ightseeing, souvenir shopping, and stuffing yourself silly are the easy parts of traveling. The hard part is making all the plans to get you there. Lucky for you, several resources make travel planning almost painless. This chapter discusses the pros and cons of travel agents, how to find bargain airfares, and the lowdown on love-'em-or-hate-'em package tours.

## *Travel Agent: Friend or Foe?*

A good travel agent is like a good mechanic or a good plumber: hard to find, but invaluable after you've found the right person. And the best way to find a good travel agent is the same way you find that good plumber or mechanic — by word of mouth. Any travel agent can help you find a bargain airfare, hotel, or rental car. But a good travel agent stops you from ruining your vacation by trying to save a few dollars. The best travel agent tells you how much time to budget for each destination, finds a cheap flight that doesn't require you to change planes three times on your way to Scotland, gets you a hotel room with a view for the same price as a lesser room, arranges for a competitively priced rental car, and even gives recommendations on restaurants.

Travel agents work on commission. The good news is that you usually don't pay the commission — instead, the airlines, accommodations, and tour companies generally pay it. The bad news is that unscrupulous travel agents may try to persuade you to book the vacations that land them the most money in commissions.

In the past few years, some airlines and resorts have begun limiting or eliminating travel agent commissions. The immediate result has been that travel agents don't bother booking these services unless a customer specifically requests them. But some travel industry analysts predict that if other airlines and accommodations follow suit, travel agents will have to start charging customers for their services.

## Finding a travel agent you can trust

This section gives you a few hints for tracking down the travel agent of your dreams.

- ✔ **Ask friends.** Your best bet, of course, is a personal referral. If you have friends or relatives who have a travel agent they're happy with, start there. Not only is this agent a relatively proven commodity, but she (or he) is also extra likely to treat you well, knowing she'll lose two customers — not just one — if she screws up your vacation.

- ✔ **Go with what you know.** If you're pleased with the service you get from the agency that books business travel at your workplace, find out whether it also books personal travel. Again, here's another relatively proven commodity — one that has a vested interest in not screwing up (even if you are just one pea in a really big corporate pod).

Because businesses tend to book travel in volume, a lot of the agencies that specialize in this kind of business act as consolidators for certain airlines or have access to other discounts that they can extend to you for your personal travel.

- ✔ **Go to the travel agent source.** If you can't get a good personal or business referral, the **American Society of Travel Agents** (www.astanet.com), the world's largest association of travel professionals, can refer you to one of its local member agents. ASTA asks that all its member agents uphold a code of ethics, and it has its own consumer affairs department to handle complaints and help travelers mediate disputes with ASTA member agencies. This doesn't guarantee that you'll get an agent you're thrilled with, but it's a giant step in the right direction and offers you a measure of consumer protection in case something goes wrong.

If you have several to choose from, keep the following in mind:

- • Look for an agent who specializes in planning vacations to your destination.

- • Choose an agent who has been in business awhile and has an established client base.

- • Consider everything about the agent, from the appearance of his or her office (if the person is local) to the agent's willingness to listen and answer questions.

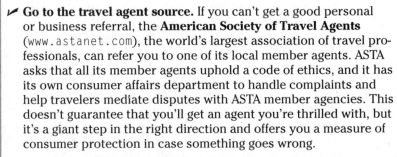

## Getting the most from your agent

To make sure you get the most out of your travel agent, do a little homework. Read about Scotland and the particular areas you plan to visit (you've already made a sound decision by buying this book), and pick some accommodations and attractions that you think you'll like. If you have access to the Internet, check airfare and package prices on the Web in advance to get an idea of what things cost. (For more info, see "Investigating the Ins and Outs of Package Tours," later in this chapter, as well as Chapter 4.)

After you've made some basic decisions and feel appropriately armed with information, take this book and your Web information to the travel agent and ask him or her to make the arrangements for you. Because agents have access to more resources than even the most complete Web site, your agent should be able to get you a better price than you can find by yourself. And your agent can issue your tickets and vouchers right on the spot. If they can't get you into the hotel or resort of your choice, your agent can recommend an alternative, and you can look for an objective review in this or any other guidebook right there and then.

 If you don't feel you're getting what you need from a particular travel agent — or you don't think he or she knows enough about Scotland to plan your trip appropriately — move on to one who makes you feel more comfortable.

# Investigating the Ins and Outs of Package Tours

Package tours are not the same thing as escorted tours (discussed in the "Deciding Whether You Need an Escort" section, later in this chapter). Package tours are simply a way to buy your airfare, accommodations, and other elements of your trip (car rentals, airport transfers, and sometimes even activities) at the same time — kind of like one-stop vacation shopping.

 For popular destinations like Scotland, packages can be a smart way to go, because they can save you a ton of money. In many cases, a package that includes airfare, hotel, and transportation to and from the airport costs you less than just the hotel alone if you booked it yourself. That's because tour operators buy packages in bulk, and then resell them to the public. It's kind of like buying your vacation at Sam's Club or Costco, except that it's the tour operator who buys the 10,000 boxes of garbage bags and resells them in bulk packs of three boxes at a price that undercuts what you'd pay at your neighborhood supermarket.

## *What's the catch?*

You almost always save money when you go the package route, but you may also have limited choices, such as a small selection of hotels or a fixed itinerary that doesn't allow for an extra day of hill climbing. Some packages offer a better class of hotels than others. Some offer the same hotels for lower prices than their competitors. Some offer flights on scheduled airlines, while others book charters. In some packages, your choices of travel days may be limited. Some packages let you choose between escorted vacations and independent vacations; others allow you to add a few guided excursions or escorted day-trips (also at prices lower than if you booked them yourself) without booking an entirely escorted tour.

Every destination in the world — including Scotland — usually has one or two packagers that tend to be better than the rest because they buy in even more bulk than the others. Not only can that mean better prices, but it can also mean more choices — a packager that just dabbles in Scotland may have only a half-dozen hotels or so for you to choose from, while a packager that focuses much (or all) of its energy on Scottish vacations may have dozens of hotels to choose from, with a good selection in every price range.

Which package is right for you depends entirely on what you want; the time you spend shopping around will be well rewarded.

## *Separating the deals from the duds*

After you start looking at packages, the sheer number of choices may overwhelm you — but don't let it. Use the tips in this section to help you distinguish one from the other and figure out the right package for you.

✔ **Read this book.** Do a little homework; read up on Scotland. Decide which cities, towns, and attractions you want to visit and choose the type of accommodations you think you'll like. Compare the *rack rates* (advertised prices) that I list in this book against the discounted rates being offered by the packagers to see whether the prices actually represent a substantial savings, or if they've just gussied up the rack rates to make the full-fare offer sound like a deal. And remember: Don't just compare packagers; compare the prices that packagers are offering on similar itineraries. The amount you save depends on the deal; most packagers can offer bigger savings on some packages than on others.

✔ **Read the fine print.** When you're comparing packages, you don't want to be comparing apples to oranges. Make sure you know exactly what's included in the price you're being quoted, and what's not. Don't assume anything: Some packagers include everything but the kitchen sink — including lots of extra discounts on restaurants and activities — while others don't even include airfare. Believe it or not, a lot of airline packages don't include airfare in the prices — these packagers know better than anybody how fares can fluctuate, and they don't want to get locked into a yearlong airfare promise.

✔ **Know what you're getting yourself into — and if you can get yourself out of it.** Before you commit to a package, make sure you know how much flexibility you have. Some packagers require iron-clad commitments, while others will go with the flow, perhaps charging minimal fees for changes or cancellations. Ask the right questions: What's the cancellation policy if your child gets sick at the last minute and you can't go? What if the office calls you home three days into your vacation? What if you have to adjust your vacation schedule — can you do that?

✔ **Use your best judgment.** Keep your antennae up for fly-by-nights and shady packagers. If a package appears to be too good to be true, it probably is. Go with a reputable firm with a proven track record.

## Finding the packager for you

The best place to start looking is the travel section of your local Sunday newspaper. Also check the ads in the back of national travel magazines such as *Travel & Leisure, National Geographic Traveler,* and *Condé Nast Traveler.* Then call a few package tour companies and ask them to send you their brochures. The biggest hotel chains, casinos, and resorts also offer packages. If you already know where you want to stay, call the hotel or resort and ask whether it offers land-air packages.

For one-stop shopping on the Web, go to www.vacationpackager.com, an incredibly extensive Web search engine where you can link up with hundreds of different package tour operators and custom design your very own package.

The following operators offer the best package tours in the business with the most options and comprehensive tours.

✔ **CIE Tours International** (☎ 800-CIE-TOUR; www.cietours.com): CIE does tours of the United Kingdom and offers escorted tours of Scotland. The Web site has a helpful tour index with package prices, descriptions, itineraries, discounts for seniors or early booking, and the like. The company organizes all varieties of tours: rail and bus, escorted, self-drive, B&Bs, and more.

✔ **Brian Moore International Tours** (☎ 800-982-2299; www.bmit.com): Brian Moore International Tours conducts escorted tours, self-drive tours, and independent customized trips. It offers a few great Scotland packages, including one for golf.

✔ **Liberty Travel** (☎ **888-271-1584** to find the store nearest you; www.libertytravel.com): One of the biggest packagers in the Northeast, Liberty Travel usually has a full-page ad in Sunday metropolitan papers.

✔ **American Express Vacations** (☎ **800-346-3607;** travel.american express.com/travel/): A no-frills site with some good bargains.

Other good resources are the airlines themselves, which often package their flights together with accommodations. When you pick an airline, you can choose one that has frequent service to your hometown or one on which you accumulate frequent-flier miles. Buying an **airline package** is a safe bet — you can be pretty sure that the company will still be in business when your departure date arrives. And you'll find that prices are comparable to what you'll get from other packagers.

# Duffing it: Golf package tours

You can take any number of customized specialty tours in Scotland, from walking tours to biking tours to fishing tours. As the home of golf, Scotland offers duffers plenty of opportunities to play during their stay. Customized package tours are a smart choice for golf fanatics, providing guaranteed tee times at some of the country's most coveted courses. Here are some of my favorites:

**Golf International:** In guaranteeing tee times at Scotland's most exclusive courses, Golf International is the leader of the pack. It's also a one-stop shop, covering not only greens fees but also accommodations, transportation, and even air-port greeters — all for one price. A one- to two-week trip costs $2,940 to $7,000. Contact: 14 East 38th St., New York, NY 10016 (☎ **800-833-1389;** www.golf international.com).

**International Travel Company:** Specializing in both African safaris (that's another book) and golf trips, ITC can customize a trip for you, covering as much or as little as you want. Prices vary greatly. Contact: 4134 Atlantic Ave., #205, Long Beach, CA 90807 (☎ **800-257-4981;** fax: 562-424-6683; www.itcgolf-africatours.com).

**Perry Golf:** With three Scotland tours (North, East, and South), Perry provides compact, excellent itineraries. What it doesn't provide are accommodations and transportation within Scotland, so you still have some work to do on your own. Call for price details. Contact: 8302 Dunwoody Place, Suite 305, Atlanta, GA 30350 (☎ **770-641-9696** or 800-344-5257; fax: 770-641-9798; www.PerryGolf.com).

**Thistle Golf (Scotland) Limited:** Offering create-your-own tours, this Scotland-based company covers tee times, accommodations, and vehicle rental. Prices depend on the touring region and the length of your stay, so call for details. Contact: Suite 423, The Pentagon Centre, 36 Washington St., Glasgow G3 8AZ (☎ **0141-248-4554;** www.thistlegolf.co.uk).

Although you can book most airline packages directly with the airline, your local travel agent can also do it for you. No matter who's doing the booking, be sure to give the airline your frequent-flier account number. Most airline packages reward you with miles based not only on the flight but on all the dollars you're spending — which can really add up and earn you credit toward your next vacation.

Among the airline packages, your options include:

- ✔ **American Airlines Vacations** (☎ **800-321-2121;** www. aavacations.com)

- ✔ **Continental Airlines Vacations** (☎ **888-898-9255;** www. coolvacations.com)

- ✔ **Delta Vacations** (☎ **800-872-7786;** www.deltavacations.com)

- ✔ **US Airways Vacations** (☎ **800-455-0123;** www. usairwaysvacations.com)

# Deciding Whether You Need an Escort

Some people love escorted tours. An escorted tour sends you on the road with a group and an escort. The tour company handles all the details; in general, your expenses are taken care of after you arrive at your destination, but you still need to cover your airfare. Escorted tours free travelers from spending lots of time behind the wheel, take care of all the little details, and tell you what to expect at each attraction. You know your costs up front, and you don't have many surprises. Escorted tours can take you to the maximum number of sights in the minimum amount of time with the least amount of hassle.

Escorted tours offer several benefits. If your mobility is limited, if you hate driving, if you like the ease and security, or if you're just the sociable type who likes to travel in a group, an escorted tour may be for you.

Other people need more freedom and spontaneity when they travel — they prefer to discover a destination by themselves, finding a gem of a restaurant or stumbling upon a charming back road. To them, getting caught in a thunderstorm without an umbrella is just part of the adventure of travel. If this sounds like you, steer clear of escorted tours.

## Knowing which questions to ask

If you do choose an escorted tour, ask a few simple questions before you buy:

- ✔ **What's the cancellation policy?** Do you have to put a deposit down? Can the tour cancel the trip if they don't get enough people? How late can you cancel if you're unable to go? When do you pay? Do you get a refund if you cancel? What happens if they cancel?

- ✔ **How jampacked is the schedule?** Do they try to fit 25 hours into a 24-hour day, or will you have ample time for relaxing, shopping, or hitting the pubs? If you don't like getting up at 7 a.m. every day and returning to the hotel at 6 or 7 p.m., certain escorted tours may not be for you.

- ✔ **How big is the group?** The smaller the group, the more flexible the tour and the less time you spend waiting for people to get on and off the bus. Tour operators may be evasive about this, because they may not know the exact size of the group until everybody has made their reservations, but they should be able to give you a rough estimate.

    Some tour companies have a minimum group size, and they may cancel the tour if they don't book enough people.

- ✔ **What's included?** Don't assume anything. You may have to pay to get yourself to and from the airport. Or an excursion may include a box lunch, but drinks cost extra. Beer may be included, but wine is not. Find out whether you're allowed to opt out of certain activities or meals — and whether the tour bus schedule is flexible. Ask also about meal preferences: Can you choose your own entree at dinner, or does everyone gets the same chicken cutlet?

When escorted-tour brochures say *double occupancy,* they almost always mean a room with twin beds rather than a queen or king — and many escorted tour packagers are unwilling to make exceptions. If you're committed to cuddling with your honey under the covers and two twin beds are going to cramp your style, be sure you're familiar with your operator's policy before you commit to a tour.

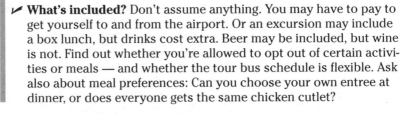

## Getting travel insurance for escorted tours

If you choose an escorted tour, think strongly about purchasing **travel insurance,** especially if the tour operator asks to you pay up front. But don't buy insurance from the tour operator! If it doesn't fulfill its obligation to provide you with the vacation you've paid for, there's no reason to think it'll fulfill its insurance obligations either. Buy travel insurance through an independent agency. (See Chapter 9 for recommended agencies and other insurance tips.)

# Choosing among escorted tour packagers

If you do decide to join an escorted tour, you have several different levels to choose from. Most of them are priced **all-inclusively,** which means you pay one price and don't have to worry about springing for your hotel or tipping your bus driver after you get there. When you're considering prices, however, always remember to check whether they include airfare — some tour operators include it with their quoted prices, while others don't.

- ✔ **CIE Tours International** (☎ 800-CIE-TOUR; www.cietours.com): See the "Finding the packager for you" section, earlier in this chapter, for details.

- ✔ **Globus** (☎ 800-221-0090; www.globusandcosmos.com): A first-class worldwide tour company, Globus has comprehensive tours of Scotland. You can book a whole package (including airfare, meals, hotels, and so on) or find your own cheap plane ticket (good for those racking up frequent-flier miles) and book only the bus-tour part. Price ranges from $950 to $1,400.

- ✔ **Cosmos** (☎ 800-221-0090; www.globusandcosmos.com): The budget arm of Globus offers downscale versions of the Globus trips (although you don't see a great price difference), with a tour guide and motorcoach on hand at all times.

You should be able to book any of these guided tours directly or through your travel agent. The companies themselves can usually refer you to a local agent if they can't book your tour directly.

# Flying to Scotland without Going Broke

Passengers sitting right next to each other on an airplane rarely pay the same fare. Rather, they pay what the market will bear on the day they book their flight.

Business travelers pay the premium rate, known as the *full fare,* because they need the flexibility to purchase their tickets at the last minute, change their itinerary at a moment's notice, or get home before the weekend. Passengers who can book their tickets long in advance, don't mind staying over Saturday night, and are willing to travel on a Tuesday, Wednesday, or Thursday pay the least, usually a fraction of the full fare — what's known in industry lingo as an *APEX* (advance-purchase excursion) fare.

The airlines also periodically hold sales in which they lower the prices on their most popular routes. These fares have advance-purchase requirements and date-of-travel restrictions, but you can't beat the prices. So keep your eyes peeled for a sale as you're planning your vacation, and pounce if you get wind of one. But don't hold your breath if you're traveling in the high season; you'll almost never see a sale around the peak vacation months of July and August — and forget Christmas.

## Surviving the APEX vortex: Some restrictions may apply

The general rule about APEX fares is this: As the ticket gets cheaper, the restrictions get tighter. For example, if you get a decent fare to Scotland in the middle of the week in the off-season, you may be charged, say, a $50 penalty for changing your flight schedule. If you luck into a sale fare at the height of the high season, don't be surprised if the schedule isn't changeable. Period.

When you're quoted a fare, make sure you know exactly what the restrictions are before you commit. If the restrictions are tight, don't buy until you're sure the schedule you've booked works for you. Otherwise, if your boss doesn't approve your vacation schedule or your kid comes down with the flu at exactly the wrong moment, you'll be stuck with some scrap paper you used to call an airline ticket.

## A drop in the bucket: Booking through bucket shops

*Consolidators* (also known as *bucket shops*) buy tickets directly from the airlines and resell them at lower prices. There's nothing shady about the reliable ones — basically, they're just big travel agents who get discounts for buying in bulk and pass some of the savings on to you, so everybody wins in the end. They get your business, and you get a cheaper airfare than you would if you bought directly from the airline or from a travel agent who doesn't act as a consolidator. It's worth the call; just don't tell your faithful travel agent you're going to the dark side!

I know what you're thinking: If a consolidator can save me $200 on the same flight my travel agent can get me, why haven't consolidators taken over the travel world? Here's the catch: Using a consolidator can be very time-consuming. The logistics and restrictions can be confusing, and you have to comparison shop, sometimes between apples and oranges, and then you have to go through the hassle of getting a live person on the phone. When you finally talk to someone live, some consolidators may not even have flights going your way when you want to go. That's the tradeoff for the great deal you may end up with.

You see consolidator ads in small boxes at the bottom of the page in the Sunday newspaper travel section. They may be legit, but be careful and make sure you know what you're getting before you give anybody your credit card number; if a fare sounds too good to be true, it probably is.

My favorite consolidators are **Cheap Tickets** (☎ 800-377-1000; www.cheaptickets.com) and **1-800-FLY-4-LESS. Council Travel** (☎ 800-226-8624; fax: 617-528-2091; www.ciee.org) is relatively easy to get through to and has also quoted some very competitive fares when I've dealt with them. Part of the Council on International Educational Exchange, Council Travel has especially good deals for travelers under age 26. Other reputable consolidators include **1-800-FLY-CHEAP** (www.lowfares.com) and **TFI Tours International** (☎ 800-745-8000), which also has good fares, but I've found their operators to be less than polite on more than one occasion.

# Surfing the Web for savings

Another way to find the cheapest fare is by using the Internet. After all, that's what computers do best — search through millions of pieces of data and return usable information.

The number of virtual travel agencies on the Internet has increased exponentially in recent years. There are too many companies to mention, but a few of the better-respected ones are **Travelocity** (www.travelocity.com), which includes maps, flights, rooms, cars, packages, currency converters, and weather forecasts; **Microsoft Expedia** (www.expedia.com), which has maps, flights, rooms, cars, and packages; **Orbitz** (www.orbitz.com); **Yahoo!** (www.travel.yahoo.com/travel); and **Priceline.com** (www.priceline.com). Priceline is a bit different from its competitors in that you bid for your desired flight; if it meets your price (with less control over the time of day you leave), you automatically purchase the flight. It's a bit riskier, but you also gamble on getting the best deal possible.

**American Express** (travel.americanexpress.com/travel/) is one of the most comprehensive Internet airline-information sources and reservations services. A few of the site's features are links to virtually every airline in the world, Internet-only airfare deals posted on one easy-to-scan page, and perhaps the best fare-finder on the Web. Call ☎ 800-253-9822 or 650-494-1557 before or after you make your reservation if you have any questions or concerns about what you see on-screen.

Each site has its own little quirks — Travelocity, for example, requires you to register — but they all provide variations of the same service. Just enter the dates you want to fly and the cities you want to visit, and the computer looks for the lowest fares. The Yahoo! site has a feature called "Fare Beater," which will check flights on other airlines or at different times or dates in hopes of finding an even cheaper fare. Expedia's site e-mails you the best airfare deals to your selected cities about once a week, if you choose.

## Figuring out who flies where

Air travelers to Scotland typically connect in London, where they catch a plane (or train) to Edinburgh or Glasgow.

### Major airlines that fly directly to Scotland

Air Canada offers direct flights to Edinburgh, allowing you to bypass London. You can fly from Toronto year-round and from Calgary, Halifax, and Vancouver during the summer. At the time of this writing, no U.S. carriers offered direct flights to Edinburgh or Glasgow.

No airlines fly directly from Australia and New Zealand to Scotland. All flights on international airlines from these two countries go through London.

### Major airlines that fly from North America to London

Several North American airlines fly to London airports, where you can catch a connecting flight to Scotland. Call more than one airline to compare prices.

- ✔ **Air Canada** (☎ **800-776-3000;** www.aircanada.ca) — from Canada only.
- ✔ **American Airlines** (☎ **800-223-7776;** www.aa.com)
- ✔ **British Airways** (☎ **800-247-9297;** www.british-airways.co.uk or www.british-airways.com)
- ✔ **Continental Airlines** (☎ **800-231-0856;** www.flycontinental.com)
- ✔ **Delta Airlines** (☎ **800-241-4141;** www.delta.com)
- ✔ **Northwest Airlines** (☎ **800-447-4747;** www.nwa.com)
- ✔ **United Airlines** (☎ **800-241-6522;** www.ual.com)
- ✔ **US Airways** (☎ **800-428-4322;** www.usair.com)
- ✔ **Virgin Atlantic** (☎ **800-862-8621;** www.fly.virgin.com)

### Major airlines that fly between England and Scotland

When you arrive in London, you'll need a short flight to Scotland. A quick comparison search among these airlines should land you an economical fare.

- ✔ **British Airways** (☎ **0845-733-3377**; www.britishairways.com) — Heathrow to Glasgow.

- ✔ **British European** (☎ **08705-676-676**; www.british-european.com) — all London airports to Aberdeen, Glasgow, and Edinburgh.

- ✔ **British Midland** (☎ **800-788-0555**; www.britishmidland.com) — Heathrow and Stansted to Aberdeen, Glasgow, and Edinburgh.

- ✔ **Ryanair** (☎ **0870-333-1231**; www.ryanair.com) — London-Stansted to Glasgow.

- ✔ **ScotAirways** (☎ **0870-606-0707**; www.scotairways.co.uk/home.htm) — London City to Dundee, Glasgow, and Edinburgh.

## Deciding which Scottish airport to fly into

Either directly or from London, you fly into Glasgow, Edinburgh, Dundee, or Aberdeen depending on the carrier you take. I recommend flying into Glasgow or Edinburgh. I prefer Glasgow, because it's easier to get in and out of, but both cities have large airports and easy transportation in and out of the airport. Also, because of the frequency of flights into these airports, you're more likely to find a cheaper fare than when you fly to a smaller city. Both are perfectly fine airports, and neither option outweighs the other in terms of proximity to a city. (For pointers on planning your itinerary, which helps you decide where you should fly in and out of, see Chapter 3.)

# Taking the Train

Taking a train from London may not be the fastest way to get to Scotland, but you may save a few quid (read: pounds) by taking the train from London instead of flying — plus you get to ogle some English countryside in the bargain. Remember, though: The five hours or so on the train (and an extra five for your return trip to London, because it's not cost-effective to fly one-way to or from London) are precious daylight hours when you could be sightseeing in Scotland. If you do ride the rails from London, ask about red-eye trips that let you sleep on the train — you won't lose sightseeing time, and, if you factor in the cost of a hotel, you'll save even more money.

The two train companies that venture north from London are:

- ✔ **Scotrail:** ☎ **0845-748-4950**; credit card bookings 0845-755-0033; info: 08457-484-950; www.scotrail.co.uk.

- ✔ **Virgin Trains:** ☎ **0870-010-1128**; www.virgintrains.co.uk.

# Chapter 7

# Getting Around Scotland

* * * * * * * * * * * * * * * * * * * * * * * * * * * * * * * * * * * * * *

## In This Chapter

▶ Deciding among cars, trains, and buses

▶ Getting to the islands by ferry

* * * * * * * * * * * * * * * * * * * * * * * * * * * * * * * * * * * * * *

*Y*ou have four choices when it comes to getting around Scotland: **car, bus, train,** and **ferry.** I recommend renting a car for the majority of your trip — it's really the best way to see the country. If your budget, length of stay, and destination choices make driving out of the question, you can easily take a bus or a train. And if you're traveling to the islands, you'll probably have to take a ferry (or, if you have a lot of money, you can fly).

## Experiencing Scotland by Car

The advantages of seeing Scotland by car are many. You'll have no timetables, plenty of legroom, and control over where you want to go. I guarantee you'll be pulling over on a regular basis to take in the scenery and snap a few thousand pictures. If that sounds like your cuppa tea, this section helps you focus on the ins and outs of renting a car, as well as what you need to know about driving in Scotland.

### Answering a few questions about your rental

Renting a car to get around Scotland is one of the most popular choices for the independent traveler. If you plan to rent and drive, here's what you should know:

> ✔ **How far in advance should you book a rental car?** In the off-season (between October and March) you should have little diffi-culty getting a car on short (or no) notice. Booking anything during the summer, however, is a different story. During the height of the tourist season, cars can be hard or impossible to come by. Also, count on prices jumping (if enough people want something, prices

are bound to skyrocket). So the earlier you book your car, the better. To stay on the safe side, book from a few weeks to a month in advance, no matter when you're visiting.

✔ **What kind of car can you expect?** A stick shift. Unlike in the States, where standard rental cars have automatic transmissions, the standard in Scotland is manual transmission. As in most of Europe, stick shifts are the norm for both car owners and renters. You *can* get an automatic, but it will cost you. Prices vary widely, so if you want an automatic, shop around for the best deal. Car-rental companies cash in on your extra demands, so learning how to drive a stick before you go may be worthwhile. A bit of good news: During the off-season, some companies offer free upgrades to automatic transmissions.

Because the driver's side is the right-hand side in Scotland, your left hand, not your right, controls the stick shift. Sounds wacky and hard to do, but we promise you'll get the hang of it in no time.

As for the class of car, you can expect three levels: **economy** (small), **compact** (medium), and **intermediate** (large). You may think you want a larger vehicle, but keep in mind that most roads are nail-bitingly narrow. You won't realize just *how* narrow until you're under way, and while winding down a street lined with cars and oncoming traffic, you'll appreciate driving a mini-mobile. Try to get the smallest car you can, taking into consideration your driving comfort, the comfort of your fellow travelers, and the amount of luggage you're carrying. Another thought: Smaller is cheaper.

Note that **air conditioning** and **unlimited mileage** are standard.

To be on the safe side, ask whether the car has a **radio.** It won't cost anything, and you probably don't want to rely on your passenger's musical ability for entertainment between sightseeing stops.

✔ **Where and when should you pick up a car?** You don't want to pay for a car you're not using. If you fly into Edinburgh or Glasgow and plan to stay in the city for two or more days, wait to get the car until you're just about to head out to the countryside. In the city, you don't need a car — and with the lack of parking, you don't want one, either. Some companies have pick-up locations in or near the city. If you're planning to leave town immediately or early the next morning, however, getting the car upon arrival is a good idea. You can set right out, and you save the time and hassle of having to go back to the airport or locate the rental agency.

A few companies allow you to pick up and drop off cars in different places, and some have non-airport pick-up locations, like Aberdeen, Inverness, and St. Andrews. Ask about your options and whether the company charges drop-off fees.

Try to pick up your car later in the day. Rentals are due back at the same time you picked them up, and if you're late, you'll be forced to pay for an extra day or (with some merciful renters) extra hours. So if you get the car at 9 a.m., it's due back at 9 a.m., and unless your hotel is next to the drop-off location, you probably won't get it there in time. Therefore, early afternoon is a good time to pick up a rental car.

✔ **How do you pay for the car?** Some companies require a deposit, generally on a credit card, when you make your reservation. If you book by phone, the clerk may ask for the card number then; otherwise you use your credit card at the rental desk. Don't be shocked if you're charged a gas deposit on your card. Just fill the tank before drop-off, and the deposit will be removed (good thing, because the refueling charge is way more than the price of a tank of gas!).

If you're not sure how long you'll need a car (if, maybe, you're thinking about coming back to Glasgow early to see more city sights), book for the shorter amount of time and extend your rental from the road with a simple phone call, rather than bringing it back early. If you've booked a car for a week but bring it back after only four days, for example, the company will post the refund to your credit card — but don't expect it to happen anytime soon. I found this out the hard way.

### Finding rental-car companies in Scotland

In this section, I list the biggest, most reputable companies that have pick-up and drop-off locations throughout the country.

✔ **Europcar/AutoEurope** (☎ **0870-607-5000;** 800-223-5555 in the U.S.; 800-12-6409 in Australia; 800-44-0722 in New Zealand; www.auto-europe.co.uk). Major locations: Edinburgh, Glasgow, Aberdeen, Dundee, Stirling, Inverness, and Perth.

✔ **National** (☎ **0870-400-4502;** fax 800-844-4991; 800-227-3876 from the United States). Major locations: Edinburgh, Glasgow, Aberdeen, Dundee, Stirling, and Inverness.

✔ **Budget** (☎ **0870-156-5656;** 800-472-3325 from the United States; reservations@budgetcarrental.ie). Major locations: Edinburgh, Glasgow, Aberdeen, Dundee, and Inverness.

✔ **Alamo** (☎ **0870-599-3000;** 800-522-9696 from the United States). Major locations: Edinburgh, Glasgow, Aberdeen, Dundee, and Inverness.

✔ **Avis** (☎ **0870-606-0100;** 800-331-1084 from the United States). Major locations: Edinburgh, Glasgow, Aberdeen, Dundee, and Stirling.

✔ **Hertz** (☎ **0870-844-8844;** 800-654-3131 from the United States). Major locations: Edinburgh, Glasgow, Aberdeen, Inverness, and Perth.

## Under 25? Renting a car in Scotland

Unlike in the States, Scotland is a place where most people under the age of 25 (but over 21) can rent a car without a problem. Keep in mind that some companies charge an *underage driver fee,* so, if you're under 25, seek out companies that don't impose that fee — make it your first question when calling. Members of Hostelling International (see Chapter 8) not only get discounts on car rentals but also are directed to companies that rent to underage drivers. Here's the scoop on your prospects:

✔ **Europcar/AutoEurope:** Must be at least 21; $15 a day extra up to age 23.

✔ **National:** Must be at least 23; no extra fee.

✔ **Budget:** Must be at least 23; no extra fee.

✔ **Alamo:** Must be at least 21; $6.53 a day extra up to age 25.

✔ **Avis:** Must be at least 23; no extra fee.

✔ **Hertz:** Must be at least 21; $17 a day extra up to age 25.

### *Getting the best deal on a rental car*

Car-rental rates vary more than airline fares. The price depends on the size of the car, the length of time you keep it, where and when you pick it up and drop it off, where you take it, and a host of other factors.

Asking a few key questions and raising a few issues can save you hundreds of dollars. Weekend rates may be lower than weekday rates, for example.

✔ **Ask whether the rate is the same for pick-up Friday morning as it is Thursday night.** If you're keeping the car five or more days, a weekly rate may be cheaper than the daily rate. Some companies may assess a drop-off charge if you don't return the car to the same rental location; others, notably National, do not. Ask whether the rate is cheaper if you pick up the car at the airport or a location in town.

✔ **Don't forget to mention the advertised rate.** If you see an advertised price in your local newspaper, be sure to ask for that specific rate; otherwise you may be charged the standard (higher) rate.

✔ **Don't forget to mention membership in AAA, AARP, frequent-flier programs, and trade unions.** These usually entitle you to discounts ranging from 5% to 30%. Ask your travel agent to check any and all of these rates. And remember: Most car rentals are worth at least 500 miles on your frequent-flier account!

As with other aspects of planning your trip, **using the Internet** can make comparison shopping for a car rental much easier. All the major booking sites — Travelocity (www.travelocity.com), Microsoft Expedia (www.expedia.com), Yahoo! Travel (www.travel.yahoo.com), Cheap Tickets (www.cheaptickets.com), and Priceline (www.priceline.com), for example — have search engines that can dig up discounted car-rental rates. Just enter the size of the car you want, the pick-up and return dates, and the city where you want to rent, and the server returns a price. You can even make the reservation through these sites.

Some companies also offer refueling packages, in which you pay for an entire tank of gas up front. The price is usually fairly competitive with local gas prices, but you don't get credit for any gas remaining in the tank. If you reject this option, you pay only for the gas you use, but you have to return it with a full tank or face charges for any shortfall. If a stop at a gas station on the way to the airport will make you miss your plane, then by all means take advantage of the fuel purchase option. Otherwise, skip it.

### Deciding on rental-car insurance

Your personal auto insurance doesn't extend to rental cars in Scotland. If your credit card company doesn't provide coverage, the price of the rental automatically includes a **collision damage waiver** (which requires you to pay for damage to the car in the event of a collision). Check with your credit card company before you go so that you can avoid paying this hefty fee (as much as $15 per day).

Car-rental companies also offer additional liability insurance (if you harm others in an accident), personal accident insurance (if you harm yourself or your passengers), and personal effects insurance (if your luggage is stolen from your car). Weigh the likelihood of getting into an accident or losing your luggage against the cost of coverage (as much as $20 per day combined, which can significantly add to the price of your rental).

# Driving in Scotland: Rules of the road

Perhaps just the idea of driving in a foreign country is overwhelming to you. Different cars, different roads, and different laws don't make for an inviting situation. And, unfortunately, these factors may be enough to keep you from driving at all. But I don't think you should be that easily swayed.

Driving a car around Scotland is a great experience — one that shouldn't be missed. This is not to say that the newness of it all won't take a little getting used to. But after you get the knack of it, you'll be driving like a pro. The sections that follow help you answer some common driving questions and curiosities — answers that I hope will allay your fears and get you on the road.

### Determining whether you need a special driver's license

To drive a car in Scotland, all you need is a valid U.S. driver's license.

### Getting along without road signs

One of the biggest complaints that tourists have about traveling around Scotland (along with the narrow roads and potholes big enough to hide small villages) is the lack of road signs. There you are, driving along, looking out for a sign that leads you to your destination, but you don't see any. Plain and simple, the reason some roads lack signs is that they get stolen. Pub owners and, yes, tourists steal signs, especially those that bear a family name or an ancestral town name, as decorations and souvenirs. It's always helpful to have a good map close at hand that includes bulleted landmarks and attractions along the route, to help you track your progress. When in doubt, however, simply stop and ask for directions.

### Knowing why some streets have more than one name

You're in a city, you're driving along such-and-such street, and then magically it has a new name. This curiosity comes up often as you navigate the streets. It is common, in fact, for street names to change. For example, the famous Royal Mile in Edinburgh between the castle and Holyrood House actually consists of five different smaller streets. Royally confusing, I say. A good map with bulleted landmarks and attractions helps you find your way around.

### Getting used to driving on the left side of the road

If you're used to driving on the right-hand side of the road, driving on the left side of the road causes an initial shock that may throw you at first. To get an idea of what it's like to drive in Scotland, simply imagine driving where you normally drive . . . and turn that image upside down. The wheel is on the right-hand side and the gear is on the left (the relative positions of the gas, clutch, and brake pedals are the same).

In highway traffic, you merge to the right, and slower traffic stays on the left. *Roundabouts* (traffic circles) are tricky, and you'll probably pop a few curbs while making sharp lefts, but don't get discouraged. Just like getting to Carnegie Hall, it takes practice, practice, practice. See the "Staying safe: Read this before you get behind the wheel!" section, later in this chapter, for important traffic rules.

No matter how great a driver you are, it's disconcerting to cruise along in the lane that in many countries would hold oncoming traffic. Thankfully, it's a temporary feeling, and soon you'll be able to comfortably drive from town to town. (Not my guarantee — just my experience!)

Consider having a good navigator along to watch for road signs so that you can focus completely on the road.

### Staying safe with two cars in one lane

Smaller roads have the tendency to shrink to a white-knuckling single lane. What happens when a car is coming from the other direction?

Black and white striped poles or small white signs reading PASSING AREA mark little pullover areas called *lay-bys*. When you see a car coming, put your blinker on and stop at the lay-by to let it pass. If it stops first, you can go ahead through. But remember, if the lay-by area is on the right-hand side, you shouldn't pull over into it, just stop the car and allow the oncoming traffic to go around you in the lay-by. It is customary for you and the other driver to exchange a wave when you pass.

### Planning your gasoline expenditures

Is gas expensive? Is Scotch alcohol?

Gas, called *petrol* in Scotland, is very costly. You'll notice that the signs at petrol stations advertise prices that seem comparable to what you see in the United States, but those are the prices per *liter*, not per gallon. So in essence you'll be paying more than four times what you would in the States. Of course, Scotland is a small country — though St. Andrews to Uig is a cross-country trip, it's nothing like driving from New York to San Francisco — but you'll still feel the pinch of the petrol on your wallet. Another reason to get a smaller car: better gas mileage.

### Laying down the law on parking

Unlike the United States, Scotland has no law prohibiting a car from being parked facing traffic. You often see cars on one side of the road parked in both directions, which makes it tough to tell if you're going the wrong way on a one-way street.

In larger towns, you may find some, but not many, parking garages. Street parking is fine, but don't think that the absence of meters means that parking is free. In Scotland you have to buy *parking disks* that indicate how long you've been in the spot. Buy disks at machines marked with a "P," which you shouldn't mistake for small phone boxes. Purchase a ticket and stick it to your window. Residential neighborhoods and some towns also require disks but have no parking-disk machines. In those cases, local corner shops usually sell parking disks.

### Figuring out when a tourist is driving

When they come to a turn, the windshield wipers start moving.

## Does your boot go in your luggage, or does your luggage go in your boot?

To save confusion about car-related words and phrases in Scotland, here's a list of the most commonly used (and most commonly confused) terms you may come across:

- **roundabouts:** Traffic circles (or rotaries if you're a New Englander). These are common, especially entering and leaving cities. Make sure you go left and yield to the right!

- **boot:** trunk

- **bonnet:** hood

- **gear stick:** stick shift

- **footpath:** sidewalk

- **motorways:** highways

- **petrol:** gasoline

## *Staying safe: Read this before you get behind the wheel!*

Here are some important traffic rules and laws to help you get around safely and legally.

- Yield to traffic coming from your right.

- The general speed limit is 60 mph (96km/h) unless otherwise posted. Standard 60 mph signs bear only a black circle with a slash mark through it. When the speed limit is other than 60 mph, you'll see a sign with a red circle and the limit written inside in black. You'll see this often when entering small towns where you should reduce your speed to 30 mph. On motorways, the speed limit is generally 70 mph.

- A flashing yellow light means yield to pedestrian traffic but proceed with caution when clear.

- A sign with a red circle and a red "X" through the middle means no stopping or parking during posted hours.

- Drivers and front-seat passengers must wear seat belts. If your car has back-seat belts, passengers must wear them.

- Drinking and driving is a serious offense and is dealt with harshly. Under no circumstances should you drink and drive.

# Crossing Scotland by Train

Scotland's **ScotRail** is an excellent rail system that connects the major towns of the country and runs into England. The advantages of train travel are that it's fast and very comfortable. On the downside, trains are more expensive and travel to fewer destinations than buses (discussed in the next section). Train travel is a comfortable way to get from one part of the country to another but is not comprehensive enough to allow you to see all the sights in between.

Year-round, you should have no problem buying **tickets** a half-hour before departure, but during the high season, call the day before to confirm availability. For tickets, call **ScotRail Telesales** at ☎ **0845-755-0033** (www.scotrail.co.uk). For 24-hour train information, call ☎ **0845-748-4950**.

The **Freedom of Scotland Travelpass** is a great bargain if you plan to rail it around the country; it even hooks up with buses and ferries to take you where the trains can't. The Travelpass comes with discount vouchers for tour buses and ferries, too. Seniors, students, and the disabled get a 33% discount, and children 5 to 15 years of age get a 50% discount. For more information and prices, call ScotRail or visit the Web site.

# Seeing Scotland by Bus

Despite their not-so-great reputation, buses are a pretty great way to see Scotland. They make many more stops than the trains, and the cost is a lot cheaper. But the usual downsides apply. Unlike when you have a rental car, you're not free to stop wherever and whenever you want. You're stuck with the same people for hours at a time. And not all buses have toilets. Regardless, the seating is comfortable, and it's a good way to meet people.

**Citylink** is the country's primary public coach line, and its vast network of routes weaves through all the principal towns of Scotland. It's much more of a tool of transportation than of tourism, however — it doesn't always stop at or even pass close to all of the tourist sights along the way. Information, prices, times, and routes can be found by calling ☎ **0141-332-9191** or by visiting www.citylink.co.uk.

Despite everything, one element of taking the bus holds true for any form of transportation: The view from the window is the same. In fact, the coach windows are huge; you can see more from them than from a car window. When you get to a major town, local transportation and walking can usually get you where you want to go.

Several coach tours travel in Scotland; the following two are reputable and cover a good deal of the country. If you want to see a particular area, especially one that's not covered by either of these companies, ask the local tourism board to recommend a good local coach service.

- ✔ **Whyte's Coach Tours** offers eight 4- to 8-day tours from April through September. Trips include the islands, the Borders, and the Highlands (see Part IV of this book), and the company also books your accommodations. Scotstown Road, Newmachar, Aberdeen AB21 7PP (☎ **0165-186-2211;** fax 0165-186-2918; www.whytescoachtours.co.uk).

- ✔ **Scotline Tours** are great if you'd like to stay in Edinburgh (see Chapter 10) and take day-trips to surrounding areas. Tours visit Loch Ness, Loch Lomond, St. Andrews, and the Borders areas (see Part IV). 87 High Street, Edinburgh EH1 1SG (☎ **0131-557-0162;** fax 0131-556-2029; www.capital-coaches.co.uk).

# Getting to the Islands, Mon

The preferable way to get from one island to the next in the Hebrides (see Chapter 17) is by ferry. Only one major company runs the major routes between islands: **Caledonian MacBrayne.** For the Orkneys and Shetlands (see Chapter 18), I recommend flying, but you can also get there with **P&O Scottish Ferries.** You can take your car on most of the ferries, but a few are vehicle-free and want to stay that way. Remember to call the day before you hope to go out, because bad weather can limit ferry travel.

- ✔ **Caledonian MacBrayne** ☎ **01475-650-100;** www.calmac.co.uk.

- ✔ **P&O Scottish Ferries** ☎ **01224-572-615;** www.poscottish ferries.co.uk.

# Chapter 8

# Deciding Where to Stay

● ● ● ● ● ● ● ● ● ● ● ● ● ● ● ● ● ● ● ● ● ● ● ● ● ● ● ● ● ● ● ● ● ● ● ● ● ● ● ● ● ●

## In This Chapter

▶ Knowing what you'll pay to stay

▶ Determining your lodging needs

▶ Deciding among hotels, B&Bs, self-catering cottages, hostels, and more

● ● ● ● ● ● ● ● ● ● ● ● ● ● ● ● ● ● ● ● ● ● ● ● ● ● ● ● ● ● ● ● ● ● ● ● ● ● ● ● ● ●

*T*his chapter provides a rundown of the types of accommodations you'll find in Scotland, helping you choose what's right for you, comfort-wise and budget-wise. Individual accommodation listings appear in each city and region chapter in this book (Chapters 10 through 18).

Of great benefit is the **Scottish Tourist Board grading system,** which covers all types of accommodations. The board's 1- to 5-star rating system of hotels and B&Bs evaluates hospitality, service, ambience, comfort, food, and the condition of the property. (The rating system doesn't cover the size or location of the place, price, or the range of facilities.) Inspectors visit all the properties every year to ensure that ratings are current. Accommodations involved in the program display a blue plaque or sticker showing the number of stars earned; look for the rating, which is usually on or by the door. If you don't see the plaque and the lodging is not in the rating system, it's not necessarily a bad place to stay, but if you do have a bad experience, the tourist board has no authority to reprimand the establishment.

## *Knowing What You'll Pay*

You can expect a wide range of prices for accommodations. So that you can easily gauge whether my options throughout this book are afford-able to you, I've listed the cost of a **double room** — what'll it cost for you and a guest to stay in one room together. The figures indicate the range of prices from the off-season (the lower price) to the high season (the highest cost). So, for example, if at the end of one review the price is, say, £40–£65 ($58–$94.30), this means that the cost of a room for two people will be anywhere between those two numbers. The range also takes into account the differences in cost of a room with a sea view, extra-large beds, and the like. Note that children of any age who occupy a bed typically pay the adult rate; listings for lodgings that offer a discount for children include that information. Almost every place listed in the book includes a **full traditional breakfast.**

Use the following scale for quick reference:

| | | |
|---|---|---|
| **$** | = | £50 or less double ($72.50) |
| **$$** | = | £50–100 double ($72.50–$145) |
| **$$$** | = | £100–200 double ($145–$290) |
| **$$$$** | = | £200 or more double ($290) |

# Castle or Cottage? Determining Your Accommodations Needs

I know, I know: You probably won't be staying in either a castle or a cottage during your trip to Scotland — although you certainly can if you want. The local tourism board will be more than happy to find just the right 30-room mansion or ivy-covered cottage in the heather. More likely, you'll be staying in one of the two most common choices for accommodations in Scotland: **hotels** and **guesthouses.**

Hotels in Scotland are comparable in variety and service to those you find back home. The other option is a *guesthouse,* which is essentially a **bed-and-breakfast.** I include more hotels than B&Bs in this guide because hotels are more often right on the tourist trail; B&Bs are peppered throughout the country, yet easy to find. You can expect friendly service, clean rooms, and a decent breakfast whichever way you go.

You can find other options as well, such as **self-catering properties** and **hostels;** the following sections tell you more about each and help you find the type of accommodation that's best for you. If you choose to color outside the lines and stay someplace not listed in Parts III and IV of this book, chances are you probably won't be disappointed. Why? Because the Scottish really are masters at the art of hospitality. Accommodating people in a warm and friendly way is something Scots all take quite seriously.

You can find out much about the country's different accommodation types at the **Scottish Tourist Board.** Its Web site lists a range of lodging choices, including hotels, guesthouses, bed-and-breakfasts, caravan and camping parks, and self-catering cottages. Go to www.visitscotland.com for more information and to get the lowdown on the latest package deals.

# Hello? Is this Scotland?

Before you can book your room, you'll need to know **how to call Scotland.** To call Scotland from anywhere in the world, dial the international access code (011 from the U.S.), then the country code (44), then the city code (for example, Glasgow is 141), and then the number.

For example, if you wanted to call one of my favorite watering holes in Glasgow, the Babbity Bowster, just to make sure they'll have enough stout ready when you get there, you would dial:

| Int'l | | Country | | City | | Number |
|-------|---|---------|---|------|---|--------|
| 011 | + | 44 | + | 141 | + | 552-5055 |

Remember, Scotland is five hours ahead of eastern standard time, so if you're trying to call a business, call between 9 a.m. and 5 p.m. their time.

# *Hotels*

The hotel experience in Scotland is similar to what you'd expect to find back home, with a few minor differences. Many places have tea- and coffee-making facilities in the rooms. Bellhops aren't common. And smaller hotels sometimes lock the doors at certain (late) hours, so you may have to ring or knock to be let in after hours. (But don't worry; they're used to it.)

Even among hotels, the range of accommodations is wide — from castles to small, family-run lodges. Hotels are used to catering to tourists and have a deserved reputation for helpfulness and friendliness. You can expect the furnishings to be comfortable, and many of the larger and chain hotels have fitness equipment, room service, and in-house pubs and restaurants.

The following chains have top-quality hotels in major cities throughout the country. If your itinerary takes you into these towns, you can answer the question of where to stay with one call:

- **Hilton Stakis Hotels:** ☎ **0141-304-1276;** fax: 0141-304-1274; reservations: 0900-383-838; 800-445-8667 from the U.S.; www.hilton. com/worldwide/uk/stakis/html.

- **Best Western International:** ☎ **0181-541-0033;** fax: 0181-546-1638; reservations: 0345-737-373; 800-528-1234 from the U.S.; www.best western.com.

- **Forte Hotels:** ☎ **0171-301-2000;** fax: 0171-301-2011; reservations: 0800-404-040.

- **Swallow Hotels:** ☎ **0191-419-4545;** fax: 0191-415-1777; reservations: 0191-419-4666; www.swallowhotels.com.

Weekends are often the cheapest time to stay at hotels in major cities. These hotels often cater to business travelers, but those loyal customers return home on the weekends. Hotels are eager to keep the house full, so they may offer great deals to tourists like you. It's definitely worth asking — it may mean saving a few bucks.

## Bed-and-breakfasts (B&Bs)

Scottish B&Bs are rumored to be some of the best in Europe, and you can see why. Bed-and-breakfast hosts in Scotland take their hospitality seriously. You get to know the owners of the B&B (likely the same folks who cook and serve your breakfast, clean your room, and lug your bags upstairs) — and you'll probably come away feeling that you've made a new friend. This makes for a pleasant, welcoming atmosphere.

A *guesthouse* is, for the most part, the same thing as a B&B, though possibly a little larger.

A big advantage of choosing a B&B over a huge hotel is the **price.** The cost of a double room averages £30 to £45 ($43.50–$58). You won't get some of the amenities of a hotel (pool, gym, room service, and so on), but really, how often do you take advantage of those, anyway?

Also, keep in mind that many B&Bs don't accept credit cards, so have enough cash on hand.

Bed-and-breakfasts aren't large — most have only four to ten rooms. The better B&Bs tend to fill up quickly during the high season, so book at least a week in advance of your trip, even sooner if you can. You may not be able to make reservations, however: Some places accept guests only on a first-come, first-served basis.

Some B&B rooms are not *en suite,* meaning they don't have a **private bathroom** (though you'll find this situation less and less these days). So if you're completely averse to sharing facilities with the folks down the hall, make sure you ask for a room with its own bathroom (which may cost a bit more).

For recommendations on the country's top B&Bs, contact **Scotland's Best B&Bs** (www.b-and-b-scotland.co.uk), an online booking service that lists only those bed-and-breakfasts receiving 4- and 5-star ratings by the Scottish Tourism Board.

## Self-catering cottages

*Cottage* is a term used loosely in Scotland: The properties offered as *self-catering* run the gamut from apartments to castles. Self-catering cottages are the equivalent of renting a condo in Florida for you and your family.

They're a place for you to drop your bags, settle in, and do things family-style. This is an option if you shy away from the hustle of moving in and out of hotels night after night and prefer to have a home base. At self-catering properties, you cook your own meals and make your own beds. If you're making the trip with a passel of children, this may be a perfect option, both convenience-wise and money-wise.

With self-catering properties, you pay one price, generally for the week. (Some rent by the weekend, for two to three days.) When you take into account the amount of money you would pay for hotels and B&Bs, staying in a self-catering lodging can cut costs considerably. Food costs also decrease when you're buying your own and cooking in. So if you're money-minded, this is an option worth checking out.

The drawback? Location. You're in one place all week, and to see the sights you must drive to them — and then drive "home." This isn't difficult if, for example, you intend to spend all your time around Loch Ness, but checking out the Borders from there would be a murderously tough day-trip.

On the other hand, staying in one place gives you the opportunity to take in all that an area has to offer — you can find a better way to get the feel of a place and live like a local. And a self-catering property is an especially worthwhile option if a big goal of your trip is to track down your family history. Plus, if you're traveling with smaller children, your daily travel time will be minimized — which can't be a bad thing!

To find a self-catering property, call the tourist board in the area you wish to visit. Or contact the **Association of Scotland's Self-Caterers** (☎ **01764-684-100;** www.assc.co.uk), which represents owners and operators of a wide range of self-catering properties, from cottages to chalets to lodges to castles.

## *Hostels*

Hostels have a reputation of being the accommodation of choice for the micro-budgeted. If the image you have of hostels is full of young, tireless travelers who don't mind going long stretches without showers or food, you're partly right (though only partly). Hostels are for **independent travelers** who cherish flexibility.

Hostels across Scotland vary in quality and services. Some offer community kitchens in which you bring in and cook your own food, and some even have private rooms with bathrooms. Families can stay in hostels, renting a room with four bunks. The majority of hostels, though, are places where people sleep dorm-style — anywhere from four to dozens of people to a room.

## Ensuring hostel security

Any time you're sleeping in a room full of strangers, take precautions to ensure the security of your personal belongings. Security isn't a major problem, but it is something to consider. Many hostels provide security lockers; if yours doesn't, however, protect your luggage and other personal belongings in other ways. Lock your luggage every night, or make your bags as difficult to get into as possible. Stack bags atop each other, for example, with the most valuable at the bottom. By the time someone's gotten to the good stuff, you'll be awake. Also, bring your wallet, passport, purse, and any other valuables into bed with you for safekeeping.

Hostels provide a blanket and pillow, and some beds have sheets, but to be safe, bring your own sheets, a sleeping bag, or a sleep sack (basically two sheets sewn together). As for bathrooms: Think of high school gym restrooms — cold tiles, a row of small sinks, toilets, and shower stalls. You may not love it, but it gets the job done.

I can't account for every hostel in Scotland, but one undeniable fact is that they're cheap. You can get a warm bed for as little as £6 ($8.70) and never pay more than £20 ($29). And you'll meet people from all over the world who are doing the same thing as you. Sure, you'll run into your share of hostels that don't exactly disinfect the toilet daily, but on the whole, they're clean places.

Some hostels take reservations, but only a day ahead. Others are first come, first sleep. If you're planning a hostel tour of Scotland, you'll benefit from contacting **Hostelling International** (☎ **202-783-6161;** www.iyhf.org) before you leave. In fact, some places accept only card-carrying members. Fees are $25 a year; $10 if you're under 18; and $15 if you're over 54. With the card, you get discounts at places affiliated with the group and even save on car rentals.

One general resource to check out is www.hostels.com. And if you know you'll be taking the backpacking route through Scotland, you may want to contact the Scottish Youth Hostel Association, 7 Glebe Crescent, Stirling FK8 2JA, ☎ **01786-891-400;** fax: 01786-891-333; info@syha. org.uk. It has special offers for budget travelers, as well as information on more than 80 youth hostels in Scotland. And while these accommodations are called "youth hostels," they allow anyone of any age, although most of the people there will be in their late teens or early 20s.

# Chapter 9

# Tying Up Loose Ends

. . . . . . . . . . . . . . . . . . . . . . . . . . . . . . . . . . . . . . . . . . . . . . . . .

. . . . . . . . . . . . . . . . . . . . . . . . . . . . . . . . . . . . . . . . . . . . . . . . .

*B*efore boarding the plane, you need to take care of a few bits of business. This chapter makes sure you get all your ducks in a row, including getting a passport.

# Papers, Please! Lining Up Your Passport and Visa

Who needs a **passport**? You, that's who! With very few exceptions, you absolutely need a passport to enter any foreign country, Scotland included. In fact, your passport is the single most important item you'll be carrying while you travel. Now that you're perfectly intimidated by this all-powerful document, I tell you how easy it is to get one.

## Getting a U.S. passport

The biggest mistake you can make is to wait too long to get a passport. It normally takes about a month from when your application is received until you receive your passport. You can request that the process be speeded up to get it within five business days, but like all the good things in life, that's not free! The cost to expedite is $35 in addition to the normal fee, and you have to have proof (that is, airline tickets) that you're leaving when you say you are. If you're flying out within two weeks, go to a passport agency instead of using the mail system to get it in time.

To **apply for your passport in person** (and you have to if it's your first time), go to an authorized office, which is often as close as a courthouse or a post office. Find the closest one to you at `http://travel.state.gov` or by calling ☎ **900-225-5674** or **888-362-8668**. If you have Internet access, use that option — calling either of the phone numbers costs money.

Passport agencies are busiest during January, and generally jumping constantly from then until fall. To get your passport quickly (and that's a relative word), the best time to apply is between September and December.

Here's what you need to bring with you to apply for your passport:

✔ A completed (but not signed) application

✔ Proof of citizenship (an old passport or a certified copy of your birth certificate)

✔ Proof of identity (a driver's license, ID card, and so on)

✔ Two identical 2" x 2" (5.1cm x 5.1cm) photographs that show the front of your head with a white background

✔ The correct fee (in cash, money order, or cashier's check):

• If you're over 16, the cost is $60, which includes a $15 execution fee. Your passport will be valid for ten years.

• For ages 15 and younger, it's $40, which includes the fee. It's valid for five years.

**To reapply by mail,** get the application from the nearest passport agency, court, authorized post office, or travel agent, or from the Internet address listed earlier in this section.

## Getting a Canadian passport

To find the nearest passport location, call ☎ **819-994-3500** from within Canada. In addition to the application, you must have a birth or citizenship certificate and two matching photos.

### What is a visa (and do you need one)?

When people hear the word "visa," many think it's a formal document that they must obtain before entering a foreign country. For some countries, it is, but not for Scotland. A visa is a stamp in your passport that is basically a country's official way of okaying your stay within its borders for a certain amount of time. When you enter Scotland, your passport will be stamped with a temporary tourist visa, good for 90 days of travel within the United Kingdom. If you want to stay longer, you must get a special visa (for example, a study visa or a work visa).

## Getting an Australian passport

Contact the Department of Foreign Affairs and Trade (☎ **131-232** within Australia; www.dfat.gov.au/passports) for all questions about how to obtain a passport.

## Getting a New Zealand passport

Contact the Department of Internal Affairs, Documents of National Identity, Passport Division (☎ **0800-22-5050,** toll-free within the country; www.passports.govt.nz). In addition to the application, you must have a birth or citizenship certificate and two matching photos.

## Keeping your passport safe

Always keep your passport with you. Never give it to someone to hold (especially if that someone is wearing a trench coat and slouch hat). Also, make a **couple of photocopies** of your passport. Leave one with someone at home, who can fax it to you if you need it, and keep one with you as you travel, stored separately from the original.

Ever seen the movie *Midnight Express*? Not having **vital documents** in a foreign country can be dangerous and scary, so don't leave it to chance. If any of your most important documents are lost or stolen, you need to be able to prove who you are. Before you leave, photocopy your passport, driver's license, Social Security card, and any other pertinent information. Make a few copies, and pass them on to friends and family, keeping one for your luggage.

In the terrible event that you do lose your passport while you're in Scotland, the first thing you should do is contact your country's embassy or consulate. The authorities need to know that someone else may be posing as you, and they can help you get a replacement passport. (You cannot return home without a passport, so getting another is a top priority.) Remember to bring any identification you have, plus a photocopy of your passport. In Scotland, embassy and consulate locations are as follows:

- ✔ **United States:** Consulate General, 3 Regent Terrace, Edinburgh, Scotland, EH7 5BW (☎ **0131-556-8315;** fax: 0131-557-6023; www.usembassy.org.uk; hours: Mon–Fri 8:30 a.m. to noon for phone inquiries only; Mon–Fri 1–5 p.m. for phone inquiries and personal appointments).

- ✔ **Canada:** Canadian High Commission, 38 Grosvenor St., London W1K 4AA, U.K. (☎ **09068-616-644;** fax: 020-7258-6506; www.canada.org.uk; hours: Mon–Fri 8–11 a.m.

✔ **Australia:** Honorary Consul, 37 George St., Edinburgh EHN2 3HN
(☎ **0131-624-3333;** fax: 0131-624-3701; www.australia.org.uk;
hours: Mon–Fri 9:30 a.m.–3:30 p.m.

✔ **New Zealand:** New Zealand House, 80 Haymarket, London
SW1Y 4TQ (☎ **0171-930-8422;** www.newzealandhc.org.uk;
hours: Mon–Fri 10 a.m. to noon and 2–4 p.m.

# Understanding the Customs of Customs

If you come to Scotland bearing gifts, you may not necessarily be that
well received: You'll encounter rules about what you can bring into
Scotland, and how much you can bring. These guidelines are strict and
may result in a mess if you try to get around them.

For starters, you can't bring any of the following into the country:
firearms, ammunition, and explosives; narcotics; poultry, domestic animals, and plants and their byproducts. In moderation, you can bring
the following: 200 cigarettes, 1 liter of liquor, and 2 ounces of perfume.
If you're flying out of or back to the United States, information about
what goods can be brought in and out is available on the U.S. State
Department's Web site: http://travel.state.gov.

# Deciding Whether You Need Travel Insurance

Three kinds of travel insurance exist: **trip-cancellation, medical,** and
**lost-luggage coverage.** Of the three, the only one you may want to
invest in is trip-cancellation insurance; the other two types make little
sense for most travelers. Rule number one: Check your existing poli-
cies before you buy any additional coverage.

**Trip-cancellation insurance** is a good idea if you've paid a large portion of your vacation expenses up front — you'll be covered if, for
whatever reason, your trip is cancelled. Trip-cancellation insurance
costs approximately 6% to 8% of the total value of your vacation.
Among the reputable issuers of **travel insurance** are:

✔ **Access America,** P.O. Box 90315, Richmond, VA 23286
(☎ **800-284-8300;** www.accessamerica.com)

✔ **Travel Guard International,** 1145 Clark St., Stevens Point, WI
54481 (☎ **800-826-4919;** www.travel-guard.com)

✔ **Travel Insured International, Inc.,** P.O. Box 280568, East Hartford,
CT 06128 (☎ **800-243-3174;** www.travelinsured.com)

✔ **Columbus Travel Insurance,** 17 Devonshire Sq., London EC2M 4SQ (☎ **0171-375-0011;** www.columbusdirect.com)

✔ **Travelex Insurance Services,** P.O. Box 9408, Garden City, NY 11530-9408 (☎ **800-228-9792**)

✔ **International SOS Assistance,** P.O. Box 11568, Philadelphia, PA 11916 (☎ **800-523-8930** or 215-244-1500). This one is a medical evacuation assistance program. If you get sick abroad, it gets you home and to the proper medical people. This is a good idea for someone with a difficult medical condition that could pose problems while abroad.

As for **medical insurance,** your existing health insurance should cover you if you get sick while on vacation (although if you belong to an HMO, check to see whether you are fully covered when away from home). If you need hospital treatment, most health insurance plans and HMOs cover out-of-country hospital visits and procedures, at least to some extent. However, many make you pay the bills up front at the time of care, and you get a refund after you've returned and filed all the paperwork. Members of **Blue Cross/Blue Shield** (☎ **800-810-BLUE**) can use their cards at select hospitals in most major cities worldwide. **Medicare** covers U.S. citizens only when traveling in Mexico and Canada. For additional health-insurance coverage, see the "Getting extra medical insurance" sidebar.

Some credit- and charge-card companies may insure you against travel accidents if you buy plane, train, or bus tickets with their cards, and some (American Express, certain gold and platinum Visas and MasterCards, and Discover cards, for example) offer automatic death or dismemberment insurance in case of an airplane crash. Call your insurers or credit- or charge-card companies if you have questions.

# Getting extra medical insurance

If you lack regular medical or homeowner's insurance, you feel that the coverage you have is insufficient, or you just think you need additional insurance, try one of the companies listed here. But don't pay for more than you need.

Companies specializing in **accident and medical care travel insurance** include:

✔ **International Medical Group,** 407 Fulton St., Indianapolis, IN 46202 (☎ **800-628-4664;** Internet: www.imglobal.com)

✔ **MEDEX International,** P.O. Box 5375, Timonium, MD 21094-5375 (☎ **888-MEDEX-00** or 410-453-6300; Fax: 410-453-6301; Internet: www.medexassist.com)

✔ **Travel Assistance International** (Worldwide Assistance Services, Inc.), 1133 15th St. NW, Suite 400, Washington, DC 20005 (☎ **800-821-2828** or 202-828-5894; Fax: 202-828-5896)

**Luggage insurance** is unnecessary in most instances because your homeowner's insurance should cover stolen luggage. If you're carrying anything really valuable, keep it in your carry-on luggage rather than checking it.

The differences between **travel assistance** and **travel insurance** are often blurred, but in general the former offers on-the-spot assistance and 24-hour hotlines (mostly oriented toward medical problems), while the latter reimburses you for travel problems (medical or otherwise) after you have filed the paperwork.

# Knowing What to Do if You Get Sick Away from Home

Finding a doctor you trust when you're in an unfamiliar place can be difficult. Try to take proper precautions the week before you depart to avoid falling ill while you're away from home. Amid the last-minute frenzy that often precedes a vacation break, make an extra effort to eat and sleep well — especially if you feel an illness coming on.

If you worry about getting sick away from home, consider medical travel insurance (see the "Getting extra medical insurance" sidebar). In most cases, however, your existing health plan will provide all the coverage you need. Be sure to carry your identification card in your wallet.

If you suffer from a chronic illness, consult your doctor before you leave home. For conditions such as epilepsy, diabetes, heart problems, asthma, or serious allergies, wear a Medic Alert Identification Tag (☎ **888-633-4298;** www.medicalert.org), which immediately alerts doctors to your condition and gives them access to your records through Medic Alert's 24-hour hotline. Membership is $35, plus a $20 annual fee.

Pack **prescription medications** in your carry-on luggage. Carry prescriptions written in generic form rather than under a brand name and dispense all prescription medications from their original labeled vials. Also, bring along copies of your prescriptions in case you lose your pills or run out.

If you wear **contact lenses,** pack an extra pair, in case you lose one.

Contact the **International Association for Medical Assistance to Travelers** (☎ **716-754-4883;** www.sentex.net/~iamat). This organization offers tips on travel and health concerns in the countries you'll be visiting. The **United States Centers for Disease Control and Prevention** (☎ **404-332-4559;** www.cdc.gov/travel) provides up-to-date information on necessary vaccines and health hazards by region or country (by mail, its booklet is $20; on the Internet, it's free).

When you're abroad, any local tourist office can provide a list of area doctors. If you do get sick, you may want to ask the concierge at your hotel to recommend a local doctor — even his or her own. This will probably yield a better recommendation than any toll-free number would. If you can't find a doctor who can help you right away, try the emergency room at the local hospital. Many emergency rooms have walk-in clinics for cases that aren't life-threatening. You may not get immediate attention, but you won't pay the high price of an actual emergency-room visit.

# Get Packing!

The only thing more important than what you bring on your trip is what you leave at home. So many hapless travelers make the easily avoidable mistake of bringing too much with them. I know how hard it is to imagine spending even one night without your creature comforts, but not only will you never use that bathtub headrest or those fur-lined self-warming slippers, but you'll forget all about them. It's guaranteed: If you bring only a quarter of what you're planning to pack, you'll have plenty! Focus on packing only the bare minimum.

For most people, packing is a necessary evil, but if you dive into this chore with the right mindset, you'll set the tone for a great trip.

## Using a packing checklist

Does the following list seem skimpy? It's not. If you want to bring an item that's not on this checklist, ask yourself whether you'll really need it. If not, that's one less thing you'll have to drag around the country. Remember, you're almost certain not to run into anyone you know. Who'll care if you wear the same pants every day and a sweater four times? Anyway, it's a world market! If you forget anything or really need it after you arrive, you can buy it there.

### Clothes

- ❏ Two pairs of pants (jeans for banging around; slacks for going out)
- ❏ A casual dress or button-down shirt (for a nice dinner or, say, Mass)
- ❏ Underwear, socks, and T-shirts (underclothes keep outer clothes cleaner longer)
- ❏ Two long-sleeve shirts
- ❏ One dark sweater — warm and potentially dressy

❏ One pair of good walking shoes (much of your time will be spent walking, and you'll want to be comfortable. Be warned, though: A few restaurants and Glasgow clubs won't allow tennis shoes, so you may think about bringing a second pair if Glasgow is on your itinerary. A pair of solid walking shoes like Rockports or Timberlands would do the trick nicely and avoid the need to carry an extra pair.)

## Toiletries

❏ Toothbrush and toothpaste

❏ Brush or comb (combs take up less space)

❏ Soap and shampoo (travel sizes should be enough for the trip, because you'll get some from hotels — though not from B&Bs and hostels)

❏ Razor and shaving cream (a light, small, travel-size shaving cream and three razors will last weeks. You may be tempted to bring an electric razor, but it could prove useless. I explain in the "Scotland unplugged: Leaving that electric nose-hair trimmer at home" section, later in this chapter.)

❏ Deodorant

❏ Medicine (bring an extra week of your prescription meds, just in case. Taking along common remedies like aspirin, Pepto-Bismol, cold medicine, or Dramamine is a good idea, rather than taking chances with equivalents or nothing at all)

❏ Glasses, contacts, and ample saline solution

❏ Feminine hygiene products

❏ Laundry bag (a pillowcase will do)

❏ Towel (a must if you stay at hostels, and you may prefer your own to those at some B&Bs)

❏ Condoms (yes, you can get them in Scotland, but U.S. brands are safer)

❏ Pocket-size tissue packs (aside from the obvious rescue from a runny nose, they make great napkins in a pinch)

❏ Odds and ends (lotion, makeup, and the like)

## The rest

❏ Passport

❏ This book (don't leave it behind!)

❏ A travel log (even if it's just a cheap spiral notebook, use it to keep track of every day of your trip. No matter how memorable your trip seems, you'll probably never remember every detail.)

❏ Camera (unless you have the disposable kind, bring extra batteries)

❑ Film (bring plenty of extra; it's much more expensive in Scotland), but keep it away from X-ray machines, which ruin film

❑ Travel alarm clock (they're standard in hotels, but you'll need one in B&Bs and hostels) or a stopwatch that has a built-in alarm clock

❑ Address list (leave behind the whole address book, and instead jot down those people you want to send postcards to)

❑ Small umbrella

❑ Paperback novel(s)

❑ Gum (for ear popping during take-off and landing)

❑ Money (traveler's checks, some cash, credit cards, calling card, ATM card)

❑ Driver's license (it doesn't hold as much power in terms of identification as it does at home, but you definitely need it to rent a car)

❑ Student or youth ID (great for discounts and backup identification)

❑ Airline tickets

Here's a good rule: Pack what you like but make sure you can carry it. Chances are no one will want to carry his or her load and take care of yours, too. There's nothing worse than being slowed down by too much luggage. So fill 'er up and lug those bags around for a while. If getting your luggage from the door to the driveway is a struggle, you can be sure you'll never make it through the airport, let alone down a crowded street. Unless you're confident you can lift, swing, carry, and pull your luggage, go back to the drawing board.

## Packing smart

No matter how many bags you bring with you, you want to utilize every inch of space you have. You also want to pack so that any leak, spill, or breakage is contained. Here are some tips on how to pack smartly and resourcefully.

✔ **Pack your clothes military style.** Atten-shun! If you want to fit as much as you can into your bags, you take up the least space by rolling up your clothes tightly, as you would a carpet. This method also minimizes wrinkles. When your clothes are neat little rolls in your bag, you can pack them around potential breakables, providing a buffer for the umpteen times your things will be thrown onto conveyor belts before getting back in your hands.

✔ **Pack big items first** and tuck in the little items after you've settled in the bulky pieces.

✔ **Share with others.** Traveling with someone else? Put one of your outfits in their luggage, and vice versa. If one of you loses a bag, the other will still have at least one outfit.

✔ **Prepare your bags for a bumpy ride.** Don't be fooled into believing that your luggage is gingerly handled with care while loaded onto and off the plane. To avoid a disaster like toothpaste in your underwear or shampoo in your shoes, put all liquids in plastic resealable bags or transfer toiletries into smaller containers. They take up much less room, and, in the nasty event that they do manage to leak, there's less to go around. There's nothing worse than finding all your clothes covered in some heady-smelling liquid.

✔ **Wear your bulkiest clothes on the plane.** This way, you have more packing room. Also, because you'll be wearing layers, you can more easily adjust to the ever-varying onboard temperatures.

## Deciding what to bring and what not to bring

If you're set on how much to pack and how to pack it, welcome to the crucial phase of packing. The biggest mistakes you can make are bringing too many clothes and the wrong kind.

✔ **Forget about anything that wrinkles easily.** Unless you'll be staying in upscale hotels, you'll be hard pressed to find an iron. Bringing your own is dead weight, and besides, it won't work in Scotland. (See the following section.)

✔ **Whites are a no-no** for travel in general and Scotland in particular: With so much rain, a white outfit wouldn't make it to the curb before becoming an abstract piece of art, with mud as the medium.

✔ **Bring casual clothes.** For the most part, Scotland is a casual country, and even if it weren't, what you'll be doing as a tourist pretty much requires warm, loose-fitting clothes. You'll spend a lot of time outside or in drafty castles and abbeys, and you want to be comfortable.

✔ **Plan to layer.** Layering is the best way to ensure your comfort no matter what the temperature. Sure, the clothes you pack depend on what time of year you'll be visiting, but even in summer, don't bother with shorts and tank tops — it's never really warm enough for that. Remember, too: From September to April, it's cold enough for sweaters and jackets. (See Chapter 2 for more on weather in Scotland.)

✔ **Plan for rain.** It does rain a good deal in Scotland, but a raincoat isn't really necessary. A compact umbrella is fine for the light yet constant drizzle that's characteristic of the country. Bringing a raincoat will take up too much space, while an umbrella is light and small.

## Cabin comfort: Making the plane ride smooth and easy

Whoever said "getting there is half the fun" was wrong. Plane rides, especially bad ones, can be particularly uncomfortable. Cramped legs, infamously bad cuisine, and a movie you can barely see can put a damper on the first leg of your trip. But you can plan ahead. Bringing just a few essential items in your carry-on bag can make the trip a smooth and easy one.

Pressurized cabins are notorious for leaving you dehydrated, so **bring a large bottle of water** to drink throughout the flight. Airlines are pretty generous on overseas flights, but even ten rounds with the drink cart won't give you enough fluids, given those tiny cups of water. Speaking of generosity, **alcohol** flows pretty freely on the flight, but beware: The accompanying dehydration will only exacerbate jet lag.

The in-flight magazine will soon wear thin, and you can't count on a new movie, so plenty of diversions are a must. A **novel, magazine,** or **crossword puzzle** is a good time-passer. And if you want to sleep, an **eye mask** and **earplugs** go a long way.

Dress comfortably, too, and bring along some **slippers** or **socks** to wear when you're curled up in your seat. Planes can get chilly, too, so carry a sweater or a jacket on board.

It could take eons for the dinner cart to make it to your row, and even then you may hate the meal, so be prepared! There's nothing worse than starving through a long flight. Pack some snacks that are filling but not too salty, like dried fruit or bagels. One plus about airplane food these days is that airlines are gracious and willing to accommodate **passenger food restrictions and limitations.** So if you're a vegetarian, are on a diet, are restricting your salt or fat intake, are allergic to certain foods, keep kosher or halal, or have some other special dietary regime, call the airline two days before you leave and request a special meal. You may be surprised at how many options you have.

Remember, you don't need 14 outfits for a two-week trip. Nearly every town has a laundry service — for a few pounds you can get your clothes washed and dried, and you'll be lugging much less.

## Scotland unplugged: Leaving that electric nose-hair trimmer at home

Don't bother bringing anything that must be plugged in or recharged. The plugs in Scotland are different. You can buy a cheap adapter, but that doesn't address the problem of different voltages.

In the States and Canada, the current is 110 volts. In Scotland, it's 240 volts. So if you plug in your hair dryer, even with an adapter, the machine could light up like a Roman candle or blow a fuse. And the other guests in the hotel may not appreciate dressing for bed in the dark! You can buy a voltage transformer (Walkabouttravelgear.com sells them), but they can be expensive and not worth the cost for a short stay.

Some travel appliances, such as shavers and irons, have a nice feature called **dual voltage** that adapt to the change, but unless your appliance gives a voltage range (such as 110v–220v), don't chance it. Most **laptop computers** have this feature, but always check with the manufacturer or owner's manual as a precaution. Plug adaptors for these appliances aren't hard to find; your local hardware store or even the airport should have what you need. Online sources for adapters include Walkabouttravelgear.com, LaptopTravel.com, TeleAdapt.com, Magellans.com, and ConnectGlobally.com. ConnectGlobally also has an excellent travel tips page.

If you bring electronic items, make sure they're battery powered. Take a battery-operated alarm clock (for when you can't get a wake-up call), battery-powered shaver (if you're averse to disposables), and personal cassette player (if you want your favorite tapes along), plus extra batteries. Otherwise, do without or be creative.

If you plan on bringing a video camera (something I don't encourage — better to be looking at and remembering the country than devoting all your attention to the camera), bring enough battery packs *and* enough videotape. Blank cassette tapes in Scotland look identical to the ones from home, but they won't work in your camera!

## Allowing room for souvenirs!

After you're all packed, any room left? Good. That's where you'll put **souvenirs.** No matter how much room you leave, though, it'll never be enough. If you can't cram everything into your luggage for the return trip, either buy an inexpensive bag or mail yourself your dirty laundry (not your souvenirs!). Mailing your laundry is safer than risking your souvenirs in the postal service, and having to wait for your clothes only puts off another load of laundry.

## Checking bags versus carrying on

Checking luggage is a convenience that lets travelers breeze through the airport and onto the plane, relatively free and easy — except when it comes time to pick up your things at baggage claim, which can be frustratingly time-consuming. Why waste precious travel time (and sanity) watching the luggage carousel go round and round, waiting for your bags? Why spend a chunk of your vacation looking for your checked baggage, when you could be well on your way to your hotel? All you need to do is pack sparingly — everything you really need will most likely pack snugly into **carry-on bags** that will fit into the over-head compartments of the plane. So instead of looking at carry-on bag-gage as a place to stow all those distractions you bring for the plane ride but never get to, consider it your ticket out of the airport, fast!

 Remember to allow for airline **restrictions** regarding carry-ons. Each airline is different, but it's pretty standard for overseas flights to allow passengers one carry-on bag (generally 10" x 14" x 36") and one smaller one, such as a purse. Always ask for your airline's regulations when you make your reservations.

If you're packing on the other extreme, you'll also encounter restrictions. For **checked baggage,** you're usually allowed **two bags,** each weighing up to **70 pounds** (again, this is in general; you'll have to check with your airline for its rules). This may sound restrictive, and no one wants to begrudge you the chance to bring all your Scottish cousins gifts from America, but you want that plane to get off the ground, don't you? And don't worry: 140 pounds is really a lot to work with. If you're worried, place your bags on the bathroom scale. That should be a close indicator.

 Of course, be prepared for the slim chance that your luggage will be **lost or delayed.** You can prepare yourself for this undesirable event, though. Simply pack a carry-on bag with a light change of clothes and necessary toiletries. This way, even if you are high and dry for a day or so, you won't frighten the natives.

# Everything but the Pony Express: Communicating with the Folks Back Home

You've just landed in Scotland. So much to do, so much to see. Still, what's the first thing you want to do? Phone home to make sure your plants will be watered and the dog walked twice a day? No problem. Calling home from Scotland is pretty easy, after you know the basics.

## Phoning home

 If possible, **never call from your hotel room.** You may foot surcharges, pay astronomical charges for local calls, and even be charged just to get your calling-card company on the line. Using the pay phone in the lobby may seem inconvenient, but on the way down, think of the money you'll save.

 You save money by making calls before or after business hours (8 a.m.–6 p.m.). This is sometimes tough to finesse when calling home because of the time difference, but it will save you some bucks if you can swing it.

You'll find two types of pay phones in Scotland, Coin-Phones and Card-Phones. You often see them side by side, and you'll find both throughout the country. You can also use U.S. calling cards or call collect.

✔ **The Card-Phone:** No calling card? No change? No problem. The Scots have a great counterpart to those phone cards you can get in any convenience store — and in fact, I think theirs is even better. These phone cards work the same as those in the U.S. (like a debit card), and you can buy one in any shop or post office. They come in varying denominations. What's different about the Scottish version is that you use it in its own phone booth, designated by the sign CARD-PHONE. When you enter the booth, slide the card in the slot as you would a credit card. A screen on the phone shows you how many units the card has left. The units decrease while you're on the phone, and of course tick off faster if you're calling overseas or during business hours.

---

# Making phone calls to and from Scotland

Making phone calls to and from Scotland is a cinch, after you master the order of things and the country codes. When you're calling numbers within Scotland, keep in mind that you can drop the city codes if you're calling in the same city. The city code 0131 precedes Edinburgh numbers, for example. But if you're calling Edinburgh from Edinburgh, skip the code.

✔ **To call Scotland:** If you're calling Scotland from the United States:

1. Dial the international access code (011)

2. Dial the country code (44)

3. Dial the city code (for example, Glasgow is 141; Edinburgh is 0131; some can be up to five digits) and then the number.

So the whole number you'd dial would be, for example, 011-44-141, followed by 000-0000 or 000-000.

✔ **To make international calls:** To make calls from Scotland to places outside the United Kingdom, you first dial 00 and then the country code (U.S. and Canada are 1, Australia is 61, New Zealand is 64). Next you dial the area code and number. For example, if you want to call the British Embassy in Washington, D.C., you dial **00-1-202-588-7800.**

✔ **For directory assistance:** Dial 192 if you're looking for numbers in the United Kingdom; dial 153 for numbers in all other countries.

✔ **For operator assistance:** If you need operator assistance in making a call, dial **114** if you're trying to make an international call and **10** if you want to call a number in the United Kingdom.

✔ **800 numbers:** Numbers beginning with 0800 within Scotland are toll-free, but calling a U.S. 1-800 number from Scotland is not toll-free. In fact, it costs the same as a regular overseas call.

Buy small denominations — say, £5 ($7.25) — so you don't buy time you won't use.

✔ **The Coin-Phone:** Coin-Phones are notorious for (1) taking your money when you still have more time or even when the call doesn't go through, and (2) cutting you off in mid-sentence while you fumble for more coins. Before you start feeding the machine all sorts of coins, read the directions. Some phones require putting the coins in before you dial; in others, you deposit the coins after the other party answers. Phones cost 20p or 30p, and the amount of time you'll get depends on how far you're calling. Have change in hand — the phone gives an extremely short warning before disconnecting.

✔ **Calling cards or calling collect:** AT&T, MCI, and Sprint are all worldwide calling cards, so using any of them in Scotland is no problem. Each has a local access number, which saves you the cost of dialing directly to the States. When you want to use your card, just call ☎ **0800-13-0011** or 0800-89-0011 for AT&T, ☎ **0800-890-2222** or 0500-890-2222 for MCI, and ☎ **0800-890-877** for Sprint. The operator then explains how to make the call.

If you have a calling card with a company other than one of those listed, you must call before you go on the trip to see whether it has a local access number in Scotland or the United Kingdom. Calling after you arrive is too late; directory assistance deals only with AT&T, MCI, and Sprint.

Phone your calling card company before you go on your trip to see whether it has an international calling card plan. It may offer a discount plan for calling overseas.

## Cyber Scotland: Using Internet cafes

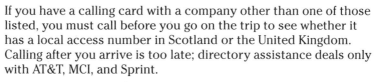

If you're going global, go all the way! By using one of Scotland's many Internet cafes, you'll be able to send quick e-mail "postcards" to your friends and retrieve your most pressing (or entertaining) incoming messages as you travel. You'll find cybercafes throughout the country; I list some of them in the "Fast Facts" sections at the end of each chapter in Parts III and IV.

CyberCaptive.com and NetCafeGuide.com offer lists of cybercafe locations in Scotland, but NetCafes.com is probably the most comprehensive. Make your list of cafe locations before you go. Not every cafe will be listed, however, so by all means ask your hotel concierge or the tourist office if you can't find one on the Web or in this book.

**America Online** is available at many Internet cafes; you just have to sign on as a guest or through www.aol.com. Best of all, there's no extra charge to you for using your AOL account abroad. If your Internet provider isn't Net-based or Net-accessible, set up a free **Hotmail** account before you go on your trip. It's easy to do. Just go to www.hotmail.com and follow directions. You'll have your free account in minutes. Give your new address to friends before you go and you'll be able to send and receive messages from any cybercafe in the world, just by going to the Hotmail Web site and entering your name and password.

The cost of Internet cafes is generally £4 to £5 ($5.80–$7.25) an hour. If you just need to pop in for a quick fix, most allow you to pay by the quarter-hour. Compared with the cost of calling home, it can't be beat.

## *Snail mail: Mailing postcards and letters*

No matter how easy it is to communicate by e-mail and calling cards, the folks back home still love getting postcards. You can find post offices in nearly every town and sometimes in odd places you wouldn't expect to find them (in people's homes, for example, or in shops). They're easy to spot: Look for a bright red storefront with red awnings, signs, and post boxes. The price of a postcard stamp is 45p (65¢); the smallest letter stamp is 47p (68¢). Mail usually takes less than a week to get to the States. If mail packages, you can save money by sending them economy, or surface mail. This comes in handy when mailing things to yourself.

**UPS** (☎ **800-575-757**) and **Federal Express** (☎ **800-535-800**) offer overnight service to Canada and the U.S. for about £32 ($46), and they have free pick-up.

Post offices are more than just places to mail postcards. You can buy phone cards and lottery tickets at them, too. You can even change money at main branches.

---

# Receiving mail in Scotland

If you need to have mail sent to you while you're on your trip in Scotland, no problem. Just have the sender address the mail with your name, care of the Post Office, Restante Office, and the town name. It'll be held for you to pick up. Larger post office branches (all of those I list in the "Quick Concierge" appendix of this book, for example) provide this service, but smaller post offices don't. If you're an **American Express** cardholder, you can also have mail sent to you at the Amex offices in Edinburgh or Glasgow (see "Fast Facts" in Chapters 10 and 11 for Amex information).

# Part III
# Edinburgh and Glasgow

All I said was it'd be nice to have a privacy fence, and Stuart was so inspired after our trip to Edinburgh, so...

## In this part . . .

This part describes the wonders of Scotland's two major cities, Edinburgh and Glasgow. The cities are vastly different, and each is worth an extended visit. Edinburgh, the capital, is famous for its big-city attractions and picture-postcard backdrop. Glasgow, once one of the greatest shipbuilding centers of the world, revels in its working-class soul and growing cosmopolitan sheen.

In this part, you find everything you need to plan your trip to Edinburgh and Glasgow, from getting there to getting around to discovering the best places to stay and dine. You get the lowdown on the cities' finest sights and attractions, as well as insider tips on quintessential Scottish pubs and quaint little teahouses.

# Chapter 10

# Edinburgh

. . . . . . . . . . . . . . . . . . . . . . . . . . . . . . . . . . . . . . . . . . . . . . . . .

## In This Chapter

▶ Getting to Edinburgh and getting around after you're there

▶ Discovering the best places to stay and eat

▶ Exploring the city's sights and attractions

▶ Shopping for quintessential Scottish souvenirs

▶ Finding the best watering holes for pints, music, and pub grub

. . . . . . . . . . . . . . . . . . . . . . . . . . . . . . . . . . . . . . . . . . . . . . . . .

*E*dinburgh isn't just the capital of Scotland — it also has enough beauty, old-world charm, history, and cosmopolitan savvy to make it a nation in miniature. From the heights of Castle Rock and Calton Hill to the lovely Princes Street Gardens in the valley to all the great restaurants, historic sites, and shops in between, Edinburgh has it all. One visit to the city, and you can see why it's called the "Athens of the North."

The best (or worst, depending on how you look at it) time to visit Edinburgh is in August, when as many as half a million people flock to the **Edinburgh Festival**'s arts explosion. (See the "Edinburgh Festival: The big summer event" sidebar, later in this chapter, for more information.) Whenever you decide to visit, plan to stay more than one night: Two days is barely enough time to see all that Edinburgh has to offer.

## Getting to Edinburgh

Getting to Edinburgh from overseas first requires getting onto the British Isles, most conveniently by plane. Currently most flights to Edinburgh from North America stop over in London. If you're coming from London, your best option is flying or taking an overnight train. Unless you really want to see the English countryside, you'll be wasting precious time driving from England. If you're coming from elsewhere in Scotland, the major bus and train routes serve Edinburgh, and the country's widest (read: three lanes) highways run into the city. No matter how you come into Edinburgh, you should have little difficulty; the city skillfully handles many tourists.

## How to get from the airport to the city

The **Guide Friday** (☎ 0131-556-2244) and the **Lothian Regional Transport** (☎ 0131-220-4111) operate buses from Edinburgh Airport to Waverley Bridge, the city center. Buses leave every 15 minutes from the terminal. The Guide Friday's **Airbus Express** costs £3.50 ($5.10) one way, £5.50 ($8) round-trip adults; £1.50 ($2.20) children (age 5–12) one way. The LRT's **Airline 100** costs £3.20 ($4.65) adults, £2 ($2.90) children (age 5–16) one way; £5 ($7.25) adults, £3.40 ($4.95) children round-trip. Both take less than 30 minutes to get to the city center and have plenty of room for luggage. Can't be bothered with a bus? A taxi ride into town costs £12 to £16 ($17–$23).

✔ **By plane: Edinburgh Airport** (☎ **0131-333-1000** or 0131-333-2167; Internet: www.baa.co.uk) is 7 miles from the city center. **British Midlands** and **British Airways** have regular flights from London.

✔ **By car:** Coming from the east, take the A1; from the southeast, the A7; from the southwest, the A71; from the west, the M8 or M9; from the north, the M90 and the Forth Road Bridge. All roads take you into the city center.

✔ **By train: Waverley Station** (☎ **0345-484-950**) is in the city center. **ScotRail** (☎ **0845-748-4950,** or 0845-755-0033 for credit-card bookings; www.scotrail.co.uk) operates trains from London, Glasgow, and elsewhere in Scotland.

✔ **By bus:** The **St. Andrew Square Bus Station** on Clyde Street serves coaches arriving from England and Wales through the U.K.'s extensive network, **National Express** (☎ **0990-808-080**), as well as buses run by **Scottish Citylink** (☎ **0990-505-050**), which serves all of Scotland.

# Getting Around Edinburgh after You're There

Making your way around Edinburgh is pretty effortless, unless you're planning to drive from sight to sight, which can be a hassle. My suggestion is to park the car and not think about it while you're in the city. If you can avoid picking up a car at all until you're ready to see the rest of the country, do that.

Edinburgh may have a few hills and dales, but it's pedestrian-friendly, and you'll likely find that foot traffic never backs up the way real traffic often does. Suffering from sore feet? Grab a bus or hail a taxi; neither is difficult to do. Still, in my mind, taking your time strolling about is preferable to watching the city's great scenery whiz by the window. The following list helps you through all your options:

✔ **On foot:** Edinburgh is a very walkable city and difficult to drive in. Also, many little alleys and passageways are accessible only on foot. So I suggest bringing a pair of comfortable shoes and start walking.

✔ **By taxi:** Major taxi stands are on Hanover Street, North St. Andrew Street, and Lauriston Place, and at Waverly Station. You can hail cabs on the streets or outside most hotels, or contact **City Cabs at ☎ 0131-228-1211** (Internet: www.citycabs.co.uk) or **Central Radio Taxis at ☎ 0131-229-2468.**

✔ **By bus:** You may want to use city buses occasionally, but because the town is so walkable, you probably won't even need them. (Listings in this guide for many of the city's venues include the bus line.) An all-day **Edinburgh Freedom Pass** lets you ride any city bus for £2 ($2.90) adults, £1.40 ($2.05) children. For more information, visit the **Waverly Bridge Transport Office (☎ 0131-554-4494**) on the bridge. For local routes to nearby towns on **Lothian** buses, call ☎ **0131-555-6363.**

✔ **By car:** Edinburgh isn't a fun town to drive in. Given all the one-way streets and the constant and confusing stream of construction detours, you're much better off parking the car in a lot and hoofing it. Whatever you do, don't try to drive on the Royal Mile, a frightening stretch of roadway where tour buses swerve back and forth to get around the cars that park on either side of the narrow street.

# Knowing What's Where: Edinburgh's Major Neighborhoods

Edinburgh has four major sections, all worth visiting. The main drag, known as the **Royal Mile,** divides the city in half. The city's top attraction, Edinburgh Castle, is on the Mile, as is the famous Palace of Holyrood.

Your orientation in Edinburgh begins with the mighty **Castle Rock,** impossible to miss when you enter the city. This landmark dates to the Ice Age, when the rock, a volcanic core, was so strong it split a huge glacier in two and formed the valleys on either side. Today, its craggy mass dominates the skyline. The rock, on which Edinburgh Castle stands, is your prime orientation point as you get around town.

Below the castle (though geographically north) are the **Princes Street Gardens** and **Princes Street.** Princes Street literally and metaphorically splits the center of Edinburgh in two. South of the Gardens begin the winding alleys and hills of **Old Town,** including the castle and the Royal Mile. North is **New Town,** with its gridlike network of streets and squares lined with classical Georgian buildings. The two smaller areas of town are **Calton,** known principally for its hill of monuments, and **Canongate,** below the Royal Mile, which is home to the lofty **Arthur's Seat.**

*Edinburgh Orientation*

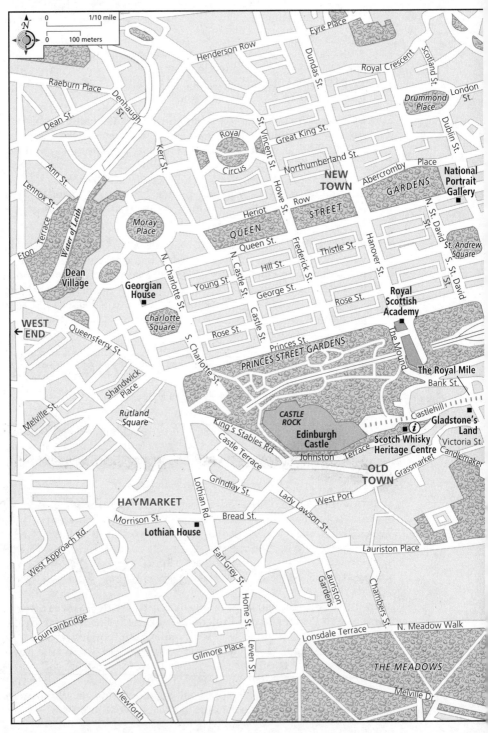

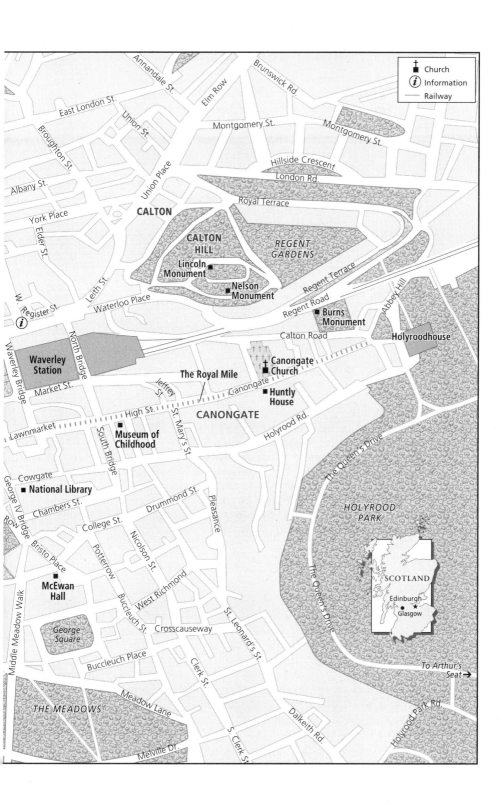

# Famous Edinburghers

Edinburgh residents include *Harry Potter* author J.K. Rowling, who has become one of the best-selling writers in history. She lives in the shadow of Edinburgh Castle and wrote her first book in one of the city's coffee shops. David Hume lived at James Court in Old Town in the 18th century. James Boswell, Robert Louis Stevenson, Sir Walter Scott, and Flora MacDonald also made their homes here. One of the city's most famous former residents, Sean Connery, grew up in the Fenton Bridge tenements. Queen Elizabeth knighted him in June 2000 at the Palace of Holyrood. The actor, most widely known for his many James Bond films, had previously dismissed the idea of knighthood as long as Scotland was denied independent rule. (See Chapter 1 for more on the political history of Scotland.)

## Old Town

Old Town runs south from Edinburgh Castle and the Royal Mile to two areas known as **Grassmarket** and **Cowgate.** You find the top attractions (such as the castle, John Knox House, St. Giles Cathedral, Canongate Tolbooth, Greyfriars Kirk, and the Museum of Scotland) in this part of town. A row of fun pubs lies in the shadow of the rock in the Grassmarket; also here are several excellent cafes.

Old Town is known for its narrow *wynds* (lanes) and stairways, which are fun to explore. You may be surprised to find a hidden underground pub or the old house of a famous writer. Castle Rock is the core of the ancient capital, where rich and poor lived in close quarters for centuries within the city walls. Sewage in the streets led to disease, and Old Town was one of the worst slums in Europe even into the 20th century. (The affectionate nickname for Edinburgh in its heavily polluted days was *Auld Reekie.*) Today, the sewage is gone, but the medieval look and feel survive. The old walls have come down, and the tourists have flocked in.

## New Town

In contrast to the winding alleys of Old Town, New Town is a neighborhood of neatly coiffed, well-planned 18th-century streets. The architecture is Georgian for the most part, and the material is mostly sandstone. Throughout the area are the city's finest hotels, restaurants, and shopping. Princes Street, Edinburgh's primary commercial avenue, runs along the edge of New Town and the Gardens that share its name — use it as the starting point for New Town exploration.

New Town was built by wealthy city residents who had become sick (literally and figuratively) of the conditions within the dirty confines of the old part of town. The neoclassical buildings and garden squares reflect an enlightened perspective on urban living, making it a unique area of development. Today, New Town is the largest classified historical monument in Britain. The Royal Scottish Academy, the Scottish National Portrait Gallery, the National Gallery of Modern Art, and the National Gallery of Scotland are here.

## Calton Hill

The debate continues over which offers the better view of the city: Edinburgh Castle or Calton Hill. The castle may win, except for one thing: It can't be in its own view. Follow New Town's Princes Street east and you'll end up at the foot of Calton Hill. Calton has more landmarks than attractions; a good walking tour of the area includes the grand Royal High School, the National and Nelson monuments, and the Regent and Royal Terrace Gardens, as well as a little exercise.

## Canongate

The Royal Mile consists of five differently named but connected streets. The one farthest from the castle is Canongate. Located on the eastern side of Old Town, this area is the home of the Palace of Holyrood, Dynamic Earth, and the new Scottish Parliament building, which was still under construction at press time. From Holyrood, you can walk or drive up Queen's Drive to the lofty heights of Arthur's Seat and Holyrood Park, a nice place to picnic or just take in the view of the surrounding countryside.

# Figuring Out Where to Stay

Edinburgh offers many hotel options, and you'll probably need some help choosing. The city has every kind of lodging, ranging from the luxurious — and expensive — to a simple room to rest your sightseeing head. In this section, I share some of Edinburgh's best accommodations — in terms of location, price, and amenities.

Unlike most lodgings in the rest of Scotland, Edinburgh hotels don't really lower their prices during the off-season (Oct–Apr). Some rates go down, but don't expect a deal at one of the city's finest hotels just because it's the dead of winter. Still, definitely ask about **weekend deals.** City hotels, which rely on business travelers to make up the bulk of their guests, often offer great package deals for the weekend. Wherever you stay, room rates include a **full traditional breakfast** (unless otherwise indicated).

## *Edinburgh Accommodations*

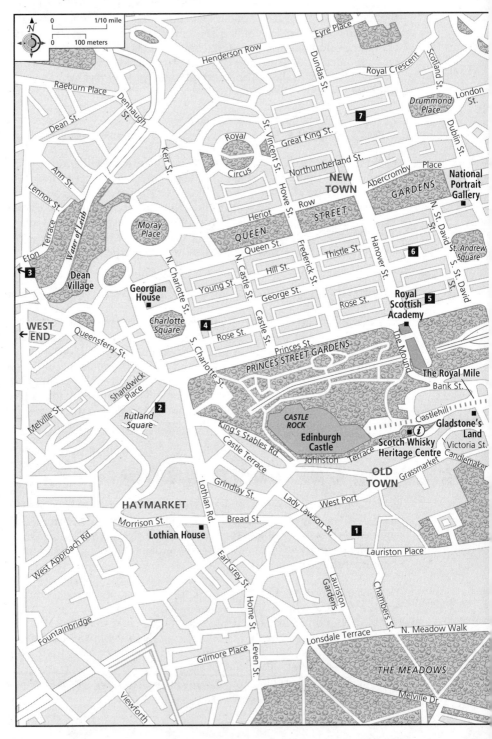

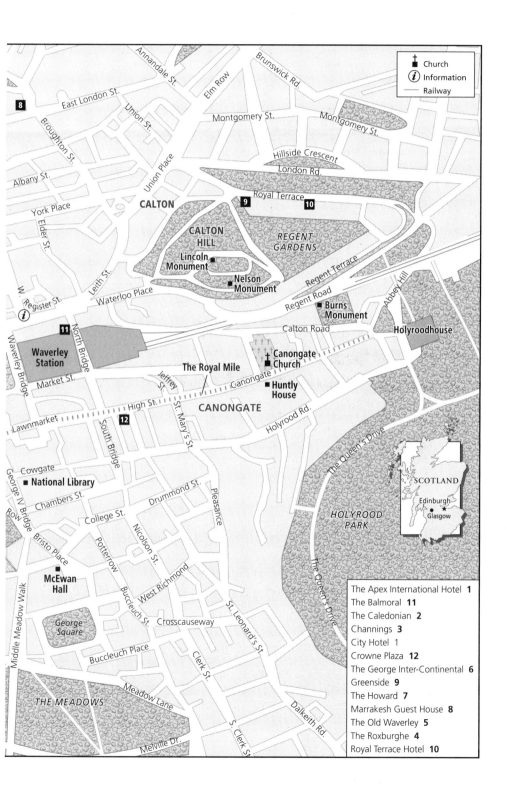

Most of the city's accommodations have **parking** available, although the room rate generally doesn't include the price of parking. If a hotel has a garage, it often extends discounts to guests. For the record, I recommend that you wait and pick up your rental car *after* you tour the city (see Chapter 7). It eliminates the hassle of parking altogether.

Given the choice — and the cash — this section gives you the accommodations that I most prefer. If you want more options, the **VisitScotland office** (☎ **0131-557-1700**) on Princes Street can help you locate accommodations based on price, location, and other factors.

### The Apex International and City Hotels
$$$–$$$$    Old Town

These two thoroughly modern hotels have some of the nicest rooms and most heavenly beds in the city, giving an upscale feeling to even the most basic unit. The rooms are smart and airy (the indirect lighting helps) and the curtains and top blanket share a sleek, stylish gray-and-white motif. The penthouse suites are particularly nice and have their own balconies with views of the castle. The City Hotel side has DVD players and wide-screen televisions. The International side caters to business travelers, with services such as word processing and Internet access. Of the three Apex hotels in Edinburgh, these two in the Grassmarket area are more convenient to the castle and the Royal Mile, so don't agree to take a room at Haymarket Terrace (farther out of town) if these aren't booked.

*31–35 and 60 Grassmarket, at Candlemaker Row.* ☎ *0131-300-3456. Fax: 0131-220-5345. E-mail:* international@apexhotel.co.uk *and* city@apexhotel.co.uk. *Internet:* www.apexhotels.co.uk. *Bus: 2, 12. Rack rates: £140–£350 ($203–$508) double. AE, DC, MC, V.*

### The Balmoral
$$$$    Old Town

Arguably the finest place to stay in Edinburgh, this century-old Victorian station house treats its guests like royalty. The hotel's immense clock tower is a fixture in the cityscape, lit up in its full architectural glory on many postcards. The location, just above the Waverley train station, is convenient, but thankfully, you won't hear any train whistles from your large, well-insulated room. You can also escape hoi polloi the people by spending some time in the huge health club, with its large heated swimming pool, gym, sauna, steam room, and beauty treatments. Every room has an interactive television, fax machine, and private bar. Will you ever want to leave?

*1 Princes St., on the east end of the street, above Waverley Station.* ☎ *0131-556-2414 or 556-1111; toll-free in U.S. 800-223-6800. Fax: 0131-557-3747. E-mail:* reservations@thebalmoralhotel.com. *Internet:* www.roccoforte hotels.com. *Bus: 4, 15, 44. Rack rates: £210–£275 ($305–$399) double. Breakfast not included. AE, DC, MC, V.*

## The Caledonian

**$$$$   Old Town**

This large red sandstone hotel has been taking good care of its guests for nearly 100 years — long before anyone heard of a hotel family named Hilton, the current owner of the grand place. The service is top quality, the unique rooms anything but cookie-cutter, and the beds are so big and comfortable that they induce a coma. The "Caley" encourages its guests to ward off doctors with a large vase of apples in the lobby. The hotel has an excellent health club with steam room, heated indoor pool, and a tanning bed. Named after the Scottish railway, the Caledonian is still steaming right along like clockwork. Parents note: Kids under 15 stay free, and the rooms have enough amenities to keep them occupied.

*Princes Street, on the west end of the street.* ☎ **0131-222-8888.** *Fax: 0131-222-8889. Internet:* www.hilton.com. *Bus: 4, 15, 44. Rack rates: £210–£260 ($305–$377) double. AE, DC, MC, V.*

## Channings

**$$$   Between West End and Old Town**

Five Edwardian town houses have been preserved and restored to create this excellent accommodation that's only a ten-minute walk from the center of Edinburgh. Located on a quiet cobblestone street, Channings is just far enough off the tourist trail to give it an exclusive retreat feel. Its residential location is its greatest selling point. The rooms and public areas are all quaintly decorated (although the facilities are modern), and the lounges have coffee or tea. Rooms on the top floor offer views of the rooftops and gardens of the neighborhood. The hotel also has an interesting collection of antique prints, sculptures, and books.

*15 South Learmonth Gardens, parallel to Queensferry Road after Dean Bridge.* ☎ **0131-315-2226.** *Fax: 0131-332-9631. E-mail:* reserve@channings.co.uk. *Internet:* www.channings.co.uk. *Rack rates: £170–£185 ($247–$268) double. AE, DC, MC, V.*

## Crowne Plaza

**$$$–$$$$   Old Town**

Located right on the Royal Mile, the Crowne Plaza is the finest hotel in Old Town. While the old brick building blends in with the street's architecture, as you enter the lobby you know you've stepped off the beaten path into high luxury. The rooms are spacious and perfectly decorated, with heated floors in the bathrooms; most rooms are nonsmoking. One of the nicest features is the leisure center with pool, gym, and solarium. Amazingly enough for its location, the Crowne Plaza even has its own parking.

*80 High St., on the Royal Mile (midway down).* ☎ **0131-557-9797** *or 0800-027-1022. Fax: 0131-557-9789. E-mail:* ResCPEdinbugh@AllianceUK.com. *Internet:*

www.crowneplazaed.co.uk. *Bus: 1, 6. Parking: Free. Rack rates: £180–£250 ($261–$363) double. AE, MC, V.*

### The George Inter-Continental

$$$$ **New Town**

This luxurious hotel in a landmark building strikes the perfect balance of old-world charm and modern service. The 200-year-old Georgian building retains much of its original splendor despite a major restoration. Each room is perfectly arranged and as comfortable as it is beautiful. Some rooms have a view of the water and the castle, but you won't be disappointed even if your room overlooks bustling George Street. The hotel has two fine restaurants, and breakfast is served in a magnificent dining room under stained-glass ceilings and chandeliers. The staff is, of course, first-rate.

*19-21 George St., near St. Andrew Square.* ☎ *0131-225-1251; toll-free in U.S. 800-327-0200. Fax: 0131-226-5644. E-mail:* edinburgh@interconti.com. *Internet:* www.edinburgh.intercontinental.com. *Bus: 4, 15, 44. Rack rates: £205–£240 ($297–$348) double. AE, DC, MC, V.*

### Greenside

$$–$$$ **Calton Hill**

This personally run hotel in a traditional Georgian terraced house is in a quiet location, close to Princes Street. The place has been renovated and offers a lot of charm for your pound. The rooms are huge and individually decorated, with good-size bathrooms. You can expect friendly service and all the usual amenities, but what makes Greenside such a popular choice is that you get hotel amenities without being in a huge hotel; in fact, it's more like a luxury B&B.

*9 Royal Terrace, facing the Royal Terrace Gardens.* ☎ *0131-557-0022 or 557-0121. Fax: 0131-557-0022. E-mail:* greensidehotel@ednet.co.uk. *Bus: 4, 15, 44. Rack rates: £75–£120 ($109–$174) double. AE, DC, MC, V.*

### The Howard

$$$$ **New Town**

Travel back in time as you step into these wonderful Georgian town houses in New Town. The individually decorated rooms, each named after an old Edinburgh street, are simply wonderful. Beautiful antique furniture, old-fashioned telephones, and large baths make for a wonderful retreat from the 21st century and the tourist crowds. The building is an architectural wonder, and the staff is always attentive and quick with a cup o' tea at any hour. The Howard also has a private place to park your car.

*34 Great King St., at Dundas St.* ☎ *0131-557-3500; toll-free in U.S. 800-323-5463. Fax: 0131-557-6515. E-mail:* reserve@thehoward.com. *Internet:* www.the howard.com. *Bus: 13, 23, 27. Parking: Free. Rack rates: £235–£275 ($341–$399) double. AE, DC, MC, V.*

### Marrakesh Guest House

**$–$$   New Town**

A super-friendly family runs this small but comfortable B&B and the Moroccan restaurant in the basement. The rooms are comfy, the bathrooms are tiny, and the breakfast — though sadly not ethnic — is quite filling. The best (or worst, if you're trying to eat lightly) feature of the place is the yummy smell emanating from below during the day. And for the location (walking distance to the center of town), you can't beat the price.

*30 E. London St., off Broughton Street.* ☎ *0131-556-4444. Fax: 0131-557-3615. E-mail:* marr@rapidial.co.uk. *Bus: 13. Rack rates: £40–£60 ($58–$87) double. AE, DC, MC, V.*

### The Old Waverley

**$$$   Old Town**

The location, about halfway down Princes Street, can't be better. Many rooms overlook the gardens and castle, and good shopping is just across the street. You don't find anything fancy or pretentious about the Waverley, but it's clean and comfortable. The rooms are cookie-cutter standard but pleasant. The staff is very helpful, and the breakfasts are huge — you'll be full 'til dinner.

*43 Princes St., at S. St. David Street.* ☎ *0131-556-4648. Fax: 0131-557-6316. E-mail:* oldwaverlyreservations@paramount-hotels.co.uk. *Internet:* www.paramount-hotels.co.uk. *Bus: 4, 15, 44. Rack rates: £130–£170 ($189–$247) double. AE, DC, MC, V.*

### The Roxburghe

**$$$– $$$$   Between Old Town and New Town**

This Georgian-style hotel is ideally located just a block from Princes and George streets on quiet and beautiful Charlotte Square. The rooms are grand, appointed in fine classical style, each with its own fireplace. The large windows make the rooms sunny, which can be a plus or minus depending on how late you like to sleep. A recent multimillion-dollar renovation added more rooms and a state-of-the-art gym with steam room and pool, the perfect refreshment after a tiring day of museums and shopping.

*38 Charlotte Sq., at George Street.* ☎ *0131-240-5500. Fax: 0131-240-5555. E-mail:* info@roxburghe.macdonald-hotels.co.uk. *Internet:* www.macdonald-hotels.co.uk. *Bus: 3, 21, 26, 31, 85. Rack rates: £120–£210 ($174–$305) double. AE, DC, MC, V.*

### Royal Terrace Hotel

**$$$–$$$$   Calton Hill**

This luxurious hotel occupies a set of interconnected terraced Georgian town houses on a crescent-shaped street. It has its own garden and views over the Firth of Forth, a 60-mile-long river. The public rooms with fireplaces and chandeliers are wonderful places to sit and plan your itinerary, but ask the staff for recommendations, as well. Rooms are impeccably decorated (some with four-poster beds), and most have spa baths. If your room doesn't have a whirlpool, you don't want to miss the health club's Romanesque plunge pool. Children under 14 stay free.

*18 Royal Terrace, facing the Royal Terrace Gardens.* ☎ *0131-557-3222. Fax: 0131-557-5334. E-mail:* reservations.royalterrace@principalhotels. co.uk. *Bus: 4, 15, 44. Rack rates: £110–£250 ($145–$363) double. AE, DC, MC, V.*

# Dining in Edinburgh

Edinburgh abounds with excellent restaurants. An influx of new citizens from all over the globe has added Asian and European influences to the standout local cuisine. That said, because Edinburgh is such a tourist mecca, you also find plenty of mediocre places to dine. My advice is not to settle. You may be in the city for only a day or two, so don't go to the closest place to your hotel or some eatery near a tourist attraction.

I've done the legwork and found the prime spots so that you don't have to waste time, money, or good taste. You can also ask your hotel concierge or B&B host, but sometimes he or she has reasons other than the quality of the food for pointing you to one restaurant over another. Asking your host is a good idea, however, if you have a hankering for something in particular but don't see it represented here.

Before you begin to choose which ale goes with what entrée, keep the following in mind: **Lunch menus** in Edinburgh often offer the same delicious food as the dinner menus, but at a better price. So have a big late lunch and snack on fast food when you get hungry in the evening.

If you're dining with children, the **best chain restaurant for kids** is **Littlejohn's.** This chain of family-style restaurants features pasta, burgers, and some Scottish cuisine at family-friendly prices. The service is good, and the breakfasts are yummy, should you decide not to take advantage of the free breakfast at your place of lodging. The Edinburgh location is 104 Hanover St. (☎ **0131-226-6300**).

### The Atrium
**$$$–$$$$   Old Town/Haymarket   Modern Scottish/International**

In a magnificent location in the atrium of an office block, this fine-dining experience is one of the best the city has to offer. The kitchen serves up the freshest of Mediterranean and Scottish cuisine. If in doubt about what to order, go for prime Angus beef or grilled salmon — but don't shy away from something more inventive, such as Parma-ham-wrapped breast of corn-fed chicken with roasted root vegetables and juniper-flavored butter sauce, or venison with Savoy cabbage and mustard *jus*. The softly lit dining room is also a popular place to be seen, so be sure to book ahead. Celebs who have enjoyed dinner in the modern, cream-colored, canvas-covered dining room include Jack Nicholson, Scottish comedian Billy Connolly, and Robert Carlyle.

*In the foyer of the Traverse Theatre, 10 Cambridge St., off Lothian Rd. ☎ 0131-228-8882. Bus: 4, 15, 44. Reservations recommended. Main courses: £11.50–£19.50 ($17–$28). AE, MC, V. Open: Mon–Sat noon to 2:30 p.m. and 6–10:30 p.m.*

## Black Bo's

**$$    Between Old Town and Canongate    Vegetarian**

This excellent vegetarian restaurant has a warm, laid-back feel. The staff is friendly and flexible, the wooden tables and chairs homey, and the crowd boisterous at times. This is the kind of place you wish was on your block so that you could eat here all the time. The mercurial menu offers veggie standards, such as delicious marinated kebabs, but also inventive dishes, like chickpea and black-olive soufflé with red pepper and ginger salsa bread-and-butter pudding. The place has so many good options that even if you're a meat-eater, you won't leave hungry.

*57–61 Blackfriars St., at Cowgate. ☎ 0131-557-6136. Bus: 1, 34, 35. Reservations accepted. Main courses: £8.25–£10.50 ($12–$15). AE, DC, MC, V. Open: Mon–Sat noon to 2 p.m.; daily 6–10:30 p.m.*

## The Grill Room

**$$–$$$$    New Town    International**

The Grill Room sits under a large and impressive stained-glass dome roof. In a grandly proportioned former bank, live music accompanies your meal, even at lunch. The white-aproned, professional wait staff serves gourmet dishes, such as navarin of lamb and seared Scotch salmon. Under the dome is a beautiful gilded island bar with a great wine selection and full bar.

*14 George St., at Frederick Street. ☎ 0131-624-8624. Bus: 4, 15, 44. Reservations recommended for dinner. Main courses: £8–£19 ($12–$15). AE, DC, MC, V. Open: Sun–Thurs noon to 9:30 p.m., Fri–Sat noon to 10:30 p.m.*

## Elephant House

**$    Old Town    Coffee Shop/Bistro Fare**

The owners have more than 600 elephant figurines and drawings in the restaurant, but that's not what brings in the lunchtime crowds. The food is innovative, excellent, and inexpensive. It includes baked strombolis and potatoes; good stuffed sandwiches, soups, and salads; and all-day breakfast. (Curiously, the menu lists no peanuts, but it does include an elephant-shaped shortbread biscuit.) The Elephant House is renowned

## Edinburgh Dining

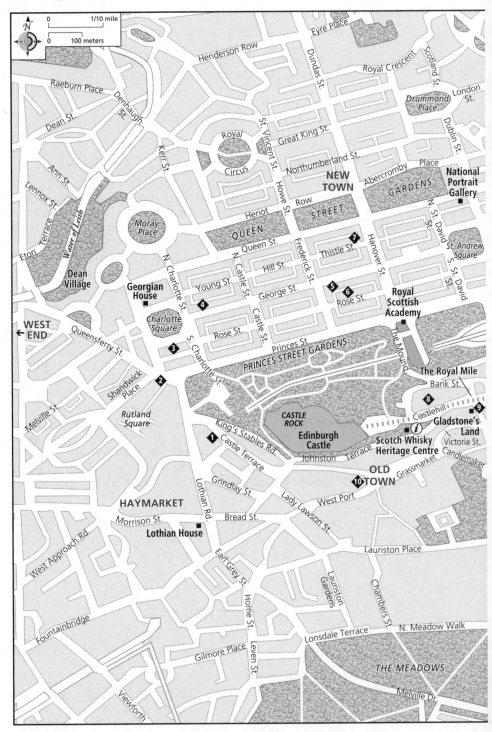

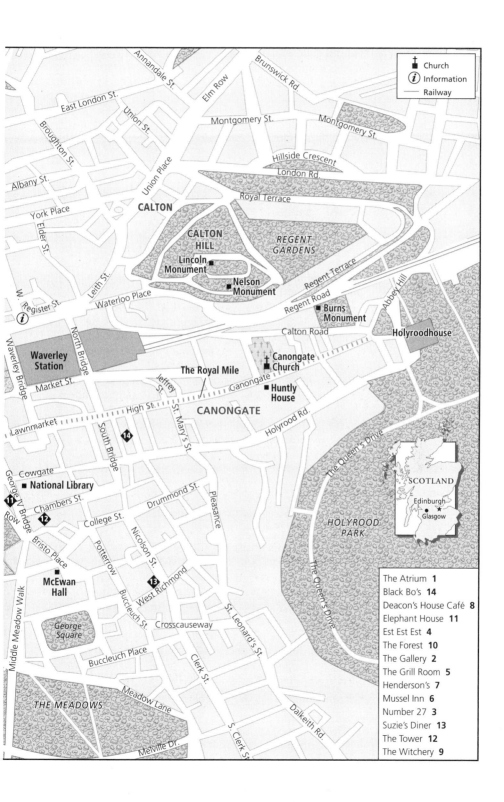

for pouring the best cup of coffee in Edinburgh and has a quality range of teas, coffees, and other hot drinks. You can even find instructions on the tables advising you how to make a perfect cup of joe or tea at home. The restaurant has a nonsmoking section, and the music is American but good — like, Frank Sinatra good. Live music is on tap Thursday evenings.

*21 George IV Bridge, near Edinburgh University and the Museum of Scotland.* ☎ *0131-220-5355. Internet:* www.desim.co.uk/elephant.htm. *Reservations not accepted. Main courses: £1.95–£3.25 ($2.85–$4.70). AE, DC, MC, V. Open: Mon–Fri 8 a.m.–11 p.m., Sat–Sun 10 a.m.–11 p.m.*

### Est Est Est

**$$–$$$   New Town   Italian**

This upscale Italian restaurant offers a well-priced choice of traditional pasta, antipasto, and pizza dishes using the old recipes and the finest ingredients. A particularly good side dish is pesto mashed potatoes. The super-friendly staff and sleek architecture give the place a happening bistro feel. The small chain, which has a location in Glasgow (see Chapter 11), gets its name from a 12th-century bishop who sent a scout into towns to write *"est"* ("it is") on the door of any inn with good wine. If the place had exceptionally great wine, the scout enthusiastically wrote, *"Est, Est, Est."* It goes without saying that this place serves good wine, but be sure not to drink yourself into the grave like the good bishop did. You also want to book ahead. Supposedly, Mick Jagger came here once and had to wait for a table because he failed to call in advance.

*135a George St., at Charlotte Square.* ☎ *0131-225-2555. Internet:* www.estestest. co.uk. *Bus: 4, 15, 44. Reservations recommended. Main courses: £6.95–£13.95 ($10–$20). AE, V. Open: Mon–Fri noon to 2:30 p.m.; Mon–Thurs 5–10 p.m., Fri 6–11 p.m.; Sat noon to 11 p.m.; Sun noon to 10:30 p.m.*

### The Forest

**$   Grassmarket   Vegetarian**

Full of hippie kids and couches, this cool little eatery and coffee shop may look like what you expect, but the food may surprise you. For jaw-droppingly cheap prices, you can get veggie-friendly, organic, and fair-trade fare, such as veggie burgers, roasted red pepper soup, couscous, fruit smoothies, cheddar pickle salad filling, and even soy milk with your cappuccino. Volunteer workers and clientele (often the same people) are surrounded by surrealist art that's painted on the wall, a poetry shelf, and a barter "swap" board.

*9 W. Port Rd., at the Grassmarket.* ☎ *0131-221-0237. Bus: 1, 34, 35. Reservations not accepted. Main courses: £1.50–£3.50 ($2.20–$5.10). No credit cards. Open: Daily 1–6 p.m.*

## The Gallery
### $$ Old Town Modern Scottish

One of the nicest aspects of this place, located in the old Rutland Hotel, is the view from the semicircular dining area. Depending on where you sit, you look down Hope Street toward Charlotte Square, Princes Street, or Edinburgh Castle. The upstairs restaurant is formal but not fancy. Although the menu is not particularly innovative, it's all good, especially the red pepper cod and the barbecued gammon steak. The desserts, especially the triple chocolate temptation, have earned local renown. The menu offers nothing for vegetarians.

*Rutland Street, off Queensferry Street. ☎ **0131-229-3402**. Bus: 3, 34, 35. Reservations not accepted. Main courses: £4.95–£8.95 ($7.20–$13). AE, DC, MC, V. Open: Daily 11 a.m.–9:30 p.m.*

## Henderson's
### $ New Town Vegetarian

Health-conscious or not, you can't go wrong at this wee bistro. It has a modern look and the innovative philosophy of serving healthy organic meals that are earth-friendly. Oh, and it's dirt cheap, too. The restaurant has a superb wine list and a small gourmet menu that changes constantly. The intimate, informal dining area (down Thistle Street) has dark wood tables sometimes lit with candles. A popular menu option is eggplant and chickpea curry, but you'd be foolish to forgo the outstanding organic oat-cakes. Also look for the Henderson's whole-foods store on the corner of Thistle and Hanover; it has served good veggie fare since the '60s and also sells prepared foods. A salad table is open all day Monday through Saturday at the Hanover Street location.

*25b Thistle St. (restaurant) and 94 Hanover St. (store), between George and Queen streets. ☎ **0131-225-2605** or 0131-225-2131. Internet:* www.hendersonsof edinburgh.co.uk. *Bus: 23, 27. Reservations accepted. Main courses £3.95–£4.95 ($5.75–$7.20). AE, DC, MC, V. Open: Restaurant and store Mon–Sat 8 a.m.–10:45 p.m.; restaurant closed Mon except during the Edinburgh Festival (Aug).*

## Mussel Inn
### $$–$$$ New Town Seafood

Always crowded, this snug little seafood treasure skips the nautical décor and puts its energy into the food. Steaming, spilling piles of mussels (served by the kilo) come in the following fun flavors: natural, shallot and white wine, fennel and bacon, smoked cheese and cider, spicy Moroccan, and Thai flavored. Also available are big platters of grilled mussels or scallops, fish dishes, oysters, chowder, salmon, and whatever else the net drags in.

*61–65 Rose St., at Frederick Street. ☎ **0131-225-5979**. Bus: 4, 15, 44. Reservations not accepted. Main courses: £5.60–£14.95 ($8.10–$22). MC, V. Open: Daily 6–11 p.m.*

# A lovely stop for a spot o' tay

Deacon's House Café in Old Town is a great place for tea or coffee rather than a full meal. The real attraction of a wee stop here is that this was home to a colorful local character, Deacon Brodie. Brodie is commonly believed to be the inspiration for Robert Louis Stevenson's *The Strange Case of Dr. Jekyll and Mr. Hyde*. This is a nice stop as you make your way down the Royal Mile.

*Brodies Close, 435 Lawnmarket, on the Royal Mile.* ☎ *0131-225-6531. Reservations not accepted. All items £5 ($7.25) or less. No credit cards. Open: Daily 9 a.m.–5 p.m.*

## Number 27

**$$$   New Town   Scottish**

The name may be unimaginative, but the menu certainly isn't. It includes superb creations such as supreme chicken filled with haggis made with whisky cream and heather honey, and rack of lamb topped with mint mousse. Located inside one of the old Georgian houses that comprise Charlotte Square, the restaurant has a splendid formal dining room and particularly wide entrance stairs that were built to accommodate the once-preferred transport of the wealthy — sedan chairs carried by Highlander servants. Gentlemen are expected to scrape their footwear clean on the iron boot scraper at the base of the lamppost.

*27 Charlotte Sq., across from the Georgian House.* ☎ *0131-243-9339. Bus: 3, 21, 26, 31, 85. Reservations required on weekends. Main courses: £10.95–£16.95 ($16–$25). AE, DC, MC, V. Open: Daily 6–11 p.m.*

## Suzie's Diner

**$   Old Town   Vegetarian**

This self-serve eatery features healthy, vegetarian-friendly options with a smile. It's a super-laid-back place that lets you decide your own portions. Suzie's serves excellent grain coffees and fruit teas to go along with unfailingly yummy entrees, such as quiches, falafel, grilled tofu in a pita, and veggie burgers, plus a salad bar and more. You can also get local wine or beer. A great place for a quick lunch, Suzie's sometimes schedules live music or belly dancing at night — so you may want to make a dinner date out of it. The place is nonsmoking through lunch.

*51–53 West Nicolson St., opposite the Pear Tree.* ☎ *0131-667-8729. Internet:* www. ednet.co.uk/~susies/. *Bus: 30, 33. Reservations not required. Main courses: £2.50–£5.75 ($3.65–$8.35). AE, V. Open: Mon–Sat 9 a.m.–9 p.m.*

### The Tower

$$$$ **Old Town** **Scottish/British**

This fine eatery inside the new Museum of Scotland is only a few years old but has established itself as a first-rate place to eat. It's known for having one of the best wine lists in the city, and the food is equally rich and well planned. The steaks are all the buzz. Tables 2 and 7 in this futuristic-looking restaurant are considered choice for their views of the castle and cityscape, but only celebs (such as Catherine Zeta-Jones or the Countess of Wessex) and loyal regulars get those, so aim for something close by. If you're a nonsmoker, you'll probably like the way the restaurant quarantines smokers in the balcony. Make sure to book ahead if you plan to dine here on the weekend. The owner of the Tower (and of the Witchery; see a review in the listing that follows) is award-winning manager James Thomson.

*Corner of Chambers Street and George IV Bridge, above the Museum of Scotland.* ☎ *0131-225-3003. Bus: 3, 7, 21, 30, 31, 53, 69, 80. Reservations recommended for dinner. Main courses: £12.95–£21.50 ($19–$31). AE, DC, MC, V. Open: Mon–Sat 10 a.m.–11 p.m., Sun noon to 11 p.m.*

### The Witchery

$$$–$$$$ **Old Town Scottish/International**

This popular Gothic-style restaurant, just steps from Edinburgh Castle, is surprisingly excellent, despite its proximity to the city's largest tourist attraction. An extensive list of top-shelf award-winning wines and whiskys accompanies the Scottish menu, which has subtle French and Mediterranean influences. Crab-stuffed salmon makes an excellent starter before you dig into steamed turbot with lime and ginger or pan-fried guinea fowl with tapenade. Give yourself a little time to explore the dining area's collection of interesting historic artifacts and relics. If you're a history buff, take note: A plaque notes that Samuel Johnson and James Boswell met and dined here in 1770.

*352 Castlehill, on the Royal Mile, just before the castle entrance.* ☎ *0131-225-5613. Bus: 1, 34, 35. Reservations recommended for dinner in the summer. Main courses: £13.95–£19.95 ($20–$29). AE, DC, MC, V. Open: Daily noon to 4 p.m. and 5–11:30 p.m.*

# Exploring Edinburgh

You won't find another city in Scotland that offers as many attractions per square foot as Edinburgh does. The Royal Mile alone has about a half-dozen different museums and churches. Stroll in any direction, and you're bound to run into something of historical note or amusement. Your kids won't be bored, your camera won't go idle, and if you're a history buff, you'll have a field day.

The only problem with so many options is deciding what you have time to see. It would take at least a few days to visit every place listed in this section — so you're going to have to make some decisions if your time is limited. I put the attractions in order of general interest, but browse the list for something you may have a special desire to see.

## Edinburgh's top attractions

### Edinburgh Castle
**Castlehill**

If you see only one thing in Edinburgh, see the castle. It has more history than you will possibly remember, panoramic views of the city, and several museums within its walls, each with its own impressive collection. The castle is also home to the **Stone of Destiny** (upon which the Scottish kings, such as David I, Macbeth, and Robert the Bruce, were crowned), as well as the **Honours,** which are the crown jewels, sword, and crown of Scotland. The castle offers guided tours, but you get a lot more out of your visit by taking the audio guided tour (£3/$4.35), which explains every aspect of the castle and prompts you at every stop to punch up extra tracks and hear more on specific topics. You'll soon be off on your own, because you pick and choose the topics that interest you.

Besides the Honours, don't miss the **Great Hall,** the creepy **prison vaults,** **St. Margaret's Chapel** (built in 1076, it's the oldest building in the city), and the **royal apartments,** where Mary Queen of Scots gave birth to the future King James IV of Scotland (also known as James I of England). If you're visiting at 1 p.m. (Monday through Saturday only), crowd into the **Half-Moon Battery** and watch the firing of the cannon. Edinburgh has set its clocks to the cannon's boom since 1861.

---

## John Knox is buried here . . . and other Edinburgh Castle trivia

You won't find this tidbit on the tour, but Protestant Reformation leader **John Knox** (his house is another attraction on the Royal Mile) is buried on the castle grounds. His grave was rather unceremoniously paved over to make room for a parking lot. He's at the Courthouse's parking lot, spot no. 43. Plus, there is a small area (ask a guard in the car park where the spot is) at the castle entrance that's technically **Canadian soil.** The story goes that when King Charles founded the Canadian province of Nova Scotia (or New Scotland), he didn't want to make the trip to christen the new baronesses, so he did so on Canadian land here. Another interesting fact: Today, Nova Scotia is home to more Gaelic speakers per capita than Scotland.

Finally — and I can't stress this enough — *go early.* Even if you hurry through the regimental museum and the vaults and ignore some of the stops along the way, you'd be hard pressed to see all the highlights in less than three hours. And when they say that they close at 6 p.m., they mean it. You'll be out the front gate at 6:01 no matter how much or how little you saw.

*Castlehill, at the top of the Royal Mile.* ☎ *0131-225-9846. Web cam:* www.camvista.com/scotland/edinburgh/ecastle.php3. *Bus: 1, 34, 35. Admission: £8 ($12) adults, £6 ($8.70) seniors, £2 ($2.90) children under 16. Open: Daily Apr–Sept 9:30 a.m.–6 p.m., Oct–Mar 9:30 a.m.–5 p.m. Time: 4–5 hours.*

### The Royal Mile
**Old Town**

The oldest street in Edinburgh, the Royal Mile was the main thoroughfare for the medieval city. Actually five small connecting streets, it got its name from the presence of a castle at one end and an abbey (now a palace) at the other. As you make your way from Edinburgh Castle to the Palace of Holyrood, be sure to explore the *closes* (alleyways) leading off the road. Some have plaques describing a famous person who once lived there (such as David Hume or Flora MacDonald), some are named after their old use (such as "fleshmarket," the old butchering center), and others open onto beautiful enclosed squares. You can also find several museums, such as **Huntly House, Museum of Childhood,** and the **John Knox House,** as well as churches, such as **Canongate** and the **High Kirk of St. Giles.** Also along the route are many pubs, cafes, and stores selling everything from plaid junk to Havana cigars to top-quality crafts and clothing. You can also witness history in the making. Although it won't open until late 2003, the new **Scottish Parliament building** (which will be home to the first independent parliament in nearly 200 years) is under construction on the Royal Mile's Holyrood end.

*Between Edinburgh Castle and the Palace of Holyrood. Web cam:* www.camvista.com/scotland/edinburgh/royalmile.php3. *Bus: 1, 6, 23, 27, 30, 34, 36. Time: 2–3 hours.*

### The Palace of Holyrood
**Canongate**

King David built the Palace of Holyrood in the 12th century as an abbey as a way to thank God for sparing his life. The name comes from its original relic (which is no longer here), a piece of Christ's cross. The story goes that David was attacked by a deer and saw a star over the stag's head — one that he took as a sign that he wouldn't be killed. The building was converted into a palace for Charles II and today is the Queen's official residence in Scotland when she is in town. The rooms and artifacts of Holyrood's history are on view. On the palace grounds are the remains of the old **Abbey,** the site of the coronation of Charles I. The highlight of the tour is the **Picture Gallery,** which holds a huge collection of portraits of Scottish monarchs.

The most gruesome chapter in Holyrood's history happened while Mary Queen of Scots lived here in the 1560s. David Rizzio, the queen's favorite secretary, was stabbed to death in her bedroom while a pregnant Mary watched in horror. Lord Darnley, Mary's third husband, killed Rizzio because he suspected them of having an affair or because he wanted to revenge Mary's refusal to make Darnley king of Scotland. (You can still see a stain, which is supposedly Rizzio's blood, just inside the window from which his corpse was thrown.) During his Jacobite rebel days, Bonnie Prince Charles threw some lavish parties here, and when Mendelssohn stayed at the palace in 1829, he was inspired to write his *Scottish Symphony.*

*Bottom of the Royal Mile.* ☎ *0131-556-1761 or 556-7371 for recorded information. Internet:* www.royalmile.com/info/holyrood.htm. *Bus: 1, 6. Admission: £6.50 ($9.45) adults, £5 ($7.25) seniors, £3.30 ($4.80) children under 16, £16.50 ($24) family (2 adults, 2 kids). Open: Daily Apr–Oct 9:30 a.m.–6 p.m., Nov–Mar 9:30 a.m.–4:30 p.m. Last admission 45 minutes before closing. Closed during royal visits. Time: 2–3 hours.*

### Arthur's Seat and Holyrood Park
**Canongate**

For a breathtaking view of the city, castle, and coast, grab your camera and head up the high cliff of Arthur's Seat in Holyrood Park, the highest point in the city. On a clear day, you can see the Highlands to the north and half of southern Scotland. You can drive to the top, but if the weather is nice and dry and you have an hour or so to spare, take the popular walk to the top — you'll appreciate the summit more that way. In the winter, the weather can get cold at the top, with snow or flurries, so be sure to dress appropriately. The park is a great place for a midday picnic, with plenty of nice paths for walks or letting the little ones romp. Can't make it all the way to the top? To the left is **St. Mary's Loch,** a lake with loads of swans and a large area that's particularly suitable for flying kites, gliding Frisbees, kicking around footballs, and generally letting off steam.

*Queen's Drive and Radical Road, south of the Royal Mile. Admission: Free. Open: Year-round, 24 hours. Time: 1–2 hours.*

### Museum of Scotland and the Royal Museum
**Old Town**

At these two museums, you get two for the price of one — you could spend the whole day at these two spots and not see the same thing twice. Six floors of displays upon displays upon displays mean you must make some tough choices about what to see. The Museum of Scotland explores the history of Scotland, from its primordial evolution to early man and Roman and Viking conquests all the way up to the religious, economic, and industrial development of the 20th century. The CD-guided tour starts automatically as you meander past the unparalleled collection of artifacts and antiquities — including rather big pieces, such as a locomotive engine and a huge steam-powered mill. One extra treat is the roof terrace, open (weather permitting) for great views of the city.

The Royal Museum is five times the size of the Museum of Scotland, and its 36 galleries make up a natural-, cultural-, and world-history museum all rolled into one. It devotes entire wings to technology, taxidermied wildlife, fish, gems, Asian art, and much more. One unique and rather bizarre item is the millennium clock, located in the main atrium. You really don't want to miss its hourly chimes.

Between the two museums, you may be on sensory overload. If anything bores you, move right along, because you have plenty more to see. Both museums also offer free guided tours, some specifically for children.

*Chambers Street. ☎ 0131-247-4422 or 247-4219. Internet:* www.nms.ac.uk. *Bus: 1, 6. Admission: £3 ($4.35) adults, £1.50 ($2.20) seniors and students, free for children under 16. Tues free after 4:30. Open: Mon, Wed–Sat 10 a.m.–5 p.m., Tues 10 a.m.– 8 p.m., Sun noon to 5 p.m. Time: 2–4 hours.*

### The Edinburgh Zoo
**Corstorphine Road**

This hilly zoo is home to more than 1,000 animals, including some rare species, such as the funny-looking *Waldrapo ibis* (if you're a birder, take note). Also here are old favorites, such as pandas, hippos, and snakes. The pride of the zoo has long been the huge penguin pool, the largest in the world. Every day from March to October, the tuxedoed birds parade at 2 p.m. to the delight of camera-snapping visitors. The zoo also has a good number of lions and primates. Special activities for kids, such as animal handling and safari tours, take place every day in July and August. The zoo also hosts special activities on holidays.

*Corstorphine Road, 3 miles west of the city center on the A8. ☎ 0131-334-9171. Internet:* www.edinburghzoo.org.uk. *Bus from the city: Red 2, 12, 26, 31, 36, 66, 69 and Green 16, 18, 80, 86, 274. Admission: £7 ($10) adults, £4.50 ($6.55) seniors, £4 ($5.80) children under 16, £20 ($29) family. MC, V. Open: Daily Apr–Sept 9 a.m.– 6 p.m., Oct–Mar 9 a.m.–5 p.m. Time: 2 hours.*

### Princes Street Gardens
**Old Town**

Seeing Princes Street Gardens may make imagining its humble origins difficult: At one time, this large floral park was a man-made loch (lake), and later the town dump, before it attained its current splendor. The infamous loch was where suspected witches were tied and thrown in — if they drowned, they were innocent; if they floated, they were taken out and burned to death. Take a little time to stroll the lovely green, and don't miss the park's floral clock, the oldest one of its kind in the world (since 1902), near the corner of Princes Street and the Mound. It consists of about 20,000 plants, and the cuckoo appears every quarter-hour. The mechanism for the clock is under the statue of the writer and wig-maker Allan Ramsay, near the Scott memorial. Notice that Ramsay is wearing a silk turban, the baseball cap of its day — its popularity stemmed from the fact that you didn't have to wear a wig.

If you want a little exercise, you can climb the 287 steps to the 200-foot Scott monument in the East Gardens for a great view of the castle. This beautiful spot in the middle of the city is a popular place for a stroll, especially among tourists who appreciate stopping to smell the flowers.

*Parallel to Princes Street, in center of town. Bus: 4, 15, 44. Open: Year-round, 24 hours. Time: 1 hour.*

### The People's Story
**Canongate**

This interesting museum is inside the Canongate Tolbooth, the old courthouse and prison for the city. It's not your typical museum, but more of a short tour through the life of Edinburgh from the 18th century to the present. Attempting to break down the fourth wall of museums by re-creating the sights, sounds, and even smells of the old city, the People's Story is a fun museum with lots of life-size figures and surround-sound effects set in an old laundry room and kitchen.

*163 Canongate, on the Royal Mile. ☎ 0131-529-4057. Bus: 1, 6. Admission: Free. Open: Mon–Sat 10 a.m.–5 p.m. Time: 1 hour.*

### Museum of Childhood
**Canongate**

Dollhouses, stuffed animals, games, and more make up the displays at this unique museum, which may be disappointing for wee ones because it's hands-off. This isn't your typical toy-store selection, but a unique collection of antique, pre-battery toys. The museum isn't just for kids; adults also enjoy the nostalgia of seeing toys from their childhood. In fact, the story behind the museum is that a man who didn't like kids built it. The exhibits also represent the not-so-fun side of childhood, so if you were fed castor oil as a child, prepare to be reminded.

*42 High St., on the Royal Mile. ☎ 0131-529-4124. Bus: 1, 6. Admission: Free. Open: Mon–Sat 10 a.m.–5 p.m. Time: 1 hour.*

### Scotch Whisky Centre
**Castlehill**

What you get here that you won't find on distillery tours is the most comprehensive demonstration of the whisky distillation process in the country. You also discover the history of the popular drink and its economic impact on the country and the world. Kids and adults alike will find the electric tram ride and audiovisual presentation fun and interesting. A conglomeration of the largest distilleries in the country runs the attraction. For an extra £10 ($15), your tour includes two drams (small shots) of whisky.

*354 Castlehill, on the Royal Mile.* ☎ *0131-220-0441. Internet:* www.whiskey-heritage.co.uk. *Bus: 1, 6. Admission: £6.95 ($10) adults, £4.75 ($6.90) seniors and students, £3.40 ($4.95) children under 16, £15 ($22) family. Open: Daily 10 a.m.–6:30 p.m. Time: 2 hours.*

### Camera Obscura
**Castlehill**

If you've never seen a *camera obscura* — a live "camera" that was invented by Leonardo da Vinci — then this will be a unique treat. And even if you have seen one of these glorified periscopes in action, you haven't seen one with so royal a view. While you wait your turn at the camera obscura atop the 17th-century tenement building, you can marvel at the holograms, optical illusions, and rooftop views of the city. The gift shop is full of both imaginative and gimmicky gifts. Take note if you have mobility issues: You must walk to the top of the tower, and there is no wheelchair access.

*Castlehill, at the top of the Royal Mile.* ☎ *0131-226-3709. Internet:* www.camera-obscura.co.uk. *Bus: 1, 34, 35. Admission: £4.95 ($7.20) adults, £3.15 ($4.60) seniors, £3.95 ($5.75) students, £2.50 ($3.65) children under 16, £14.50 ($21) family. Open: Apr–June and Sept–Oct daily 10 a.m.–6 p.m.; July–Aug Mon–Fri 9:30 a.m.–6 p.m., Sat–Sun 10 a.m.–6 p.m.; Nov–Mar daily 10 a.m.–5 p.m. Time: 1 hour.*

### The Royal Yacht Britannia
**Leith**

This decommissioned royal yacht gives you an interesting, informative firsthand look at how the royal family lived. The furniture may be a bit tacky and the technology antiquated, but you can see the Royal Apartments and walk where the Queen once did, giving the place a Graceland-on-water feel. The included audio tour is very good. The gift shop stocks items fit for fans of the royals, from Princess Diana wrapping paper to Britannia cooking aprons.

Because the yacht lies some distance from downtown Edinburgh, you're best bet for getting to the site is with one of the bus tours and hopping off and on again.

*Ocean Drive, Leith.* ☎ *0131-555-5566. Internet:* www.royalyachtbritannia. co.uk. *Admission: £7.75 ($11) adults, £5.95 ($8.65) seniors, £3.75 ($5.45) children under 16, £20 ($29) family. Open: Daily Apr–Sept 9:30 a.m.–4:30 p.m., Oct–Mar 10 a.m.– 3:30 p.m. Time: 1 hour.*

## Other fun stuff to do

### Dynamic Earth

Neither Edinburgh- nor Scotland-related, this unique exhibit (the only one of its kind in Europe) demonstrates the history of the earth's formation. Adult visitors will find plenty to read, and kids may find the pyrotechnics more interesting. The building is an attraction in itself. The large white pavilion-shaped structure set before the background of Arthur's Seat contains a large sphere (the "Showdome") — home to the main exhibit.

*Holyrood Road, below the Royal Mile.* ☎ *0131-550-7800. Internet:* www.dynamic earth.co.uk. *Admission: £8.95 ($13) adults, £5.50 ($8) seniors and children under 16, £6.50 ($9.45) students, £25 ($36) family. Open: Apr–Oct 10 a.m.–6 p.m. daily, Nov–Mar Wed–Sun 10 a.m.–5 p.m. Time: 2 hours.*

### Royal Botanic Garden

In a country full of gardens, this may be the best. Created in 1670, the manicured landscape now occupies 70 acres and makes for a nice walking tour. Exhibits include an Alpine House, a demonstration garden, an arboretum, a rock garden, and even a peat garden. Not just for plant lovers, the Royal Botanic Garden is a godsend for parents: It has acres of grass, no cars, and absolutely no dogs. You can feed the squirrels and ducks or marvel at the large glass houses with huge goldfish. Kids will also enjoy the Exhibition Hall, with its decent hands-on educational exhibitions, and a playground opposite the West Gate.

*Inverleith Row, north of Stockbridge.* ☎ *0131-552-7171. Bus: 8, 19, 23, 27, 37. Admission: Voluntary donation. Open: Daily May–Aug 10 a.m.–8 p.m., Mar–Apr and Sept–Oct 10 a.m.–6 p.m., Nov–Feb 10 a.m.–4 p.m. Time: 2 hours.*

### John Knox House

Knox was the father of the Protestant Reformation movement in Scotland, and this is one of the oldest houses on the Royal Mile, dating to medieval times. But the name is a misnomer — John Knox likely never lived here. One known owner, James Mossman, was the goldsmith to Mary Queen of Scots and later hanged for his loyalty to her. It's not the most fascinating museum, containing a lot of period furniture and Knox family memorabilia, but it is worth the stop. Part of the exhibit includes a re-creation of a conversation between Knox and Mary. The Church of Scotland runs the building.

*43/45 High Street, on the Royal Mile. ☎ 0131-556-9579. Bus: 1, 6. Admission: £2.25 ($3.25) adults, £1.95 ($2.85) seniors and students, £.75 ($1.10) children under 16. Open: Year-round Mon–Sat 10 a.m.–4:30 p.m., plus July–Aug Sun noon to 5 p.m. Time: 1 hour.*

## Writer's Museum

Printing presses, first editions, and other mementoes of Edinburgh's great literary figures are on display at this literary shrine. Fans will delight in seeing Robert Burns' writing desk, Sir Walter Scott's pipe and chess set, and early editions of Robert Louis Stevenson novels. If you're interested in the seedier side of the lives of these literary luminaries, I suggest the literary pub tour described under the "Seeing Edinburgh by guided tour" section, later in this chapter.

*Lady Stair's House, Lawnmarket, on the Royal Mile. ☎ 0131-529-4901. E-mail:* enquiries@writersmuseum.demon.co.uk. *Bus: 1, 6. Admission: Free. Open: Mon–Sat 10 a.m.–5 p.m. Time: 1 hour.*

## Huntly House Museum

If Edinburgh Castle doesn't sate your appetite for local artifacts, check out the Huntly. Included in the modest but interesting collection is the actual collar of Scotland's most famous dog, Greyfriars Bobby, the loyal pup that continued to visit his master's grave years after he was buried. Other local items on display at this small but busy museum include local silver and glassware and an important religious protest document, the National Covenant of 1638.

*142 Canongate, on the Royal Mile. ☎ 0131-529-414. Bus: 1, 6. Admission: Free. Open: Mon–Sat 10 a.m.–5 p.m. Time: 1 hour.*

## Scottish National Portrait Gallery

Before you go inside this world-class art gallery, notice the statues on top of the front entrance: Queen Victoria and two sphinxes guard the treasures within. Among the unique items in the gallery's permanent collection are a Gainsborough, portraits by Scottish artists Ramsay and Raeburn (from Mary Queen of Scots, to Sean Connery), 16th-century Celtic harps, and mysterious walrus ivory chessmen from the Middle Ages that were found on the Isle of Lewis.

*1 Queen St. ☎ 0131-225-7534. Bus: 18, 20, 41. Admission: Free. Open: Mon–Sat 10 a.m.–5 p.m., Sun 2–5 p.m. Time: 1 hour.*

## National Gallery

Edinburgh's other art gallery (besides the National Portrait Gallery; see the preceding listing) is compact but expertly picked. The permanent collection ranges from the Renaissance to the post-Impressionist period, and contains many of the masters of their times. Paintings by Velázquez,

## Edinburgh Attractions

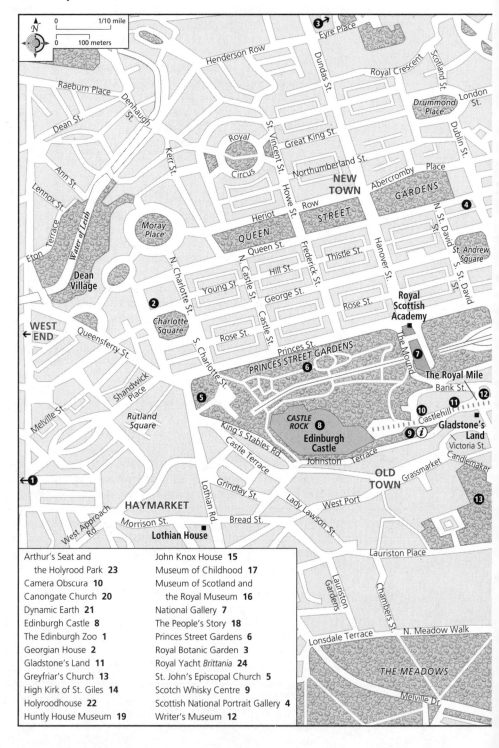

| | |
|---|---|
| Arthur's Seat and the Holyrood Park **23** | John Knox House **15** |
| Camera Obscura **10** | Museum of Childhood **17** |
| Canongate Church **20** | Museum of Scotland and the Royal Museum **16** |
| Dynamic Earth **21** | National Gallery **7** |
| Edinburgh Castle **8** | The People's Story **18** |
| The Edinburgh Zoo **1** | Princes Street Gardens **6** |
| Georgian House **2** | Royal Botanic Garden **3** |
| Gladstone's Land **11** | Royal Yacht *Brittania* **24** |
| Greyfriar's Church **13** | St. John's Episcopal Church **5** |
| High Kirk of St. Giles **14** | Scotch Whisky Centre **9** |
| Holyroodhouse **22** | Scottish National Portrait Gallery **4** |
| Huntly House Museum **19** | Writer's Museum **12** |

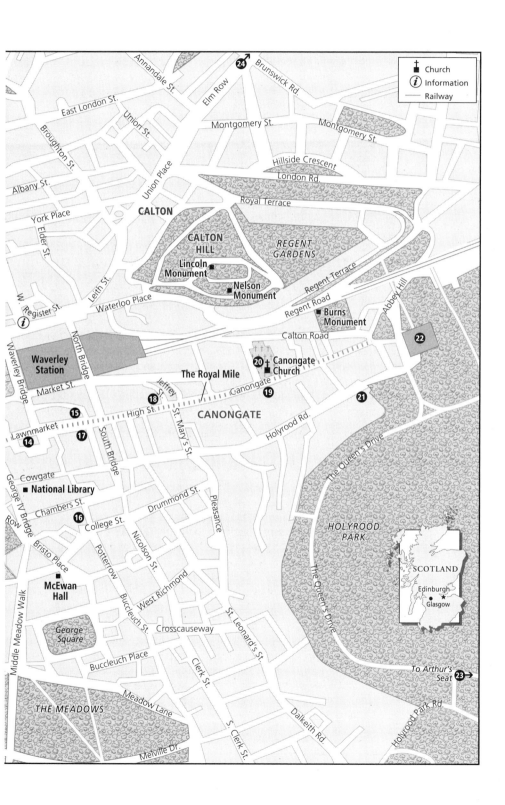

Church
Information
Railway

Annandale St.
Brunswick Rd.
24
Elm Row
East London St.
Union St.
Montgomery St.
Montgomery St.
Broughton St.
Union Place
Hillside Crescent
London Rd.
Albany St.
Royal Terrace
York Place
**CALTON**
Elder St.
**CALTON HILL**
*REGENT GARDENS*
Leith St.
Lincoln Monument
Nelson Monument
Regent Terrace
Abbey Hill
W. Register St.
Waterloo Place
Regent Road
Burns Monument
Calton Road
22
North Bridge
**Waverley Station**
20
Canongate Church
Waverley Bridge
Market St.
**The Royal Mile**
Jeffrey St.
Canongate
19
21
18
St. Mary's St.
**CANONGATE**
15
High St.
Lawnmarket
17
14
South Bridge
Holyrood Rd.
The Queen's Drive
Cowgate
George IV Bridge
Row
■ **National Library**
Chambers St.
Drummond St.
Pleasance
16
College St.
*HOLYROOD PARK*
Bristo Place
Potterrow
Nicolson St.
■ **McEwan Hall**
West Richmond
*SCOTLAND*
Buccleuch St.
Edinburgh
Middle Meadow Walk
*George Square*
Crosscauseway
St. Leonard's St.
Glasgow
The Queen's Drive
Buccleuch Place
Clerk St.
To Arthur's Seat 23
*THE MEADOWS*
Meadow Lane
Holyrood Park Rd.
S. Clerk St.
Dalkeith Rd.
Melville Dr.

El Greco, Raphael, Cézanne, Rembrandt, Turner, Degas, Monet, and Van Gogh — the list reads like a who's who of classic art. The gallery is also the premier repository of Scottish art.

*2 The Mound. ☎ 0131-556-8921. Bus: 3, 21, 26. Admission: Free. Open: Mon–Sat 10 a.m.–6 p.m., Sun 2–5 p.m. Time: 1 hour.*

### Gladstone's Land

This refurbished 17th-century home near the top of the Royal Mile has the only intact example of once-prevalent medieval arches. Notice that the windows are half glass and half shuttered with wood — a throwback to the days when glass was an expensive luxury. The stately rooms and painted ceilings are amazing. It may not be everyone's cup of tea — kids will be bored — but it is an impressive preservation.

*477B Lawnmarket. ☎ 0131-226-5856. Bus: 1, 34, 35. Admission: £3.20 ($4.65). Open: Apr–Oct Mon–Sat 10 a.m.–5 p.m., Sun 2 p.m.–5 p.m. Closed Nov–Mar. Time: 1 hour.*

### Georgian House

Like Gladstone's Land (see the previous listing), this refurbished home is a walking tour back in time. Located on New Town's Charlotte Square, the period house demonstrates the lifestyle of an affluent family in the late 18th century. You don't have to be an interior decorator to appreciate the paintings, Wedgwood china, and Chippendale and Hepplewhite furniture.

## Edinburgh Festival: The big summer event

As the closest thing Scotland has to Mardi Gras, this international festival is the highlight of the Scottish calendar. Started in 1947 as a stage for peace and unity in Europe, the festival has grown to citywide proportions and now includes an unofficial **Fringe Festival.** A book, film, music, comedy, and theater festival all at the same time, it has about 14,000 events going on through the month of August. The main festival takes place in all the big theaters in the city, from schools to the streets (particularly High Street). The main venue is the **Famous Grouse House,** 16 Chambers St. Every year, the program expands to include all the best in Scottish and international folk music, theater, and arts, and includes numerous concerts, *ceilidhs,* and late-night fun and food.

Be prepared for crowds. The population of Edinburgh, about half a million, reputedly doubles in August. The main office, which sells all tickets, is at the Hub, Castlehill, in an old church near the castle at the top end of the Royal Mile (☎ 0131-473-2000; Internet: www.edinburghfestivals.co.uk or www.eif.co.uk); Fringe Festival (☎ 0131-226-5257; www.edfringe.com); Military Tattoo (☎ 0131-225-1188). Bus: 1, 34, 35. Office open Apr–July Mon–Sat 9:30 a.m.–5:30 p.m.; Aug Mon–Sat 9 a.m.–8 p.m., Sun 10 a.m.–5 p.m.

*7 Charlotte Sq., on the north side.* ☎ *0131-225-2160. Bus: 3, 21, 26, 31, 85. Admission: £4.20 ($6.10) adults, £2.80 ($4.10) seniors, students, and children under 16. Open: Daily Apr–Sept 10 a.m.–6 p.m., Oct–Dec 11 a.m.–4p.m. Time: 1 hour.*

# Churches in Edinburgh

## High Kirk of St. Giles

Frequent guided tours explore this beautiful church on the Royal Mile, a religious site since the ninth century. It's short on artifacts but long on architecture; of particular note are the stunning stained-glass windows. Just inside, you'll notice a statue of Reformation leader John Knox, who was minister here from 1560 to 1570. Also take a look at the corner Thistle Chapel, with the carved coat of arms of 16 knights above.

*High Street, on the Royal Mile.* ☎ *0131-225-9442. E-mail:* stgiles@hotmail.com. *Bus: 1, 6. Admission: Free; donation requested. Open: Mon–Sat 9 a.m.–5 p.m., Sun 1–5 p.m. Time: 1 hour.*

## Canongate Church

This is where the late Queen Mum went to church when she visited Edinburgh. The architecture is distinctively Danish, but the real attraction is the well-groomed graveyard at the back. You're free to walk through and view the graves of such luminaries as the poet Robert Fergusson, Robert Burns' girlfriend Agnes McLehose (affectionately known as Clarinda), Adam Smith (author of *The Wealth of Nations*), and David Rizzio, a favorite aide to Mary Queen of Scots (whom Mary's husband tortured and killed in the Palace of Holyrood).

*Canongate, on the Royal Mile.* ☎ *0131-556-3515. Bus: 1, 6. Admission: Free. Open: June–Sept Mon–Sat 10:30 a.m.–4:30 p.m. Church closed Oct–May; graveyard open. Time: 1 hour.*

## Greyfriars Church

The most important historical event that took place here was the signing of the National Covenant of 1638, outlawing Roman Catholicism in the country. The signers, mostly Congregationalists, were later imprisoned in the church. Poet Allan Ramsay is buried here, and so is John Gray, an Edinburgh policeman. Gray owned a dog called Grayfriars Bobby, who accompanied his master on the beat and continued to visit his grave for 14 years after Gray was buried here. Today, dogs are no longer allowed on the grounds. (The listing for the little Scottish terrier's statue appears later in this chapter under "Edinburgh Landmarks.")

The church was the first one to be built in the city after the Reformation, and its grounds formerly belonged to the friars of St. Francis, or Greyfriars — hence its name.

*West Crosscauseway, at the bottom of George IV Bridge.* ☎ *0131-667-0867. Bus: 2, 12, 23, 24, 27–29, 40–42, 45–47. Admission: Free. Open: Apr–Oct Mon–Fri 10:30 a.m.–4:30 p.m., Sat 10:30 a.m.–2:30 p.m.; Nov–Mar Thurs 1:30–3:30 p.m.; other times by arrangement with the Visitors Office. Time: 1 hour.*

### St. John's Episcopal Church

Built in the Windsor style, this stunning church is worth a stroll inside just to see the vaulted ceilings and detailed architecture. The other big feature of the Gothic church is the 12 stained-glass windows devoted to the apostles; you can see the windows especially well at night when they're lit up from inside. This place is also a popular festival venue because of its excellent acoustics. An August craft fair takes place in the graveyard. Spooky, huh?

*Princes Street, on the west end.* ☎ *0131-229-7565. Bus: 4, 15, 44. Admission: Free. Open: Mon–Sat 10 a.m.–5 p.m. Time: 1 hour.*

# Edinburgh landmarks

### Calton Hill

Robert Louis Stevenson claimed that Calton Hill offered the best view of the city because you can see both Arthur's Seat and the castle from its peak. The hill, with its row of Greek columns on top, is an odd landmark, reminiscent of an uncompleted Roman temple. Local citizens tried to build a Parthenon on the hill in 1822, but the project ran out of money after only 12 columns. The truncated pseudo-temple, known as the National Monument, honors the Scottish dead from the Napoleonic wars. In addition to the Parthenon, an obelisk monument commemorates the political reformers of the 19th century, and a statue of Abraham Lincoln honors Scots who died in the American Civil War. It is the largest statue of Lincoln outside of the United States. Also on the hill is the Old Cemetery, home of the tomb of the philosopher David Hume. (The Nelson Monument, also on Calton Hill, is listed later in this section.) The 350-foot hill is a good open space for fresh air and a light climb up and down.

*Regent Road. From Princes Street (which becomes Regent Road), take Regent Terrace up to the top. Time: 1 hour.*

### The Execution Spot

The little area now known as Grassmarket was the cattle market of 17th-century Edinburgh. But it was also the sight of the public gallows. At one end of the median strip of Grassmarket (street) are a walled area and a stone marker with an "X" on it, marking the spot. One of the people to be hanged here (although legend says he survived the sentence by paying the hangman to quickly release him) was Deacon Brodie, the man who many believe was the real-life Dr. Jekyll and Mr. Hyde — and who helped design the gallows. The Grassmarket of today is a student hangout area with cheap Italian restaurants and a few pubs. One pub, The Last Drop, is a grim reminder of the neighborhood's infamous past.

*Grassmarket, south of the castle.*

## Forth Rail Bridge

This fine bridge in the heart of the city is a great photo backdrop, but as you cross you may want to keep in mind the permanent casualty inside it. As the story has it, a man on the construction crew fell down one of the tubular pylons. Unable to rescue him, his co-workers eventually fed him a strychnine sandwich to put him out of his misery — and in the bridge he still rests.

*South Queensferry, 10 minutes west of the city on the A90.*

## Greyfriars Bobby

This memorial fountain to Greyfriars Bobby, the loyal terrier who guarded his master's grave for 14 years, is one of the city's most treasured landmarks. The small statue and fountain for the wee dog is in Bobby's likeness. Disney even made a movie about the loyal pup in the 1950s.

*Candlemaker Row, opposite the National Museum of Scotland.*

## Nelson Monument

This Napoleonic War memorial honors Admiral Nelson, the victor at the Battle of Trafalgar. Built in the shape of an upturned telescope, this monument to the great naval officer offers stunning views of the city if you're adventurous enough to hike up the 143 steps. At 1 p.m. every day, you'll notice the large ball pulled up on the cruciform mast at the top of the monument. This relates to the timed cannon shot from Edinburgh Castle, to which locals have been setting their watches since 1861.

*Lothian Road, top of Calton Hill. ☎ 0131-556-2716. Admission: £2 ($2.90). Open: Mon–Sat 10 a.m.–3 p.m.*

## Royal High School

Sir Walter Scott and Alexander Graham Bell both attended school in this grand, neoclassical building. The Greek-style structure was almost the meeting place for Scotland's new parliament, but the building was too small (the new parliament building is currently under construction on the Royal Mile). The school is closed now and not open to the public.

*Regent Road, below Calton Hill.*

### Stevenson House

This is the last place Robert Louis Stevenson and his family lived before he moved to the South Pacific to escape the damp weather that was exacerbating his ill health. He lived here for 23 years. You can't see it through the trees, but in the private Queen's Gardens across the street from his house is a lake with an island in the middle, believed to be the inspiration for one of his most popular novels, *Treasure Island*. The house is not open to the public.

*17 Heriot Row, above Queen Street and Gardens.*

### Sir Walter Scott

Dubbed the "space rocket," this amazingly large and elaborate structure resembling a cathedral spire is visible from all over the city. Inside the 200-foot rocket is the lounging statue of Mr. Scott and his dog, Maida. Carved figures inside the monument represent heroes from Scott's works, including Ivanhoe and Rob Roy. For a fee, you can walk to the top of the monument.

*Princes Street Gardens.* ☎ *0131-539-4068. Admission: £2.50 ($3.65). Open: Mar–May Mon–Sat 9 a.m.–6 p.m., Sun 10 a.m.–6 p.m.; June–Oct Mon–Sat 9 a.m.–8 p.m., Sun 10 a.m.–6 p.m.; Nov–Feb Mon–Sat 9 a.m.–4 p.m., Sun 10 a.m.–4 p.m.*

### The Watchtower

Notice the castle-like spire overlooking the graveyard of St. Cuthbert's Church. Families of those interred here built the watchtower to discourage the body snatchers who once pillaged the graves in order to make a tidy profit selling cadavers to medical students. The families chipped in for guard's pay — 6 pence a week and all the whisky he could drink (to help allay the more frightening aspects of the job). One questions how effective the guard must have been while enjoying a liquid paycheck.

*Lothian Road, next to St. John's Church near the corner of Princes Street.*

# Seeing Edinburgh by guided tour

If you haven't the time in Edinburgh to fully appreciate on your own enough of the attractions listed in this chapter, or if you're looking to experience Edinburgh with others who share your interests, a guided tour may be for you. Here are some of the best:

✔ **Guide Friday** (☎ 0131-556-2244) offers a fun ride around the city in one of its fleet of open-top, double-decker green-and-tan buses. The commentaries are colorful and full of interesting footnotes, and the guides are knowledgeable and willing to answer questions. But the best part about the tour is that your all-day ticket (£6.50/$9.45) allows you to get on and off as you please. Don't make it your only tour of the city (I recommend taking any of the remaining tours in this list), but use it as a good overview with a quick guide to the top spots. The circuit includes the castle, the Royal Mile, the Palace of Holyrood, Grassmarket, Princes Street, and Charlotte Square. Tours run from 7 a.m. through dusk. Buses leave from Waverley Bridge, but you can get on at any one of the stops. Minimum time is one hour if you do just a circuit and stay on the entire route.

✔ On the **McEwan's Literary Pub Tour** (☎ 0131-226-6665; www.scot-lit-tour.co.uk), the drinking is optional, but the laughs and learning are not. This humorous and intellectual pub crawl covers the literary heights and lowbrow debaucheries of all the great local writers. Your two hosts banter in a battle of wits that leaves you the winner. Hear the words and tales of Robert Louis Stevenson, Sir Walter Scott, Robert Burns, and more, and walk where they stumbled. As the local newspaper *The Scotsman* puts it, this tour offers something more than "the usual tartan tat." Funny, interesting, and punctuated with drinks, this a popular tour, and for good reason. The tour leaves from the Beehive pub on Grassmarket in Old Town and winds through the Royal Mile, ending at Milne's pub in New Town. Tour hours: June and September daily 6 and 8:30 p.m.; July and August daily 2, 6, and 8:30 p.m.; April, May, and October Thursday through Sunday 7:30 p.m.; November through March Friday 7:30 p.m. Tickets (£7/$10 adults, £5/$7.25 students and children) are for sale at the Beehive or in advance at the tourist office on Princes Street. Time: 2 hours.

✔ The subject matter may be gory, but **The Witchery Tour** (☎ 0131-225-6745) around the Royal Mile is very funny. Light on history — unless you count the history of witchcraft, the plague, and torture — it's a good laugh, plus you get to keep the booklet of witch tales. Although the tour is family friendly, toddlers may be frightened by the "jumper-ooters" — actors who surprise you when you least expect it. The two tours, "Ghosts & Gore" and "Murder & Mystery," are similar and overlap in content, so don't take both. Tours leave from in front of the Witchery Restaurant, 352 Castlehill, on the Royal Mile, and stay along the Royal Mile. The Ghost Tour leaves daily at 6:30 p.m. and 8 p.m. from May through August. The Murder Tour leaves daily at 9 p.m. and 10 p.m. year-round. Each costs £7 ($10) adults, £5 ($7.25) students, seniors and children. Time: 1 hour, 15 minutes.

✔ Walking tours often meet in the evening, but **Robin's Tours** (☎ 0131-557-9933) of the city and hidden vaults, during the day, are a good way to walk off your hearty breakfast. There are three tours in all. The Grand Tour covers New Town and the Royal Mile, but not the underground vaults, and the others cover either just the Royal Mile or the vaults. You can't see the vaults on your own, so if you aren't claustrophobic, you may want to check them out. Otherwise, the grand tour is a great overview of town, giving you plenty of time afterward to go back and revisit some of the attractions. Tours run daily; meet outside the Tourist Office on Princes Street. The Hidden Vaults Tour: 11:30 a.m. and 2 p.m. May through September; 2:30 p.m. October to April. The Royal Mile Walk leaves at 11 a.m. year-round. The Grand Tour leaves at 10 a.m. year-round. Tickets cost £5 ($7.25) adults, £3 ($4.35) students, seniors, and children. Time: 2 to 5 hours.

✔ Of all the history tours in Edinburgh, **Mercat Tours** (☎ 0131-557-6464; www.mercattours.co.uk) is the original. Experts, not actors, lead these interesting tours. The lineup includes a history tour, one that goes through the underground vaults, and a few macabre tours covering the ghosts of Edinburgh's creepy side. If you're faint of heart or traveling with kids, take note that the Ghosts & Ghouls Tour includes a drink afterward, and, like the Ghost Hunter Trail, includes the vaults and ends in a graveyard. The three most popular tours are the Royal Mile, Underground Vaults, and the Ghost Hunter Trail. Tours leave from Mercat Cross, next to St. Giles Cathedral, daily year-round. Royal Mile Tour: £6 ($9) adults, £5 ($7.25) students and seniors, £4 ($5.80) children. April through September 11 a.m. and 2 p.m., October to March 11:15 a.m. Ghost Hunter Trail: £6 ($8.70) adults, £2 ($2.90) students and seniors, £1 ($1.45) children. April to September 9:30 a.m. and 10:30 p.m., October to March 9:30 a.m. Vault Tour: £5 ($7.25) adults, £4 ($5.80) students and seniors, £3 ($4.35) children. April to September hourly between 11 a.m. and 4 p.m., October to March noon and 4 p.m. Time: Royal Mile and Ghost Hunter Trail: 2 hours. Vault Tour: 1 hour.

# "I see dead people"

**Mercat Tours** (☎ 0131-557-6464; www.mercattours.co.uk) has a monopoly on one particularly gruesome piece of subterranean real estate. **Mary King's Close,** underneath what are now the City Chambers, was the street where bubonic plague sufferers were quarantined in 1645, after an outbreak had killed off a third of the city's population. The city closed the entrances to the street, and the sick were left there to die. After all were dead, two butchers were sent in to chop the bodies and bring them out. Locals consider it the most haunted street in Scotland. If you take the tour of Mary King's Close, you may see toys and dolls lying about, left for the spirit of Annie, just one of the children sent to the Close and sealed in with the other doomed. Contact Mercat for prices and other details of this new tour.

# Shopping in Edinburgh

Edinburgh has two main areas that offer a good variety of specialty shops and a range of stores. The first is the **Royal Mile,** where tourist-centric souvenir shops sell items from "tartan tat" to upscale gifts and crafts. The boutiques and fashionable shops on New Town's **Princes Street,** between the Princes Mall and the Jenners department store, are also worth an afternoon of serious shopping.

In most cases, unless otherwise noted, the shops in this section accept credit cards. The most common are Visa and MasterCard; many places take American Express, but few honor Discover (it's not common in Europe) or Diner's Club. Shops usually open at 9 or 10 a.m. and close between 5:00 and 6:30 p.m. Some stay open as late as 9 p.m., but only in high season. Most keep shorter hours on Sunday. The listings in this section note exceptions.

If you're on a mission to fill up that empty suitcase you brought along, start at one of the following two places and then make your way around the city.

- **Jenners,** 48 Princes St., across from the Scott Monument (☎ **0131-225-2442**). This is the primo spot on your shopping crawl. Edinburgh's answer to London's Harrods or New York's Bloomingdale's, the upscale establishment is the oldest independent department store in the world (dating to 1838). The Victorian building contains all the modern apparel and gift items you could want and is also known as the best place in Scotland for china.

- **Princes Mall,** Princes Street (☎ **0131-557-3759;** www.princes mall-edinburgh.co.uk). The partially underground mall has a good number of shops, including Benetton, The Body Shop, Hector Russell kiltmaker, and the Whisky Shop. You'll find everything from clothes and gourmet food to gifts and souvenirs. It's conveniently located below the tourist information center, next to Waverley Station and the Waverley Bridge.

In the following sections, I share some of my favorite shopping stops in Edinburgh for eats, gifts, souvenirs, clothing, and that hard-to-describe, uniquely Scottish something.

## Books

**Bauermeister Booksellers,** 19 George IV Bridge (☎ **0131-226-5561**), is a great initial stop for out-of-towners — in addition to a good collection of fiction, it stocks a helpful selection of tourist guides, maps, and magazines. It's also just off the Royal Mile, putting the two-floor store right on the tourist trail. Open Monday to Friday from 9 a.m. to 8 p.m., Saturday from 9 a.m. to 5.30 p.m., and Sunday noon to 5 p.m.

Instead of the usual tourist fluff, take home an interesting coffee-table book about Scotland from **Beyond Words,** 42–44 Cockburn St. (☎ 0131-226-6636). This quiet little bookshop specializes in big photography volumes. The expert staff can help you find what you need. Open Tuesday to Saturday from 10 a.m. to 8 p.m., Sunday and Monday from noon to 5 p.m. Bus: 1, 6, 34, 35.

The popular chain **James Thin,** 53–59 South Bridge (☎ 0131-622-8222; E-mail: enquiries@jthin.co.uk), has several branches, but this store is the original and the best. The huge flagship opened in 1848 and has everything under the sun (90,000 titles at last count), including an extensive collection of Scottish literature. The four floors of browsing bliss hold a reasonably priced secondhand section (on the top floor), ambrosia for bargain-hunters. Open Monday to Friday from 9 a.m. to 10 p.m., Saturday from 9 a.m. to 5:30 p.m., and Sunday from 11 a.m. to 5 p.m. Bus: 100.

**West Port Books,** 145 West Port (☎ 0131-229-4431), is the antithesis of large chain bookstores. It has no easy layout or well-marked sections, but that's the fun of the place. The labyrinthine shop overflows with an odd range of secondhand books, old records, and sheet music. Open Monday to Wednesday from 10:30 a.m. to 5:30 p.m., and Thursday to Saturday from 11:15 a.m. to 5.30 p.m.

## Clothing

**Cashmere Store of Scotland,** 2 St. Giles St., Royal Mile (☎ 0131-225-5178), and 67 George St. (☎ 0131-226-4861), is the place for classic and contemporary cashmere coats, sweaters, scarves, gloves, and more. If you want top-quality cashmere, you've come to the right place. Not many bargains, but you won't be hard-pressed to find something you'll love.

More than just a clothes shop, **Edinburgh Old Town Weaving Co.,** 555 Castlehill, on the Royal Mile, next to the castle (☎ 0131-226-1555), is a shopping event, and one the kids won't whine through, either. It's one thing to see weaving in action, but tartan weaving is a complicated and beautiful process. Master craftsman Geoffrey Tailor makes the kilts, and the shop stocks all kinds of clothes as well as gifts and jewelry. If you're not interested in taking home a kilt or traditional costume, you can dress up and have your picture taken as a unique souvenir. If you want your very own tartan — designed just for you and registered with the Scottish Tartans Society — you can buy that, too.

**Hector Russell,** 95 Princes St. (☎ **0131-225-3315**), 137–141 High St. (☎ **0131-558-1254**), and Princes Mall (☎ **0131-558-8021**), is renowned as the best kiltmaker in the business. No wonder visitors and locals alike flock to his shops. Not ready for a kilt, you say? You'll find plenty of other well-crafted formal wear and wooly clothes to browse through. Open daily from 9 a.m. to 5:30 p.m., until 10 p.m. May to September. AE, DC, MC, V.

## Crafts and jewelry

Looking for an excellent collection of antique jewelry and clocks? At **Alistir Tait,** 116a Rose St. (☎ **0131-225-4105**), the materials are largely local, and the selection is unique. One of the most popular items is an elaborate pendant called a _luckenbooth;_ the store has one of the city's largest collections of these much-desired items. Call for hours. Bus: 3, 31, 69.

**Hamilton & Inches,** 87 George St. (☎ **0131-225-4898**), is an expert silver- and goldsmith that has been in operation since 1866. It has modern jewelry as well as pieces with a more traditional look. Many shoppers come to pick out porcelain and china dishware (a perfect wedding gift). The building's gilded Georgian columns are a treasure by themselves. Closed Sunday. Bus: 41, 42.

The Orkney-based knitwear designer **Judith Glue,** 64 High St. (☎ **0131-556-5443**), sells knitted gift items as well as Scottish crafts such as jewelry, ceramics, and stationery. Just next door is Judith's interior shop, which carries all kinds of funky home furnishings to take back to your abode. Bus: 1, 6.

## Food and spirits

You'll feel like a kid in a you-know-what as you peruse the jars of treats at **Casey's Confectioners,** 52 St. Mary's St. (☎ **0131-556-6082**). The Art Deco confectionery opened in 1954, and little has changed since. Not sure what to buy? Choose small sample bags for your shopping walk, and you'll no doubt find a favorite you'll want to take home. Closed Sunday. Credit cards not accepted. Bus: 1, 6.

One word: haggis. **MacSweens of Edinburgh,** 118 Bruntsfield Place (☎ **0131-229-9141**), is the best place to get it in Edinburgh. If the idea of eating certain animal parts (and the staff will tell you just what's in there if you want to know) gives you the willies, take home some spicy vegetarian haggis, instead. The haggis can't be too bad — a member of the MacSween clan tastes every batch. Closed Sunday and Monday.

**Royal Mile Whiskies,** 379 High St. (☎ 0131-225-3383), is an excellent spirit shop with a classic range of whiskys; you'll find more than 300 varieties to make a lot of friends with or just enjoy (responsibly) while you're visiting Scotland. Open Monday to Saturday from 10 a.m. to 10 p.m., and Sunday from noon to 10 p.m. AE, MC, V.

## Music and musical instruments

**Bagpipes Galore!,** 82 Canongate, on the Royal Mile (☎ 07000-474-737; E-mail: pipes@bagpipe.co.uk; Internet: www.bagpipe.co.uk), sells more bagpipes than any other company in the United Kingdom. If you're thinking about getting a set of starter pipes, this is a good place. The shop offers high-end bagpipes, but you can also get a good deal on a pair for under £100 ($145). Closed Sunday from October to April.

**Blackfriars Music,** in Bagpipers Centre, 49 Blackfriars St., off the Royal Mile (☎ 0131-557-3090), is a great one-stop shop for all things musical. It carries a good selection of cassettes, CDs, and related books and accessories. Most people come for the selection of new and used bagpipes and other folk instruments.

The best and coolest record store in the city is **Fopp,** 55 Cockburn St. (☎ 0131-220-0133). Forget the Virgin Megastore on Princes Street — you can find Virgin stores in the States — this is where locals in the know go. Downstairs is home to Scotland's largest stock of new vinyl, with handy turntables for your use; the street level holds CDs. The prices are competitive, and the bargain bins are full of great finds. Whether you're looking for traditional Scottish music or hard-to-find U.K. pop hits, this is your record store. Open Monday to Saturday from 9:30 a.m. to 7 p.m., and Sunday from 11 a.m. to 6 p.m.

## Souvenirs

**All Things Scottish,** 9 Upper Bow, on the Royal Mile (no phone), is hard to miss, with its frighteningly life-size piper in the window. Clan magnets, tartan everything, and books on Scottish history are the standard fare. You can find some nice items, but this is not the place for much more than souvenirs. Look around, and you may find something particularly tacky.

**Scottish Crafts,** 328 Lawnmarket, High Street, on the Royal Mile (☎ 0131-225-4152), is in direct competition with All Things Scottish for the lowest common denominator. Crafts has more cheesy Scottish-related gifts than you can shake a stick at. It's all tartan and touristy, but you'll find exactly the kinds of things the extended family expects you to bring home. Open daily from 9 a.m. to 7:30 p.m. Bus: 1, 6, 34, 35.

# Doing the Pub Crawl (And Other Nightlife)

Edinburgh doesn't have a raucous nightlife. Or at least not one that is tourist-friendly. You're better off sticking to one of the many friendly pubs that enjoy a good reputation among locals and visitors alike. You'll never hit them all (at least not without some serious effort), but here are the best of the best.

## Great pubs: The best of the bunch

Edinburgh may not have an up-all-night, dance-club nightlife, but it does have plenty of pubs and enough vitality to please most visitors looking for some fun.

### Indigo Yard

**The hippest bar scene**

This cool, happening joint for drinking and eating consists of a large courtyard covered by a glass canopy. The concept gives the place a fresh, airy feel. Patrons range from students to yuppies, and the drinks reflect that variety — beer, wine, shooters, and pitchers of cocktails. The place gets busy and the music is low key — instant atmosphere.

*7 Charlotte Lane, just off George Street.* ☎ *0131-220-5603. Open: Daily 8:30 a.m.– 1 a.m. Bus: 34, 35.*

### The Hebrides Bar

**The best music club**

The Hebrides is traditionally a meeting place for singers and pipers. Even when they have no live music, organized or otherwise, you'll still be entertained: The pub boasts one of the finest collections of folk music cassettes around. The bar also has an impressive array of whiskys and a knowledgeable staff to answer any questions you may have.

*17 Market St.* ☎ *0131-225-3282. Open: Mon–Sat 9 a.m.–1 a.m.; Sun 12:30 p.m.–1 a.m. Bus: 5.*

### Three Sisters

**The best late-night bar**

Open until 3 a.m., this is the top spot for the after-hours crowd. It's three bars in one — Irish, American, and Gothic — and there's something for everyone, including a beer garden on the front courtyard. The most comfortable of the three bars is the Irish-themed one. The television set shows a series of entertaining old Guinness commercials. The American bar has a good shooters menu, and if you manage to drink nine of them, you get a free T-shirt. The food is good, and if you come for breakfast before 11 a.m., you get a free pint of stout or a Bloody Mary. The sad tale of the three sisters, Kitty, Maggie, and Cath, is too long and complicated to outline here, but the whole saga appears on the back of the menu.

*139 Cowgate, in the Tailors Hall Hotel.* ☎ *0131-622-6800. Bus: 1.*

### Why Not!
### The top club

Shouldn't that be a question mark ("Why Not?")? Oh, well. This is the most user-friendly club in town. The weekend line can get a bit long, but don't be discouraged — just make sure you're well dressed (tennis shoes and jeans don't make the cut). The club is in the basement of the Dome Bar and Grill — look for the side entrance through the ornate gates. The room once held the vaults of the old Bank of Scotland, and according to legend, the place has a ghost — I hope it knows how to groove.

*14 George St.* ☎ *0131-624-8633. Open: Thurs–Sun 10 p.m.–3 a.m. Cover: £3–£15 ($4.35–$22). Bus: 4, 15, 44.*

## Other recommended bars and pubs

Most bars and pubs are open Sunday through Thursday from 11 a.m. or noon until 11 p.m. or midnight, usually closing later on Friday and Saturday. The listings in this section note exceptions.

✔ **Bannerman's,** 212 Cowgate (☎ 0131-556-3254). If you need a cozy break from the cold or rain, this is the place to go. I don't know which is warmer, the bar or the staff. The old brick building somehow manages to keep out the draft, and the decor of this former 18th-century wine cellar is a cross between tavern chic and college dorm comfort. Watch out for the huge pillowy couches — they're known to steal the pence out of a few pockets. Bannerman's schedules music a few nights a week, ranging from jigs and reels to "join-in" songs. Bus: 34, 35.

✔ **Bar Oz,** 14 Forrest Rd., Cowgate (☎ 0131-220-1816). It may be an Australian bar (read: beer comes in cans), but it's not as cheesy at it sounds. So, no worries, mate. Locals come mostly to watch sports — the mammoth television screen shows everything — younger folks come for the music and dancing, and everybody else comes because it's a nice little bar. Bus: 34, 35.

✔ **Beehive,** 18–20 Grassmarket (☎ 0131-226-6665). The Beehive brings to mind the old English poem: "Within this hive, all alive / Good liquor makes us funny / The flaw is if you are dry, so / Step in and try the honey." Now that you've learned something, go inside and forget it with a couple pints. The Beehive has been a stopping point for visitors since the 1700s, when it was a stable house. Now it's a fun pub with a beer garden. If you're hungry, step into the Honey Pot dining room and try some beef-and-ale pie. Bus: 2, 12.

✔ **Cafe Royal Circle Bar,** 17 West Register St., off St. Andrews Square (☎ **0131-556-1884**). One of the most famously popular bars in the city. A young but sophisticated crowd packs the large island bar every day of the week. The classic look of the place, with its grand Victorian dark-wood interior and antique paintings, belies the anything-but-somber attitude. There's no music, but you won't really notice. The bar keeps a good selection of malt whiskys and cask-conditioned ales ready.

✔ **Deacon Brodie's Tavern,** 435 Lawnmarket, top of the Royal Mile (☎ **0131-225-6531**). Named for the reputed inspiration for Stevenson's Dr. Jekyll and Mr. Hyde, this fine pub is all Jekyll and no Hyde. The traditional pub and wine cellar lounge is always hopping with locals and out-of-towners. If you're a fan of the macabre, note that the bipolar Deacon was buried on this very spot. For more information on his dual personality, head around back through the alley to read a bit more. Bus: 1, 34, 35.

✔ **The Ensign Ewart,** 521 Lawnmarket, top of the Royal Mile (☎ **0131-225-7440**). The closest pub to Edinburgh Castle, this small place often fills with tourists who are making their way to or from the city's big attraction. It's a warm, dry respite from a sometimes-chilly castle tour. The kitchen serves a cheap lunch and excellent apple pie. Kilt brooches line the beams of the ceiling, and Irish music is on the jukebox for those who like a little Van Morrison with their pint and haggis. If you like stout, as I do, have the local Orkney Dark Island stout on tap. Several nights each week in August, guest singers take the floor to entertain — and patrons are encouraged to join in the choruses of old and new favorites. Get there early for a good seat.

✔ **Greyfriar's Bobby Bar,** 34A Candlemaker Row, near George IV Bridge (☎ **0131-225-8328**). You've been to the church. You've posed next to the statue. Now have a beer in the bar — the best part of the Greyfriars Bobby trifecta. Named after Edinburgh's legendarily faithful terrier, the lively three-level pub attracts students, locals, and tourists. The coolest part of the traditional watering hall is the free jukebox. Cheers to the dawg! Open Monday to Saturday from 11 a.m. to 1 a.m., and Sunday from 12:30 p.m.–1 a.m.

✔ **Jekyll and Hyde,** 112 Hanover St. (☎ **0131-225-2022**). The drinks and service are on the doctor's side of the coin, but the decor gives over to the dark side. The creepy black building sports old light fixtures and Victorian furniture, reminiscent of the home of the Addams Family. The food menu is a kitschy scream as well; try a "sadistic sandwich" or a "feast of the underworld." Bus: 23, 27.

✔ **Jolly Judge,** 7a James Court, just off the Royal Mile (☎ 0131-225-2669). This place is very small — so small, in fact, that you are welcome to take your pint outside and enjoy it in the enclosed square. Look for the chubby magistrate's face along the Royal Mile and go down the little close at James Court to find it. This subterranean watering hole was a pub about 300 years ago but spent most of the last three centuries as a tailor shop. While you're sipping your drink, notice the recently rediscovered original ceiling beams, which are from an 18th-century sailing ship — if, that is, you find room to enjoy your drink inside.

✔ **The Last Drop,** 74/78 Grassmarket (☎ 0131-225-4851). The name of the place doesn't refer to the last drop of whisky (thank goodness) but rather the last drop of the hangman's noose. Its blood-red façade is only yards from the location of the city's old gallows. And if that's not enough to make you appreciate the finer things in life, like good beer, great Scotch, and service with a smile at the nearby pub, then I don't know what is. The place gets busy and a bit smoky on the weekends and is popular with students when school is in session. Open Monday to Saturday from 11 a.m. to 1 a.m., and Sunday from 12:30 p.m. to 1 a.m. Bus: 2, 12.

✔ **Milne's,** 35 Hanover St. (☎ 0131-225-6738). Once a popular hangout for writers and socialists, this pub was dubbed "Kremlin Cove" and the "Poet's Pub" back in the day. Now it's just a fun place to hang out, comrade, with several good local brews on tap. The back part of Milne's stretches upstairs to the most comfortable part of the bar. The place is not named for *Winnie the Pooh* author A.A. Milne, but it was a gathering place for local writers, such as the socialist Robert Louis Stevenson. Among old Victorian advertisements and pictures of the city are some poems and mementoes bragging on the Milne's heyday.

✔ **Oxford Bar,** 8 Young St., behind the west end of George Street (☎ 0131-539-7119). This small, old-fashioned bar is the favorite haunt of local literary celeb Ian Rankin. Fans of mystery and crime books will get a kick out of being in the real pub where Rankin's fictional Detective Inspector John Rebus goes to drink off his rough days on the beat. It's a good thing Rebus isn't *really* here, though, because he'd be taking up precious room at the little bar.

✔ **Peartree House,** 38 W. Nicholson St., near George IV Bridge (☎ 0131-667-7533). In the historic Peartree House, this smallish pub doesn't have to worry about crowding, thanks to its best selling point: the huge beer garden! A wall and gate enclose the garden, open year-round but most popular in the summer. In addition to regular ales and whiskys, the pub also makes a mean margarita.

✔ **Rose St. Brewery,** 57 Rose St. (☎ 0131-220-1227). First off, it's not a brewery. And the cask ale selection is unreliable. But that's the only thing wrong with this lively pub on wee Rose St. During the day, the outdoor seating is full of pint drinkers getting some sun; at night, the place is full of friendly locals of a good age range (read: no young hooligans and no old-timers who stare at the tourists). The jukebox holds top-40 '80s and '90s selections, and the bar staff is attentive and friendly. What more could you ask for? Well, home brews, I guess. Open Monday to Friday from 11 a.m. to 1 a.m., Saturday from 9 a.m. to 1 a.m., and Sunday from 12:30 p.m. to 11 p.m.

✔ **White Hart,** 34 Grassmarket (☎ **0131-226-6997**). Located inside the oldest inn in Edinburgh, this tiny pub can also boast of having served three literary legends in its long potable history. Sir Walter Scott and the poets William Wordsworth and Robert Burns (the national poet of Scotland) all had a few pints here in their day (although not at the same time, contrary to one incorrect local legend). In 1791, Burns spent his last night in Edinburgh at the inn. Bits of his poetry are written on the small roof beams of the pub. The name comes from the white stag that attacked King David, prompting his construction of Holyrood Abbey. White Hart is a student hangout during the school year, as evidenced by the many drink specials and stash of board games behind the bar, which you may enjoy, as well. It also schedules live music occasionally. Call for hours. Bus: 2, 12.

✔ **The World's End,** 2–6 High St., on the Royal Mile (☎ **0131-556-3628**). This bar's name is not a prophecy of doom but instead, signifies the spot on the Royal Mile where the old medieval city ended at the city wall. If you were a 16th-century Edinburgh resident, this would have been the edge of your world. And while you are free to have a pint anywhere in town these days, you will find this one of the nicest places to do it. The decor is tartan upholstery and carpet. If you're in town on Tuesday, check out the popular quiz night. Bus: 1, 6.

# *Going to the theater*

Interested in catching a little theater while you're in town? The large, classic venue is the **Playhouse Theatre,** 18–22 Greenside Place (☎ **0131-557-2590**). It books classical entertainment, such as opera and ballet, but also offers experimental theater, musicals, and the occasional rock concert. **The Royal Lyceum Theatre,** Grindlay Street (☎ **0131-229-9697**), is an old Victorian building enlivened by a range of top-notch performances, from new Scottish plays to Shakespeare. If you're solely interested in the vanguard, the **Traverse Theatre,** on Cambridge Street (☎ **0131-228-1404**), is two theaters in one. It shows only first-run plays by U.K. playwrights.

## Going to the cinema

You'll find lots of places to catch a flick, or, as the Scots say, go to "the cinema," in Edinburgh. Many of the movies shown, however, played months before in the States. (American films get a later European release.) The reverse is true, however, for local films: Scottish and other European films usually open here first, so you'll be seeing them ahead of your friends back home.

For mainstream movies, there's the **ABC Cinema,** 120 Lothian Rd. (☎ **0131-228-1638**). The **Filmhouse,** 88 Lothian Rd. (☎ **0131-228-2688**), is an art house showing independent and foreign films. The **Cameo Cinema,** 38 Home St., near Tollcross (☎ **0131-228-4141**), shows art and cult films.

# Fast Facts: Edinburgh

### Area Code
The area code for Edinburgh is **0131.** You need to dial the area code only if you are calling from outside the city.

### American Express
The office, 139 Princes St. (☎ 0131-225-7881), 5 blocks from Waverley Station, is open year-round Mon–Fri 9 a.m.–5:30 p.m., Sat 9 a.m.–4 p.m.

### ATMs
ATMs are available throughout the city.

### Currency Exchange
You can exchange money at travel agencies, hotels, and some post offices, but the best rates are at banks. If you have American Express traveler's checks, you can exchange them without paying any commission at the Amex office (see listing in this section). Both the **Royal Bank of Scotland** (☎ 0131-556-8555) and the **Bank of Scotland** (☎ 0131-442-7777) have branches in St. Andrew Square.

### Dentists
Both of the main hospitals in town have dental clinics: **Royal Infirmary of Edinburgh** (☎ 0131-536-4900) and **Western General Hospital** (☎ 0131-537-1338). A **dental hospital** (☎ 0131-543-4903) is at 31 Chambers St., off South Bridge.

### Embassies/Consulates
**United States Consulate General,** 3 Regent Terrace, Edinburgh, Scotland, EH7 5BW (☎ 0131-556-8315; Fax: 0131-557-6023; Internet: www.usembassy.org.uk). Hours: Mon–Fri 8:30 a.m. to noon for phone inquiries only; Mon–Fri 1–5 p.m. for phone inquiries and personal appointments.

**Australian Consulate,** Melrose House, 69 George St., Edinburgh EH2 2JG (☎ 0131-624-3333; Fax: 0131-624-3701; Internet: www.australia.org.uk). Hours: Mon–Fri 9:30 a.m. to noon and 2–5 p.m.

**Canadian High Commission,** MacDonald House, 38 Grosvenor Sq., London, England W1X 0AA (☎ 020-7258-6600). Hours: Mon–Fri 8–11 a.m.

## Emergencies

Dial **999** for police, fire, or ambulance.

## Eyeglasses

**Boots Opticians,** 101-1-3 Princes St. (☎ 0131-225-6397). Hours: Mon–Sat 9 a.m.–6 p.m.

## Genealogy Resources

**The Lothians Family History Society,** Lasswade High School Centre, Eskdale Drive, Bonnyrigg, Midlothian EH19 2LA.

## Hospitals

South of town is the **Royal Infirmary of Edinburgh,** 1 Lauriston Place, south of Grassmarket (☎ 0131-536-4000). North of the town center is the **Western General Hospital,** Crewe Street South, (☎ 0131-537-1330).

## Information

**Tourist Office,** 3 Princes St., above the Princes Mall and next to Waverley Station (☎ 0131-557-1700). Open: July–Aug Mon–Sat 9 a.m.–8 p.m., Sun 11 a.m.–8 p.m.; May–June and Sept Mon–Sat 9 a.m.–7 p.m., Sun 11 a.m.–7 p.m.; Apr and Oct Mon–Sat 9 a.m.–6 p.m., Sun 11 a.m.–6 p.m. Another office is in the airport's main terminal (☎ 0131-333-2167). An unofficial Old Town Information Centre is in Tron Kirk, High Street (☎ 0131-225-1637). The area tourism Web site is www.edinburgh.org.

## Internet Access

**Electric Frog,** 42–44 Cockburn St., between the Royal Mile and Princes Street, in the center of Old Town (☎ 0131-226-1505; Internet: www.electricfrog.co.uk). Hours: Mon–Sat 10 a.m.–10 p.m. Cost: £2.50 ($3.65) for 30 minutes.

**International Telecom Centre,** 52 High St., on the Royal Mile (☎ 0131-558-7114; Internet: www.btinternet.com/~itcl). Hours: Daily 9 a.m.–10 p.m. Cost: £4 ($5.80) per hour.

**Web 13,** 13 Bread St., near Lothian Road (☎ 0131-229-8883; E-mail: queries@web13.co.uk; Internet: www.web13.co.uk). Open: Mon–Fri 9 a.m.–10 p.m., Sat 9 a.m.–6 p.m., Sun noon to 6 p.m. Cost: £5 ($7.25) per hour.

## Mail

The main post office is inside the St. James Shopping Centre off Leith Street (☎ 0345-223-344). Open: Mon 9 a.m.–5:30 p.m., Tues–Fri 8:30 a.m.–5:30 p.m., Sat 8:30 a.m.–6 p.m. You can receive mail at the American Express office (see "American Express," earlier in this section). The service is free to cardholders; all others pay a small fee. You can collect letters at the regular post office by having the sender address them to "Poste Restante," c/o you.

## Maps

Tourist offices (see "Information," earlier in this section) distribute free basic maps and sell more detailed maps.

## Newspapers/Magazines

Newsstands and convenience stores sell local papers, such as *The Scotsman,* and international magazines; some also carry the *International Herald Tribune, USA Today,* and *The Wall Street Journal.*

## Pharmacies

**Boots,** 48 Shandwick Place, west end of Princes Street (☎ 0131-225-6757). Open: Mon–Sat 8 a.m.–9 p.m., Sun 10 a.m.–5 p.m.

## Photo

**1 Stop Photo,** 205 High St., on the Royal Mile (☎ 0131-225-1661; E-mail: info@1stopphoto.co.uk). Open: Mon–Fri 8:30 a.m.–6 p.m., Sat 9 a.m.–6 p.m., plus Sun 11 a.m.–6 p.m. Apr–Oct.

## Police

Dial **999** in case of emergencies. The police headquarters (☎ 0131-311-3131) is on Fettes Avenue north of town.

### Restrooms

Public toilets, safe and relatively clean, are available throughout the city.

### Safety

Edinburgh is a generally safe city. As in any large city, watch your purse and keep an eye on your wallet. The transit system, while not that helpful to a tourist, is very safe; little old ladies ride it.

### Smoking

You can smoke just about anywhere except in museums. Some restaurants have non-smoking sections, but don't count on it. At most hotels, you can ask for a nonsmoking room.

### Taxis

Taxis are numerous and available throughout the city. You don't have to queue up; just hail one. **City Cabs:** ☎ 0131-228-1211. **Central Radio Taxis:** ☎ 0131-229-2468.

# Chapter 11

# Glasgow

● ● ● ● ● ● ● ● ● ● ● ● ● ● ● ● ● ● ● ● ● ● ● ● ● ● ● ● ● ● ● ● ● ● ● ● ● ● ● ● ● ● ● ● ● ● ● ●

## In This Chapter

▶ Getting into Glasgow and getting around after you're there

▶ Discovering the best places to stay and eat

▶ Exploring the city's sights and attractions

▶ Planning the top stops for your own shopping crawl

▶ Finding the best pubs and clubs for pints, music, dancing, and grub

● ● ● ● ● ● ● ● ● ● ● ● ● ● ● ● ● ● ● ● ● ● ● ● ● ● ● ● ● ● ● ● ● ● ● ● ● ● ● ● ● ● ● ● ● ● ● ●

**G**lasgow is a city in transition. Although it's the largest city in the country, it has long been overshadowed by the more tourist-savvy capital city of Edinburgh, only an hour away. Sure, Edinburgh boasts the big attractions and picture-postcard backdrops, but Glaswegians argue that there's simply no comparison — that Edinburgh is English-centric and touristy, while their town is full of *real* Scots. They're proud of their working-class roots, which they say give Glasgow the soul and character its counterpart lacks.

Glasgow's architecture, restaurants, nightlife, theater, and accommodations certainly rival Edinburgh's. You'll find plenty of great attractions and things to do and see in this excellent city. And as Glasgow gets further and further from its blue-collar roots, the city grows increasingly cosmopolitan. It's really not a question of either/or — make time to see *both* cities.

## Getting to Glasgow

Glasgow is centrally located in terms of transportation options. Most flights into Glasgow Airport from North America connect in London, but some major airlines do offer direct service from the U.S. and Canada. Continental operates year-round nonstop flights to Glasgow via Newark from 96 airports across North America, American operates a daily Chicago-to-Glasgow flight from May to October, and Northwest Airlines operates a Boston-to-Glasgow flight in the summer.

# How to get from the airport to the city center

If you're driving, the airport is just off junction 28 of the M8 motorway. The M8 will take you straight into town. To get to the Buchanan Street Bus Station from Glasgow Airport, take Citylink (☎ **8705-505-050**) bus no. 900 or 901. Buses leave every 10 minutes between 8 a.m. and 5 p.m. Monday to Saturday and less frequently during off-peak times. The trip into town takes about 20 minutes and costs £2.80 ($4.10). A taxi ride into town costs £15 to £17 ($22–$25).

If you're traveling from London, you can easily take the train to the downtown station or fly to Glasgow Airport. If you're coming from elsewhere in Scotland, highway, train, and bus routes serve the city in all directions. The bus station is a couple of blocks from George Square, and the two main train stations are both in the heart of the city. There is no best way to come into Glasgow — it all depends on the time you have and the flexibility you desire — but there's no bad way to get to Glasgow, either.

✔ **By plane: Glasgow Airport** (☎ **0141-887-1111**) is 9 miles from the town center. Most major airlines flying from North America into Glasgow require a transfer in London (or, less frequently, Manchester or Birmingham), using their own planes or connecting carriers. British Midland and British Airways have regular flights from London.

✔ **By car:** Glasgow lies 40 miles west of Edinburgh. From the west, take the M8; from the south, use M74, a continuation of M8 that goes right into the city. Take the A77 from the northeast and the A82 from the northwest. The A80 also goes into the city.

✔ **By train:** Glasgow's **Central Station** and **Queen Street Station** are both in the city center. As a rule, trains from the southern region of Scotland and Britain arrive at Central Station; Queen Street Station gets service from the north. Trains from London, Glasgow, and elsewhere in Scotland run on **ScotRail** (☎ **0845-748-4950;** 0845-755-0033 for credit card bookings; www.scotrail.co.uk).

✔ **By bus:** The **Buchanan Street Bus Station** (☎ **0141-332-7133**), on Killermont Street (two blocks above the Queen Street train station), serves coaches arriving from England and Wales through Britain's extensive network, **National Express** (☎ **0990-808-080**), as well as buses serving the whole of Scotland run by **Scottish Citylink** (☎ **0990-505-050;** www.citylink.co.uk).

# Getting Around Glasgow after You're There

In Glasgow, park the car and explore on foot. Buses crisscross the city, but for the most part, you can easily walk from one area of town to the next. The exception is the West End, which is accessible by the Underground train. Between a comfortable pair of shoes and the Underground, you can get just about anywhere in a jiffy. Taxis are abundant in case you'd like to get from point A to point B lickety-split.

- ✔ **On foot:** Glasgow is very pedestrian friendly. Some streets have entire blocks closed to traffic (Sauchiehall, Buchanan, and Argyle streets), and the city is not too large to walk from one end to the other.

- ✔ **By Underground:** The **Underground** (☎ 0141-332-7133 or 226-4826; Internet: www.virtualglasgow.com/transport-u.htm), affectionately known to Glaswegians as the "clockwork orange" for its orange trains, is a subway system consisting of two circular lines — an inner and an outer circle. Trains run every 4 to 8 minutes depending on the time of day. They operate Monday through Saturday from 6:30 a.m. to 10:35 p.m., and Sunday from 11 a.m. to 6 p.m.

  The fare is £.65 (95¢) per ride anywhere on the system. It's a fast and efficient way to go from one end of town to the other and less confusing than the bus. Between the Underground and walking, you'll be able to get nearly everywhere in town.

- ✔ **By taxi:** You can hail cabs on the streets or outside most hotels. Try **Glasgow Wide Taxis** (☎ 0141-332-6666 or 332-7070), which takes credit cards; or **TOA Taxis** (☎ 0141-332-7070).

- ✔ **By car:** Between the Underground, the occasional taxi, and your own rubber soles, you don't really need a car in the city. If you're spending more than a day in Glasgow, save yourself the rental cost. Except for the occasional dead end and bad traffic, Glasgow isn't difficult to get around in a car — but parking is expensive and such a headache that driving yourself is not a convenient way to get around downtown.

- ✔ **By bus:** You may want to use city buses occasionally, but they can be confusing because several different companies run them. Besides, the town is so walkable that you probably won't need to use them at all. Buses run frequently through the day, less often after 11 p.m. For more information, call one of the city travel centers: **St. Enoch Square** (☎ 0141-226-4826) and **George Square** (☎ 0141-204-4400). The major bus station is the **Buchanan Street Bus Station,** Killermont Street. Fares are usually £1.20 ($1.75), and you need exact change.

# Knowing What's Where: Glasgow's Major Neighborhoods

In the first half of the century, Glasgow's prime location on the River Clyde made it one of the greatest shipbuilding centers in the world; the *QEII*, *Britannia*, and *Cutty Sark* were built here. But the decline of ship-building led to an economic depression in the 1960s (nearly everyone, including you, flies across the Atlantic now). Recent efforts to revitalize the city and attract new business and industry seem to be working beautifully. They've certainly impressed the college crowd: Glasgow has been voted "coolest city" in the U.K. in a poll in Great Britain. New restaurants and bars open all the time to meet the demand.

Glasgow has long been considered the least British city in Great Britain — a point emphasized by the unique Glaswegian dialect. And lest you think Glasgow is an industrial city devoid of nature, the city actu-ally has more green spaces per resident than any other city in Europe. It's no surprise that the name *Glasgow* means "sweet green place."

The city may seem relatively flat, but Glasgow was actually built on 37 hills (called *drumlins*). Unlike Edinburgh's Old Town, with its winding streets, Glasgow consists of a relatively user-friendly grid. In fact, it has 260 public squares and parks, many of them gifts to the city from local industrialists.

Glasgow has no major landmarks to help you orient yourself, but if you figure out a few major streets, you'll have little trouble getting from one area to the next. The pedestrian-friendly **Sauchiehall Street** (pro-nounced "Sucky-hall") goes straight from the major theater district of the city all the way out to the west end of town, with many restaurants and bars along the way. In the heart of the old city is **George Square,** just above the shopping district known as Merchant City. The **River Clyde** doesn't cut through the center of town but stretches from Glasgow Green out to the tall-ship docks. **High Street,** on the east end of town, runs from Glasgow Cathedral to Glasgow Green and the river. (It was once the site of a battle led by William "Braveheart" Wallace.) **Kelvin Way** bisects the collegiate West End neighborhood and serves as a point of reference in that part of town.

## Glasgow Center

Although pinpointing the exact center of the city is difficult, the area I'm referring to is easy to define by what it's *not*. Glasgow Center is basically the area north of the River Clyde, west of Medieval Glasgow and Merchant City, and east of the West End (all defined in the following sec-tions). The major thoroughfare running north-south is Buchanan Street and the east-west thoroughfare is Sauchiehall Street. (Both are largely

*Glasgow Orientation*

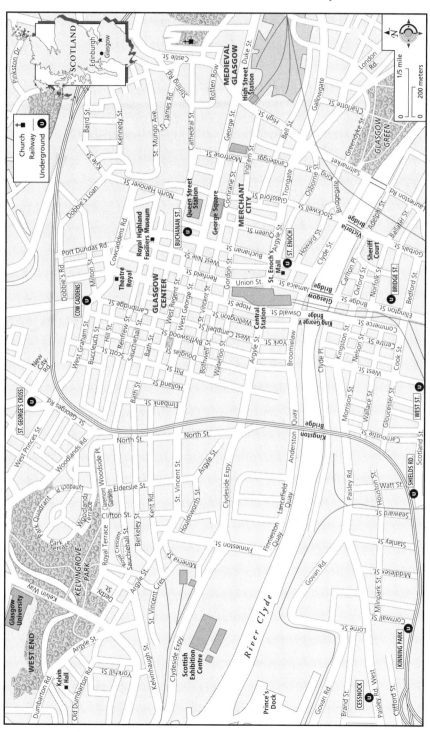

closed to traffic.) Within this region are the majority of the city's attractions (such as the Mackintosh-designed School of Art and the Tenement House), as well as many of the city's best hotels, bars, and restaurants. The area also includes the city's theater district and its main train stations and bus station.

## The West End

The hip side of town has as its main influence the University of Glasgow. With that comes great new restaurants and trendy bars. Getting out west takes extra effort, made worthwhile by the major galleries and museums located here.

- ✔ The Kelvingrove Museum is Scotland's answer to the Smithsonian.
- ✔ The Museum of Transportation is surprisingly fascinating and fun.
- ✔ The Huntarian Art Gallery is home to original Mackintosh works.
- ✔ The large Botanic Garden is the perfect place to bliss out after hoofing it through the area.

In this neighborhood, the Underground is a godsend. You are only minutes away from the West End on the speedy orange trains.

## Medieval Glasgow

The heart of the oldest section of the city is the Cathedral of St. Kentigern, a magnificent church enshrining St. Mungo, the patron saint of Glasgow. Next door to the cathedral is the excellent St. Mungo Museum of Religious Life and Art, and behind both of them is the fascinating macabre attraction, the Necropolis graveyard. If you travel south on historic High Street, you go past Merchant City and the old city Tolbooth and reach Glasgow Green and the River Clyde. Farther east, you find the bizarre bazaar section called the Barras and the excellent museum devoted to Glaswegian life, the People's Palace.

## Merchant City

This bustling section of town between George Square and the river is the city's major shopping district (as if you couldn't guess from its name). The major road going through Merchant City is Argyle Street, stretching from the Tolbooth and the old gallows of the city's once foreboding walls all the way past Central Station. In addition to all the shops and a couple of malls, this part of town has a few great dining, club, and theater finds. Technically, this nabe includes the magnificent City Chambers (city hall), as well as an abundance of excellent Georgian and Victorian architecture left over from the days when wealthy tobacco barons ran the economic center of Glasgow.

## Alongside the River Clyde

Unlike London's Thames or Dublin's Liffey, the River Clyde does not course through the heart of the city; it lies several blocks from the main attractions. But for many years, this region was the heart of industrial Glasgow. The western end still holds throwbacks, such as the tall ships and the paddleboat Waverley, and it's a nice walk to the eastern end of town and the Glasgow Green, the city's largest and most famous park. In between are a few good bars and restaurants, offering easy access to the river's edge. While Clyde isn't the prettiest part of town, it's certainly worth a visit.

# Figuring Out Where to Stay

Glasgow has a good range of accommodations in various parts of town. In this section, I try to give a fair range of the best accommodations, but if you want more options or have particular needs not met by my picks, the **Scottish Tourism Board office** (☎ **0141-204-4400**) on George Square can help you find lodgings based on price, location, and other factors for a small fee.

## The top hotels and B&Bs

### Glasgow Hilton International
$$$   **West End**

This elegant hotel has the distinction of being located in the country's tallest (24-story) building — a sleek modern façade that contrasts with much of Glasgow's architecture. The hotel offers top views of the city and the River Clyde. It's within walking distance of most of the town, in a good location between the city center and the West End. The professional staff and well-tailored rooms leave nothing to want, and because it's part of a major international chain, the hotel is used to meeting the needs of guests from all over the globe. In particular, the concierge offers excellent local recommendations. The hotel even has an all-Japanese floor, decorated with Japanese wallpaper, art, and sculpture. Take a look.

*1 William St., at Waterloo Street.* ☎ ***0141-204-5555***. *Toll-free in the U.S.: 800-445-8667. Fax: 0141-204-5004. Bus: 62. Rack rates: £170–£180 ($247–$261) double. AE, DC, MC, V.*

### Kelvin Park Lorne
$$   **West End**

This hotel in the trendy West End is a fun choice. It even offers in-house movies! It's in a great location: Nearly all the top attractions lie in this part of town. The rooms range from standard to first class, but all have

## *Glasgow Accommodations*

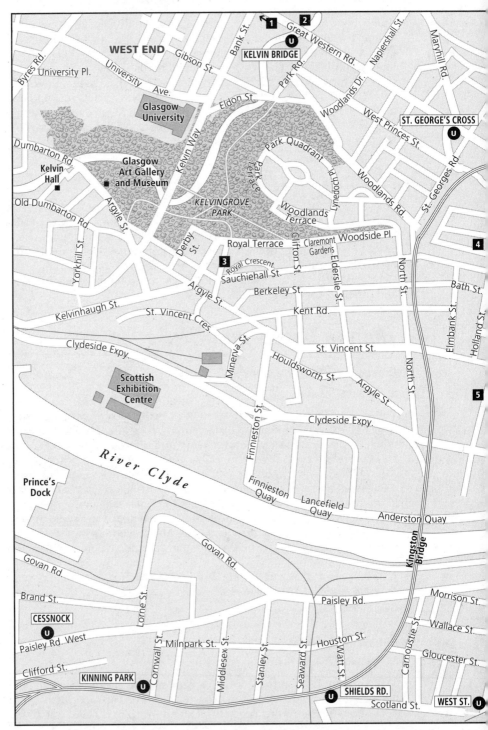

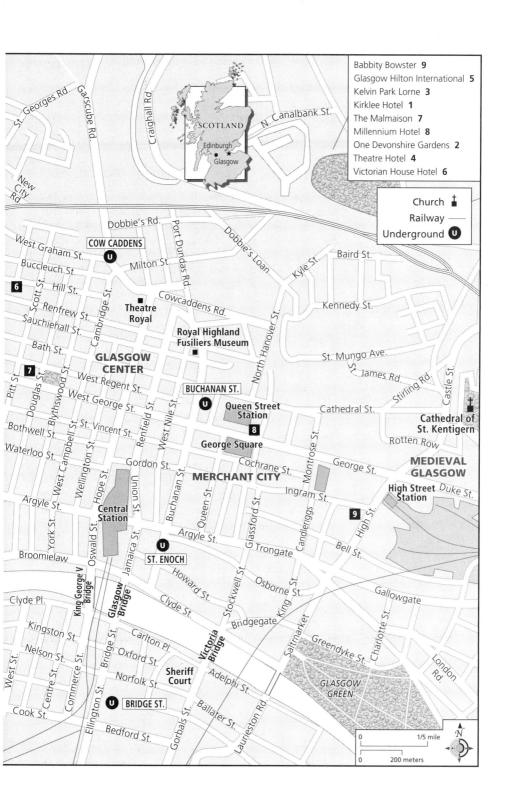

Babbity Bowster **9**
Glasgow Hilton International **5**
Kelvin Park Lorne **3**
Kirklee Hotel **1**
The Malmaison **7**
Millennium Hotel **8**
One Devonshire Gardens **2**
Theatre Hotel **4**
Victorian House Hotel **6**

Church ⛪
Railway ——
Underground Ⓤ

SCOTLAND
Edinburgh
★ Glasgow

St. Georges Rd.
Garscube Rd.
Craighall Rd.
N. Canalbank St.
New City Rd.
Dobbie's Rd.
**COW CADDENS** Ⓤ
Port Dundas Rd.
Dobbie's Loan
West Graham St.
Buccleuch St.
Milton St.
Baird St.
Kyle St.
Hill St.
Scott St.
Renfrew St.
Cowcaddens Rd.
Kennedy St.
**Theatre Royal**
Cambridge St.
Sauchiehall St.
Bath St.
**Royal Highland Fusiliers Museum**
North Hanover St.
St. Mungo Ave.
**GLASGOW CENTER**
West Regent St.
St. James Rd.
Stirling Rd.
Castle St.
Pitt St.
Douglas St.
Blythswood St.
West George St.
Renfield St.
West Nile St.
**BUCHANAN ST.** Ⓤ
**Queen Street Station**
Cathedral St.
**Cathedral of St. Kentigern**
St. Vincent St.
Bothwell St.
West Campbell St.
Wellington St.
Hope St.
**8**
**George Square**
Montrose St.
Rotten Row
**MEDIEVAL GLASGOW**
Waterloo St.
Gordon St.
Cochrane St.
George St.
**MERCHANT CITY**
Ingram St.
**High Street Station**
Duke St.
Argyle St.
**Central Station**
Union St.
Buchanan St.
Queen St.
Glassford St.
Candleriggs
**9**
High St.
York St.
Jamaica St.
**ST. ENOCH** Ⓤ
Argyle St.
Trongate
Bell St.
Broomielaw
Howard St.
Osborne St.
Gallowgate
**Glasgow Bridge**
King George V Bridge
Oswald St.
Clyde St.
Stockwell St.
King St.
Saltmarket
Charlotte St.
London Rd.
Clyde Pl.
Bridgegate
Greendyke St.
Kingston St.
Carlton Pl.
Bridge St.
Oxford St.
**Victoria Bridge**
**GLASGOW GREEN**
Nelson St.
West St.
Centre St.
Commerce St.
Norfolk St.
**Sheriff Court**
Adelphi St.
Cook St.
**BRIDGE ST.** Ⓤ
Gorbals St.
Ballater St.
Lauriston Rd.
Ellington St.
Bedford St.

0        1/5 mile
0    200 meters
N

the same facilities and are roomy and comfortable. Make sure to ask for a nonsmoking room if you're inclined; if you need your laundry washed or dry-cleaned, the staff will take care of that on the premises.

*923 Sauchiehall St., 1 block south of Kelvingrove Park.* ☎ *0141-314-9955. Fax: 0141-337-1659. Internet:* www.regalhotels.co.uk/kelvinparklorne. *Bus: 9, 16, 42. Rack rates: £65–£85 ($94–$123) double. AE, DC, MC, V.*

## The Malmaison
### $$$  Glasgow Center

Owned by the same capable chain as One Devonshire Gardens (see the review of that hotel later in this section), this stylish hotel is a converted church. The modest-size rooms, designed in Art Deco style, offer nice duvet blankets, cable television, and CD players. The beautiful staircase in the lobby exemplifies the hotel's excellence. The in-house brasserie serves excellent food, prepared with a heavy French accent, which makes sense: "Malmaison" is the name of Napoleon's home.

*278 West George St., at Pitt Street.* ☎ *0141-572-1000. Fax: 0141-572-1002. E-mail:* glasgow@malmaison.com. *Internet:* www.malmaison.com. *Bus: 11. Rack rates: £120–£155 ($174–$225) double. AE, DC, MC, V.*

## Millennium Hotel
### $$$$  Merchant City

The Millennium Hotel is the oldest building on George Square. Formerly 18th-century town houses, it has been around since the square was residential and was called the Copthorne Hotel until a £5.5-million refurbishment and a reopening with the new name in 2000. It's the only place where you can sleep right on the square. The huge, earth-tone rooms hold comfortable beds with quilted duvets. Nice extras in the spacious rooms include satellite and movie channels on the telly, personal safe, trouser press, and iron. The hotel also has a little cardiovascular (workout) room, baby-sitting service, laundry service, and 24-hour room service. The Millennium is a footnote in the history books: U.S. involvement in World War II began here when British Prime Minister Winston Churchill met with an envoy to U.S. President Franklin D. Roosevelt in Room 21 to secure America's participation.

*40 George Sq., off George St.* ☎ *0141-332-6711. Toll-free from the U.S.: 800-465-6486. Fax: 0141-332-4264. E-mail:* sales.glasgow@mill-cop.com. *Internet:* www.mill-cop.com *or book at* www.relax.with-us.com. *Underground: Buchanan Street. Rack rates: £175–£225 ($254–$326) double. AE, DC, MC, V.*

## One Devonshire Gardens
### $$$  West End

Located on a leafy street of Victorian terrace houses, the Gardens offers you an amazing stay that you won't soon forget. The staff and food are top-notch, and the location is excellent. This oasis of hospitality shines brightest in the lovely rooms. The management is not stingy with towels, it supplies bathrobes (always a nice touch), and sofas and chairs are soporifically plush. You also get satellite television, a minibar, CD player, and high-powered showers — and most rooms have thick king-size mattresses. Each unit is different; the best (and most expensive) is the Garden Suite, with private access to the terrace garden. Don't take my word for it; listen to composer Leonard Bernstein, who called it "pure theatre, truly inspirational." Elizabeth Taylor and Luciano Pavarotti also stayed here, and neither was heard to complain.

*1 Devonshire Gardens, off Great Western Road.* ☎ *0141-339-2001. Fax: 0141-337-1663. E-mail:* devonshire5@aol.com. *Internet:* www.one-devonshire-gardens.com. *Underground: Hillhead. Rack rates: £130–£158 ($189–$229) double. Breakfast not included. AE, DC, MC, V.*

## Runner-up accommodations

### Babbity Bowster
#### $–$$  Merchant City/Medieval Glasgow

This excellent place is not only one of my favorite bars; it also operates one of the best B&Bs in the city. The quintessentially Scottish accommodation offers hospitality and food made with care — and you don't have to travel far if you're thirsty. The rooms are rather basic, but you can't do much better on this end of town. The three-story lodging is on a pedestrian courtyard between Merchant City and Medieval Glasgow on the east side of Glasgow. The renovated 18th-century town house offers all the usual amenities. The only bad thing is that you can't go to bed early and expect the bar patrons to pipe down for you.

*16–18 Blackfriars St., just off High Street.* ☎ *0141-552-5055. Fax: 0141-552-7774. Underground: Buchanan Street. Rack rates: £45–£65 ($65–$94) double. AE, MC, V.*

### Kirklee Hotel
#### $$  West End

Blurring the line between hotel and B&B, this fine nine-bedroom hotel has the charm and intimacy of a bed-and-breakfast but the efficiency and amenities of a hotel. The redbrick house, built in 1904 for one of Glasgow's shipping families, sits on a lovely tree-lined street of Victorians in a residential area of the West End. The rooms are quiet, spacious, and tastefully decorated. You can't miss the house; it's the one with the amazing roses out front. The best thing about the Kirklee? Three words: breakfast in bed.

*11 Kensington Gate, off Great Western Road.* ☎ *0141-344-5555. Fax: 0141-339-3828. E-mail:* kirklee@clara.net. *Internet:* www.scotland2000.com/kirklee/. *Underground: Hillhead. Rack rates: £68 ($93) double. AE, DC, MC, V.*

### Theatre Hotel
**$$–$$$   Glasgow Center**

This turn-of-the-20th-century town house has been converted into a lovely hotel, and every room is nicely put together. The original paneling and stained glass have been restored, and the beds are as comfortable as they look. The front desk staff is very helpful — either providing what you need or pointing you in the right direction. Parents note: Family suites are well priced at £75 ($109). Between the satellite TV, breakfast in bed, and mattresses worthy of jumping up and down, the whole family will enjoy the stay.

*27 Elmbank St., just off Sauchiehall Street.* ☎ **0141-227-2772**. *Fax: 0141-227-2774. E-mail:* theatrehotel@clara.net. *Internet:* www.theatrehotel.clara. net. *Underground: Cowcaddens. Rack rates: £75–£119 ($109–$173) double. MC, V.*

### Victorian House Hotel
**$   Glasgow Center/West End**

When you walk in, you'll be pleased to see that the inviting bright-yellow reception area matches the friendly and accommodating staff. The rooms are not as nice, but they are comfortable and quiet. One of the best aspects of the Victorian is its ideal location near Charing Cross, putting it smack between the hustle and bustle of the city center and the hipness of the West End. It's basically in walking distance of everything and in view of the Mackintosh-designed Glasgow School of Art. For the price, you can't beat it.

*212 Renfrew St., at Scott Street.* ☎ **0141-332-0129**. *Fax: 0141-353-3155. Bus: 57. Rack rates: £38–£52 ($55–$75) double. AE, DC, MC, V.*

## Dining in Glasgow

Glasgow has no shortage of excellent places to dine. Whether you want high-class European cuisine, traditional Scottish, or something exotic, you won't be disappointed. I've scoured the city looking for the best eats, and I offer them in this section. By no means is this list complete. New places open all the time. If you're looking for something not covered here, be sure to ask your hotel concierge or B&B host.

**Lunch menus** in Glasgow often offer the same delicious food as the dinner menus, but at a better price. So have a big late lunch and snack on fast food when you get hungry in the evening.

If you're dining with children, the best chain restaurant is **Littlejohn's.** This chain of family-style restaurants features pasta, burgers, and some Scottish cuisine at family-friendly prices. The service is good, and the breakfasts are yummy. The Glasgow location is 17 Vinicombe St. (☎ **0141-339-2333**).

# The top restaurants

### Air Organic

**$$$**   **Glasgow Center/West End**   **Upscale Organic**

Voted one of the best in Europe, this restaurant is a welcome respite from traditional Scottish fare. The main dining room is in '60s Space Race design, looking like the shuttle lounge from the film *2001: A Space Odyssey,* with some wheatgrass and world music thrown in. Before your meal, the pleasant wait staff brings you hot-from-the-oven rolls and a carafe of water flavored with herbs and cucumbers. The dishes are full of strong flavors and fresh organic ingredients, from peppered bluefin tuna salad to imaginative watermelon Thai curry to spinach and mushroom risotto. The cook's emphasis is on bringing out the natural flavors of food instead of drowning them in sauces. The restaurant offers a good wine selection and, if it's not raining, outdoor seating complete with space heaters.

*36 Kelvingrove St., at the corner of Sauchiehall Street. ☎ 0141-564-5200. Bus: 9, 16, 42. Reservations recommended for dinner. Main courses: £12–£18 ($18–$26). AE, MC, V. Open: Mon–Thurs noon to 3 p.m. and 5–11 p.m., Fri and Sat noon to midnight.*

### Esca

**$$–$$$**   **Merchant City/River Clyde**   **International**

This funky little restaurant has the unusual theme of "night and day." The wall of the dining area features a large sun and moon, and the comfortable, artsy furniture (and the silk flowers on the tables) are red and blue. Sounds funky, but the end result is clean and neat. The food defies any regional category. You can get pizza and pasta, but also a fat juicy steak and excellent vegetarian options such as the heavenly feta-and-spinach soufflé. Meal presentation is fancy, but there's nothing pretentious about the place. Esca also makes a mean margarita and a thirst-quenching sangria. The soundtrack is classic '50s and '60s — Sinatra, Tom Jones, and the like.

*27 Chisolm St., off Tron Street. ☎ 0141-553-0880. Underground: St. Enoch. Reservations accepted. Main courses: £5.50–£13.50 ($8–$20). AE, DC, MC, V. Open: Mon–Fri noon to 10 p.m., Sat noon to 5 p.m.*

### Grassroots Cafe

**$**   **West End/Charing Cross**   **Vegetarian**

This small dining area is the yummy restaurant half of Grassroots Wholefoods Market, the best in the city. Cheerful, hip college students serve meals made with the care and attention that you'd expect from a restaurant that chooses organic produce and caters to all manner of vegetarians and those with food allergies. The humus is a must, the sandwiches arrive on thick hearty bread, the salads are divine, and soups are savory. If your B&B breakfast leaves you wanting more, the veggie fry is a

## Glasgow Dining

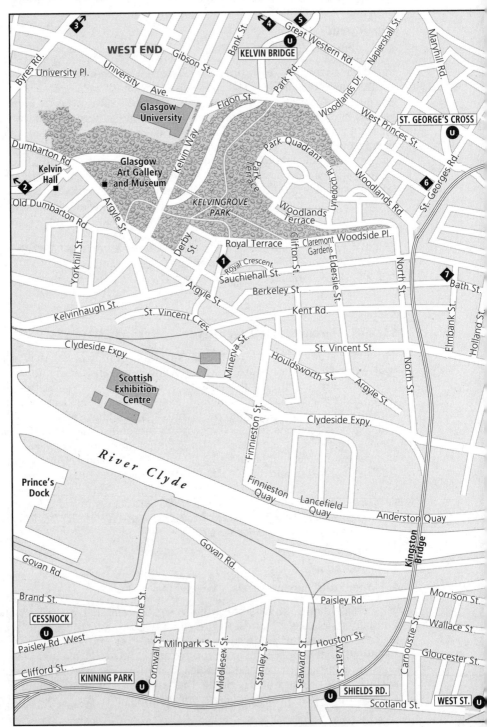

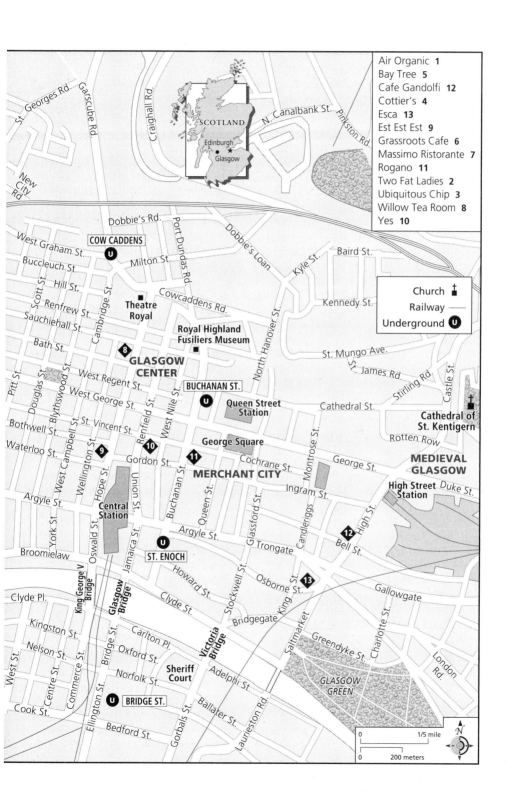

Air Organic **1**
Bay Tree **5**
Cafe Gandolfi **12**
Cottier's **4**
Esca **13**
Est Est Est **9**
Grassroots Cafe **6**
Massimo Ristorante **7**
Rogano **11**
Two Fat Ladies **2**
Ubiquitous Chip **3**
Willow Tea Room **8**
Yes **10**

Church
Railway
Underground

popular choice for brunch. An informal spot, the cafe is full of art and always plays a cool alternative soundtrack.

*97 St. George's Rd.* ☎ *0141-333-0534. Internet:* www.grassroots.shop. *Underground: St. George's Cross. Reservations not accepted. Main courses: £3.95–£5.95 ($5.75–$8.65). AE, DC, MC, V. Open: Daily 10 a.m.–10 p.m.*

### Rogano
**$$$   Merchant City   Seafood**

One of the oldest and glitziest restaurants in the city, Rogano has long been Glasgow's fine-dining choice for celebrities as dissimilar as Mick Jagger, Joan Collins, and Winston Churchill. The Versace-clad staff serves such delicacies as sautéed foie gras, steamed sea bream, and seared scallops. The Art Deco–style restaurant, built to look like the interior of the *Queen Mary,* provides a separate vegetarian menu, but most come for the house specialties. They include fish soup, monkfish tails, and smoked salmon with scrambled eggs. Although you won't get to sit there, have your waiter point out the celebrated "power table," no. 16 — the best seat in the house and the most sought-after table in Scotland. The less formal Café Rogano, downstairs, serves a similar seafood menu.

*11 Exchange Place.* ☎ *0141-248-4055. Underground: Buchanan Street. Reservations recommended for dinner. Main courses: £7.50–£11.50 ($11–$17). AE, DC, MC, V. Open: Mon–Sat noon to 2:30 p.m. and 6:30–10:30 p.m.*

### Two Fat Ladies
**$$$–$$$$   West End   Seafood**

This small, high-class restaurant walks a fine line between traditional and daring. The menu changes weekly, but you're likely to find inventive staples such as Cullen Skink (a traditional fish stew), steamed mussels, grilled mackerel with wasabi, and teriyaki salmon. Desserts are out-of-this-world good. The dining room is also a treat. High ceilings and Rubenesque art make you feel as if you're a guest in a lavish dining room from a more mannered era. The name of the restaurant comes from the address, not the owners. Apparently "88" in bingo-speak is called "two fat ladies." This well-established, highly recommended seafood restaurant has only seven tables — so booking ahead is advised.

*88 Dumbarton Rd.* ☎ *0141-339-1944. Bus: 16, 42, 5. Reservations recommended for dinner. Main courses: £8.95–£23.50 ($13–$34). AE, DC, MC, V. Open: Fri–Sat noon to 2 p.m.; Tues–Sat 6–10 p.m.*

### Ubiquitous Chip
**$$$   West End   Nouvelle Scottish**

You could describe the popularity of this excellent restaurant as cultish. The many regulars swear that this is the best place to eat in the city.

Word is out, but fortunately, popularity hasn't ruined the place. Trees and plants fill the airy atrium dining room, where the brick floor and wood tables give the place a rustic feel. The cuisine includes succulent choices such as venison haggis, blood-red breast of pigeon, and cod with chili oil. The wine list is encyclopedic — one of the best in the city. Make sure to reserve ahead; this place is booked on weekdays.

*12 Ashton Lane, off Byres Road, behind the Underground station. ☎ 0141-334-5007. Underground: Hillhead. Reservations recommended for dinner. Main courses£7.65–£15.45 ($11–$22). AE, DC, MC. Open: Daily noon to 2:30 p.m. and 5:30–11 p.m.*

### Yes
**$$–$$$   Merchant City   Modern Scottish**

Yes quickly earned a reputation as one of the finest places to eat in the city after it opened several years ago. You can sit upstairs amid sleek, modern table settings and Deco chairs, or scoot into a large booth downstairs. In either place you'll find excellent modern Scottish cuisine and live music. If you're feeling adventurous, you can order the four-course "Surprise Menu." Otherwise, go for safe bets such as rack of lamb with mushroom risotto or seared chicken breast. Yes doesn't kid around with the express lunch — your order will be ready in just 15 minutes. For dinner, make sure to book a reservation in advance.

*22 West Nile St. ☎ 0141-221-8044. Bus: 66. Reservations accepted. Set prices: £15.95 ($23) for 2 courses; £18.95 ($28) for 3 courses; £22.50 ($33) for 4 courses. AE, DC, MC, V. Open: Daily noon to 2:30 p.m. and 7–10:30 p.m.*

# Runner-up restaurants

### Bay Tree
**$$–$$$   West End   Middle Eastern/Vegetarian**

This funky restaurant is a Glasgow legend for its gourmet vegetarian and vegan cuisine. The heavily Middle Eastern menu also offers stand-bys, such as veggie burgers. The white walls and simple furnishings give the place a cool, calm feel, and the happy-go-lucky staff enhances the ambience. Don't be surprised to see members of the student crowd just hanging out with a book and a cup o' joe — the place is well known among locals but has yet to be spoiled by the tourist crowds. There's no meat on the menu, but the food is so good that even if you're am enthusiastic meat eater, you probably won't notice.

*403 Great Western Rd. ☎ 0141-334-5898. Underground: Kelvinbridge. Reservations not required. Main courses: £6–£18.95 ($8.70–$28). AE, DC, MC, V. Open: Mon–Sat 8:30 a.m.–9 p.m.; Sun 10 a.m.–8 p.m.*

# A drink with jam and bread

The Willow Tea Room is a must stop on the tourist trail. Not only did Glasgow's world-renowned architect, Charles Rennie Mackintosh, design the upstairs tearoom, but he also created the original waitress uniforms. Oh, yes, the Willow Room makes a great cup of tea, and the dessert menu is worth a nibble. The tearoom gets its name from Sauchiehall (the street), which means "meadow of the willow tree." Below the tearoom is a Mackintosh gift shop.

*217 Sauchiehall St., Glasgow Center. ☎ 0141-332-0521. Underground: Cowcaddens. Bus: 57. Reservations not accepted. Main courses: £2.50–£5.50 ($3.65–$8). Open: Daily 9:30 a.m.–4 p.m.*

## Cafe Gandolfi
$$  **Merchant City   Scottish/French**

When a great coffee shop serves excellent food, the result is instant success. Although Cafe Gandolfi is one of the places to be seen in the city, it has retained its cozy coffee-shop feel. Note the stained-glass windows, unique carved wooden furniture (commissioned by local artist Tim Stead), and black-and-white photos of other cafes. Perfect cappuccinos accompany excellent wine and filling meals such as linguine with red pepper, roasted pine nuts, and Gorgonzola, or honey-marinated chicken with saffron couscous. Not interested in being typecast, the cafe serves standard items, such as a thick New York pastrami sandwich, as well as inventive creations, such as grilled goat cheese salad. It also has light meal selections. Another draw is the delicious, dark, bitter Traquair House Ale — it goes well with any meal. Be sure to book ahead.

*64 Albion St. ☎ 0141-552-6813. Underground: St. Enoch. Reservations recommended for dinner. Main courses: £4.50–£10.50 ($6.55–$15). AE, MC, V. Open: Mon–Sat 9 a.m.–11:30 p.m.; Sun noon to 11:30 p.m.*

## Cottier's
$$–$$$  **West End   American Southwestern**

Located in a converted church, this great place is a restaurant, bar, cafe, and beer-garden complex serving mostly authentic Southwest cuisine. The eclectic menu of spicy dishes is American Southwestern, with some Mediterranean and Chinese influences. It includes tasty enchiladas, fajitas, stuffed salmon, and char-grilled *poussin*. The space retains a rustic and somewhat spiritual ambience, even with the addition of lights, art, and bars. There's live music most nights and a few outdoor tables when the weather is nice. On Sundays, the wicked good brunch includes items such as eggs Benedict and Cajun kedgeree served up with the morning papers.

*93/95 Hyndland St., near Highburgh Road. ☎ 0141-357-5827. Underground: Hillhead. Reservations not required. Main courses: £8.50–£12.95 ($12–$19). AE, DC, MC, V. Open: Daily noon to 10 p.m.*

### Est Est Est

$$–$$$   **Glasgow Center   Italian**

This is as high-class and formal as Italian gets. And it's not all presentation; the food is tops as well. The sleek, well-priced menu offers traditional pasta, antipasto, and pizza dishes using old recipes and the finest ingredients. One exceptional side dish is pesto mashed potatoes. The two huge dining rooms with wall-to-wall windows overlooking Bothwell Street don't make for private, intimate eating — on the other hand, it's a good place to people-watch. This small chain (there is another location in Edinburgh; see Chapter 10) gets its name from a 12th-century bishop who sent a scout into towns where he wrote *"est"* ("it is") on the door of any inn that had exceptional wine. One place with particularly great wine garnered an enthusiastic, *"Est, Est, Est."*

*21–25 Bothwell St. ☎ 0141-248-6262. Internet:* www.estestest.co.uk. *Underground: Central Station. Reservations accepted. Main courses: £5.95–£12.95 ($8.65–$19). AE, DC, V. Open: Mon–Fri noon to 2:30 p.m.; Mon–Thurs 5–10 p.m., Fri 6–11 p.m.; Sat noon to 11 p.m.; Sun noon to 10:30 p.m.*

### Massimo Ristorante

$$–$$$   **Glasgow Center   Italian**

*Primo!* Hit this Italian bistro for large, well-priced versions of the real thing; even the menus are written in Italian. Don't skip the wine: The owner, Massimo, picks a new house red of the month, and it's always a carefully chosen winner. A below-street-level dining area has been transformed into a faux-stone grottolike room, decorated with small tokens from the old country. To start, try one of the delicious crostini, toasted Italian bread with your choice of toppings. The large selection of main courses covers all tastes; some standouts include fusilli primavera (spiral pasta with roasted peppers, courgettes, and black olives) and scaloppini funghi (veal in creamy mushroom sauce). The restaurant also serves a good variety of pizza.

*57 Elmbank St. ☎ 0141-332-3227. Bus: 62, 64. Reservations recommended for dinner. Main courses: £6.95–£12.95 ($10–$19). AE, DC, MC, V. Open: Daily 11 a.m.–9 p.m.*

# Exploring Glasgow

It may not have the big attractions of Edinburgh, but Glasgow offers enough interesting activities to do to justify at least two days in the big city. Excellent museums, art galleries, and unique items rival that of the "other" city. The best part? Most of the attractions are free!

While some cities have a clear "A" and "B" list, Glasgow has a solid line-up of good picks. Figure out exactly what you want to see so that you can plan a good route that covers all the bases. I've put the attractions in order of general interest, but you should browse the list for something you may have a special desire to see.

# Taking in Glasgow's top attractions

### St. Mungo Museum of Religious Life and Art
**Medieval Glasgow**

The eclectic and, at times, controversial little museum near Glasgow Cathedral is an introductory lesson in comparative religion. Idols and items of ritual represent all the major traditions, making this museum the only one of its kind in the world. Buddha, Ganesha, Shiva, and the rest are here, as well as a Chinese robe worn in the Bernardo Bertolucci film *The Last Emperor.* The jewel of the museum is Salvador Dali's famous (or infamous) painting *Christ of St. John of the Cross.* Behind the £6-million museum in the shadow of the Necropolis is Britain's only Japanese Zen garden.

*2 Castle St.* ☎ *0141-553-2557. Bus: 2. Admission: Free. Open: Mon–Thurs, Sat 10 a.m.–5 p.m.; Fri and Sun 11 a.m.–5 p.m. Time: 90 min.*

### Huntarian Art Gallery
**West End**

The main gallery, housing paintings, coins, pottery, and prints, is not very large or diverse, but it has some rare pieces and attracts some good items on loan from other museums. The best-known artist featured is James McNeill Whistler. The museum has the largest collection of his work in Europe, even his old paints and brushes (although his most famous work, *Whistler's Mother,* is not here). Charles Rennie Mackintosh is the other celeb at the Huntarian. Displays include drawings as well as reconstructions of the interiors of his own home. The newest wing devoted to the local architect and designer, Mackintosh House, is very impressive. Outside, next to the University Library, is a small sculpture garden.

*82 Hillhead St., University of Glasgow.* ☎ *0141-330-5431. Internet:* www.gla.ac.uk/Museum/. *Underground: Hillhead. Admission: Free. Open: Mon–Sat 9:30 a.m.–5 p.m.; Mackintosh House closed 12:30–1:30 p.m. Time: 2 hours.*

### The Huntarian Museum
**West End**

The focus of the first public museum in Glasgow is the history of the planet through Scottish eyes. There are Scottish dinosaur fossils, a Glasgow meteorite, and area rocks and minerals. More recent displays include altars and pieces from the Roman occupation of Scotland in the second century, an exhibit on the exploits of Captain Cook, and a world-famous Coin Gallery. The University of Glasgow owns the museum, which bears the name of its benefactor, William Hunter, a former student.

*University of Glasgow, Gilbert Scott Building.* ☎ *0141-330-4221. E-mail:* recep tion@museum.gla.ac.uk. *Internet:* www.gla.ac.uk/Museum/HuntMus/. *Underground: Hillhead. Admission: Free. Open: Mon–Sat 9:30 a.m.–5 p.m. Time: 90 min.*

## Museum of Transport and Technology
**West End**

The name makes it sound boring, but this large museum is an informative treat for people of all ages. It's a life-size monument to the city's proud transportation and technological history, with an excellent collection of cars, motorcycles, trams, buses, boats, and trains. Glasgow was one of the great shipbuilding ports in the world — the *Queen Mary* and the *QEI* and *II* were built here. In addition to the huge warehouse of vehicles, the museum has a reproduction of a 1938 city street with period shops and cars.

*1 Bunhouse Rd., Kelvin Hall.* ☎ *0141-287-2720. Internet: www.gla.ac.uk. Underground: Kelvin Hall. Admission: Free. Open: Mon–Thurs, Sat 10 a.m.–5 p.m.; Fri and Sun 11 a.m.–5 p.m. Time: 2 hours, 30 min.*

## People's Palace and Winter Gardens
**Medieval Glasgow**

A museum devoted to life in Glasgow since the 1750s may not sound that intriguing, but the social, political, and historical exhibits are very entertaining. Sections give candid and humorous looks at topics such as "The Bevvy" (drinking), public hangings, and "The Patter" (the "what-did-he-say?" Scots way of talking). While adults are having a good smile and learning a thing or two, the kids will be fully engaged with the many hands-on exhibits that encourage playing and re-creating life in Depression-era Glasgow. With old films, interactive computers, and more, the museum has plenty of bells and whistles (and World War II air-raid sirens) to keep everyone entertained. The winter gardens, a collection of tropical fauna, are worth a walk-through; they occupy a large greenhouse room believed to be designed after the upturned hull of Horatio Nelson's ship, *Victory.* The People's Palace building dates to 1898, when it was designed to be the cultural center of the city and built on the East End at a time when that area was the most overcrowded and unsanitary part of the city. A £1.2-million refurbishment of the French Renaissance-style structure restored it to its former magnificence.

*Glasgow Green.* ☎ *0141-554-0223. Bus: 14, 18, 20, 62. Admission: Free. Open: Mon–Sat 10 a.m.–5 p.m., Sun 11 a.m.–5 p.m. Time: 2 hours.*

### Glasgow Cathedral
**Medieval Glasgow**

This multilevel cathedral is the most important religious site in the city. The construction of the country's first stone cathedral began in 1136 in the presence of King David of Scotland on the spot where St. Mungo built his chapel in A.D. 500. The only pre-Reformation Gothic structure still standing in Scotland may be light on artifacts, but it has an impressive array of architecture: fine vaulted crypts, large nave windows, trefoils, and chapels, as well as a modern (1940s) collection of stained glass. Underneath the main church is the cathedral's most important shrine, the burial site of St. Mungo, the patron saint of Glasgow. The cathedral's well is believed to be the one that Mungo used to perform baptisms.

*2 Castle St., at the eastern end of Cathedral Street.* ☎ *0141-552-8198. Bus: 2. Admission: Free. Open: Apr–Sept Mon–Sat 9:30 a.m.–6 p.m., Sun 1–5 p.m.; Oct–Mar Mon–Sat 9:30 a.m.–4 p.m., Sun 1–4 p.m. Time: 2 hours.*

### Necropolis
**Medieval Glasgow**

One of the best views in the city is across the Bridge of Sighs in the Necropolis, the graveyard of the Merchants' House of Glasgow and Glasgow's first planned cemetery, which opened in 1832. If you're a fan of cemeteries, you may be interested to know that this one was modeled after Père Lachaise in Paris. As you explore the grounds, keep your eye out for some interesting monuments, like that of Alexander McCall, a rare Celtic cross designed by Charles Rennie Mackintosh. Actor and manager John Henry Alexander's tomb shows a final curtain falling and contains the Shakespearean quotation, "All the world's a stage and all the men and women merely players." The highest and oldest monument in the Necropolis belongs to John Knox, the leader of the Scottish Reformation.

*Castle Street; drive up John Knox Street from Castle Street or walk the Bridge of Sighs from behind the cathedral.* ☎ *0141-287-3961. Bus: 2. Admission: Free. Open: Daily dawn to dusk. Time: 1 hour.*

### Glasgow Green
**Medieval Glasgow**

The Green is the oldest public park in Great Britain, granted to the public in 1450, and the sight of many a political demonstration. Golf was played at one point, Bonnie Prince Charlie reviewed his Jacobite troops here, and until 1865 public executions took place here. For the last hanging, 80,000 men, women, and children attended. It's a quiet place now, home to joggers and host to the odd concert or public sport. The park has two major monuments: a hard-to-miss gray obelisk in memory of Horatio Nelson, and a smaller one nearby, commemorating James Watt, the inventor of the steam engine. Watt reputedly came up with the idea during a Sunday morning stroll in the Green.

*Greendyke Street. ☎ 0141-553-1092. Bus: 14, 18, 20, 62. Admission: Free. Open: Daily dawn to dusk. Time: 1 hour.*

## Museum of Modern Art
**Merchant City**

As modern art galleries rate, this one is top-notch. A lot of items come and go, but you can always find a great deal of innovative — at times controversial — eye candy on the premises. From the mirror room in the lobby to the top-floor air gallery, the variety and innovation of the pieces is impressive. They usually include something of Eduard Bersudsky's kinetic collection. The building, which doesn't look the slightest bit modern, was once the Royal Exchange and was originally built as a home for William Cunninghame, one of the wealthy local tobacco merchants. A statue of Wellington on horseback stands guard out front (and usually has a parking cone cheekily stuck on its head).

*Queen Street. ☎ 0141-229-1996. Underground: St. Enoch. Admission: Free. Open: Mon–Sat 10 a.m.–5 p.m., Sun 11 a.m.–5 p.m. Time: 90 min.*

## Glasgow School of Art
**Glasgow Center**

This is one of the best art schools in the world, and the Art Nouveau design of the main building is an attraction in itself. The famed local architect Charles Rennie Mackintosh won the competition to design the building at the age of 28. You can tour the building (the only way to see the interior) and marvel at his unique style — from the furniture and halls to the magnificent library. You don't have to be a fan of architecture to enjoy the guided tour and appreciate the genius of Mackintosh. The architect's influence is apparent everywhere in Glasgow, including the Willow Tea Room on Sauchiehall Street, which he designed (see the "A drink with jam and bread" sidebar, earlier in this chapter).

*167 Renfrew St. (between Douglas and Pitt streets). ☎ 0141-353-4526. Internet: www.gsa.ac.uk. Underground: Cowcaddens. Guided tour: £5 ($7.25) adults, £3 ($4.35) seniors, students, and children. Tours: July–Aug Mon–Fri 11 a.m. and 2 p.m., Sat–Sun 10:30 a.m., 11:30 a.m., and 1 p.m.; Sept–June Mon–Fri 11 a.m. and 2 p.m., Sat 10:30 a.m. and 11:30 a.m. Time: 90 min.*

## City Chambers
**Merchant City**

Located on George Square, the Venetian-style city hall is even more impressive on the inside than out. Even if you don't take the free tour, at least pop your head in to see the cruciform front hall (the only part open to visitors who don't take the tour). The ceiling tilework and the magnificent marble columns appear throughout the building. In fact, the palatial interior has been used in many films as a stand-in for both the Vatican and the Kremlin, as well as for an interior shot in *Dr. Zhivago*. A tour of the Italian Renaissance building includes the city council chambers, where local officials vote, and the beautifully detailed banquet hall. The City Chambers were built in the 1880s; Queen Victoria officially opened them. The office of the city's Lord Provost (essentially the mayor) is here as well. Outside, Yanks will note a little Statue of Liberty atop the façade, just below the flag.

*George Square.* ☎ *0141-287-2000. Underground: Buchanan Street. Admission: Free. Open: Tours offered Mon–Fri 10:30–2:30. Time: 1 hour, 30 min.*

## Locating other fun stuff to do

### Provand's Lordship

The oldest house in Glasgow was built before Columbus sailed to the New World. Mary Queen of Scots and her son, James I, both stayed in the restored residence, which the easily spooked consider haunted. The house, which also had turns as a candy shop and a home to the city hangman, contains 17th-century period furniture. A medieval-themed garden containing medicinal herbs is on the grounds.

*3 Castle St., across from the St. Mungo Museum.* ☎ *0141-552-8819. Bus: 2. Admission: Free. Open: Mon–Sat 10 a.m.–5 p.m., Sun 11 a.m.–5 p.m. Time: 1 hour.*

### Tenement House

Step into a time machine and see what life was like in overcrowded early-20th-century Glasgow. This museum of tenement life in the Victorian age is a bit quirky; imagine if your grandmother had moved into her home in 1911, as owner Agnes Toward did here, and never changed a thing over the decades. Tenements were once Glasgow's principal housing, and this gives you a good idea of how cramped (you may even say claustrophobic) they could be. The museum has steep steps that may be hard for wheelchair users to tackle.

*145 Buccleuch St., Garnethill, near Charing Cross and Sauchiehall Street.* ☎ *0141-333-0183. Underground: Cowcaddens. Admission: £3.50 ($5.10) adults; £2.50 ($3.65) seniors, students, and children under 16. Open: Mar–Oct daily 2–5 p.m. Closed Nov–Feb. Time: 90 min.*

### Botanic Gardens

This highly popular tourist attraction is a 40-acre collection of tropical plants, herb gardens, flowerbeds, and orchids. Walk around or bring a picnic lunch. The amazing main glass-house structure, the Kibble Palace, an education, conservation, and research center, is worth checking out. Inside are palm trees, ferns, and rain-forest conditions.

*730 Great Western Rd.* ☎ *0141-334-2422. Underground: Hillhead. Admission: Free. Open: Garden: Daily dawn to dusk. Kibble Palace: Daily 10 a.m.–4:45 p.m. Time: 1 hour.*

### House for an Art Lover

This unique museum sits in the beautiful Bellahouston Park next to the Victorian Walled Gardens. Charles Rennie Mackintosh designed the building in 1901, but it wasn't built until after his death. Many of the art pieces change periodically; also on display are a permanent exhibit about the history of the place, posthumously built Mackintosh crafts, and a music room.

*10 Dumbreck Rd., Bellahouston Park.* ☎ *0141-353-4770. Internet:* www.house foranartlover.co.uk. *Underground: Ibrox. Bus: 9A, 39, 54, 59, 36. Admission: £3.50 ($5.10) adults; £2.50 ($3.65) seniors and students; £1 ($1.45) children under 16. Open: House: Sat–Sun 10 a.m.–4 p.m. Cafe and shop: Daily 10 a.m.–5 p.m. Time: 1 hour.*

### The Tall Ship at Glasgow Harbour

You won't be going anywhere, but you're free to explore the remarkable *Glenlee,* built in Port Glasgow in 1896. 1896? Yeah, but don't worry, it won't sink into the River Clyde; it was totally refurbished and made shipshape before its reopening in 1999. The *Glenlee*'s onboard exhibition details her cargo-trading history and the people who owned and sailed the ship. The *Glenlee* has circumnavigated the country 4 times and rounded Cape Horn 15 times. The pumphouse visitor center on the dock contains exhibition galleries, a nautical souvenir shop, and a restaurant. An excellent guided tour (included in the admission price) begins at 2 p.m. on Tuesday, Wednesday, and Thursday.

*100 Stobcross Rd.* ☎ *0141-339-0631. E-mail:* info@thetallship.com. *Internet:* www.glenlee.co.uk. *Bus: 26. Admission: £4.50 ($6.55) adults; £3.25 ($4.70) seniors, students, and children under 16; £6.95–£9.95 ($10–$14) family. Open: Daily 10 a.m.–5 p.m. Time: 90 min.*

## Surveying Glasgow's landmarks

### George Square

The square is considered the center of the city. It's the place of celebration and of city-sponsored events on most weekends. The statue of Sir Walter Scott stands 80 feet high in the middle; other statues include a young Queen Victoria (who officially opened the square in 1888) and Prince Albert on horseback, inventor James Watt, and poet Robbie Burns. Interestingly, the main spot occupied by Scott was intended for George III (for whom the square is named), but he went mad before the statue was completed, and it was scrapped.

*George and Vincent streets. Webcam:* www.glasgow.gov.uk/webcam/ webcam.htm. *Underground: Buchanan Street.*

## Glasgow Attractions

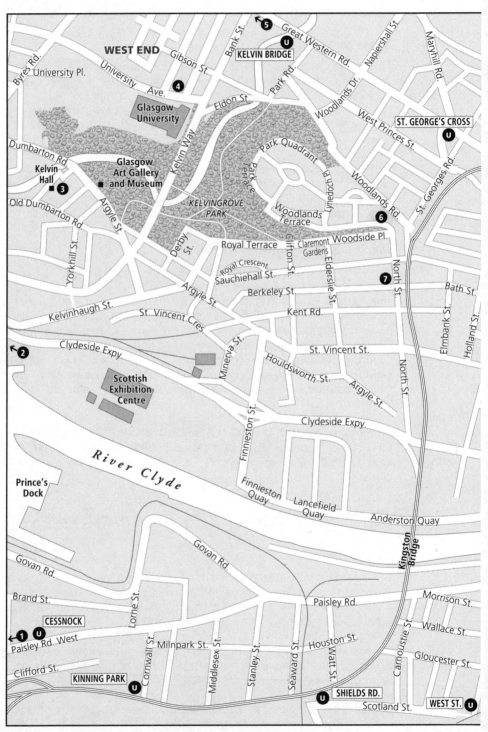

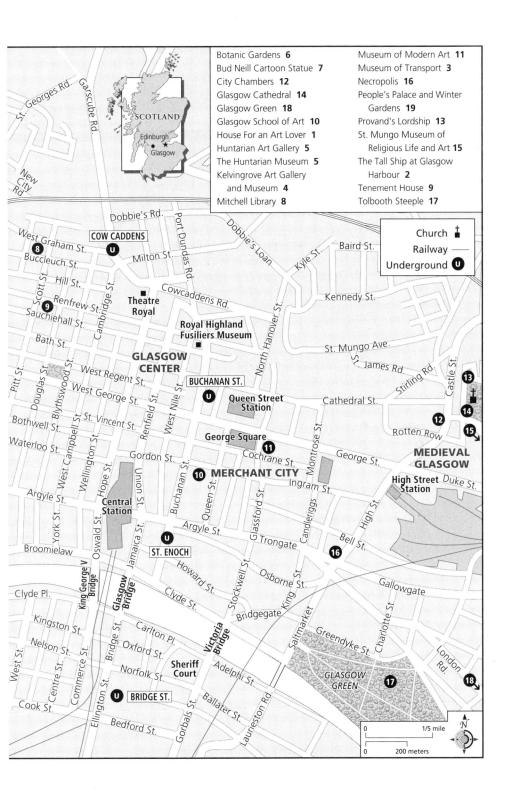

Botanic Gardens **6**
Bud Neill Cartoon Statue **7**
City Chambers **12**
Glasgow Cathedral **14**
Glasgow Green **18**
Glasgow School of Art **10**
House For an Art Lover **1**
Huntarian Art Gallery **5**
The Huntarian Museum **5**
Kelvingrove Art Gallery
   and Museum **4**
Mitchell Library **8**

Museum of Modern Art **11**
Museum of Transport **3**
Necropolis **16**
People's Palace and Winter
   Gardens **19**
Provand's Lordship **13**
St. Mungo Museum of
   Religious Life and Art **15**
The Tall Ship at Glasgow
   Harbour **2**
Tenement House **9**
Tolbooth Steeple **17**

Church ✝
Railway ——
Underground **U**

SCOTLAND

Edinburgh
Glasgow

# The legend behind Glasgow's coat of arms

What's with those fish and bells? You'll see many examples of the city's coat of arms throughout the city, including a modified version on many lampposts. The best ones are just inside the door of the City Chambers and on the front of the Royal Concert Hall.

The coat of arms, with its fish, tree, bird, gold rings, and bell, may look a tad odd, but it has some interesting stories behind it. At the top of the armorial insignia is St. Kentigern (better known as Mungo, the patron saint of Glasgow), and on the other three sides are salmon with gold rings in their mouths surrounding a tree with a bird and bell in it.

The fish and rings are from a legend that tells of St. Mungo's recovery of a ring that was to be a gift from the Queen of Cadzow to her husband. The king, suspecting malfeasance, stole the ring from a sleeping knight who was caring for the gift and threw it into the River Clyde. The next day, he demanded the ring from his wife, and when she could not produce it, he threatened to kill her. Mungo instructed one of his monks to go fishing and return with the first one caught — and that salmon contained the ring.

The tree represents the one that Mungo was able to light on fire by praying over it after the sixth-century firestarter monk was put in charge of the monastery's holy fire and some dastardly hooligans put it out. The bird represents a wild robin tamed by Mungo's master, St. Serf, that Mungo brought back to life after it was accidentally killed. The bell represents one that the pope gave to Mungo; the treasure rang often before it disappeared. A popular children's song surrounds the coat of arms: "Here is the bird that never flew. / Here is the tree that never grew. / Here is the bell that never rang. / Here is the fish that never swam."

## Tolbooth Steeple

Before the construction of City Chambers on George Square, the *tolbooth* (a place where citizens paid rent to the city) housed the town council and was also the city jail and execution spot. According to one local legend, a murderer was brought to the steeple to be hanged, but the executioner could not be found, and as a result the criminal was offered the hangman's job and given a pardon. It's no coincidence that the tolbooth is on a road called Gallowgate: The beginning of the road marks the location of the old city wall, outside of which hanged bodies were displayed as a warning to visitors. All that remains of the old tolbooth is the impressive steeple with blue clock faces.

*Corner of Trongate and High Street. Underground: St. Enoch.*

## Bud Neill Cartoon Statue

Neill was a local poet and cartoonist who drew a popular cartoon of two goofy-looking cowboys and their two-legged horse. When Neill passed away, the local community erected a statue of his immortal characters in his honor. It's one of the oddest statues in Scotland.

*At the intersection of Woodlands Road and W. End Park Street (across from Halt Bar), West End. Underground: Kelvinbridge.*

### Mitchell Library

This is the largest public library in Europe and contains more than a million volumes. It's more famous for having the world's largest collection of poems by Robert Burns. Above the library is the statue of Minerva, the goddess of learning and wisdom. Be sure to check out the ornate back of the library.

*North Street at Berkeley Street.* ☎ *0141-287-2931. Bus: 23, 57. Open: Mon–Fri 9 a.m.–9 p.m., Sat 9 a.m.–5 p.m.*

# Seeing Glasgow by guided tour

If you're more inclined to be led around Glasgow than to find your own way, here are a few guided tours that may suit you:

- ✔ **Friday Bus Tour** (☎ **0141-284-7644**; E-mail: Glasgow@guidefriday.com; Internet: www.hoponhopoff.com) is an international group that does an unfailingly good job of covering all the bases and throwing in trivia about Glasgow. The circuit stretches from the East End Barras and Glasgow Green as far west as Glasgow University, stopping at Glasgow Cathedral, People's Palace, Mitchell Library, the Huntarian Museum, and the Transport Museum.

    Make sure you stick your hand out if you want the bus to stop; the Friday buses share bus stops with regular buses. You can pick up the green-and-tan buses at many places along the route; the East and West End legs start and stop on George Square (opposite the City Chambers).

    The bus comes every 30 minutes between 9:30 a.m. and 6 p.m. daily April through October and less frequently in the off-season. Tickets cost £7.50 ($11) adults, £6 ($8.70) seniors and students, £2.50 ($3.65) children under 16, £17.50 ($25) family. Time: 90 minutes.

- ✔ **The Glasgow Tour** (☎ **0141-204-0444**; www.scotguide.com) is very similar to the Friday tour except that it stops to see the Tall Ship at Glasgow Harbor and is sanctioned by the tourist board. The tour guides are knowledgeable and enjoy answering questions. You can pick up the bright, multicolored buses at many places along the route and on George Square (opposite the City Chambers).

    The bus comes every 30 minutes between 9:30 a.m. and 4:30 p.m. daily March through October and less frequently in the off-season. Your ticket is valid for 24 hours, so if you get on in the afternoon, you can still ride the next morning. Tickets cost £7.50 ($11) adults, £6 ($8.70) seniors and students, £3 ($4.35) children under 16, £17 ($25) family. Time: 90 minutes.

✔ **Mercat Walks** (☎ **0141-772-0022;** E-mail: ask@mercat-tours. co.uk; Internet: www.mercat-tours.co.uk) are ghoulish and chilling tours run by historians, not actors, but they still manage a theatrical flair. You'll hear the tales of body snatchers, ghosts, murderers, and hangmen. The tours of the macabre side of Glasgow include a night visit to Glasgow Cathedral and the grave-yard, so young kids and the easily scared may not want to join. If this gives you the creeps, you can take the afternoon history walk.

Tours begin at the tourist office on George Square; all run daily. Gruesome Glasgow leaves at 7 p.m., Ghosts and Ghouls at 9 p.m., and Historic Glasgow at 2 p.m. Tickets cost £5 ($7.25) adults, £4 ($5.80) seniors and students, £3 ($4.35) children under 16, £13 ($19) family). Time: 90 minutes.

✔ **The *Waverley*** (☎ **0141-243-2224**) is the only seagoing paddle steamer in the world. Known affectionately as the "Pride of the Clyde," the steamer takes visitors along the river out to sea. From the heated lounges and bars or anywhere along the sides, you'll get great views of the Clyde's pretty fjord scenery. There are many different routes, so call ahead to find out the ones on the days you'll be visiting.

The steamer leaves from Waverley Terminal, Anderston Quay, an easy walk or cab ride from downtown. The price depends on the length of your trip, ranging from £9 to £35 ($13–$51); children under 16 are half price, under age 3 are free, and seniors get a £2 ($2.90) reduction.

# *Shopping Glasgow*

Glasgow is a great city for shopping. The three main streets lined with shops are Buchanan, Argyle, and Sauchiehall — all of which will keep you busy for days of shopping for clothes and gifts. **Argyle Arcade** is an enclosed gallery of jewelry shops. **Princes Square** also abounds with unique boutiques.

The city has two large malls: the **Buchanan Galleries,** at the intersec-tion of Buchanan and Sauchiehall, with 80 shops; and **St. Enoch's Mall,** at the intersection of Buchanan and Argyle, which is even larger (and sits under the largest glass roof in Europe). Neither compares in size and scope with the East End outdoor mall and bazaar called the Barras (from the word "wheelbarrow," which merchants rented to peddle their wares).

The **Barras,** at Gallowgate and Kent Streets, is the largest enclosed market in Europe — and for non-native eyes, it is an experience in itself. More than 800 booths sell everything from tartan tourist wares and homemade clothes to old books and antiques. There is a lot of junk as well, easily overlooked by any discriminating shopper. But it's old-world shopping, with men hawking packs of tobacco through the crowds and an entertaining butcher who sells his meat like an auctioneer. You'll find plenty of food and even two pubs within the Barras' walls. Open weekends until sunset. (Bus: 14, 18, 20, 62.)

Unless otherwise noted, most shops in this section accept credit cards. The most common are Visa and MasterCard; many places take American Express, but few honor Discover (it's not common in Europe) or Diner's Club. Shops usually open at 9 or 10 a.m. and close between 5 and 6:30 p.m. Some stay open as late as 9 p.m., but only in high season. Most keep shorter hours on Sunday. The listings in the following sections note exceptions.

Here are some of my favorite shopping stops in Glasgow for gifts, souvenirs, clothing, and uniquely Scottish items.

## *Antiques*

**Lansdowne Antiques,** 10 Park Rd. (☎ **0141-339-7211**), is a renowned spot for excellent vintage wood furnishings, lamps, and all sorts of ornaments. The pieces aren't cheap — but well-preserved objects demand high prices. Underground: Kelvinbridge. Open: Monday to Friday from 10:30 a.m. to 5:30 p.m., Saturday and Sunday from 11 a.m. to 5 p.m.

## *Books*

The famous bookshop **John Smith and Son,** 57 St. Vincent St. (☎ **0141-221-3095**), is known for having the largest selection of Scottish titles in the city. So if, for some reason, this guide doesn't have all the info you need, you'll find it there. Open: Monday to Friday from 10:30 a.m. to 5:30 p.m.; Saturday and Sunday from 11 a.m. to 5 p.m.

## *Clothes*

**James Pringle Weavers,** 130 Buchanan St. (☎ **0141-221-3434**), is a quality Scottish specialty shop. It carries many of the same sweaters, gifts, and trinkets you'll find in other such shops but also a few unique items, such as lamb-shaped slippers made of baby's wool, and tartan nightshirts. Although the Edinburgh Woollen Mill Company owns the shop, Pringle Weavers has been around since 1780, and the staff is unfailingly helpful and knowledgeable. Call for hours.

The high-end clothing store **Hector Russell,** 110 Buchanan St. (☎ **0141-221-0217**), stocks tweed jackets, sweaters, and, of course, kilts. Russell is the oldest kilt-making establishment in Scotland — this shop has been in operation since 1881, and believe me, after 120 years, they've worked out all the kinks. The staff is wonderfully friendly, too, without ever crossing the "pushy" line. Call for hours.

## Crafts and jewelry

**Papyrus,** 296–298 Sauchiehall St. (☎ **0141-353-2182**), with a branch at 374 Byres Rd. (☎ **0141-334-6514**), is an eclectic gift shop with a plentiful supply of cards, books, Mackintosh gifts, and jewelry — a little bit of everything for everyone. You'll surely find something unique, although it probably won't have much to do with Scotland. Closed Sunday.

**Henderson the Jeweler,** 217 Sauchiehall St. (☎ **0141-331-2569**), is perhaps the only excellent jewelry store not in the Argyle Arcade. This shop is renowned for its wide range of silver jewelry and Mackintosh-style gifts. It's in the same building as the Willow Tea Room, discussed in the "A drink with jam and bread" sidebar, earlier in this chapter.

## Food

**Peckham's Delicatessen,** 100 Byres Rd. (☎ **0141-357-1454**), with a branch at Central Station (☎ **0141-248-4012**), is a great place to stock up for a lovely picnic in the Botanic Gardens or Glasgow Green. You'll find great gourmet items to take home, as well. Peckham's sells sausages, cheeses, and Irn-Bru, the Scottish equivalent of Coke, but ten times as popular.

## Music and musical instruments

You know **Fopp,** 358 Byres Rd. (☎ **0141-357-0774**), is the best and coolest record store in the city because it overflows with students in search of the latest and hippest. Forget the Virgin Megastore on Union Street — the excellent collection includes vinyl records with handy turntables for your use as well as an extensive CD collection. The prices are competitive, and the bargain bins are full of great finds. Whether you're looking for traditional Scottish music or hard-to-find U.K. pop hits, this is your record store. Underground: Hillhead. Open: Monday to Saturday from 9:30 a.m. to 7 p.m., and Sunday from 11 a.m. to 6 p.m.

If you're looking to make your own music, **Southside Music,** 599 Cathcart Rd., Govanhill (☎ **0141-423-5474**), is the best place in town to take home an inexpensive pair of pipes or another new or used instrument. The shop sells sheet music and instruction guides to get you started. Southside may be best known for its collection of vintage guitars. Call for hours.

## Souvenirs

**Robin Hood Gift House,** 11 St. Vincent Place, just off George Square (☎ 0141-221-7408), is an excellent shop with a good range of items. You'll find the typical touristy stuff but also nice items such as chess sets and wool blankets. Other big sellers are clan history books, shortbread, whisky, and books on Robert Burns. Underground: Buchanan Street. Closed Sunday.

And don't forget **Scotch on the Rocks** at St. Enoch's Centre (☎ 0141-248-1502). I love the name of this place. The goods are great as well. From tartan cufflinks and china Loch Ness monsters to Celtic jewelry and Caithness glass, everything is handcrafted in Scotland. Underground: St. Enoch. Open: Monday to Saturday from 9 a.m. to 6 p.m., Thursday until 8 p.m., and Sunday from 11 a.m. to 5:30 p.m.

# Doing the Pub Crawl: Pubs, Clubs, and Other Nightlife

"Oh show me, the way, to the next whisky bar . . . ." You shouldn't leave Glasgow without taking a traditional pub crawl through the streets of the city. Glasgow has a good mix of traditional watering holes and new hip joints — you can't go wrong. Nightlife is one of the city's best selling points. You may have to spend more than one night in the city just so you can hit all the top spots.

## Best of the bunch

### Nice and Sleazy
**The hippest bar scene**

Neither nice nor sleazy, this cool bar has diner-style seating in booths with shining steel tables and chairs, along with funky Chinese lantern-style lighting. The jukebox is terminally hip — don't be discouraged if you don't recognize a lot of the bands — and so are some of the drink specials. House concoctions (named for movies, actors, and a few inside jokes, I assume) include the Gary Coleman, a surprisingly tasty combination of rum, coke, and Guinness. You'll hear live music most nights, both upstairs and down, and can play pool. The only complaint: It tends to get a bit hot in here, so don't wear your new woolly jumper.

*421 Sauchiehall St.* ☎ *0141-333-9637. Bus: 57. Open: Daily 11:30 a.m.–11:45 p.m.*

### O'Neill's

**Best late-night bar**

It may have an Irish theme, but this boisterous pub is known for its after-hours '70s, '80s, and '90s music nights, which attract a good spread of patrons. Many of the city's bars close at midnight, but O'Neill's pours the creamy Guinness 'til 2 or 3 a.m. By last call, everyone in the place is singing, smiling, and dancing. The bar calls this "Irish hospitality," but it's simply what happens when good stout and great music mix in the wee hours.

*447 Sauchiehall St. (☎ 0141-353-0436). Cover: £3 ($4.35) Thurs, £5 ($7.25) Fri and Sat. Bus: 57.*

### The Riverside Club

**Best dancing (even if you have two left feet)**

Don't be intimidated by the cover charge or all the dancing. The Riverside will be one of the most memorable experiences of your trip, as long as you're not afraid to let go and dance. For more than a dozen years, this large hall has hosted a toe-tappin' Scottish *ceilidh,* and its musicians have taught fun and fast-paced Scottish dancing to visitors from all over the globe. It doesn't matter if you have two left feet and no ear for music; you'll be having too much fun to notice that no one here is Fred Astaire. And you won't be expected to know the steps, either — the staff will teach you. Go after 9 p.m. when everyone is dancing.

*Fox Street, off Clyde Street. ☎ 0141-643-0685 or 0141-248-3144. Underground: St. Enoch. Open: Thurs–Sat 6 p.m. to midnight.*

### The Victoria Bar

**Best music bar**

The "Vicky" is not your sharp-corners-and-scratchless-furniture type of place. This very traditional pub on one of Glasgow's oldest streets doesn't beckon with neon or "Drink Special" signs outside. It is an authentic classic pub and far enough off the beaten tourist path that you actually get to meet Scots. You can sing with them, as well — pickup players often encourage the whole place to sing along. It's great fun and the real deal. Don't confuse this place with the cheesy nightclub called Victoria's on Sauchiehall Street.

*159 Bridgegate, near the corner of Clyde Street, by the river. ☎ 0141-552-6040. Open: Daily 11 a.m. to midnight.*

## Recommended pubs

Here are a few of the city's finest pubs to end your day of seeing the best of Glasgow.

✔ **Babbity Bowster,** 16–18 Blackfriars St. (☎ 0141-552-5055). This fine little pub arranges plenty of outdoor seating in its shady and cool alley. The theme and the beer are Irish, and the only tough choice you must make is whether to have a Guinness or the slightly sweeter stout, Murphy's. The staff is the friendliest group I've ever met in a pub. Even after closing, they don't shoo anybody out while they clean up for the night, and they give a nice goodbye to patrons as you exit. The historic French-style building features a genuine Roman Doric doorway and traditional Scottish painted ceiling beams. In case you're wondering, Babbity Bowster is an old Scottish dance that may have been the lambada of its day. Underground: St. Enoch.

✔ **Bar 91,** 91 Candleriggs (☎ 0141-552-5211). This cool bar is more European than Scottish. The tables, chairs, and bar are urban chic, and pieces of modern art dot the walls. Although it can get a bit crowded, especially during happy hour (which features good drink specials), the bar is never understaffed, so you never have to wait long for a drink — unless you're getting a Guinness. Merchant City's only Art Deco bar is across from the City Chambers. Underground: St. Enoch.

✔ **Brunswick Cellar,** 239 Sauchiehall St. (☎ 0141-353-0131). This cool subterranean bar seems a million miles away from the hustle and bustle of shoppers on the street above. The dim, candlelit cellar will give you temporary blindness if you're stepping out of the sun, but as you orient yourself you'll have no trouble finding the well-stocked bar and a comfortable place to sit. The cavernous atmosphere incorporates a steady background of dance music (not loud enough to disturb conversation) and television sets, sometimes showing Hollywood movies. If you go for the excellent happy hour between 3 and 8 p.m. (when drinks cost £1–£1.20/$1.45–$1.75), don't be surprised if it's still light out when you return to the surface. Bus: 57.

✔ **Budda Bar,** 142 St. Vincent St. (☎ 0141-243-2212). This subterranean bar is a nirvana of plush couches and pillows under dim lights with a soundtrack of chill rock 'n' roll. Get enlightened by the well-made cocktails, which are a little bigger than the juice-glass-size mixed drinks you get in most places. On Friday and Saturday nights, 20- and 30-somethings crowd in for a drink before heading upstairs to the bar's own nightclub. You can't miss the bar; a gold silhouette of the big-bellied Buddha and a neat wooden idol mark the spot at street level. Bus: 6, 8, 16.

✔ **The Cas (Bāh),** 1 Lyndoch St., at Woodlands Road, Charing Cross, West End (☎ 0141-564-1801). Not just a clever name, this U-shaped bar below the Music Academy Restaurant is a hip feature of the West End bar scene. The tree-trunk tables and masonry walls are, well, different, and there is foosball! Located in the trendy West End district, the place tends to fill with a young crowd on weekends.

And if you're a woman, and go on a Monday night and have a couple of pints, you drink free on Tuesdays. No kidding; the bar calls it the Venus Fly Trap. Underground: St. George's Cross.

✔ **Fialte,** 79 St. Vincent St. (☎ **0141-248-4989**). If the name of the pub doesn't give it away (it's Gaelic for "welcome"), the Guinness posters along the walls will clue you in that this is an Irish pub. And why would you want to go to an Irish pub while in Scotland? Well, there's no such thing as a Scottish-style pub, and English pubs went out of style in the '80s along with break-dancing. So, get down there, drink some of the dark stuff, and sing along to the traditional Irish music that plays most nights. Bus: 6, 8, 16.

✔ **Halt Bar,** 160 Woodlands Rd. ☎ 0141-564-1527). Although the Halt looks generic, with its typical booths and tables and local pictures on the walls, it is one of the more popular watering holes in the West End. It draws an impressive mix of patrons, from the old guys who refuse to stop drinking at their local bar no matter how popular it gets, to students who frequent the bar for the all-day happy hour between 11 a.m. and 6 p.m. (all pints £1.50/$2.20). Live local bands jam on Friday and Saturday nights, football shows on the big screen, and a popular quiz night (the latest pub fad) takes place on Sunday evenings. Underground: Kelvinbridge.

✔ **Republic Bier Halle,** 9 Gordon St. (☎ **0141-204-0706;** www. republicbierhall.com). This boisterous underground beer hall is not your typical Glasgow pub. The international menu features a few Scottish microbrews, such as spicy Fraoch and fruity Grozet, and many of the best brews from around the world — not the macro-brews you may think, but good local picks. If you're feeling homesick for the States, have the San Franciscan staple, Anchor Steam, or go for something more exotic, such as a Casablanca (Moroccan, natch), a Greek Marathon, or a Cuban Hautey (can't get *that* in the United States). If you're overwhelmed about what to choose, don't fret: They also have my favorite beer in the whole wide world: Chimay, made by Belgian Trappist monks (and with a high alcohol content). You can also order mixed drinks or wine — but isn't that like asking for a Leprechaun trinket in a Scottish gift shop? Anyway, you can't fail to have a good time at the Bier Hall. Underground: Buchanan Street.

✔ **The Saracen Head,** 209 Gallowgate, near Barrowlands (☎ **0141-552-1660**). It claims to be the oldest pub in Glasgow (other places disagree), but it technically doesn't have a liquor license. No, you don't need a password to get in to drink bathtub gin — the pub doesn't require a license because of an old law that exempts places where royalty stayed. Calling itself a pub-museum, the Saracen Head has the skull of the last man accused of witchcraft in Scotland, who was burned alive, as well as a poem by Robert Burns. The history and odd items in the "museum" are the only criteria for putting this place on the tourist route. Otherwise, it's just a dinky little pub, not unlike the common forgettable local establishments — with one more notable exception, a lethal con-coction called White Tornado cider (not too far removed from that bathtub gin). Closes at 10:30 p.m. weekdays. Bus: 14, 18, 20, 62.

✔ **Scotia Bar,** 112 Stockwell St. (☎ **0141-552-8681**). This fun pub is one of the oldest in Glasgow — hence the not-so-pretty exterior. Don't be surprised to see patrons of all ages mingling; it's the kind of place that appeals to everybody. The service and the locals are friendly, and the seating is comfortable. When the pub closes at midnight, you can head upstairs for another couple hours for more drinks, a good jukebox, and pool, but you must actually *play* pool, a condition of the after-hours liquor license. The man at the door will even ask you if you plan to play and have you sign the guest registry. Underground: St. Enoch.

✔ **Waxy O'Conner's,** 46 West George St. (☎ **0141-354-5154**). A labyrinth of a bar, this fun watering hole has five levels of rooms and bars for you to explore. Based on a popular London bar of the same name, the interesting design is supposed to represent a church inside a large tree. Wherever you look, it's a cavern of tree limbs and stained glass — Robinson Crusoe meets Sunday school. The teak pulpits and pipe organs upstairs are nice touches. The weekend DJs play a lot of American top-40 hits — which can be a good and bad thing — and the bar staff is very fast and knows how to pull a good pint of Murphy's. If you go, leave a trail of breadcrumbs so that you can get out later. Finding the place is no trouble; just look for the two Olympic-style torches flickering out front. Bus: 11.

## Recommended clubs

If walking all over town didn't send you running for the nearest comfort-able spot to kick up your feet, one of these nightspots may do the trick.

✔ **Destiny,** 18 Cambridge St., just off Sauchiehall Street (☎ **0141-353-6555**). Smoke and mirrors, literally. Things don't get moving until after midnight most nights, when the fog machines come on and the laser lights get going. This multilevel club has two dance floors and good DJs — and feels like being inside a human pinball machine. Lights shine from the floor, strobe lights blink, and glow-ing crystal balls hang from the ceiling. The place is big enough that it never gets too crowded, except at the bar — I've honestly never waited so long for a drink. But what can you do? It's out of your hands; it's Destiny. Bus: 57. Open: Daily 10 p.m.–3 a.m.

✔ **The Garage,** 490 Sauchiehall St. (☎ **0141-332-1120**). It's hard to miss this place: Just look for the truck cabin crashing through the wall above the entrance. The place is one big room full of pyrotechnics and two bars, decorated with little except a surfing skeleton and dummies crashing through the walls (in keeping with the outside decor). Plenty of seating and tables line the edge and the balcony overlooking the dance floor, in case you need a breather or just want to people-watch. The Garage is a great place for a show if you can catch one, and the acoustics lend themselves to great dancing, as well. Bus: 57.

## Going to the theater

Glasgow is home to the Scottish Opera, the Scottish Ballet, the Royal Scottish Opera, and plenty of great theater. **The Tron,** 63 Trongate (☎ 0141-552-4267; www.tron.co.uk), is a large theater that schedules a good variety of classic and newer plays, and is never afraid to be a little controversial. There's nothing amateur about it, so you can't go wrong. It also has a restaurant and two bars for the pre- and post-theater crowds. The name comes from the fact that the structure was once the home of the city's public weighing machine, or *tron.* **The Theatre Royal,** Hope Street and Cowcaddens Road (☎ 0141-332-9000), is a magnificent venue that books both opera and ballet. **The King's Theatre,** 297 Bath St. (☎ 0141-248-5153), shows mostly musicals. **The Royal Concert Hall,** 2 Sauchiehall St. (☎ 0141-287-5511; information hotline ☎ 0141-353-8050; www.grch.com), schedules classical music, comedy, rock concerts, and more.

## Going to the movies

Glasgow has a couple of excellent movie houses that are especially welcoming on a rainy afternoon.

For mainstream movies, try the **ABC Film Centre,** Sauchiehall Street (☎ 0141-332-9513), or the **Odeon Film Centre,** Renfield Street (☎ 0141-332-3413; www.odeon.co.uk). For classic, independent, art, and foreign films, head to the excellent **Glasgow Film Theatre,** 12 Rose St. (☎ 0141-332-6535).

# Fast Facts: Glasgow

**American Express**

The **Amex** office is at 115 Hope St., near the corner of Bothwell (☎ 0141-226-3077; Bus: 38, 45, 48, 57). Open: Mon–Fri 8:30 a.m.– 5:30 p.m., Sat 9 a.m. to noon (until 4 p.m. Sat June–July).

**Area Code**

The area code for Glasgow is **0141.** You need to dial the area code only if you're calling from outside the city.

**ATMs**

ATMs are available throughout the city.

**Currency Exchange**

You can exchange money at travel agencies, hotels, and some post offices, but the best rates are to be found at banks. If you have American Express traveler's checks, you can exchange them without paying any commission at the Amex office (see previous listing).

## Dentists

The **Glasgow Dental Hospital** is at 378 Sauchiehall St. (☎ 0141-211-9600; Bus: 57). Open Mon–Fri 9:15 a.m.–3:15 p.m., Sun 10:30 a.m. to noon.

## Emergencies

Dial **999** for police, fire, or ambulance.

## Eyeglasses

**Dolan & Aitchison,** 7 Union St. (☎ 0141-204-4394).

## Genealogy Resources

**Glasgow & West of Scotland Family History Society,** Unit 15, 32 Mansfield St., Glasgow G11 5QP (☎ 0141-339-8303).

## Hospitals

The major hospital is the **Royal Infirmary,** 82–86 Castle St. (☎ 0141-211-4000 or 0141-332-1925; Bus: 2, 2A). The other hospital is the **Western Infirmary,** Dumbarton Road (☎ 0141-211-2000).

## Information

Tourist Information Centre, 11 George Sq. (☎ 0141-204-4400; E-mail: enquiries@ seeglasgow.com; Internet: www.see glasgow.com).

## Internet Access

**Gameland,** 1060 Argyle St. (☎ 0141-226-2220; E-mail: gamelandweb@email.com; Internet: www.gamelandweb.com). Open: Mon–Sat 8 a.m.–10 p.m., Sun 8 a.m.–8 p.m. Cost: £2 ($2.90) for 30 minutes.

**Comms Port,** 471 Great Western Rd. (☎ 0141-339-6909; Internet: www.commsport.com; Underground: Kelvinbridge). Open Mon–Wed 8 a.m.–8 p.m., Thurs–Sat 8 a.m.–9 p.m., Sun 9 a.m.–8 p.m. Cost: £3 ($4.35) per hour. Look for the opening of a new location at 205 Sauchiehall St.

**Surfin Internet Café,** 81 St. Georges Rd., Charing Cross (☎ 0141-332 0404; E-mail: nav010@hotmail.com; Internet: www.surf-in.co.uk). Open 24 hours. Cost: From £1 ($1.45) per hour.

## Mail

The main branch of the post office is at 47 St. Vincent's St. (☎ 0141-204-3689; Underground: Buchanan Street; Bus: 6, 8, 16). Open: Mon–Fri 8:30 a.m.–5:45 p.m., Sat 9 a.m.–5:30 p.m. You can receive mail at the American Express office (see listing earlier in these Fast Facts). The service is free to cardholders; all others pay a small fee. You can also collect letters at the regular post office by having the sender address them to "Poste Restante," c/o you at the post office.

## Maps

The tourist office (see "Information," earlier in this section) distributes free basic maps and sells more detailed maps.

## Newspapers/Magazines

Newsstands and convenience stores sell local papers, such as *The Scotsman,* and international magazines; some also carry the *International Herald Tribune, USA Today,* and *The Wall Street Journal.*

## Pharmacies

**Boots,** 200 Sauchiehall St. (☎ 0141-332-1925; Bus: 57). Open: Mon–Wed 8:30 a.m.–6 p.m., Thurs 8:30 a.m.–8 p.m., Fri–Sat 8:30 a.m.–6 p.m., Sun 11 a.m.–5 p.m.

## Police

Dial **999** in case of emergencies. The police headquarters is at 173 Pitt St. (☎ 0141-532-2000).

## Restrooms

Public toilets, safe and relatively clean, are available throughout the city.

### Safety

Glasgow is a generally safe city. It suffers more personal theft than Edinburgh because its drug problem is worse. As in any large city, watch your purse and keep an eye on your wallet. The only neighborhood to avoid is the high-rise housing north of Charing Cross (at the east side of the West End).

### Smoking

You can smoke just about anywhere except in museums. Some restaurants have nonsmoking sections, but don't count on it. At most hotels, you can ask for a nonsmoking room.

### Taxis

Taxis are numerous and available throughout the city. You don't have to queue up; just hail one. **Glasgow Wide Taxis:** ☎ 0141-332-6666 or 0141-332-7070. **TOA Taxis:** ☎ 0141-332-7070.

# Part IV
# The Major Regions

The 5<sup>th</sup> Wave     By Rich Tennant

"Looks like our trip into the town of Argyll will be delayed while we let one of the local farmers pass with his sheep."

# In this part . . .

**M**ost travelers don't just visit Edinburgh and Glasgow (discussed in Part III) and stop there. They travel to the outer regions of Scotland, thrilling to the grandeur of castle ruins, green Highland hills, and rugged glens.

The Borders region overflows with history and historic sites such as abbey ruins and ancient castles. Argyll and the Islands are home to Inveraray, a charming port town, and Oban, a bustling harbor town where the Highlands meet the Islands. Fife and the Central Highlands have excellent attractions within easy reach of Glasgow and Edinburgh. St. Andrews is the golf mecca of the world, and Stirling is a mini-Edinburgh with a good variety of wining and dining options as well as impressive landmarks. In the heathered hills of Tayside and Grampian lies the heart of castle country, and you can tour the many Scotch whisky distilleries on the fabled Whisky Trail. The West Highlands region, the most visited area in Scotland after Edinburgh and Glasgow, is the home of Loch Ness and its reticent resident, Nessie. Hop from island to island on ferries that go between the beautiful Hebridean Islands, and enjoy the quiet, largely unspoiled landscape. Finally, a unique trip awaits you as you head northward to the Shetlands and Orkney Islands, areas that offer glorious views, castle ruins, and locally made crafts.

# Chapter 12

# The Borders

● ● ● ● ● ● ● ● ● ● ● ● ● ● ● ● ● ● ● ● ● ● ● ● ● ● ● ● ● ● ● ● ● ● ● ● ● ● ● ● ● ● ● ● ●

## In This Chapter

▶ Finding the best places to stay, eat, and shop in the Borders

▶ Discovering where Sir Walter Scott and Robert Burns lived

▶ Visiting the famous Borders abbeys

▶ Getting the lowdown on Robbie Burns's favorite pub

● ● ● ● ● ● ● ● ● ● ● ● ● ● ● ● ● ● ● ● ● ● ● ● ● ● ● ● ● ● ● ● ● ● ● ● ● ● ● ● ● ● ● ● ●

*T*he Borders region, so named simply because it borders England, often escapes visitors' attention, partly for good reason. Because most tourists enter Scotland by plane or train, arriving in either Glasgow or Edinburgh, they tend to go north after visiting the country's two largest cities. Most of the big attractions and towns are not in the Borders but in the Islands, Highlands, and Fife. With limited time in the country, seeing everything is difficult, so many choose to spend time in the north rather than in the south.

That's a shame, because even though the Borders are largely agricultural, the area has several great attractions.

## Orienting Yourself to the Borders

For anyone on a castles-and-cathedrals tour of Scotland, the Borders is an important area to visit. King David I commissioned four abbeys in the Borders, and many of the castles in the area have seen their share of skirmishes with the English. Also, two of Scotland's most famous locals spent their last years in the rural Borders region: Sir Walter Scott and national poet Robert Burns.

Attractions aside, the Borders has an abundance of land for animal grazing. Sheep, in fact, outnumber people three to one. The Dumfries and Galloway regions are large dairy-producing areas, and the Borders is known for the breeding of a rare species of an otherwise common dog, the Border terrier.

Because even the bigger Borders towns of Dumfries, Melrose, and Peebles are quite small compared with towns in other regions of the country, the area has few standout restaurant, pub, and shopping areas. More often than not, your hotel will be one of your best options for dining and drinking. I include hotels that offer excellent fare and friendly pubs.

Give yourself a day or two to drive through the region. Pick the attractions you want to see, figure out a convenient place to stay overnight, and make the Borders a long side trip from Glasgow or Edinburgh. Just be sure not to discount the whole region without taking a look at this chapter.

## Getting to the Borders

You have a few options for getting in and out of the Borders region. Although buses and (to a lesser extent) trains run from Glasgow and Edinburgh, your best way to fully explore this spread-out area is to drive. You can cover a lot of ground in a car. Following are the primary options for getting there and getting around:

- ✔ **By car:** Take the A68 from Edinburgh toward Kelso, Jedburgh, and Melrose. To get to Dumfries from Glasgow, take the A77 to the A76 south. From the eastern towns, take the A708 to the A701.

- ✔ **By bus: Citylink** (☎ **0990-808-080**) buses cover all the major towns in the Borders region mentioned in this chapter.

- ✔ **By train: ScotRail** (☎ **0345-484-950**) travels to a few towns in the Borders region, including Berwick-upon-Tweed, Lockerbie, Dumfries, and Stranraer. You have to rely on buses to get you to smaller towns from there.

- ✔ **By ferry: Sealink Ferries** (☎ **01776-702-262**) travel between Stranraer and Belfast, Northern Ireland.

## Knowing Where to Stay

Most of the accommodations in the region are bed-and-breakfasts. The vast majority have few outstanding qualities — most are simply spare bedrooms in people's homes. You can visit or call a local tourist board if you want to book one, but don't expect an unforgettable breakfast or the world's best bed.

The selections in this section are some of the best accommodations for your money in the region. All are moderately priced, which is typical for the region, and many have great food for dinner and a full bar for a friendly pint or nightcap. Some have earned star ratings from the Scottish Tourist Board; see Chapter 8 for a description of the rating system.

## The Borders and Galloway Regions

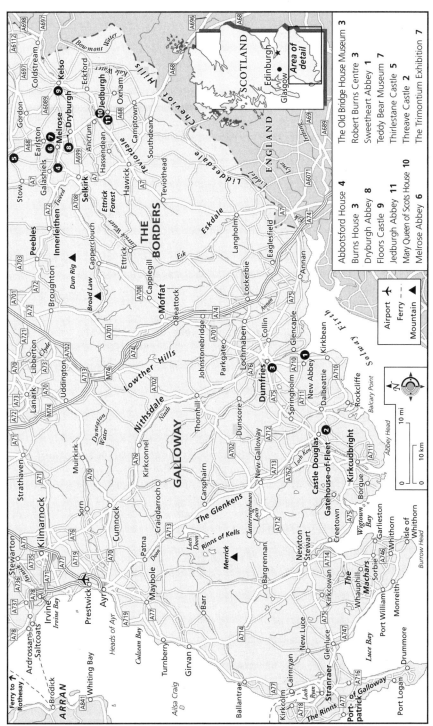

| | |
|---|---|
| The Old Bridge House Museum **3** | Abbotsford House **4** |
| Robert Burns Centre **3** | Burns House **3** |
| Sweetheart Abbey **1** | Dryburgh Abbey **8** |
| Teddy Bear Museum **7** | Floors Castle **9** |
| Thirlestane Castle **5** | Jedburgh Abbey **11** |
| Threave Castle **2** | Mary Queen of Scots House **10** |
| The Trimontium Exhibition **7** | Melrose Abbey **6** |

Airport ✈
Ferry – – –
Mountain ▲

N ↑

0 ___ 10 mi
0 ___ 10 km

## Burts Hotel
### $$ Melrose

This small, whitewashed hotel is best known for its excellent service and even better food. Locals and guests from other hotels pack the dining room. The cute building dates to 1722, but don't worry — the modest-sized rooms have color television, telephones, and other modern amenities. Burts also has a car park, unlike other accommodations in Melrose.

*Market Square, in the center of town.* ☎ **01896-822-285.** *Fax: 01896-822-870. Internet:* www.burtshotel.co.uk. *Rack rates: £94 ($136) double. AE, DC, MC, V.*

## Cairndale Hotel
### $$$ Dumfries

This early-20th-century resort hotel with a stone facade is a wonderful place to go for a little R&R. The rooms are very comfortable, but the best features of this place are the hot spa and heated indoor pool. The most fun months are May through October, when the hotel has traditional music and dancing on the weekends. Management added a conference center to appeal to a business clientele, but the Cairndale still knows how to treat vacationing guests right.

*132–136 English St., just off High Street.* ☎ **01387-254-111;** *toll-free in U.S. 800-468-3750. Fax: 01387-250-555. E-mail:* sales@cairndalehotel.co.uk. *Internet:* www.cairndalehotel.co.uk. *Rack rates: £105 ($152) double. AE, DC, MC, V.*

## Ednam House Hotel
### $$ Kelso

The Ednam occupies a great location overlooking the River Tweed in the heart of Kelso town. The Georgian mansion has a warming fire and is awash in fishing mementoes and other old furnishings and antiques, giving it a visiting-the-grandparents feel — and you'll be looked after just as if you were staying with relatives. Make sure to take high tea in the garden and have a meal in the restaurant — the river view is one of the best parts of the place.

*Bridge Street, just off the town square, one block north of the Kelso Bridge.* ☎ **01573-224-168.** *Fax: 01573-226-319. Rack rates: £52–£99 ($75–$144) double. MC, V.*

## Glenfriar's Hotel
### $$$ Jedburgh

All six rooms in this small hotel are very comfortable. The building is a charming Georgian home full of antiques and lovely furnishings. The beds are comfortable (the bigger rooms have four-poster beds), and the baths are roomy enough for a nice hot soak. Ms. Jenny Bywater runs the whole show and will take care of your every need.

*Friarsgate, next to St. John's Church.* ☎ **01835-862-000**. *E-mail:* glenfriars@edenroad.demon.co.uk. *Internet:* www.edenroad.demon.co.uk. *Rack rates: £100 ($145) double. MC, V.*

## Millars
$$$ **Melrose**

A three-star hotel that probably deserves that fourth one for the excellent rooms, big beds, gourmet food, and attentive hospitality, Millars Hotel is the newest excellent place to stay in town. The Millars (Carle and Kenny) have transformed the small hotel into a well-furnished and comfortable space that includes outdoor seating and a private bar. You'd be hard pressed to find a better dinner in town either, evidenced by the locals who eat in their dining room. And all rooms are non-smoking.

*Market Square, in the center of town.* ☎ **01896-822-645**. *Fax: 01896-823-474. E-mail:* Millars.Hotel@btinternet.com. *Internet:* www.millarshotel.com. *Rack rates: £85 ($123) double. AE, DC, MC, V.*

## Moffat House Hotel
$$ **Moffat**

This 18th-century mansion sits in the center of a garden in the heart of Moffat town. The red-and-black-painted stone building is hard to miss, and lovely trees grace the back. Each individually decorated room is well stocked with amenities. The food is excellent Scottish cuisine. A literary footnote: It is believed that poet James MacPherson (controversially thought to be the poet Ossian) wrote his disputed works here.

*High Street, in the city center.* ☎ **01683-220-039**. *Fax: 01683-221-288. E-mail:* moffat@talk21.com. *Internet:* www.moffathouse.co.uk. *Rack rates: £70–£94 ($102–$136) double. DC, MC, V.*

## Peebles Hydro
$$ **Peebles**

Once a Victorian "hydropathatic" hotel that claimed to cure whatever ailed you with a hot spring and mineral waters, the hotel is no longer in the health-spa business. Its main features, as the name suggests, are its hydro-centric options: a pool for the kids and a whirlpool and sauna for the adults. The hotel has lots of hallways and 30 acres of grounds for young ones to explore. Other activities at this chateau-style hotel include archery, snooker, and bicycling, plus organized activities specifically for kids. Oh, and the rooms are spacious and quite comfortable.

*Innerleithen Road, on A72 just outside Peebles.* ☎ **01721-720-602**. *Fax: 01721-722-999. Rack rates: £74.50–£91 ($108–$132) double. AE, DC, MC, V.*

## Selkirk Arms
$$  **Kirkcudbright**

Located in a small country house on a residential street, the Selkirk is a typically quaint accommodation. The 1770s Georgian structure holds charming rooms with contemporary furniture and amenities. Take in the large secluded garden and the nice lounge, both good spots for reading a little Robbie Burns — who stayed here when he wrote the poem "Selkirk Grace."

*Old High Street, on the east side of the street.* ☎ *01557-330-402. Fax: 01557-331-639. Rack rates: £75–£80 ($110–$115) double. AE, DC, MC, V.*

## The Spinney Guest House and Lodges
$  **Jedburgh**

This is what staying in the countryside is all about. The lodges are converted log cabins, and are as cozy as they sound, with pinewood furniture and plush beds. The farmhouse sleeps two or three — perfect for a small family — and the owners. The Frys will cook you a filling breakfast, or you can cook for yourself in the small kitchen area.

*Langlee, on the A68, 2 miles south of Jedburgh.* ☎ *01835-863-525. Fax: 01835-864-883. Rack rates: £20–£25 ($29–$36) double. Closed Nov–Feb. No credit cards.*

## Station Hotel
$$  **Dumfries**

The Station's Victorian sandstone building lies near the railroad station and the center of town. The comfortable 100-year-old rooms are renovated but maintain a certain rustic charm. The hotel's dining room and ornate staircase are also throwbacks to auld lang syne. Don't worry about being close to the rail station; there aren't any late-night trains. If you're looking for a good bite to eat, check out Somewhere Else. That's the actual name of the hotel's inspired Italian/Mexican bistro.

*49 Lovers Walk, just off Lockerbie Road, the main road from Glasgow (look for the train station).* ☎ *01387-254-316. Fax: 01387-250-388. Rack rates: £70–£90 ($102–$131) double. AE, DC, MC, V.*

## Torbay Lodge Guest House
$  **Dumfries**

This four-star guesthouse's top feature is proprietor Aileen Abernathy. She greets you coming and going, gives you all the insider tips on the town, and cooks a tasty breakfast. The rooms are large for a guesthouse, the furnishings are new and tasteful, and you can get lost in the beds — all for a very reasonable price. The redbrick house and garden lawn make this one of the cutest guesthouses in Dumfries.

*31 Lovers Walk, just off Lockerbie Road, the main road from Glasgow.* ☎ *01387-253-922. Internet:* www.torbaylodge.co.uk. *E-mail:* enquires@torbay lodge.co.uk. *Rack rates: £46 ($67) double. MC, V.*

# Dining in the Borders

The Borders lacks the larger towns that attract many outstanding restaurants. As a result, most of the dining options are in hotels. Many of the accommodations in the preceding section have great dining; here are a few other standouts in the region.

## Auld Alliance

$$–$$$    **Kirkcudbright    Scottish/French**

This restaurant is well known in the area for its oversize queen scallops with Ayrshire bacon and Galloway cream. Other good calls include chicken pâté or salmon — caught in the nearby River Dee. Everything is unfailingly fresh and made with care. Interestingly, the family-owned establishment was built with stones from the city's old castle ruins.

*5 Castle St., across from McClellan Castle.* ☎ *01557-330-569. Reservations recommended. Main courses: £8.50–£15.50 ($12–$23). No credit cards. Open: Apr–Oct daily 6:30–9:30 p.m. Closed Nov–Mar.*

## Globe Inn

$    **Dumfries    Scottish**

A popular place to eat and drink, the Globe is probably most famous as a favorite watering hole of the national poet, Robert Burns. Don't just enjoy a libation; options on the great lunch menu, including roast beef, breaded trout with almonds, and veggie-friendly vegetable roast, are all tasty and well priced. Dessert is a must, as well; try rhubarb pie or the house specialty, hot custard. You'll be sitting just where the great poet himself once enjoyed a pint and a bite.

*56 High St.* ☎ *01387-252-335. Internet:* www.globeinndumfries.co.uk. *Main courses: £4.20–£5.40 ($6.10–$7.85). No credit cards. Open: Mon–Sat noon to 3 p.m.; reservations required for dinner.*

## Horse Shoe Inn

$$–$$$    **Eddleston    Scottish**

This fun little pub, restaurant, and hotel draws big crowds for its excellent cuisine. The country feel of the place matches the food — hearty steaks, salmon grilled on the bone, and steak-and-stout pies, accompanied by traditional Scottish sides such as oatcakes and fresh brown bread. The place can get busy on weekends, so be sure to call ahead.

*Eddleston, 4 miles north of Peebles on the A703 toward Edinburgh. ☎ 01721-73-0225. Reservations recommended. Main courses: £5–£15.50 ($7.25–$23). AE, DC, MC, V. Open: Daily 7:30 a.m.–3 p.m. and 6–10 p.m.*

# Exploring the Area

The Borders offers a rich array of attractions for the visitor. Three of the four famous **Borders abbeys,** Dryburgh, Jedburgh, and Melrose, are in this area (the fourth, Kelso, is practically rubble and not worth the trip). Whether you prefer literary spots such as Burns House and Sir Walter Scott's Abbotsford, historic castles and abbeys, or simply picturesque grazing land, plan your trip around the attractions you want to see. The following sights are listed alphabetically.

### Abbotsford House
**Roxburghshire**

Sir Walter Scott built this impressive home, where he lived for the last ten years of his life. It was once the site of a farmhouse, and the spot where Mary Queen of Scots officially abdicated her throne. Built in 1822, the house boasts all the architectural treats of its time — turrets, battlements, and gables. Inside is a collection of Scott memorabilia — his death mask, clothes, and some of his most treasured items, such as a gun once owned by Rob Roy, a sword belonging to the Earl of Montrose, armor, and a collection of more than 9,000 rare books. The lovely home bankrupted Scott, and he spent his last years writing to get out of debt. His descendants live there today.

*Hwy. B6360, off the A72, between Galashiels and Melrose. ☎ 01896-752-043. Admission: £4 ($5.80) adults, £2 ($2.90) children under 16. Open: June–Sept daily 9:30 a.m.–5 p.m.; Mar–May and Oct Mon–Sat 9:30 a.m.–5 p.m., Sun 2–5 p.m. Closed Nov–Feb. Time: 2 hours.*

### Burns House
**Dumfries**

Of the two museums devoted to Scotland's national poet, Robert Burns, this is the one he lived and died in. (The other is the Robert Burns Centre; see listing later in this section.) Burns was only 37 when he passed away in 1796 in this sandstone house, which is now on the pilgrim trail for the poet's fans. The house has been preserved to look as it did when he lived there, and contains such personal articles as Burns' gun and writing chair, as well as original manuscripts, letters, and printed editions. Incidentally, Burns died after his doctor recommended that he bathe in a local well. The Burns House guides have a key to the poet's sarcophagus at nearby St. Michael's Church and can take you over to see it.

*Burns Street, between Shakespeare and St. Michael's streets.* ☎ **01387-255-297.** *Admission: Free. Open: Apr–Sept Mon–Sat 10 a.m.–5 p.m., Sun 2–5 p.m.; Oct–Mar Tues–Sat 10 a.m.–1 p.m. and 2–5 p.m. Time: 2 hours.*

## Dryburgh Abbey
**Near St. Boswells**

It's no wonder Sir Walter Scott chose to spend eternity resting here. The abbey ruins, amid giant cedar trees, lies on the bonnie banks of the River Tweed. Of the four famed Borders abbeys, Dryburgh was the largest, arguably the most beautiful, and probably the most attacked by English troops. Its pleasant green surroundings make a lovely spot for a picnic lunch. Scott was interred at the side chapel in 1832.

*Off the A68, 8 miles southeast of Melrose on the B6404 near St. Boswells.* ☎ **01835-822-381.** *Admission: £2.80 ($4.10) adults, £2 ($2.90) seniors and students, £1 ($1.45) children under 16. Open: Apr–Sept daily 9:30 a.m.–6:30 p.m.; Oct–Mar Mon–Sat 9:30 a.m.–4 p.m., Sun 2–4:30 p.m. Time: 2 hours.*

## Floors Castle
**Near Kelso**

One of the few fully intact and occupied castles in the Borders, Floors is the largest inhabited castle in all of Scotland. Home to the Duke and Duchess of Roxburghe and their family, the castle overlooks the river. Your route will take you past countless paintings, tapestries, and furnishings from all over the continent. After viewing the impressive collection, venture outdoors and walk one of the nature trails through the woods or along the River Tweed. The walled garden also has new playground equipment for the kids. King James II was killed by "friendly fire" on the grounds when a cannon accidentally shot off; many years later, the castle was used in the film *Greystoke: The Legend of Tarzan, Lord of the Apes.*

*Hwy. A697, 2 miles northwest of Kelso.* ☎ **01573-223-333.** *E-mail:* estates@ floorscastle.com. *Internet:* www.floorscastle.com. *Admission: £5.50 ($8) adults, £4.75 ($6.90) seniors and students, £3.25 ($4.70) children under 16, £15 ($22) family. Open: Apr–Oct 10 a.m.–4:30 p.m. Closed Nov–Mar. Time: 3 hours.*

## Jedburgh Abbey
**Jedburgh**

Of the four Borders abbeys commissioned by King David I in the 1100s, Jedburgh is the most intact. The most complete parts of the Romanesque and Gothic ruins are the tower and large Catherine window. The impressive visitor center covers the full story of the monastery's long history, including the archaeological dig of a 12th-century underground "comb" on the grounds.

*Hwy. A68.* ☎ *01835-863-925. Admission: £3.30 ($4.80) adults, £2.50 ($3.65) seniors and students, £1.20 ($1.75) children under 16. Open: Apr–Sept 9:30 a.m.–6:30 p.m., Oct–Mar Mon–Sat 9:30 a.m.–4:30 p.m., Sun 2–4:30 p.m. Time: 2 hours.*

### *Mary Queen of Scots' House*
**Jedburgh**

As the story goes, Mary was on a trip in 1566 to visit her betrothed, the Earl of Bothwell, when she became ill with fever. She stayed in this house for a month and a half to recover. Now the building is a visitor center that tells the tragic story of her life and features magnificent tapestries, oil paintings, antique furniture, coats of arms, armor, and some of the Queen's possessions — all dating to the mid–1500s.

*Queen Street.* ☎ *01835-863-331. Admission: £2.50 ($3.65) adults, £1.50 ($2.20) seniors and students, free for children. Open: Mar–Nov Mon–Sat 10 a.m.–4:30 p.m., Sun 1–4 p.m. Closed Dec–Feb. Time: 2 hours.*

### *Melrose Abbey*
**Melrose**

Legend has it that the heart of Robert the Bruce is buried somewhere on the grounds of this abbey, which is in ruins. A 1996 archaeological dig uncovered a small conical lead casket along with a plaque saying that a heart had been found inside in 1921. The remains of one of the wealthiest abbeys in the country retain a regal beauty. The red sandstone Gothic alcoves and medieval statues and gargoyles (including one pig playing the bagpipes) make for an interesting walking tour. The abbey was built in the 1100s at the behest of Scotland's first king, David I (it's one of the famous Borders abbeys), and was later destroyed by the English and rebuilt by Robert the Bruce in the 14th century. None other than the famous novelist Sir Walter Scott led a 19th-century restoration project. Be sure to take the excellent free audio tour.

*Abbey Street, just off the main square, Market Square.* ☎ *01896-822-562. Admission: £2.80 ($4.10) adults, £1 ($1.45) children under 16. Open: Apr–Sept Mon–Sat 9:30 a.m.–6:30 p.m., Sun 2–6:30 p.m.; Oct–Mar Mon–Sat 9:30 a.m.– 4:30 p.m., Sun 2–4:30 p.m. Time: 90 min.*

### *The Old Bridge House Museum*
**Dumfries**

The 1660 sandstone house built into the Devorgilla Bridge is the oldest building in Dumfries. Today, it's a museum devoted to Scottish life of centuries past. A mid–19th-century kitchen, antique dental tools, and furniture from the last 400 years are among the interesting items on display. The Victorian bedroom and nursery have been impressively restored.

*Mill Road.* ☎ *01387-256904. Admission: Free. Open: Apr–Sept Mon–Sat 10 a.m.–5 p.m., Sun 2–5 p.m. Closed Oct–Mar. Time: 1 hour.*

### Robert Burns Centre
**Dumfries**

This excellent museum in the town's 18th-century watermill covers the poet's last years in the town. On display are many interesting items, such as a cast of Burns' skull, a scale model of 1790s Dumfries, and an eerie and a sentimental audiovisual presentation of the poet's life. It even shows the nasty well that was the downfall of the poet's health. Also on display are original documents and relics belonging to Burns. The center has a cafe and bookshop.

*Mill Road, on the west bank of the River Nith.* ☎ *01387-264-808. Admission: £1.50 ($2.20) adults, £.75 (90¢) seniors, students, and children under 16. Open: Apr–Sept Mon–Sat 10 a.m.–8 p.m., Sun 2–5 p.m.; Oct–Mar Tues–Sat 10 a.m.–1 p.m., Sun 2–5 p.m. Time: 1 hour.*

### Sweetheart Abbey
**New Abbey**

These impressive remains, which date to the 13th century, are worth the short jaunt from Dumfries. An unusual story lies behind the construction of the red sandstone structure. The Lady of Galloway, Devorgilla, founded the abbey in 1273 in memory of her husband. She carried his embalmed heart around with her for 22 years, and when she was buried here in front of the altar, the heart went with her — thus the name Sweetheart Abbey. Sweet, eh? Actually, it's a little frightening. But don't let that stop you from checking out these picturesque ruins.

*Hwy. A710, New Abbey village, 7 miles south of Dumfries.* ☎ *01387-850-397. Admission: £1.80 ($2.60) adults, £1.30 ($1.90) seniors and students, £.75 ($1.10) children under 16. Open: Apr–Sept Mon–Sat 9:30 a.m.–6:30 p.m., Sun 2–6:30 p.m.; Oct–Mar Mon–Wed and Sat 9:30 a.m.–4:30 p.m., Thurs 9:30 a.m.–1 p.m., Sun 2–4:30 p.m. Time: 1 hour.*

### Teddy Bear Museum
**Melrose**

Who doesn't like teddy bears? This must be the single largest repository for all things teddy. The exhibits cover the history and heritage of British teddy bears since the turn of the 20th century. From 100-year-old bruins to the latest designer bears, all the top celebs are here, such as Winnie the Pooh and Paddington. You can watch teddies being made in the downstairs shop and buy them in the store upstairs.

*The Wynd.* ☎ *01896-822-464. Admission: £1.50 ($2.20). Open: Summer Mon–Sat 10 a.m.–5 p.m., Sun noon to 5 p.m.; winter Fri–Sun 11 a.m.–4 p.m. Time: 1 hour.*

### Thirlestane Castle
**Lauder**

This 16th-century castle was built on the banks of the Leader River where an older fort once sat. The English built the castle during an oddly named period of fighting called the War of Rough Wooing. This home to the Earls and Duke of Lauderdale surrendered just two years after it was built, but fortunately it was not destroyed. The current castle boasts impressive ceiling work in the main rooms and a historic toy collection. Also housed here is the Border Country Life Museum, an exhibit on the history of the area dating to prehistoric times.

*Lauder, off Hwy. A68, 10 miles north of Melrose.* ☎ *01578-722-430. E-mail:* admin@thirlestanecastle.co.uk. *Internet:* www.thirlestanecastle.co.uk. *Admission: Castle and grounds: £5.30 ($7.70) adults, £3 ($4.35) children under 16, £13.50 ($19.60) family. Grounds only £1.50 ($2.20). Open: Apr–Oct 10:30 a.m.–4:15 p.m. Closed Nov–Mar. Time: 1 hour.*

### Threave Castle
**The River Dee**

One of the coolest things about this massive tower is how to get here. You ring a bell to call a boatman, who ferries you to the impressive ruins in a rowboat. The castle, on an island in the middle of the River Dee, was built by a former Lord of Galloway named Archibald the Grim (apparently for his battlefield disposition). His castle is a little grim, too; there's not much to see inside, but it is fun to walk about the artillery fortification around the base of the structure. Though sacked over the years, it was last used in the 19th century as a prison for Napoleonic War soldiers. Birders enjoy an opportunity to get up close and personal with the swallows that nest in the ruins. *Note:* Leave your best shoes at home; the path from the parking area to the boat pickup can get muddy when it rains.

*Three miles west of Castle Douglas on A75 (follow signs from the roundabout).* ☎ *0831-168-512. Admission: Ferry and entrance £2.20 ($3.20) adults, £1.60 ($2.30) seniors and students, £.75 ($1.10) children under 16. Open: Apr–Sept Mon–Sat 9:30 a.m.–6 p.m., Sun 2–6:30 p.m. Closed Oct–Mar. Time: 1 hour.*

### The Trimontium Exhibition
**Melrose**

Whose is the last voice you'd expect to hear in the Borders, talking about a lost Roman legion that once explored this area? If you said Leonard Nimoy's, you'd be right. It's here at this small, interesting museum devoted to Trimontium, the legendary three-peaked Roman fort and annexes of the ancient Tweed Valley. Once the Roman army's headquarters in Scotland, Trimontium now looms over Melrose. Among the collection of first- and second-century artifacts are a Roman skull and face-mask, tools, weapons, and pottery. The audiovisual presentation by Mr. Nimoy is interesting, too — sort of like a lost episode of "In Search Of."

*Ormiston Institute, Market Square.* ☎ ***01896-822-651.*** *Admission: £1.50 ($2.20) adults; £1 ($1.45) seniors, students, and children under 16; £4 ($5.80) family. Open: Daily 10:30 a.m.–1 p.m. and 2–4:30 p.m. Time: 1 hour.*

# Shopping in the Borders

None of the Borders towns has a major shopping district. The closest you'll get is High Street in the midsize town of Dumfries, which has a row of small craft shops and clothing stores. Dumfries does offer something special: free electric scooters and wheelchairs to shoppers with disabilities; just call ☎ **01345-090-904.**

Kelso is the home of **Pettigrews** (☎ **01573-224-234;** Internet: www. pettigrews.com), which produces a vast range of delicious gourmet Scottish food at its factory here. You can find Pettigrews products at the following stores in Kelso: Mayfield Garden Centre, Mitchells Deli (Bridge Street), Teviot Fish (Horsemarket), and Safeway (Roxburgh Street). Or simply order such homemade goodies as shortbread, meringues, preserves, chutneys, and mustards from the Pettigrews Web site. The premier item is lemon curd.

Following are a few great picks that are worth visiting even if they're off the beaten path.

✔ **Benny Gillies Bookshop,** 31-33 Victoria St., Kirkpatrick, Durham, on the B794 from the A75 from Castle Douglas (☎ **01556-502-531**). This old-world shop holds an awesome collection of rare and secondhand Scottish literature and reference books. Unique prints, hand-painted maps, lithographs, and engravings are also on sale, making for excellent, special souvenirs to frame and hang in your living room. Open: May through October Monday to Saturday from 10 a.m. to 5 p.m. and year-round by appointment; call ahead.

✔ **Broughton Gallery,** Broughton Place, Broughton (☎ **01899-830-234**). This fine little gallery has a good selection of Scottish items you won't find anywhere else. Most of the pieces are by living artists and include paintings, glassware, ceramics, jewelry, and even toys. The gallery will frame any paintings or prints you purchase. The shop is in an old tower house. Open: Late March through mid-October and mid-November to December 25, Thursday to Tuesday from 10:30 a.m. to 6 p.m.

✔ **Lochcarron of Scotland Cashmere and Wool Centre,** Nether Mill, Galashiels (☎ **01896-75-2091**). The biggest thing going on in this small Borders town is this shop and mini-museum of fine woolens and tweeds. The shop carries well-made items and, if you believe the owner, the world's largest range of woolen tartans and cashmere. If you feel like learning more about the manufacture of knitwear, you can take the mill tour (£2.50). Open: Year-round Monday to Saturday from 9 a.m. to 5 p.m., plus Sunday from noon to 5 p.m. from June to September. No tours on weekends.

✔ **Selkirk Glass,** on the A7, Selkirk (☎ **01750-20-954**). This factory shop and showroom is a popular place for bargain hunters — factory prices for most of the glassware are cheaper than you'll find at wholesale shops. You can watch skilled craftsmen making glassware in the factory, as well. Open: Monday to Saturday from 9 a.m. to 5 p.m., and Sunday from 11 a.m. to 5 p.m.; closed holidays.

✔ **Singing Potter,** 20 High St., Moffat (☎ **01683-20-793**). Gerard Lyons is both a potter and a singer — an opera singer, to be exact. His pottery studio is well known not just for its excellent crafts, but for Mr. Lyons' tendency to break into song. Both decorative and functional, the pieces range from candlestick holders to mugs. If the former Scottish Opera virtuoso isn't belting out a tune while you're there, you can always buy a tape of him singing. Open: Monday to Saturday from 9 a.m. to 5 p.m.

# Doing the Pub Crawl

Most of the pubs in the Borders region are local, nondescript corner watering holes. Every town has one or two, and whether it's unimpressive or nice, a pub is a great place to meet the locals on an evening out. Ask your hotel concierge or guesthouse host to recommend a pub near your accommodation, walking distance preferred.

The leader of the pack and worth special note is the **Globe Inn,** 56 High St., Dumfries (☎ **01387-252-335;** Internet: www.globeinndumfries. co.uk). Mentioned earlier in this chapter under "Dining in the Borders," the Globe draws tourists with its main claim to fame: This was the poet Robert Burns' favorite local pub. Head straight for the snug. You can see old prints of the inn back when the Burns drank here in the wood-paneled area before the dining room. You can even sit in Burns' favorite seat, just to the left of the fireplace. If she's not busy, Jane, the lovely barkeep, can take you upstairs to see where Burns and the daughter of the Globe Inn's owner shared a bed and conceived one of the poet's illegitimate children. Worth asking.

# Fast Facts: The Borders

### Area Code

The area codes for major towns: Jedburgh is **01835**; Kelso is **01573**; Melrose is **01896**; Selkirk is **01750**; Peebles is **01721**; Moffat is **01683**; Dumfries is **01387**; Castle Douglas is **01556**; Kirkcudbright is **01557**; Stranraer is **01776**. You need to dial the area code only if you are calling from outside the town you want to reach.

### Emergencies

Dial **999** for police, fire, or ambulance.

### Genealogy resources

**Dumfries & Galloway Family History Research Centre**, 9 Glasgow St., Dumfries (☎ 01387-248-093; E-mail: KylBet@ aol.com).

### Hospitals

**Dumfries & Galloway Royal Infirmary,** Bankend Road, Dumfries (☎ 01387-246-246).

### Information

Scottish tourism centers include: Murray's Green, **Jedburgh** (☎ 01835-863-435); Town House, The Square, **Kelso** (☎ 01573-223-464); and 64 Whitesands, **Dumfries** (☎ 01387-253-862). Summer offices: Abbey Street, **Melrose** (☎ 01896-822-555); Halliwell's House, **Selkirk** (☎ 01750-720-054); 23 High St., **Peebles** (☎ 01721-20-138); Churchgate, **Moffat** (☎ 01683-220-620); Abbey Street, **Castle Douglas** (☎ 01556-502-611); Harbour Square, **Kirkcudbright** (☎ 01557-330-494); Burns House, Harbour Street, **Stranraer** (☎ 01776-702-262). The **Scottish Borders Tourist Board,** has a location in Campbell House, Bankend Road, Dumfries (☎ 01387-20-555 or 01387-25-0434; Internet: www. scot-hborders.co.uk/tourism/).

### Internet Access

**Dumfries Internet Centre**, 26/28 Brewery St., next to the Whitesands, Dumfries (☎ 01387-259-400; E-mail: ditc@ndirect.co.uk; Internet: www.t2lg.net). Open: Mon–Fri 9 a.m.–5 p.m., Sat 10 a.m.–5 p.m. Cost: £2 ($2.90) per 30 minutes.

### Mail

The main post office in Dumfries is at 34 St. Michael St. (☎ 01387-253-415).

# Chapter 13

# Argyll and the Islands

. . . . . . . . . . . . . . . . . . . . . . . . . . . . . . . . . . . . . . . . . . . . .

*In This Chapter*

▶ Getting to Argyll and out to the islands

▶ Seeking out the best places to stay and eat

▶ Discovering outdoor fun and visiting the top castles, distilleries, and museums

▶ Shopping as you island hop

▶ Finding the best pubs

. . . . . . . . . . . . . . . . . . . . . . . . . . . . . . . . . . . . . . . . . . . . .

he Argyll and the Islands region stretches from Glasgow northwest
to the Hebridean Islands. Many visitors stop in the area briefly on
their way to parts farther north, but you'll find enough to see and do
to justify spending a few days. Here you'll drive and island hop amid
picture-postcard scenery and stellar attractions.

## Orienting Yourself to Argyll and the Islands

**Inveraray,** centrally located in the Argyll region, is a charming port
town with a nice castle and a couple of decent accommodation
options. Even if you don't stay overnight, it's a good place to stop for
lunch or tea or to recharge your batteries. The largest town in this
chapter, **Oban** (pronounced "O-bin"), is the gateway to the northern
Hebridean Islands and the flagship city in this region. The bustling
harbor town — where the Highlands meet the Islands — offers plenty of
dining and shopping options and has no shortage of B&Bs. A rather
Roman-looking coliseum — the odd pride and joy of this midsize town —
marks the cityscape.

Of the southern islands covered in this chapter, **Arran** is the largest and
most worth your time. Often called "Scotland in miniature," the island
offers diverse scenery, fine hiking, and lovely views. The smaller islands
of **Jura, Gigha** (pronounced "*gee*-a," with a hard "g"), and **Islay** (pronounced "*eye*-lay") are largely rural — great if you're a bird fancier —
devoid of big attractions, and off the beaten tourist track. If you have
the time to island hop, you should see these unspoiled places, as well.

The equally laid-back **Kintyre Peninsula** makes a nice stop on the way to the islands and has a few good attractions to justify a jaunt along its 40-mile length.

Take a half-day to cover each of the two largest attractions in this chapter, the outdoor hot spots **Loch Lomond** and **Argyll Forest Park.**

# Getting There

You can travel on trains and buses throughout the Argyll region, but you'll find they offer limited access to many of the area's attractions. Your best option is to drive. The islands are accessible by ferry, and you'll want to take a car onto Arran so that you can drive when you get there.

- **By plane: British Airways Express** (☎ 0345-222-111) flies from Glasgow to Machrihanish airport on the Kintyre Peninsula and to the Isle of Islay. **Loganair** (☎ 0141-889-1111) flies to Campbeltown, also on the Kintyre Peninsula.

- **By ferry: Caledonian MacBrayne** (☎ 08705-650-000; fax: 01475-635-235; E-mail: reservations@calmac.co.uk; Internet: www.calmac.co.uk) offices in this region include Brodick (☎ **01770-302-166**; fax: 01770-302-618), Coll (☎ **01879-230-347**; fax: 01879-230-447), Colonsay (☎ **01951-200-308**; fax: 01951-200-217), Dunoon (☎ **01369-706-491**; fax: 01369-706-491), Port Ellen (☎ **01496-302-209**; fax: 01496-302-557), Tiree (☎ **01879-220-337**), and Oban (☎ **01631-566-688**; fax: 01631-566-588). Ferries to Arran go from Ardrossan or Rothesay into Brodick or (in the summer only) Claonaig into Lochranza. Ferries to Islay go from West Tarbert to Port Askaig. To get to Jura, you must take a **Western Ferry** (☎ **01496-840-681**) from Islay's Port Askaig to Feolin. To get to Gigha, a private ferry (☎ **01583-505-251**) connects the town of Tayinloan on the Kintyre Peninsula to Ardminish on the island.

- **By car:** From Glasgow, take the A82 north to Loch Lomond and Tarbet. From Tarbet, take the A83 to Inveraray and down the Kintyre Peninsula. From the A83, pick up the A816 in Lochgilphead to go through the Kilmartin Valley and on to Oban. The A841 loops around Arran. If you want to rent a car on Arran, call **A.C. Hendry** (☎ **01770-302-835**) in Brodick.

- **By train: West Highlands Lines** (☎ 0345-484-950) travels only to Oban from Glasgow. To get to the Loch Lomond town of Tarbet, take **ScotRail** (☎ 0845-748-4950; www.scotrail.co.uk). An electric train (☎ 0345-484-950) from Glasgow runs to Ardrossan, where you catch the ferry to Arran.

- **By bus:** From Glasgow, **Citylink** (☎ 0141-332-7133) serves Oban, **National Express** (☎ 0990-808-080) travels to Inveraray, and **Western S.M.T.** (☎ 0141-226-4826) coaches go to the Kintyre Peninsula.

## Argyll and the Islands

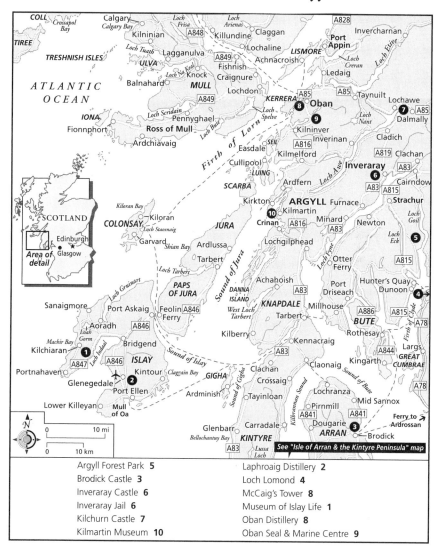

| | |
|---|---|
| Argyll Forest Park **5** | Laphroaig Distillery **2** |
| Brodick Castle **3** | Loch Lomond **4** |
| Inveraray Castle **6** | McCaig's Tower **8** |
| Inveraray Jail **6** | Museum of Islay Life **1** |
| Kilchurn Castle **7** | Oban Distillery **8** |
| Kilmartin Museum **10** | Oban Seal & Marine Centre **9** |

# Knowing Where to Stay in Argyll

You may want to stay on the mainland in Inveraray or Oban for convenience's sake, so I include the top options in those towns. Also in this section are a few other choice accommodations on the islands, in case you
decide to spend the night out there — or are forced to because you've
missed the last ferry back. The following picks reflect a wide range of
prices, although all are good deals for what you get. Several of these
lodging options are also good dining picks — particularly useful when
you're stuck on an island or in a town with few other dining options.

### Alexandra Hotel
#### $$ Oban

On the northern end of the Oban seafront, this hotel affords views of the town and the water throughout. This stately accommodation was once one of the largest buildings in town. Refurbished and modernized, the rooms are fine and simply furnished. If you're waiting out a bit of bad weather, you can play a little table tennis or snooker, or simply paddle around in the large heated indoor pool. The friendly staff will make your stay very comfortable, and there is 24-hour room service. The hotel has recently added accommodations for travelers with disabilities.

*North Pier, Oban.* ☎ *01631-562-381. Fax: 01631-564-497. Rack rates: £37.50–£70 ($43–$102) double. AE, DC, MC, V.*

### The Argyll Hotel
#### $$ Inveraray

This waterfront hotel overlooking the picturesque Inveraray harbor is a pretty, white-stone building with green trim. Inside you'll find a lovely atrium sitting room, a cozy formal dining area, and the beautiful wood-and-gilt Argyll Bar. Each room is nicely put together, with blond wood furniture and bright sheets and curtains. If you have the option, book a room with a view of Loch Fyne. Originally built in 1750 to accommodate guests of nearby Inveraray Castle, the Argyll is still putting up the castle's many visitors.

*Front Street, Inveraray.* ☎ *01499-30-2466. Fax: 01499-30-2389. E-mail:* reception@ the-argyll-hotel.co.uk. *Internet:* www.the-argyll-hotel.co.uk. *Rack rates: £86 ($94) double. AE, DC, MC, V.*

### Barcaldine House
#### $$$ Barcaldine

Just 20 minutes north of Oban, on a huge estate complete with forest walks (for avid walkers and birders), this mansion is a primo choice for the area. The rooms are huge, as are the bathtubs, and the common rooms are massive. My favorite, the warm and inviting billiards room, is full of games if you don't fancy pool. The hotel also has adorable self-catering cottages for longer stays. The place is under new ownership, and one of the excellent caretakers is a "Taste of Scotland" commended chef, so meals are simply amazing. I thoroughly enjoyed my vegetarian breakfast, complete with veggie sausages. And for all this baronial living, the price is unbeatable.

*Just off the A828 between Oban and Glancoe.* ☎ *01631-720-219. E-mail:* barcaldine@breathe.co.uk. *Internet:* www.countrymansions.com. *Rack rates: £90–£130 ($131–$189) double. MC, V.*

## The Isle of Arran and the Kintyre Peninsula

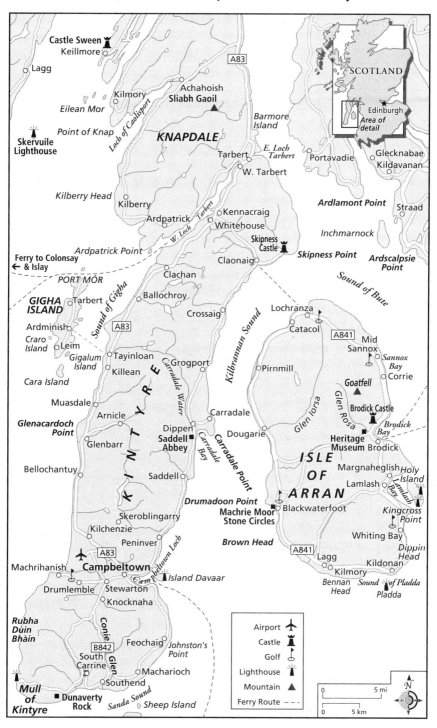

Castle Sween
Keillmore
Lagg
Kilmory
Eilean Mor
Achahoish
Sliabh Gaoil
A83
SCOTLAND
Edinburgh
Area of detail
Barmore Island
Point of Knap
Skervuile Lighthouse
KNAPDALE
E. Loch Tarbert
Tarbert
W. Tarbert
Portavadie
Glecknabae
Kildavanan
Kilberry Head
Kilberry
Ardpatrick
Kennacraig
Whitehouse
Ardlamont Point
Straad
Inchmarnock
Ardpatrick Point
Ferry to Colonsay
← & Islay
PORT MÒR
Skipness Castle
Claonaig
Skipness Point
Ardscalpsie Point
Clachan
Sound of Bute
GIGHA ISLAND
Tarbert
Ballochroy
A83
Crossaig
Lochranza
Catacol
A841
Mid Sannox
Sannox Bay
Ardminish
Craro Island
Leim
Gigalum Island
Tayinloan
Killean
Grogport
Pirnmill
Corrie
Cara Island
Muasdale
Arnicle
Carradale
Goatfell
Glen Rosa
Brodick Castle
Brodick Bay
Glenacardoch Point
Glenbarr
Dippen
Saddell Abbey
Dougarie
Glen Iorsa
Heritage Museum
Brodick
Bellochantuy
Saddell
ISLE OF ARRAN
Margnaheglish
Holy Island
Lamlash
Lamlash Bay
Drumadoon Point
Skeroblingarry
Kilchenzie
Peninver
Machrie Moor Stone Circles
Blackwaterfoot
Kingcross Point
Brown Head
Whiting Bay
A841
Dippin Head
Machrihanish
A83
Campbeltown
Island Davaar
Lagg
Kilmory
Kildonan
Drumlemble
Stewarton
Knocknaha
Bennan Head
Sound of Pladda
Pladda
Rubha Dùin Bhàin
Conie Glen
B842
Feochaig
Johnston's Point
South Carrine
Macharioch
Mull of Kintyre
Southend
Dunaverty Rock
Sanda Sound
Sheep Island

| | |
|---|---|
| Airport | ✈ |
| Castle | ♜ |
| Golf | ⛳ |
| Lighthouse | ⌁ |
| Mountain | ▲ |
| Ferry Route | --- |

0    5 mi
0    5 km
N

### Columba Hotel
#### $$ Oban

Sitting at the water's edge in the center of Oban, the Columba offers an excellent location if you want to shop and eat out — but you can also just stay in to enjoy the view. The decor of the Victorian-style hotel is contemporary, in contrast to the old redbrick building. Staff members are as eager to help with trip planning and restaurant options as tourist office employees. The Columba does not have a pool or steam room of its own, but guests have free use of the facilities of its sister hotel, the Alexandra, just a short walk along the water. John McCaig, who built the town's famous landmark, McCaig's Tower, also built the Columba.

*North Pier, Oban.* ☎ *01631-562-183. Fax: 01631-564-683. Rack rates: £75–£95 ($109–$131) double. AE, MC, V.*

### Columba Hotel
#### $$ Tarbert

In the pretty little port village of Tarbert, gateway to the Kintyre Peninsula, this handsome Victorian hotel sits above Loch Fyne. The décor is rustic, evoking the feel that you have stepped back in time to the American Old West. The huge rooms are full of antique furniture and overlook the pretty waters. You may even see the occasional seal out your window. The reading room is lovely for a spot of tea, and the fireplace in the pub is the perfect spot to relax with a pint. All that said, the real highlight is the food. Book the dinner and B&B package, because the meals are probably the best in town and you don't want to limit your dining pleasure to the excellent breakfast.

*East Pier Road, Tarbert, on the A83.* ☎ *01880-820-808. E-mail:* info@columba hotel.com. *Internet:* www.columbahotel.com. *Rack rates: £75.90–£91.90 ($110–$133) double. AE, MC, V.*

### The George Hotel
#### $ Inveraray

Treat yourself to a great night's rest and relaxation in this old stone house, which has been refurbished with the latest in modern conveniences. The rooms are large and finely decorated; some still have the original stone walls and wooden beams. The George has been putting up happy patrons since 1775 and has been run by the same family for the last 135 years.

*Main Street, Inveraray.* ☎ *01499-30-2111. Fax: 01499-30-2098. Rack rates: £25–£32.50 ($36–$47) double. AE, DC, MC, V.*

*Oban*

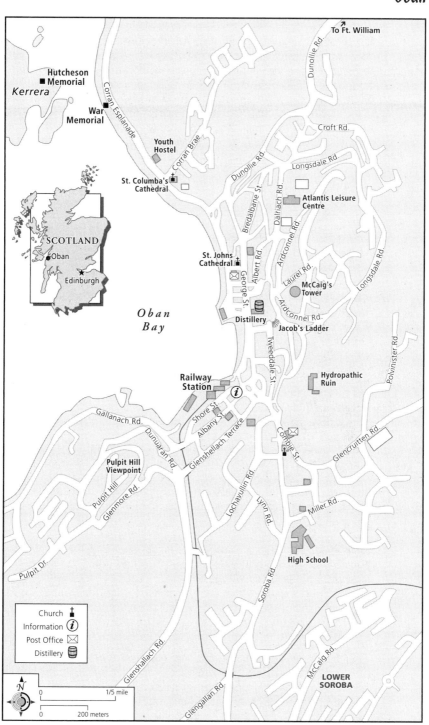

Oban Bay

Kerrera

Hutcheson Memorial

War Memorial

Corran Esplanade

Corran Brae

Youth Hostel

St. Columba's Cathedral

SCOTLAND

Oban

Edinburgh

To Ft. William

Dunollie Rd.

Croft Rd.

Longsdale Rd.

Dunollie Rd.

Bredalbane St.

Dalriach Rd.

Atlantis Leisure Centre

Ardconnel Rd.

Longsdale Rd.

St. Johns Cathedral

Albert Rd.

George St.

Laurel Rd.

McCaig's Tower

Distillery

Ardconnel Rd.

Jacob's Ladder

Tweeddale St.

Polvinister Rd.

Railway Station

Shore St.

Albany St.

Gallanach Rd.

Dunuaran Rd.

Glenshellach Terrace

Hydropathic Ruin

Combie St.

Glencruitten Rd.

Pulpit Hill Viewpoint

Pulpit Hill

Glenmore Rd.

Lochavullin Rd.

Lynn Rd.

Miller Rd.

Pulpit Dr.

Soroba Rd.

High School

Glenshallach Rd.

Glengallan Rd.

McCaig Rd.

LOWER SOROBA

Church

Information

Post Office

Distillery

N

0        1/5 mile

0        200 meters

### Gigha Hotel
**$$–$$$ Isle of Gigha**

If you plan to spend a night on the isle of Gigha, this may be your only real choice, and it's not a bad one. Close to the ferry terminal and overlooking Kintyre, the beautiful whitewashed stone building is an oasis of hospitality and comfort. Sit back, relax, and watch the sunset — this is what island life is all about. The food alone, made with fresh local produce, is worth the trip. The hotel contains the only pub on the island.

*Ardminish, Isle of Gigha.* ☎ *01583-505-254. Rack rates: £90–£110 ($131–$160) double. MC, V.*

### Greencourt Guest House
**$$ Oban**

Of the dozens of B&Bs and guesthouses in Oban, this one stands out for its extra warm reception and the lovely view over the town's bowling green. Mr. and Mrs. Garvins have owned the place for just a few years, but they are already experts on hospitality and comfort. Nonsmokers will appreciate the nonsmoking policy. Unlike many other homes along the winding streets of Oban, Greencourt has its own parking area.

*Benvoulin Lane, Oban.* ☎ *01631-56-3987. Fax: 01631-57-1276. E-mail:* stay@ greencourt-oban.fsnet.co.uk. *Internet:* www.greencourt-oban. fsnet.co.uk. *Rack rates: £44–£58 ($30–$38) double. No credit cards.*

### Harbour Inn
**$$ Isle of Islay**

The views of the bay are among the highlights of this little inn. Each of the four rooms is impeccably decorated — the floral Victorian Garden, the nautical Captain's Table, the plaid-clad Tartan room, and the Seaside, my favorite. The hotel pub, a wonderful room with stone walls and a fireplace, is the center of Islay social life, so be sure to pop in for some local color and a well-pulled pint.

*Main Street, The Square, Bowmore, Islay.* ☎ *01496-810-330. Fax: 01496-810-990. E-mail:* harbour@harbour-inn.com. *Internet:* www.harbour-inn.com. *Rack rates: £75 ($109) double. AE, MC, V.*

### Jura Hotel
**$$ Isle of Jura**

This basic, family-run hotel is the top accommodation on the island of Jura. The handsome gray building overlooks Small Isles Bay; be sure to ask for a room at the front. The hotel has the best pub on the island — and it's the *only* hotel on the island. Check out the Antlers Tearoom for high tea.

*Craighouse, near Feolin, Jura.* ☎ **01496-820-243.** *Fax: 01496-820-249. E-mail:* jura hotel@aol.com. *Internet:* http://stay.at/jurahotel/. *Rack rates: £70 ($102) double. AE, DC, MC, V.*

### Kilmichael Hotel
**$$$   Isle of Arran**

This small country-house hotel is the best accommodation on the island. The 300-year-old building is the oldest on Arran. The lovely, spacious rooms hold antique wood furniture, fresh-cut flowers, and pleasant pastel upholstery and drapes. The sitting room, formerly a chapel, has an impressive stained-glass window; you'll enjoy sitting by one of the fireplaces on a blustery day. The hotel also has an interesting collection of Japanese ornaments — but the tasty cuisine in the dining room is traditional Scottish.

*Brodick, Arran, on a private road off the main road, the A841.* ☎ **01770-302-219.** *Fax: 01770-302-068. E-mail:* enquiries@kilmichael.com. *Rack rates: £120–£160 ($174–$232) double. MC, V.*

### Kinloch Hotel
**$$   Isle of Arran**

You'll never be bored at the family-owned Kinloch. It offers a large indoor heated pool, sauna, squash court, and snooker. The pretty building is Victorian in design, and each simply decorated room holds an intercom in case you need to reach the staff. Each side of the hotel affords a nice view: The back overlooks the hotel gardens, and the front overlooks the sea.

*Blackwaterfoot, Arran, on the A841.* ☎ **01770-860-444.** *Fax: 01770-860-447. E-mail:* mail@kinloch-arran.com. *Internet:* www.kinloch-arran.com. *Rack rates: £78.40–£98 ($114–$142) double. AE, DC, MC, V.*

### Loch Fyne Hotel
**$   Inveraray**

Just north of town, this old stone house perches on a lovely spot over the loch. It offers big rooms, a friendly desk staff, and a large pool and steam room. The last time I visited, the pool was full of kids. The lovely rooms aren't fancy, but little couches and lovely views of the water make for a relaxing time between trips to the Jacuzzi or sauna. The food in the restaurant is quite good, and the price is excellent.

*On the A83, just above the center of Inveraray.* ☎ **01499-302-148.** *Fax: 01499-302-348. Rack rates: £35–£45 ($51–$65) double. AE, DC, MC, V.*

### Manor House
$$$   Oban

The Duke of Argyll once owned the granite Manor House, on the coast road. Despite its stony, formal exterior, the house is warm and inviting inside. The tasteful rooms have excellent views of Oban Bay, fine antiques, and floral linens. From the landing pad outside, the lighthouse employees take off every day by helicopter (though not during sleeping hours). The Manor House is well known for its excellent cuisine, so be sure to check the menu before you decide to eat in town.

*Gallanach Road, beyond the ferry, along the water.* ☎ **01631-562-087.** *Fax: 01631-563-053. E-mail:* manorhouseoban@aol.com. *Internet:* www.manorhouse oban.com. *Rack rates: £104–£144 ($151–$209) double. AE, MC, V.*

### Minard Castle
$$   Minard

You'll find this mansion on Loch Fyne to be the ideal spot for recharging your batteries — provided you don't miss the sign off the main road a few miles north of Inveraray pointing you down the long drive to the castle. The stately, austere interior belies the light and airy accommodations. You can stroll the castle grounds; take a walk through the garden or down by the lake. Hosts Reinold and Marion are pleasing and helpful. The outstanding breakfasts provide all the fuel you'll need for a day of sightseeing. The castle has only a few guest rooms, so be sure to book ahead.

*Minard, between Lochgilphead and Inveraray off the A83.* ☎ **01546-88-6272.** *Internet:* www.oas.co.uk/ukcottages/minardcastle/. *Rack rates: £80 ($116) double. MC, V.*

### Port Askaig Hotel
$$   Isle of Islay

The interior of this 18th-century house is quite modern and nicely decorated, with rooms that aren't fancy but are still fine. The hospitality is typical for the island: friendly and accommodating. The grounds extend out to the Sound of Islay; you can take a stroll or request a room with a sea view. The place is within walking distance of the ferry terminal. I recommend that you eat dinner here; the produce is home grown. The hotel's Snug Bar is not a place for kids — it features what some may consider "erotic" art on the walls.

*Port Askaig, Islay, on the A846.* ☎ **01496-840-245.** *Fax: 01496-840-295. Rack rates: £45–£72 ($65–$104) double. No credit cards.*

# Dining in Argyll and the Islands

In addition to hotel dining rooms, which are _de rigueur_ in this part of the country, here are several other options that are sure to tickle the taste buds.

### Anchorage Restaurant

$$–$$$   **Kintyre Peninsula**   **Mediterranean/Seafood**

It's no surprise to find that the Anchorage has won many awards and that people come from miles around to dine here: The Mediterranean-themed seafood restaurant has the freshest cuisine. The traditional stone building was once a customhouse, which explains its proximity to the water. The house specialties include monkfish and scallops, but everything is fresh from the water, and the excellent selection of white wines perfectly complements each meal.

_Harbour Street, Quayside, Tarbert._ ☎ **01880-820-881.** _Reservations recommended. Main courses: £6.50–£14.95 ($9.45–$22). MC, V. Open: Daily 7–10 p.m._

### Café na Lusan

$   **Oban**   **Vegetarian**

You get a double helping here: good food and good music. The fresh, organic, and local dishes include yummy staples like falafel and hummus, veggie burgers, and desserts, as well as organic wine and fair-trade coffee. The cafe also has its own independent record label and places its own cool, hip soundtrack. You can also check your e-mail here. It's a lovely place to spend the afternoon.

_9 Craigard Rd._ ☎ **01631-567-268.** _E-mail:_ cafenalusan@hotmail.com. _Internet:_ www.cafenalusan.com. _Reservations not accepted. Main courses: £2.30–£7.95 ($3.35–$12). Open: Tues–Thurs 11 a.m.–8 p.m., Fri–Sat 11 a.m.–10 p.m., Sun noon to 7 p.m._

### The Cairn

$$–$$$   **Kilmartin**   **Modern Scottish**

You'll find this unassuming cafe in an 18th-century farmhouse across from the Kilmartin Museum. The dining room, with a small bar, is a cozy spot for good gourmet meals. Follow an imaginative starter, such as baked banana with bacon and curry mayo, with a top-notch entree — perhaps duck breast on fresh spinach and mushrooms, or local Loch Fyne haddock. It may be on the pricey side, but you get what you pay for.

*Main Road.* ☎ *01546-510-254. Reservations not accepted. Main courses: £5.95–£13.95 ($8.65–$20). AE, DC, MC, V. Open: Wed–Mon noon to 3 p.m. and 6:30 p.m. to closing.*

### Gallery Restaurant
$$–$$$    Oban    Modern Scottish

You can't miss this colorful green-trimmed yellow building on the main road as you enter Oban. The table and chairs are rather IKEA-looking, but the ordinary decor contrasts with the gourmet takes on classic Scottish dishes. Using only fresh local produce and game, the Gallery turns traditional foods into something extraordinary. Don't miss starters such as seared pigeon breast and warm duck confit. The main dishes are all quite nice, particularly roast Crianlarich venison loin and Aberdeen Angus sirloin, both cooked to perfection.

*Gibraltar Street.* ☎ *01631-564-641. Reservations accepted. Main courses: £8.25–£12.25 ($12–$18). MC, V. Open: Summer daily 9:30 a.m.–4 p.m. and 6–9:30 p.m. Winter daily 9:30 a.m.–4 p.m.*

### The George
$$    Inveraray    Traditional Scottish

This wonderful restaurant in a fine hotel feels (and is) a couple of centuries old, with its stone floors and peat fires. The chef serves only authentic Scottish cuisine, such as steak pies and the ploughman's platter, along with fresh local produce. It's not formal, but it's definitely as nice a place as you'll find in Inveraray. Save a little room for a pint or two at the excellent George Bar — a warming pub that's good for chatting the night away in the snugs or playing a bit of billiards.

*In the George Hotel, Main Street East.* ☎ *01499-30-2111. Reservations not required. Main courses: £5.50–£9.75 ($12–$14). AE, DC, MC, V. Open: Daily 11 a.m.–9:30 p.m.*

### Loch Fyne Oyster Bar
$$–$$$    Cairndow    Seafood

Locals from all over rave about this popular place for the best seafood you'll find in the area. Located just northeast of Inveraray, the converted farm is easy to spot on the main road. The wooden booths near the big glass windows overlook the loch — the very waters from which your dinner was likely caught. An all-day kipper breakfast is popular, and if you have to wait to be seated, be sure to browse the nice gift shop next door.

*At the head of Loch Fyne on the A83, Clachan.* ☎ *01499-60-0264 or 01499-60-0217. Reservations recommended. Main courses: £4.95–£14.95 ($7.20–$22). AE, DC, MC, V. Open: Daily 9 a.m.–10 p.m.*

### McTavish's Kitchen
**$–$$$    Oban    Traditional Scottish/Seafood**

McTavish's attracts a good bit of local publicity, which makes it a popular place for tourists. Yes, it is by the water, and yes, it does have live Scottish dancing and music, but that's as good as it gets, and it's not even that great. The food, heavy on seafood and traditional Scottish dishes, is rather dull and cooked with little enthusiasm, and the place is usually packed with tourists — which only overextends the waitstaff. Children won't mind the wait, however: The paper to color on and bagpipes are sure to distract them. Unless you don't mind the cheese and a load of other tourists, you may want to shy away from McTavish's.

*34 George St. ☎ **01631-56-3064**. E-mail:* oban@mctavishs.com. *Internet:* www.lochaber.almac.co.uk/mctavishs. *Reservations recommended. Main courses: £7.35–£14.75 ($11–$21). Show: £1.75 ($2.55) adults, £1 ($1.45) children if you dine during show hours. MC, V. Open: Daily noon to 2 p.m. and 6–10 p.m. Show: May–Sept daily 8:30–10:30 p.m.*

# Exploring the Area

When it comes to island hopping, the islands become the attractions. But this area also has some particularly great stops worth visiting as you make your way through.

### Argyll Forest Park
**Southern Highlands**

Set in the middle of the region, this 60,000-acre outdoor attraction is worth taking the time to visit. It's a great place to stretch your legs. From lowland forest trails to the lofty peaks of the "Arrochar Alps," the terrain offers options for all skill levels and enough wildlife to please the kids and animal lovers among you. The park is home to acres of wildflowers, violets, bluebells, primroses, woodland birds, and even seals, otters, and other sea life in the lochs. You can explore on your own or take a seasonal ranger-led walk or safari. For park information and trail maps, visit the tourist center in Dunoon or contact the park office in Arrochar.

*Near Arrochar. ☎ **01369-840-666**. Arrochar Tourist Information Center. 7 Alexandra Park, Dunoon. ☎ **01369-703-785**. Admission: Free. Open: Daily dawn to dusk. Time: 2–5 hours.*

### Brodick Castle
**Isle of Arran**

You'll want to bring the camera to this impressive red sandstone castle, which once belonged to the Dukes of Hamilton. It sits by the bay and mountains, surrounded by acres of park and gardens. The castle occupies the site of an old Viking fortress, and the oldest parts of the building date to the 13th century. The stately rooms hold an impressive collection of silver, porcelain, paintings, and sports trophies. Each room has both expert guides (people) and fun "junior guides" (information sheets) to make the castle interesting for easily bored youths. Give yourself time to see the award-winning walled woodland gardens of exotic and sweet-smelling flowers. The castle also has a fun playground.

*Brodick, Isle of Arran, 1 mile north of the pier. ☎ 01770-302-202. Admission: £7 ($10) adults; £5.30 ($7.70) seniors, students, and children under 16. Open: Castle: Daily Apr–June and Sept–Oct 11 a.m.–4:30 p.m., July–Aug 11 a.m.–5 p.m. Gardens: Daily Apr–Oct dawn to sunset. Closed Nov–Mar. Time: 2 hours.*

### Inveraray Castle
**Inveraray**

This picture-perfect castle with fairy-tale spires and riveted roofs sits on lovely grounds near Loch Fyne. From the impressive Armoury Hall to the fine collection of French tapestries and furniture, the building holds much to marvel over. The castle and its collection belong to the clan Campbell, and the castle was once the home of the Duke and Duchess of Argyll. The grounds are lovely, particularly in the fall when the leaves change color. Check out the small Combined Operations Museum in the stables, which covers the history of Inveraray's role in preparing troops for the D-Day invasion.

*Inveraray. ☎ 01499-30-2203. E-mail: enquires@inveraray-castle.com. Internet: www.inveraray-castle.com. Admission: £5.50 ($8) adults, £4.50 ($6.55) seniors and students, £3.50 ($5.10) children under 16, £14 ($20) family (2 adults, 2 kids). Open: Apr–June, Sept–Oct Mon–Thurs, Sat 10 a.m.–1 p.m. and 2–5:45 p.m., Sun 1–5:45 p.m., closed Fri; July–Aug Mon–Sat 10 a.m.–5:45 p.m., Sun 1–5:45 p.m. Time: 2 hours.*

### Inveraray Jail
**Inveraray**

This somewhat eerie but fun museum takes on the history of Scottish crime and punishment. Wax figures and recorded voices re-create life in the old jail cells. A historic courtroom is straight out of the 1820s; from there you get a glimpse of torture and death — hot-iron branding and public whipping to (gulp) "ear nailing." The murderers and madmen aren't real, but little ones may find the prison section more frightening than fun.

*Church Square, Inveraray. ☎ 01499-302-381. E-mail: inveraryjail@btclick. com. Admission: £4.95 ($7.20) adults, £3.20 ($4.65) seniors and students, £2.50 ($3.65) children under 16, £13.65 ($20) family. Open: Daily Apr–Oct 9:30 a.m.–6 p.m., Nov–Mar 10 a.m.–5 p.m. Time: 1 hour.*

## Kilchurn Castle
**Loch Awe**

These stunning ruins dating to the 16th century are as much fun to get to as they are to explore — you can either walk up a steep path from the car park or hop on the steamboat ferry for the short ride from the Loch Awe pier. The castle, on the head of Loch Awe, has great views and is a popular place to take pictures, so don't leave the Nikon in the car. Built by Sir Colin Campbell, Kilchurn was one of the strongholds of this area, once controlled by Clan Campbell.

*Car park: Hwy. A85 east of Loch Awe. Ferry:* ☎ *01838-200-440. Admission: Free. Ferry: £4 ($5.80) adults, £3 ($4.35) children under 16. Open: Daily Apr–Nov dawn to dusk; call ahead at beginning and end of season. Closed Dec–Mar. Time: 2 hours.*

## Kilmartin House Museum
**Kilmartin**

Scotland traces its early civilizations to this area, and the Kilmartin House Museum beautifully preserves that history and culture. You'll discover several items of interest in this scattered museum, from a replica of St. Columba's boat to a workshop where you can see old skills in action. A great audiovisual presentation on the significance and sights of the Kilmartin Valley is interesting and artistically done, and the museum is full of fine artifacts, from bells to brooches, from the early settlements of the area. As you walk through, you'll hear snippets of ancient Scottish music. This historically significant valley was where travelers coming from Ireland first landed and settled on Scottish soil. The museum cafe offers regional food, traditional Scottish drinks, and coffee.

*Hwy. A816 between Lochgilphead and Oban, Kilmartin, Argyll.* ☎ *01546-51-0278. Internet:* www.kilmartin.org. *Admission: £4.50 ($6.55) adults, £3.50 ($5.10) seniors and students, £1.50 ($2.20) children under 16, £10 ($15) family. Open: Daily 10 a.m.–5:30 p.m. Time: 2 hours.*

## Laphroaig Distillery
**Port Ellen**

This is the home of a distinctive whisky that most people either love or loathe. Personally, I love it. It has a peaty flavor, with a whiff of sea air (some say they can even taste a little seaweed). Even if you aren't a fan of the whisky, this is a great distillery to visit. You'll have to make an appointment for a tour, but it's worth the phone call, because the guides are excellent — full of good anecdotes and information. The free tour includes a complimentary dram of whisky. You can also join the "Friend" program and own a piece of the distillery grounds.

*Near Port Ellen, on the road to Ardbeg.* ☎ *01496-302-418. Admission: Free. Open: By appointment. Time: 90 minutes.*

### Loch Lomond

One of the largest and prettiest lakes in Scotland, Loch Lomond is known worldwide for the song "The Bonnie Banks o' Loch Lomond," with its famous verse, "Ye'll take the high road, and I'll take the low road, and I'll be in Scotland before ye," a lament for love lost on "bonnie, bonnie Loch Lomond."

You'll drive by the 23-mile-long lake, dotted with small islands, as you make your way from Glasgow to Inveraray and Oban. You should take the time to see a little more than just the scenery — although the scenery is admittedly great. On the southern end of the lake are the small town of Balloch and the 200-acre Balloch Castle Country Park, with woods and gardens to explore and a visitor center with exhibits on the history of the lake.

The best way to see Loch Lomond is by cruise ship. The best are Sweeney's Cruises' *Silver Marlin*, which leaves from Balloch, and Cruise Loch Lomond, from the northern Loch Lomond town of Tarbet. Both cruises offer excellent live commentary. The *Silver Marlin* goes to the wooded island of Inshmurrin; Cruise Loch Lomond includes a visit to Rob Roy MacGregor's cave, where both Rob Roy and Robert the Bruce are said to have hidden from their enemies. Other options, if you're the outdoors type, include rented kayaks, canoes, or dinghies, or even water-skiing instruction from Lomond Adventures in Balfron.

*Sweeney's Cruises, next to the tourist information center, Riverside, Balloch. ☎ 01389-752-376. Cruise Loch Lomond, Tarbet Pier, on Hwy. A82 ☎ 01301-702-356; E-mail: cl1702356@aol.com. Lomond Adventures, Balfron ☎ 01360-440-690.*

### McCaig's Tower
**Oban**

The distinguishing landmark of the Oban cityscape, this Romanesque structure seems out of place looming high above the small town. Local banker John McCaig commissioned it around 1900 to employ three stone-masons who were out of work. Though never completed, the arches were going to house statues of McCaig's family. You are free to walk through the monument and enjoy the best view of the town, bay, and surrounding area, especially at sunset. Floodlights illuminate the tower at night.

*Oban, between Duncraggan and Laurel roads. Admission: Free. Open: Daily, 24 hours.*

### Museum of Islay Life
**Isle of Islay**

This interesting little museum in an old church focuses on the history of the island and island life, as well as the whisky-making process. The artifacts range from hundreds of years ago to the present. It may seem a little thrown-together, but it is interesting and gives context to your visit to Islay. If you still have questions, don't hesitate to ask the competent staff.

*Port Charlotte, Islay.* ☎ *01496-850-358. Admission: £1.60 ($2.30) adults, £1.10 ($1.60) seniors and students, £.85 ($1.25) children under 16. Open: Apr–Oct Mon–Sat 1–5 p.m., Sun 2–5 p.m. Closed Nov–Mar. Time: 1 hour.*

### Oban Distillery
**Oban**

It may not be the largest or most distinguished distillery in Scotland, but Oban (founded in 1794) is conveniently located in the heart of town and offers an informative tour of one of the oldest malt whisky makers in the country. In addition to seeing distillers at work and a decent audiovisual presentation, you'll get an idea of how regional Scottish whisky is: The proximity to the sea certainly affects the taste of Oban whisky. Like most distillery tours, this one ends with a complimentary dram (small shot) of the hard stuff and an opportunity to take a bottle home with you.

*Stafford Street, Oban.* ☎ *01631-572-004. Admission: £2.50 ($3.65). Open: July–Sept Mon–Fri 9:30 a.m.–8:30 p.m., Sat 9:30 a.m.–5 p.m., Sun noon to 5 p.m.; Easter–June and Oct Mon–Sat 9:30 a.m.–5 p.m.; Nov–Easter Mon–Fri 9:30 a.m.–5 p.m. Time: 90 minutes.*

### Oban Seal & Marine Centre
**Oban**

This seal sanctuary is a heart-warming nursery and hospital for stray, sick, and injured seal pups. The center takes care of the cute creatures before releasing them back into the wild. Highlights of the animal rescue center include daily lectures and feedings. In addition to the seals, the marine center has many exhibits on the natural habitats of sea creatures, including sharks. The setting, among tall, shady pine trees by the water's edge, is stunning — more reminiscent of northern California than Scotland.

*Barcaldine, Oban, on the shores of Loch Creran.* ☎ *01631-720-386. Admission: £6.50 ($9.45) adults, £4.95 ($7.20) seniors and students, £3.95 ($5.75) children under 16. Open: Daily 10 a.m.–5 p.m. Time: 2 hours, 30 minutes.*

# Shopping in Argyll and the Islands

Though none of the towns in the region is large enough to have a shopping area or district, Arran Island has something of a mall that's worth a stop.

✔ **Duchess Court Shops,** near Brodick, Arran (☎ 01770-302-831). This handful of nice specialty shops includes the **Island Cheese Shop** (☎ 01770-302-788), where you can watch the staff make the delectable fromage and buy other gifts and beer and wine; **Arran Aromatics** (☎ 01770-302-595), a factory shop and store for perfumes and gourmet soaps; and the gift shop **Something Special** (☎ 01770-302-991). It's rare to find a shopping crawl in the islands, so this is a good opportunity to get a bit out of the way. The items here are Scottish made.

✔ **Alexander MacIntyre & Co.,** Main Street East, Inveraray (☎ 01499-302-115). This place is the real deal. It's the perfect spot to get that wooly jumper (sweater) to keep you warm on a cool night as the mist comes in. This small shop has a huge selection, so be thorough in your browsing. Call for hours.

✔ **Caithness Glass,** Railway Pier, Oban (☎ 01631-563-386). This world-famous glass shop is a great place to find a unique memento. The colorful menagerie of items never fails to disappoint and maintains the highest level of quality. No piece with even the slightest imperfection leaves the factory. Open: March through October, Monday to Saturday from 9 a.m. to 5 p.m., plus Sunday from 11 a.m. to 5 p.m. from April to October; November to February, Monday to Saturday from 10 a.m. to 5 p.m.

✔ **Chalmer's,** George Street at Argyll Street, Oban (☎ 01631-562-053). A great place for souvenirs, Chalmer's overflows with just the kind of Scottish gifts you must take home. The best part about this shop is the range of items, from upscale gifts such as blankets and jewelry to more touristy items such as Loch Ness monsters and cheesy T-shirts. Call for hours.

✔ **Crafty Kitchen,** Ardfern, midway between Oban and Lochgilphead (☎ 01852-500-303 or 01852-500-689; E-mail: jan@craftyk.co.uk). This is one of the coolest and most memorable stores you'll find in the country. The place is part craft shop, part cafe, part gallery, and part post office. The crafts are unique and thoroughly Scottish. You'll also find a good selection of books, cards, and ethnic crafts (and a portion of the used-book sales goes to a local charity). The cafe serves delicious vegetarian fare, and the art gallery features Scottish artists and craftspeople. Open: April to October, Tuesday to Sunday from 10 a.m. to 5:30 p.m.; November and December, Saturday and Sunday from 10 a.m. to 5 p.m.

✔ **Islay Woolen Mill,** Bridgend (☎ 01496-840-646). This famous mill is about the only thing going on in the tiny town of Bridgend. The shop, in a wooded hollow by the river, makes all sorts of fine tweeds, warming items such as woolen hats and scarves, plus yards and yards of fine cloth. You can even tour the small factory. Fans of the film *Braveheart,* take note: This mill made all the tartan and tweed clothing worn in the film. Open: Monday to Saturday from 10 a.m. to 5 p.m.

✔ **Inveraray Woolen Mill,** The Anvil, Front Street, Inveraray (☎ **01499-302-166**). A self-described "Pandora's box" of Scottish gifts, the mill does have a great variety of items — more of a smorgasbord, I'd say. Among the quality gifts: Edinburgh crystal, cashmere, knitwear, woolly hats and gloves, and gourmet edibles. The architect who did much of Edinburgh's New Town designed the white-washed building. Call for hours.

# Doing the Pub Crawl

You'll find no shortage of pubs in Oban, the largest town in this area, but elsewhere the choices are limited. In less-visited areas such as the Kintyre Peninsula and the islands, the pubs are basic watering holes catering to the locals. In some small towns, in fact, the hotel pub is the only place to grab a dram of whisky or a pint.

✔ **Brodick Bar,** Brodick, Arran, just off Shore Road near the post office (☎ **01770-302-169**). This fun little bar is a great place for friendly face time with the locals. The all-wood pub pours delicious ale and has a reputation for serving excellent pub grub — especially uniquely topped pizzas. During the day, you can get a light lunch; in the evening, the kitchen serves bistro food to accompany Scottish-brewed beer. Like all old-school pubs, the Brodick Bar closes on Sundays. Open Monday to Saturday from 11 a.m. to midnight.

✔ **The Commercial,** Campbeltown (☎ **01586-553-703**). There's not a whole lot going on in Campbeltown, even though it is the capital of the Kintyre Peninsula and was once a bustling town and home to more than 30 distilleries. The bar of note is the Commercial — by day a quiet pub; at night, the social mecca of the region. Try to visit on a Thursday, Friday, or Saturday, when the place is a-hoppin' with live music. The top choice behind the bar is the popular oatmeal lager. Another plus: no cover charge, even for live music. Open: Monday to Saturday from 11 a.m. to 1 a.m., and Sunday from 12:30 p.m. to 1 a.m.

✔ **Coasters,** Corran Esplanade, Oban (☎ **01631-566-881**). Note the (ironic) lack of coasters in this smallish pub near the water. With four satellite televisions showing different games, it's a popular place to watch local and American sports. During the day, locals come for the good grub. The menu also has kiddie meals. Coasters is a fine after-dinner pub, as well: Skip dessert at the restaurant, and come here for some traditional sticky toffee pudding or hot apple pie and a nightcap. Call for hours.

✔ **Lorne Hotel Bar,** 43 Stevenson St., Oban, across a small bridge, off Combie Street (☎ **01631-562-484**). This popular bar can fill rather quickly, especially on weekends when it books live music. The crowd is a mix of young and old, and the atmosphere is amiable. A few booths hold seats, but otherwise it's standing room only around the big circular marble-and-copper bar in the center of the place. The service is quick and friendly, and the evenings offer nonstop entertainment, especially when football matches beam in on the huge TV screen. Open: Daily from 11 a.m. to 1 a.m.

✔ **Oban Inn,** Stafford Street, Oban (☎ **01631-562-484**). This classic whitewashed pub has a warm, old-fashioned elegance. Near the water just off the town's main street, it's a popular place for locals and visitors alike. The upstairs bar is a little quieter, but the downstairs room, with flags and exposed wooden beams, is a better place to meet people. The pub has an excellent selection of whisky and decent pub grub. Open: Daily from noon to 1 a.m.

# Fast Facts: Argyll and the Islands

## Area Code

The area code for the islands of Jura and Islay is **01496**, Inveraray **01499**, Oban **01631**, Arran **01770**, and Tarbert **01880**. You need to dial the area code only if you are calling from outside the city you want to reach.

## Emergencies

Dial **999** for police, fire, or ambulance.

## Genealogy Resources

**Glasgow & West of Scotland Family History Society,** Unit 15, 32 Mansfield St., Glasgow G11 5QP (☎ 0141-339-8303).

## Hospitals

**Argyll & the Isles Hospital,** off Soroba Road, south end of town, Oban (☎ 01631-567-500).

## Information

Tourist offices include: In the Old Church, Argyll Square, **Oban** (☎ 01631-563-122); Front Street, across from the water,

Inveraray (☎ 01499-302-063). Summer offices: Near Brodick pier, **Arran** (☎ 01770-302-140; Internet: www.arran.uk.com); Harbor Street, **Tarbert** (☎ 01880-820-429); Balloch Road, **Balloch** (☎ 01389-753-533); and at the Square, Bowmore, **Islay** (☎ 01496-810-254). The **regional tourism office**, 7 Alexandra Parade, Dunoon (☎ 01369-701-000; Internet: www.visit scottish.heartlands.org).

## Internet Access

**Cafe na Lusan,** 9 Craigard Rd., Oban (☎ 01631-567-268; E-mail: cafenalusan@ hotmail.com; Internet: www.cafe nalusan.com). Open: Tues–Thurs 11 a.m.–8 p.m., Fri–Sat 11 a.m.–10 p.m., Sun noon to 7 p.m. Cost: £1 ($1.45) for 15 minutes.

## Mail

The two major post offices are: Corran Esplanade, Oban (☎ 01631-562-430), and Main Street South, Inveraray (☎ 01499-302-062).

# Chapter 14

# Fife and the Central Highlands

· · · · · · · · · · · · · · · · · · · · · · · · · · · · · · · · · · · · · · · · · · · · · · ·

*In This Chapter*

▶ Getting to the Central Highlands and the Kingdom of Fife

▶ Easing your tired dogs in cozy hotels

▶ Dining on local seafood and visiting the fisheries museum next door

▶ Discovering the former stomping grounds of Rob Roy, William Wallace, and Robert the Bruce

▶ Shopping for woolens and kilts

▶ Pulling a pint down at the pub

· · · · · · · · · · · · · · · · · · · · · · · · · · · · · · · · · · · · · · · · · · · · · · ·

*T*hese two regions (one of them was a bona fide kingdom) teem with excellent attractions — and all are within easy reach of Glasgow and Edinburgh. If you're planning to include the Upper Highlands or the northeast region in your trip, you can't help but pass through either Fife or the Central Highlands. Don't just drive by, however; plan to stay awhile. The region has no shortage of attractions, accommodations, and fine wining and dining.

## Getting Oriented to Fife and the Central Highlands

Each of the two regions has a flagship city: **St. Andrews** for Fife, and the royal town of **Stirling** for the Central Highlands. Most of the attractions, pubs, restaurants, and hotels reviewed in this chapter are in or near these two fine towns. The chapter also discusses the **Trossachs,** a small region east of Loch Lomond that was once the stamping grounds of the legendary Rob Roy MacGregor (see Chapter 1).

If you've ever held a golf club, St. Andrews needs no introduction. Home to the oldest course in the world — as well as the association that decides the rules for the sport — St. Andrews is the golf mecca of the world. But it's much more than that. It's also a college town, with cobble-stone streets full of great restaurants and pubs accommodating students and golfers alike. This town by the sea also has no shortage of wonderful views.

Stirling is a famously royal town that was established by King David and was at one time the capital of Scotland. Its castle, a former home to Scottish royalty that includes Mary Queen of Scots, remains intact. The surrounding area has seen its share of battles between freedom fighters and the British. William Wallace, who has the most stunning monument in the country here, and King Robert the Bruce led decisive victories in and around Stirling. Bonnie Prince Charlie and his Jacobites tried to sack the city a few times but were never able to take the castle. This quaint town looks like a mini-Edinburgh and offers a good variety of wining and dining options along with other attractions and impressive landmarks.

At the very least, I recommend spending a day and night in each town. One glance at the many attractions and top-notch tourist facilities in the Central Highlands and the Kingdom of Fife should be enough to convince you to stick around even longer.

# Getting There

You won't necessarily need a car to experience this region's main attractions. If your visit is a side trip from Edinburgh or Glasgow, for example, consider taking the train or bus. The major towns — namely, Stirling and St. Andrews — are easily accessible by train and bus, and both cities are navigable by foot. If you want to see an attraction outside the towns, you can take a short jaunt on a train or coach. If your trip to the region is part of a journey to points farther north, however, then by all means, drive.

✔ **By car:** From Glasgow to Stirling, take the A80 to the M80; from Edinburgh, take the M9. To get to St. Andrews from Edinburgh, cross the Forth Bridge and catch the A92 to the A91. From Glasgow to St. Andrews, follow the directions to Stirling, then take the A91. The A91 connects Stirling and St. Andrews. To get to Callander from Stirling, catch the A84.

✔ **By train:** From Glasgow, Edinburgh, or Aberdeen to Stirling, take ScotRail (☎ 0845-748-4950; Internet: www.scotrail.co.uk). There is no train service to St. Andrews or the Trossachs.

✔ **By bus:** From Glasgow, Edinburgh, Aberdeen, and Inverness, Citylink (☎ 0990-505-050) buses travel to Stirling. **Midland Bluebird** (☎ 01324-613-777) serves Aberfoyle and Callander from Stirling and Glasgow. To get to St. Andrews from Edinburgh, Dundee, or Stirling, take **Scottish Fife** (☎ 01334-474-238).

# Knowing Where to Stay

It's a good idea to decide what you want to see and in what order before you pick your accommodations. For more choices, such as smaller B&Bs (there are tons of them, most comfortable but undistinguishable), consult the local tourism board for assistance.

### Craw's Nest Hotel
$$   **Anstruther**

Once an old minister's house, the Nest traded holiness for hospitality when the building became a fine hotel. It offers a little something for everyone: a games room for the young and young at heart, four-poster beds for romantic couples, and two rooms specially designed for travelers with disabilities. If you like to boogie, the hotel is also home to the largest dance floor in the region. Ask for a room in the wing overlooking the waters of the Forth and the Isle of May.

*Bankwell Rd., off Pittenweem Road.* ☎ *01333-310-691. Fax: 01333-312-216. E-mail:* enquiries@crawsnesthotel.co.uk. *Internet:* www.crawsnesthotel.co.uk. *Rack rates: £60–£94 ($87–$136) double. AE, DC, MC, V.*

### Cromlix House
$$$–$$$$   **Kinbuck**

This accommodation is a sportsman's dream. Principally a hunting lodge, the Cromlix draws fishermen and hunters with 3,000 acres of woodlands stretching to the River Allan. The owners even organize fishing and hunting trips. The three-story Victorian house is a piece of work; the sitting rooms and guest rooms are decorated with fine art and period furniture, and common areas such as the library and conservatory have been restored.

*On the B8033 from the A9, 10 miles north of Stirling.* ☎ *01786-822-125. Fax 01786-825-450. Rack rates: £135–£260 ($196–$377) double. AE, DC, MC, V. Closed Jan.*

### Golden Lion Hotel
$$   **Stirling**

Location, location, location. This 200-year-old building in the heart of Stirling houses one of the most popular accommodations in the area. Since its early days as a coaching inn, the Golden Lion has been roaring with hospitality. Now refurbished, the oldest and largest hotel in town is also quite modern. There's nothing fancy about the cookie-cutter rooms, but it's clean, and for its proximity to attractions (only a couple of blocks from the castle), the price can't be beat. Another plus: a free parking garage.

*8–10 King St., Stirling.* ☎ *01786-475-351. Fax: 01786-472-755. Rack rates: £64–£78 ($93–$113) double. AE, DC, MC, V.*

### The Inn at Lathones
**$$$ Lathones**

This is the oldest coaching inn in the St. Andrews area and is set in a picturesque spot just 5 miles from the famous golf town. It may be 400 years old, but it is thoroughly modern, and the rooms are equipped with stereos and huge baths. The bungalow-style inn has sidewalks that take you from one whitewashed building to the next. The main house, with a restaurant and front desk, is a comfortable area with fireplaces and sitting rooms. In an effort to cater to families, the inn offers a fun game room, an outdoor play area, and larger rooms that are ideal for a family of three or four.

*Five miles north of St. Andrews on the A915.* ☎ *01334-840-494. From the U.S.: 800-544-9993. Fax: 01334-840-694. E-mail:* lathones@teinn.co.uk. *Internet:* www.theinn.co.uk. *Rack rates: £120–£160 ($174–$232) double. AE, DC, MC, V.*

### Montague House
**$$–$$$ St. Andrews**

Nearly every building on Murray Place is a guesthouse or B&B, but Montague is the standout — though the price doesn't reflect it. Each of the seven comfortable rooms is nicely appointed and creatively painted. If you book far enough in advance, ask for the Ceol-na-Mara ("Sound of the Sea") room, which has a bay window overlooking the water. Montague House is well located, between old town and the beaches. The breakfasts, which include a daily special in addition to the normal great choices, are to die for. The huge guestbook speaks for itself. The Hunters, who've had the place for just a couple of years, are both locals and stay on top of the latest great place to eat. If Montague is booked, you'll find runners-up on the block.

*21 Murray Park, just off North Street.* ☎ *01334-479-287. Fax: 01334-475-827. E-mail:* info@montaguehouse.com. *Internet:* www.montaguehouse.com. *Rack rates: £50–£120 ($73–$174) double. MC, V.*

### Portcullis
**$$ Stirling**

This fun little B&B lies in the shadow of Stirling Castle. The rooms are comfortable but unpretentious, and the staff is extremely friendly. The Portcullis has been around for hundreds of years and has the rustic feel of an old coach inn and tavern. The downstairs bar is a plus or a minus, depending on your point of view — it's perfect for a nightcap, not so perfect if you want to be in bed before 10 p.m. Flowers grow in the lovely walled-in beer garden.

*Castle Wynd.* ☎ *01786-47-2290. Fax: 01786-44-6103. E-mail:* thenolport@aol.com. *Rack rates: £78–£82 ($115–$121) double. AE, MC, V.*

### Roman Camp
**$$$  Callander**

Although not as gladiatorial as its names implies, this cozy old hotel near Roman ruins is one of the more interesting places to stay in the area. Built in 1625 as a home for the Dukes of Perth, it hasn't changed much since, retaining charming low ceilings, creaking corridors, and snug furniture. The drawing room and conservatory have lovely period furniture and antiques. The River Teith runs through 20 beautiful acres of grounds; you're welcome to fish, but stay clear of the grazing sheep and cows.

*Off Main Street from the A84.* ☎ *01877-330-003. Fax: 01877-331-533. Rack rates: £110–£159 ($160–$231) double. AE, DC, MC, V.*

### Rufflets
**$$$  St. Andrews**

It's easy to see why this ivy-covered country-house hotel from the 1920s is popular among honeymooners. The ten acres of beautiful grounds and gardens are perfect for a stroll or a photographic backdrop. Located on the edge of town, it's a wonderfully quiet place off the tourist trail. The rooms are handsome and large, with all the amenities, and the staff is professional and accommodating. The restaurant is also excellent, so if you don't feel like driving back into the city center, stay put for dinner.

*Straithkinness Low Road. Take Argyll Street to Straithkinness Low Road and pass the university playing fields. On the B939.* ☎ *01334-472-594. Fax: 01334-472-594. E-mail:* reservations@rufflets.co.uk. *Internet:* www.rufflets.co.uk. *Rack rates: £130–£170 ($189–$247) double. AE, DC, MC, V.*

### Smugglers Inn
**$$  Anstruther**

Back in the day, this was a popular watering hole for smugglers. The building dates to the 13th century. Although the rooms are small and the floorboards uneven, the classic whitewashed structure with black trim is quite comfortable and homey. The nautical theme is a bit kitschy, but don't worry, matey, it doesn't extend into the guest rooms. It has only nine rooms, so booking ahead is a wise idea.

*High Street.* ☎ *01333-310-506. Fax: 01333-312-706. E-mail:* smuggs106@aol.com. *Rack rates: £50–£62 ($73–$90) double. AE, DC, MC, V.*

### St. Andrews Old Course Hotel
**$$$$  St. Andrews**

As you'd expect, this deluxe five-story hotel caters to golfers, but it has plenty of luxurious offerings for golf widows and orphans, as well. Most of the no-expense-spared rooms overlook the water and the links. The hotel is fairly new, but the architecture and wood-and-marble furnishings give the place a vintage feel. Among the luxury extras are a steam room, pool, and pro shop. Services include massage, laundry, baby-sitting, and 24-hour room service. In addition to in-house golf pros, the hotel also has staff therapists and beauticians on hand in case it's your ego or self-image that's causing your poor putting.

*Old Station Road, on the A91.* ☎ *01334-474-371. Fax: 01334-477-668. E-mail:* reservations@oldcoursehotel.co.uk. *Internet:* www.oldcoursehotel. co.uk. *Rack rates: £225–£369 ($326–$535) double. AE, DC, MC, V.*

### Stirling Highland Hotel
### $$$ Stirling

Ever fall asleep in class? Then you're familiar with the ether-like effect of school. At the Stirling, in an old converted high school, you can catch a good night's sleep or a much-needed nap in the classroom without facing detention. This well-managed accommodation is in easy hoofing distance of the castle (only 700 yards away) and all the decent restaurants in town. The architecture is Victorian and the furnishings heavy on tartan and floral patterns. The leisure room is quite nice, featuring a pool, steam room, gym equipment, table tennis, and more. The appropriately named Scholar's restaurant and the Headmaster's Study bar are pleasant, as well.

*Spittal Street.* ☎ *01786-27-2727. Fax: 01786-27-2829. E-mail:* stirling@ paramount-hotels.co.uk. *Internet:* www.paramount-hotels.co.uk. *Rack rates: £150 ($218) double. AE, DC, MC, V.*

# Dining in Fife and the Central Highlands

In dining as in accommodations, you may gravitate toward St. Andrews or Stirling. I include a couple of choice picks outside those towns, as well.

One place in particular deserves recognition lest you overlook it as you decide w here you should dine. **The Cellar,** in the ancient fishing village of Anstruther, has the best seafood in the Trossachs — and maybe in the whole country.

The regions in this chapter have few good options for family dining. The standby, and a fine one at that, is **Littlejohn's.** It offers pasta, burgers, and some Scottish cuisine at family-friendly prices. The service is good, and the breakfasts are yummy. Littlejohn's is at 73 Market St., St. Andrews (☎ 01334-475-444), and at 52 Port St., Stirling (☎ 01786-463-222).

*The Kingdom of Fife*

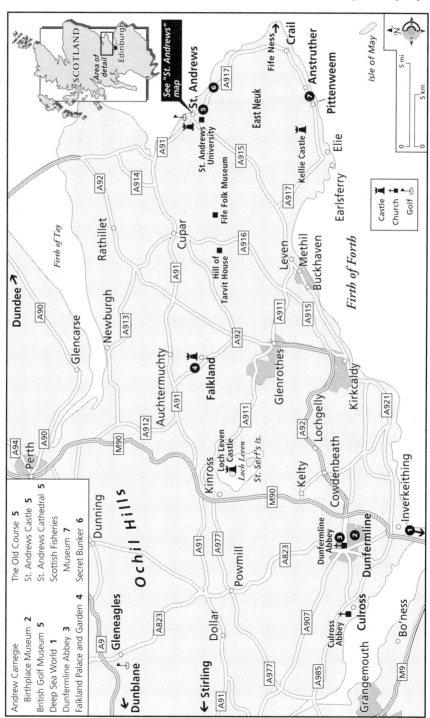

SCOTLAND

Area of detail

Edinburgh

See "St. Andrews" map

Isle of May

Crail

Fife Ness

St. Andrews

Anstruther

Pittenweem

East Neuk

St. Andrews University

Elie

Kellie Castle

Earlsferry

Fife Folk Museum

Cupar

Leven

Methil

Buckhaven

Firth of Tay

Rathillet

Hill of Tarvit House

Firth of Forth

Newburgh

Glencarse

Dundee

Glenrothes

Auchtermuchty

Falkland

Kirkcaldy

Lochgelly

Perth

Loch Leven Castle

Loch Leven

St. Serf's Is.

Kinross

Kelty

Cowdenbeath

Inverkeithing

Dunning

Ochil Hills

Powmill

Dunfermline Abbey

Dunfermline

Bo'ness

Gleneagles

Dollar

Culross Abbey

Culross

Dunblane

Stirling

Grangemouth

Andrew Carnegie Birthplace Museum **2**
British Golf Museum **5**
Deep Sea World **1**
Dunfermline Abbey **3**
Falkland Palace and Garden **4**
The Old Course **5**
St. Andrews Castle **5**
St. Andrews Cathedral **5**
Scottish Fisheries Museum **7**
Secret Bunker **6**

Castle
Church
Golf

N

5 mi

5 km

### Balaka
$$$  **St. Andrews**  **Bangladeshi**

If this high-class restaurant is good enough for the Scottish James Bond, it's good enough for you. You'll be amazed by the smells that greet you even before you reach the wonderful dining room. Inside you'll see a signed photograph of Sir Sean Connery's happy mug. The takeout menu features a quote by Gandhi about the importance of serving the customer — but last time I was there, the service was curt and the food slow to arrive. Prices were higher than on my last visit, as well, but the food is still outstanding. Not familiar with Bangladeshi dishes? You can't go wrong with the delicious Persian curry *moglai,* sweet and sour *dhansaak,* or *karai* (tandoori chicken or lamb). For dessert, try *kulfi,* an Indian ice cream. If you get post-pub hunger pangs, the restaurant stays open very late.

*3 Alexandra Place, St. Andrews.* ☎ *01334-47-4825. Internet:* www.balaka.co.uk. *Reservations recommended. Main courses: £7.65–£13.95 ($11–$20). AE, DC, MC, V. Open: Daily noon to 3 p.m. and 5 p.m.–1 a.m.*

### Barton Bar and Bistro
$  **Stirling**  **International**

This great little bistro is a favorite among the students, attracted, no doubt, by the burger and beer specials. The main room has a bar and high ceilings, which make it look like a cross between a French cafe and an old-fashioned ice cream parlor. The well-stocked menu has several all-day breakfasts (including a huge veggie breakfast and American-style pancakes) plus French bread pizzas, specialty burgers, veggie burgers, and other delectables such as the Bistro tortilla tower. The portions are large, the beer is cold (try the creamy Belhaven Ale), and the jukebox plays classic rock 'n' roll.

*3 Barton St., across from the post office.* ☎ *01786-446-930. Reservations not accepted. Main courses: £3.20–£4.95. ($4.65–$7.20). MC, V. Open: Mon–Sat 10:30 a.m.–8:30 p.m., Sun noon to 8:30 p.m.*

### The Cellar
$$–$$$$  **Anstruther**  **Seafood/Scottish**

This is the best seafood restaurant in the region and perhaps even the country. In an ancient fishing village, next door to a fisheries museum, this is a hotspot for delicacies from the sea. In addition to staples such as crab, scallops, and lobster, the mostly seafood menu includes dishes such as crayfish and mussel bisque, and monkfish with herb and garlic sauce. The stone cellar restaurant is unassuming and comfortable, with candlelight and fireplaces. The young, unpretentious staff is among the friendliest I've encountered, and the selection of white wines is excellent. The Cellar is highly popular with locals and visitors alike, so book ahead no matter what day of the week or time of year.

*24 E. Green, off the courtyard behind the Fisheries Museum.* ☎ *01333-310-378. Reservations recommended. Fixed-price lunch: £15 ($22). Fixed-price dinner: From £28.50 ($42). AE, DC, MC, V. Open: Year-round Tues–Sat 7–9 p.m.; summer Tues–Sat 12:30–2 p.m.*

## Herman's

$$$ **Stirling Austrian/Scottish**

This simply decorated restaurant with interesting art on the wall (trust me — you'll just have to see it) has a unique menu that's influenced by Austria and Scotland. So will it be *jager schnitzel* or roast Barbary duck breast? The aproned staff is excellent and helpful in decoding the menu. Choosing is tough, but don't forgo the wonderful Austrian desserts, which are to die for. You can't beat the location, just across the street from Holy Rude Church.

*58 Broad St.* ☎ *01786-45-0632. Reservations recommended. Main courses: £11.50–£16.50 ($17–$24). AE, DC, MC, V. Open: Mon–Fri noon to 2:30 p.m. and 6–10 p.m.; Sat–Sun noon to 10 p.m.*

## Kam's Garden

$$–$$$ **Stirling Cantonese**

Good Cantonese food in the middle of Scotland? Why not? All the usual suspects are here, cooked to perfection: an array of prawn dishes, savory barbecued duck, and several vegetarian-friendly options, such as the enlightening vegetable-heavy Buddha Dish. The dining area may be forgettably plain, but the food is not. One complaint: The service was friendly but a bit slow, so if you're in a hurry, you may want to eat elsewhere.

*4 Viewfield Place.* ☎ *01786-44-6445. Reservations recommended. Main courses: £5.50–£12.95 ($8–$19). MC, V. Open: Mon–Sat noon to 2 p.m.; Mon–Thurs 5:30– 11 p.m., Fri–Sat 5:30–11:30 p.m., Sun 5–11 p.m.*

## Kind Kyttock's Kitchen

$ **Cross Wynd Teahouse/Vegetarian**

This is the kind of serendipitous place travelers love to stumble upon during a day of sightseeing. No need to stumble now. This lovely teashop in a 17th-century cottage is great for a warming cup of brew or a light lunch. Particularly tasty is the Scotch broth soup served with some delicious homemade bread or oatcakes. A small art gallery in the kitchen features local artists.

*Cross Wynd.* ☎ *01337-857-477. Reservations not accepted. Main courses: £1.90–£5.45 ($2.80–$7.90). AE, MC, V. Open: Tues–Sun 10:30 a.m.–5:30 p.m.*

## La Posada

**$$ St. Andrews Mexican**

This restaurant has a fine full menu of large hunger-killing dishes. Interesting standouts include *manchamanteles* (sloppy chicken), pork and pecan nut burrito, and fabulous vegetarian chili. The bar makes a mean margarita. As if the food weren't enough of a sell, La Posada also has plenty of outdoor seating, the occasional salsa class, and an all-you-can-eat lunch buffet Mondays, Wednesdays, and Fridays. If your Spanish is a little rusty, *posada* means an inn or a gathering place. *¡Andele!*

*Inchcape House, St. Mary's Place.* ☎ *01334-47-0500. Reservations recommended. Main courses: £5.25–£9.25 ($7.60–$13). AE, DC, MC, V. Open: Daily noon to 2:30 p.m. and 5–9:30 p.m.*

## Olivia's

**$$$ Stirling Scottish**

Carnivores will love Olivia's. The restaurant serves a limited selection of well-prepared meals, with an emphasis on meaty dishes such as un-sheepish roast rack of spring lamb and pan-fried saddle of lamb. The smallish but formal dining area is open and bright, thanks to the large window at the entrance. It may not be big, but it is comfortable, and an ever-changing art gallery graces the walls.

*5 Baker Street, Stirling.* ☎ *01786-446-277. Reservations required. Main courses: £9.95–£16.95 ($14–$25). DC, MC, V. Open: Summer daily noon to 9:30 p.m.; winter Tues–Sat noon to 9:30 p.m.*

## The Victoria

**$ St. Andrews International**

This upstairs restaurant in Old St. Andrews looks like an ice cream shop, with its big bar, high ceilings, and cool marble and iron tables. Alas, no ice cream is on the menu, but you can get large burgers, excellent homemade meat pies, and plenty of vegetarian items, such as the Southwestern veggie burger, chili, wraps, or fajitas. And you'll have few complaints about the prices or the friendly service. On a warm day, soak in the air out on the lovely beer terrace.

*1 St. Marys Place.* ☎ *01334-476-964. E-mail:* victoriabar@maclay.co.uk. *Reservations not accepted. Main courses: £2.75–£6.25 ($4–$9). AE, DC, MC, V. Open: Mon–Sat 10 a.m.–7:45 p.m., Sun noon to 5 p.m.*

## The Vine Leaf

**$$$$ St. Andrews Seafood/Scottish**

This lovely restaurant in a garden is one of the nicest and most upscale places to eat in town. The back-alley entrance may seem quaint, but the elegant, contemporary dining room and the very professional wait staff will impress you. The oft-changing menu is inventive. If it's on the menu, you must try the ostrich! The specialties are seafood and game, such as succulent halibut Florentine baked with spinach and grilled cheese glaze, and roast rack of Scottish lamb; vegetarian options are available. The wine selection is always top shelf. Make sure to book ahead; it gets crowded all year long.

*131 South St. ☎ 01334-47-7497. E-mail:* vineleaf@tesco.net. *Reservations required. Set prices: £19.95 ($28) for 2 courses; £23.95 ($35) for 3 courses. AE, DC, MC, V. Open: Tues–Sat 7–10 p.m.*

# Exploring the Area

Although it's a small region, both the Central Highlands and the Kingdom of Fife boast some of the best and most interesting attractions in the country, from the Old Course at St. Andrews and the city's stunning cathedral and castle ruins to the mighty Stirling Castle and Wallace Monument. Other attractions, such as the SS *Sir Walter Scott* boat trip in the Trossachs and the Secret Bunker, will likely leave indelible memories.

Want to save a buck or two? Some attractions have two-for-one joint tickets. You can pay a single discounted price for St. Andrews Castle and St. Andrews Cathedral, for example, or for Stirling Castle and Argyll's Lodging. In the case of Stirling Castle, this discount works only if you visit Argyll's Lodging first. If you visit the Castle first, you end up paying for both.

## Setting your sites on the top attractions

### Andrew Carnegie Birthplace Museum
**Dunfermline**

The rags-to-riches story of America's steel magnate and philanthropist began here. The museum is in the cottage where Carnegie was born, and the exhibits tell his story with artifacts, documents, and photographs. At one point, Carnegie was the richest man in America, but he gave away $350 million to schools and libraries. For his hometown, he bought the land of a rich baron (where the young Andrew wasn't able to play because it was gated) and turned it into the public Pittencrieff Park, which is next to the museum. Dunfermline also received the first of more than 2,000 public libraries Carnegie built, and Scotland's very own Carnegie Hall.

*Moodie Street, at the corner of Priory Lane ☎ 01383-724-302. Admission: £2 ($2.90) adults, £1 ($1.45) seniors, free for children. Open: Apr–Oct Mon–Sat 11 a.m.–5 p.m., Sun 2–5 p.m. Closed Nov–Mar. Time: 90 minutes.*

### Argyll's Lodging
**Stirling**

Sir William Alexander, the founder of Nova Scotia (or "New Scotland"), built this 17th-century town house, one of Scotland's finest Renaissance homes. The house has been preserved as it would have looked in 1680, when the 9th Earl of Argyll lived there following Sir William's death. Although you won't see many items belonging to Archibald Argyll and his family, you get a very good idea of how the other half lived more than 300 years ago.

*Castle Wynd.* ☎ *01786-461-146. Admission: £3 ($4.35) adults, £2.25 ($3.25) seniors and students, £1.20 ($1.75) children. Open: Daily Apr–Oct. 9:30 a.m.–6 p.m., Nov–Mar 9:30 a.m.–5 p.m. Time: 1 hour.*

### Bannockburn Heritage Centre
**Stirling**

This famous battlefield site was the scene of King Robert the Bruce's victory over the English troops of Edward II. The decisive win secured Scottish independence (at least for a little while) from the British crown. The museum contains life-size statues of William "Braveheart" Wallace and Robert the Bruce, as well as a fascinating large-scale model of the Battle of Stirling Bridge. The audiovisual presentation does an excellent job of re-creating the battle and Bruce's story. Robert the Bruce picked the battle site — in his day it was a marsh, and English horses got stuck in the muck, helping to secure victory for the Scots.

*Glasgow Road, off M80* ☎ *01786-812-664. Admission: £2.30 ($3.35) adults, £1.50 ($2.20) seniors and children, £6.10 ($8.85) family. Open: Apr–Oct daily 10 a.m.–5:30 p.m.; Mar, Nov–Dec 23 daily 10:30 a.m.–4 p.m. Closed Dec 24–Feb. Time: 3 hours.*

### British Golf Museum
**St. Andrews**

Even non-golfers will find this museum devoted to the history and popularity of the game interesting. Exhibits reveal the evolution of equipment and rules and remarkable facts and feats of the last 500 years of the game. Interactive touch-screen computers take you through the lives of famous players and even test your golf acumen. Be warned: There is a lot more to read than watch. The museum won the four-star "Excellent Standard" award from the Scottish Tourist Board in 1999. Although I wouldn't classify the museum as "kid-friendly," there is a section at the end where they can putt and dress up in turn-of-the-century outfits, which would occupy little ones while you read your way through.

*Bruce Embankment.* ☎ *01334-478-880. Admission: £4 ($5.80) adults, £2 ($2.90) children, £9.50 ($13.80) family. Open: Daily Apr–mid-Oct 9:30 a.m.–5:30 p.m., mid-Oct–Mar 11 a.m.–3 p.m. Time: 2 hours.*

## Stirling, Loch Lomond, and the Trossachs

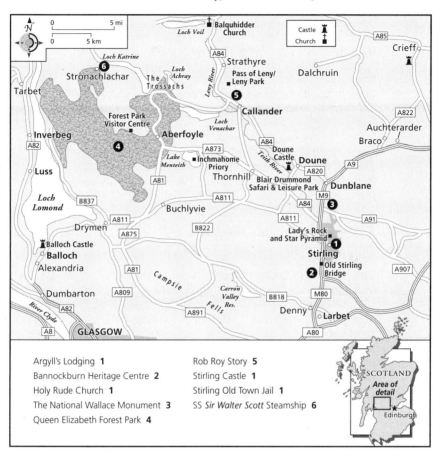

| 0          5 mi |
| --- |
| 0     5 km |

Loch Voil
Balquhidder Church
Castle ♜
Church ▐
A85
Crieff
Loch Katrine
Strathyre
A84
Stronachlachar
Loch Achray
The Trossachs
Pass of Leny/ Leny Park
Dalchruin
Tarbet
Leny River
Forest Park Visitor Centre
Callander
A822
Inverberg
Aberfoyle
Loch Venachar
Auchterarder
A82
Lake Menteith
Inchmahome Priory
A84
Doune Castle
Braco
Luss
A873
Doune
A9
Thornhill
A820
Loch Lomond
B837
A81
Blair Drummond Safari & Leisure Park
Dunblane
Buchlyvie
A811
M9
A811
A811
A91
Drymen
A811
B822
Lady's Rock and Star Pyramid
A84
Balloch Castle
A875
Stirling
Balloch
Old Stirling Bridge
A907
Alexandria
A81
Campsie
Carron Valley Res.
Dumbarton
A809
Fells
B818
M80
Denny
Larbet
A82
A891
A80
A8
GLASGOW

| | |
| --- | --- |
| Argyll's Lodging **1** | Rob Roy Story **5** |
| Bannockburn Heritage Centre **2** | Stirling Castle **1** |
| Holy Rude Church **1** | Stirling Old Town Jail **1** |
| The National Wallace Monument **3** | SS *Sir Walter Scott* Steamship **6** |
| Queen Elizabeth Forest Park **4** | |

SCOTLAND
Area of detail
Edinburgh

## Deep Sea World
### North Queensferry

There may be nothing inherently Scottish about this aquarium, but it is far too interesting to pass up. You'll walk through 1 million gallons of water in a series of underwater tunnels. ("Hey, is that a leak?" is the standard gag.) This submerged safari has the largest collection of amphibians in the U.K. and Scotland's largest collection of piranha. One particularly interesting exhibit is a tour of the world's different climates, which includes unusual creatures, such as the most deadly frog in the world. Make sure to take a guided tour and stay for a feeding.

*Take the first exit after crossing the Forth Bridge from Edinburgh.* ☎ **0930-100-300**. *Internet:* www.deepseaworld.com. *Admission: £6.25 ($9.10) adults, £3.95 ($5.75) children. Open: Daily Apr–Oct 10 a.m.–6 p.m., Nov–Mar 11 a.m.–5 p.m. Time: 2–3 hours.*

### Dunfermline Abbey and Palace
**Dunfermline**

This three-in-one site contains an intact abbey built by King David I and the ruins of both a monastery and a royal palace. The palace, which saw the birth of King James VI's son Charles I, is small but fun to explore and has a nice view of the town through the window ruins. The abbey, which once held the body of St. Margaret (David I's mother) before she was taken off to France and Italy as relics, has a newer section that holds the body of King Robert the Bruce.

*St. Margaret St., at Priory Lane* ☎ *01383-73-9026. Admission: £2.20 ($3.20) adults; £1.60 ($2.30) seniors, students, and children under 16; £15.90 ($23) family. Open: Apr–Sept daily 9:30 a.m. –6 p.m. Oct–Mar Mon–Wed, Sat 9:30 a.m.–4:30 p.m.; Thurs 9:30 a.m. to noon; Fri, Sun 2–4:30 p.m. Time: 2 hours.*

### Falkland Palace and Garden
**Falkland**

This hunting lodge and country home to eight (and counting) Stuart monarchs is an impressive specimen of Renaissance architecture. Among the rulers who resided on these stunning grounds were a young Mary Queen of Scots and her father, James V, who died here. The collection of artifacts inside is not as impressive as the architecture and painted ceilings. The jewels are the ornate Chapel Royal and the internationally lauded gardens. Also on the grounds is the world's oldest tennis court still in use. Queen Elizabeth II officially owns the palace, which the Scottish government maintains.

*High Street. Just off the M90, at Junction 8.* ☎ *01337-857-397. Admission: £4.50 ($6.55) adults, £3 ($4.35) seniors, students, and children. Open: Apr–Oct Mon–Sat 11 a.m.–5:30 p.m., Sun 1:30–5:30 p.m. Closed Nov–Mar. Time: 3 hours.*

### Holy Rude Church
**Stirling**

Among the many interesting aspects of this medieval church are bullet holes in the walls and on grave markers from the 1651 Stirling invasion by Cromwell's troops. John Knox preached the Reformation here, and the inside features illuminating stained glass, 15th-century oak beams, and one of the oldest and grandest organs in the country. *Rude* (or *rood*) means "cross," and "holy rude" is the medieval term for Christ's cross. The grounds have one of the oldest bowling greens in Scotland and access to Lady's Rock and the Star Pyramid (see listing later in this chapter).

*St. John Street.* ☎ *01786-47-5275. Admission: Free. Open: May–Sept 10 a.m.–5 p.m. Closed Oct–Apr. Time: 1 hour.*

## *The National Wallace Monument*
### Stirling

Drive anywhere near Stirling, and you're likely to see this tower, which commemorates William "Braveheart" Wallace, overlooking the surrounding plains. The view from the top of the 220-foot (and 246 steps!) tower is of Wallace's old fighting grounds, such as the Stirling Bridge, where the "Guardian of Scotland" won a decisive battle against the English in 1297. Inside the monument are exhibits on the exploits of William Wallace, as told by an automatronic head of Scotland's favorite hero. It's nearly as silly as it sounds. Also here are an audiovisual display on battles that took place in the region and occasional talks on ancient weaponry. Built in the 1860s, the monument saw its popularity soar after the release of the 1995 movie *Braveheart*. If you don't want to drive to it, Stirling Castle offers excellent views of the monument. The top is not wheelchair accessible. A free shuttle runs from the visitor center to the base of the monument.

*Alloa Road, Abbey Craig. Take Causewayhead Road from Stirling to where it meets Alloa Road (A907).* ☎ *01786-47-2140. E-mail:* nwm@aillst.ossian.net. *Admission: £3.95 ($5.75) adults, £2.75 ($4) seniors and children, £3 ($4.35) students, £10.75 ($16) family. Open: Jan–Feb, Nov–Dec 10:30 a.m.–4 p.m.; Mar–May Oct 10 a.m.–5 p.m.; June 10 a.m.–6 p.m.; July–Aug 9:30 a.m.–6:30 p.m.; Sept 9:30 a.m.– 5 p.m. Time: 90 minutes.*

## *The Old Course*
### St. Andrews

This is probably the most famous golf course in the world, a fact that would make it an attraction even for non-golfers. Mary Queen of Scots actually played here. If you're just looking, note the two famously difficult holes: the "Sea" hole (11th) and the "Road" hole (17th) — the only hole I know that you must play off the road. The clubhouse is home to the Royal & Ancient Golf Association, which has the final say on the official rules of the sport. It's not open to the public, but the course is, and you can play it if you win a lottery for tee times. Each day at 2 p.m., ballots are chosen for those who hope to play the next day. You must also have an official certificate of your handicap or a letter of introduction from your own club. Amateurs shouldn't play the course, out of courtesy to professionals. If you don't win the lottery, don't worry — this is the largest golf complex in Europe, and you can play other fine courses, such as the New Course, the Jubilee, or the Strathtyrum. The Balgrove is a nine-hole course for kids (no parents allowed, except to caddy). Film buffs, take note: The grounds were used in the opening running scene of *Chariots of Fire*.

*The corner of Golf Place and The Links Road.* ☎ *01334-475-757. Admission: Greens fees £72 ($104). Open: Mon–Sat year-round; closed Sun. Time: 4 hours.*

### Queen Elizabeth Forest Park
**Aberfoyle**

Between Loch Lomond and the Highlands and over the Forth Valley, the Queen Elizabeth Forest Park is 50,000 acres of hills, lakes, and woods. It's as fine a natural backdrop as you'll get in the country. The forests teem with wildlife, and many trails wind through. If nature walks aren't your thing, the park has plenty of picnic spots. You can drive through on the scenic Achray Forest Drive if you like. The park visitor center has maps showing trails and picnic areas.

*David Marshall Lodge, off the A821.* ☎ *01877-382-258. Admission: Free. Open: Park: Year-round daily dawn to dusk. Visitor Center: Daily Mar–mid-Oct 10 a.m.–6 p.m. Closed Nov–mid-Mar. Time: 4 hours.*

### Rob Roy Story
**Callander**

There are two Rob Roy MacGregors. One is the legendary figure of Sir Walter Scott's novel and the movies, the tartan Robin Hood. And then there is the real Rob Roy, the cattle thief and blackmailer. This museum in the Trossachs region, home of the Clan MacGregor, covers both versions of the famous clan leader. Rob Roy was certainly a hero to his people and an outlaw in defiance of the English. Life-size figures tell the tale of MacGregor's feud with the Duke of Montrose, and exhibits cover the man's life and legend.

*Ancaster Square, off Main Street (A84).* ☎ *01877-330-342. E-mail:* robroy&t@ aillst.ossian.net. *Admission: £2.90 ($4.20) adults, £2.05 ($3) seniors, £2.40 ($3.50) students, children free, £6.35 ($9.20) family. Open: June daily 9:30 a.m.–6 p.m.; July–Aug daily 9 a.m.–8 p.m.; Sept daily 10 a.m.–6 p.m.; Mar–May, Oct–Dec daily 10 a.m.–5 p.m.; Jan–Feb Sat–Sun 11 a.m.–4 p.m. Time: 2 hours.*

### St. Andrew's Castle
**St. Andrews**

Now splendid cliff-top ruins, the castle was originally built in 1200 for the archbishop of St. Andrews and later used as a prison. The visitor center traces the history of the building through an interesting audiovisual display and contains exhibits on castle attack strategies and Scottish life in the Middle Ages. More fun is walking through the ruins and inside the siege tunnels. The "bottle dungeon," a large pit 24 feet down, was a holding cell where prisoners checked in but never checked out. History buffs will note a marker just outside the castle on the spot where Protestant reformer George Wishart was burned at the stake. Another famous reformer, John Knox, was preaching here when the castle was destroyed, kicking off Mr. Knox's tenure as a ship slave.

If you visit both St. Andrews Castle and St. Andrews Cathedral, you can buy a discounted joint ticket at either spot. The price is £4 ($5.80) adults, £3 ($4.35) seniors, £1.25 ($1.80) children.

*North Castle Street, The Scores.* ☎ *01334-477-196. Admission: £2.80 ($4.10) adults, £2 ($2.90) seniors, £1 ($1.45) children. Open: Daily Apr–Sept 9:30 a.m.–6:30 p.m., Oct–Mar 9:30 a.m.–4:30 p.m. Time: 2 hours.*

### St. Andrews Cathedral
**St. Andrews**

These jaw-droppingly spectacular ruins between the water and the town are great fun to explore and capture on film. The history of what was once the largest building in Scotland goes back to the 11th century, when St. Andrews was just a wee settlement. The cathedral became a shrine for medieval pilgrims, and Protestant reformers later pillaged it. The one intact section is St. Tule's Tower, which houses a small museum. You can climb the tower for the best view in town. The visitor center's museum contains a collection of Celtic and medieval carved stones and exhibits on the history of the cathedral.

 St. Andrews Cathedral and St. Andrews Castle offer a discounted joint ticket for £4 ($5.80) adults, £3 ($4.35) seniors, £1.25 ($1.80) children. It's available at either place. If you just want to explore the grounds of the cathedral, they're free.

*Eastern end of North Street, off Pends Road.* ☎ *01334-472-563. Admission: £2.20 ($3.20) adults, £1.60 ($2.30) seniors, £.75 ($1.10) children under 16. Open: Daily Apr–Sept 9:30 a.m.–5:45 p.m., Oct–Mar 9:30 a.m.–3:45 p.m. Time: 2 hours.*

### Scottish Fisheries Museum
**Anstruther**

Built on an ancient fishing site, this museum is a lot more interesting than it sounds. On the quay outside are more than a dozen boats that are part of the collection, and inside are informative exhibits on every aspect of the Scottish fishing trade, including whaling, and a re-creation of a fisherman's cottage. Locals built the museum in tribute to their proud history and industry. Also here is a monument for Scottish fishermen who have been lost at sea.

*Harbourhead, Anstruther, 9 miles south of St. Andrews.* ☎ *01333-310-628. Admission: £3.40 ($4.95) adults, £2.30 ($3.35) seniors and children, £9.50 ($14) family. Open: Apr–Oct Mon–Fri 10 a.m.–5:30 p.m., Sun 11 a.m.–5 p.m.; Nov–Mar Mon–Fri 10 a.m.–4:30 p.m., Sun 2–4:30 p.m. Time: 1 hour.*

### Secret Bunker
**Troy Wood**

Remember the Cold War? The Secret Bunker is the former underground nuclear command center where Scotland's leaders would have lived in the event of a nuclear war. The farmhouse building doesn't look like much, but that's just a false front to the entrance of the fortified compound 100 feet underground. Kept from public knowledge for more than four decades, the nuclear bomb shelter has been declassified. In addition to the main communications center, the labyrinthine compound also contains a television studio, movie screening rooms, dorms, a mess hall, and a chapel (rentable if you want a unique marriage ceremony). A maze of tunnels connects everything; although you're free to explore, I recommend taking the informative guided tour (included in the admission price) and watching the interesting audiovisual display.

*Crown Buildings, Troy Wood, 5 miles south of St. Andrews.* ☎ *01333-310-301. Admission: £5.95 ($8.65) adults, £5.35 ($7.80) children. Open: Daily Apr–Oct 10 a.m.– 5 p.m. Tours 1:30 and 3:30 p.m. Closed Nov–Mar. Time: 2 hours.*

### SS *Sir Walter Scott* Steamship
**Loch Katrine**

For 100 years, this old-fashioned ship has taken passengers along Loch Katrine to marvel at the beauty of the Trossachs. A bit of floating history, the ship is the last screw-driven steamship on the inland waters of Scotland. It runs between the Trossachs Pier and Stronachlachar and passes an eyeful of stunning views along the way. The ship is named after the renowned author who made Loch Katrine famous in his poem *The Lady in the Lake*. Be warned, however: This popular trip can get overcrowded in the summer, so if you can, go on a weekday.

*Loch Katrine, Trossachs.* ☎ *01877-376-316. Admission: Morning trip: £6.50 ($9.45) adults, £3.75 ($5.44) children, £16 ($23) family. Afternoon trips: £5 ($7.25) adults, £3.25 ($4.70) children, £14.50 ($21) family. Departures: Daily Apr–Oct 11 a.m., 1:45 p.m., 3:45 p.m. Time: 4 hours.*

### Stirling Castle
**Stirling**

Long the home of the kings of Scotland, this beautiful Renaissance castle was the residence of Mary Queen of Scots, her son, James IV of Scotland (and later James I of England), and other Stuart monarchs. A natural fortress guarding the lowest point of the Forth Loch, the castle on a hill was the region's strategic military point throughout much of the 13th and 14th centuries. Take your time and explore the whole place. Unless you take a guided tour (included in the admission price), you can wander about as you please, and perhaps even stumble upon a few hidden underground rooms that aren't marked. Don't miss the beautiful gardens of wildflowers and roses, or the picture-worthy views from the walks along the castle walls and preserved halls. Several areas make perfect picnic spots — so grab some food in town and enjoy a meal on royal ground. Don't skip the informative introductory center (little ones will love the padded jousting room). An extensive museum highlights the wartime activities of the Argyll and Sutherland Highlander regiments. Both Mary Queen of Scots and James V were crowned in the Chapel Royal.

*Upper Castle Hill. ☎ 01786-450-000. Admission: £7 ($10.15) adults, £5 ($7.25) seniors, £2 ($2.90) children. Open: Daily 9:30 a.m.–6 p.m. Time: 3 hours.*

### Stirling Old Town Jail
**Stirling**

Who wants to be treated like a prisoner? Here's the chance you've been waiting for: a tour of a 150-year-old city jail led by actors in costume who put you through the paces as an inmate. The kids will love it — especially if one of the prisoners tries to escape — and adults will find the exhibits on the jail cells interesting. Prior to the opening of this "modern" prison, the Tolbooth jail held prisoners in cramped, unsanitary conditions. Everyone will enjoy the views from the roof — except Jock Rankin, the hangman and your tour guide. Who knew incarceration was such fun? In the winter, the tour is self-guided.

*St. John Street, at the top of the street where it meets Castle Wynd. ☎ 01786-450-050. Admission: £3.95 ($5.75) adults, £3 ($4.35) students, £2.75 ($4) seniors and children, £10.75 ($16) family. Open: Daily Apr–Sept 9:30 a.m.–6 p.m., Oct and Mar 9:30 a.m.–5:30 p.m., Nov–Feb 9:30 a.m.–5p.m. Time: 90 min.*

# Exploring regional landmarks

### St. Andrews University
**St. Andrews**

The oldest university in Scotland became even more popular in 2001 when Prince William started classes here as a freshman. The lovely campus houses one of the best colleges in the U.K. You're free to meander the grounds, but I recommend taking the official tour, which covers the university's history and takes you into a few buildings. The tour leaves St. Salvator's Chapel on Butts Wynd.

*Between the Scores and North Street. (☎ 01334-462-245). Tours: Mid-June–Aug Mon–Fri 11 a.m. and 2:30 p.m. Admission: £4.50 ($6.55) adults, £3.50 ($5.10) seniors and students.*

### Lady's Rock and Star Pyramid
**Stirling**

Located in the Stirling Castle cemetery, Lady's Rock was once a popular vantage point from which to watch tournaments in the valley below. One of the more interesting items is the Star Pyramid, a large stone monument commemorating religious martyrs.

*Enter through the castle esplanade or from Castle Wynd, next to Holy Rude Church.*

### Castle Back Walks
**Stirling**

Running along Stirling's old town walls, arguably the best preserved in Scotland, is one of the finest urban walkways in Europe. This wheelchair- and walker-friendly promenade affords lovely views of the city and has plenty of exit points into town. Interestingly, the town wall was built in 1547 after King Henry VIII announced that he would force a marriage between his son, Edward, and the then-infant Mary Queen of Scots.

*Pick up the walk off Castle Wynd or by the tourist office on Dunbarton Road.*

### The Beheading Stone
**Stirling**

How ghastly! You couldn't possibly skip this one, even if getting there is a bit of a walk. But a walk is better than being dragged to meet your maker on a slab of rock. These days, the Beheading Stone is under an iron cage, lest this old capital punishment become vogue again. In 1425, King James I had Murdoch, Duke of Albany, and his two sons executed for misuse of power. What would today's politicians say to that?

*Follow the Back Walk (which follows the Old Town walls) around the castle, or use the shorter path at the roundabout at Union and Cowan streets.*

### The Old Stirling Bridge
**Stirling**

This stone bridge over one of the narrowest points in the River Forth replaced a wooden bridge that was the central point of contention in a 1297 battle between William Wallace and his band of Scots and the English. Wallace secured victory over the English in 1297 by destroying the wooden bridge. The current bridge dates from the late 15th century. It's accessible on foot from the town center, but driving is easier.

*From Goosecroft Road, where the bus and rail stations are, make a right on Union Street at the roundabout.*

*St. Andrews*

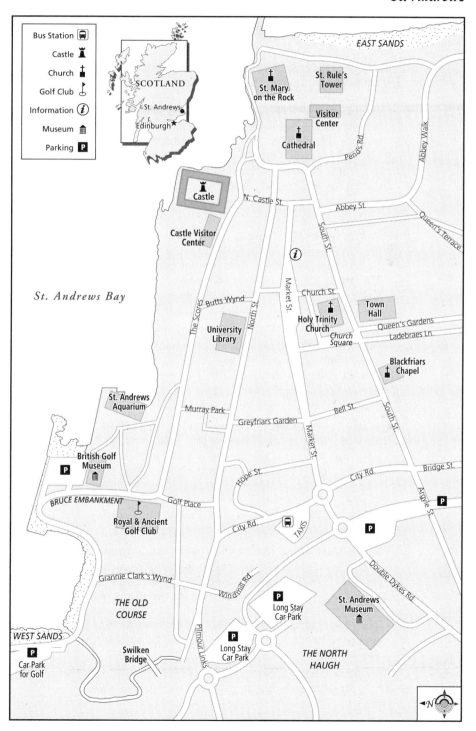

Bus Station
Castle
Church
Golf Club
Information
Museum
Parking

SCOTLAND

St. Andrews
Edinburgh

EAST SANDS

St. Mary
on the Rock

St. Rule's
Tower

Visitor
Center

Cathedral

Pends Rd.

Abbey Walk

Castle

N. Castle St.

Abbey St.

Castle Visitor
Center

South St.

Queen's Terrace

*St. Andrews Bay*

The Scores

Butts Wynd

Market St.

North St.

Church St.

Holy Trinity
Church

Town
Hall

Queen's Gardens

University
Library

Church
Square

Ladebraes Ln.

Blackfriars
Chapel

St. Andrews
Aquarium

Murray Park

Greyfriars Garden

Bell St.

Market St.

South St.

British Golf
Museum

Hope St.

City Rd.

Bridge St.

BRUCE EMBANKMENT

Golf Place

Argyle St.

Royal & Ancient
Golf Club

City Rd.

TAXIS

Grannie Clark's Wynd

Double Dykes Rd.

THE OLD
COURSE

Windmill Rd.

Long Stay
Car Park

St. Andrews
Museum

WEST SANDS

Pilmour Links

Long Stay
Car Park

THE NORTH
HAUGH

Car Park
for Golf

Swilken
Bridge

N

# Shopping in Fife and the Central Highlands

Neither Stirling nor St. Andrews has a shopping district, but you'll find a fair number of shops worth checking out in or near both towns.

✔ **Crail Pottery,** 75 Nethergate, Crail. (☎ **01333-450-413**). Three generations of potters are on hand, creating a wide range of hand-thrown pottery. Whether it's porcelain, teapots, jardinières, or gardenware, you'll find high-quality pieces. The pottery shop is in a wonderful flowery medieval yard with plenty of examples of the artists' handicraft lying about. Open: Monday to Friday from 8 a.m. to 5 p.m., and Saturday and Sunday from 10 a.m. to 5 p.m. Closed holidays.

✔ **McCutcheons,** 51 Baker St., Old Town Stirling (☎ **01786-461-771**). Indubitably the finest bookseller in the region. Books date from 1473 to the present — you name the topic, and the staff will find it. The prices are reasonable, so if you're looking for a good Scottish antiquarian book as a gift, or if you simply like to get lost in old bookstores (as I do), this is your place. Call for hours.

✔ **Jim Farmer,** 1 St. Mary's Place, Market Street, St. Andrews (☎ **01334-476-796**). Heads up, golfers. Did you lose a few too many balls in the water? Need a new pitching wedge, or just a fancy set of club warmers? Jim will take care of you and maybe even help you take a stroke or two off your game. Shirts, hats, T-shirts, shoes, and more are on hand. Call for hours.

✔ **Scotts Delicatessen,** 22 Barnton St., Stirling (☎ **01789-451-671**). This new little shop holds everything for you if you're a foodie who wants to slip a few fine Scottish ingredients and dishes past customs. From cakes and toffee to fresh haggis, meals and spirits, this tidy tartan shop has exactly what you've probably been looking for since you ate it for dinner or breakfast. Open: Monday to Thursday from 8 a.m. to 8 p.m., Friday and Saturday from 10 a.m. to 10 p.m., and Sunday from noon to 6 p.m.

✔ **St. Andrew's Fine Art,** 84A Market St., St. Andrews (☎ **01334-474-080**). One of the finest art galleries in the country, this shop seems much too small to hold all its excellent pieces — contemporary art crowds the walls. Whether you prefer prints or watercolors, oils or drawings, you'll find something to spark your interest here. The shop has specialized in Scottish art since 1800, but its stock goes well beyond the usual landscapes to include unique modern pieces. Call for hours.

✔ **R.R. Henderson,** 6–8 Friar Street, Stirling (☎ **01786-473-681**). Principally a kilt-making shop, this store also has a good range of other apparel, such as woolly mittens, tweed jackets, and cashmere sweaters. What sets Henderson's apart from other shops of its type is that it will custom-make tartans for you. You can also rent an entire kilt outfit (starting at £39.99/$58 a day) if you're in the area for a special occasion or think it'd be fun to sport the local look. Call for hours.

✔ **Barbara Davidson Pottery,** Muirhall Farm, Larbert, 9 miles south of Stirling on the A18. (☎ **01324-554-430**). Ms. Davidson's pottery studio, one of the most popular in the country, is in on 18th-century farm. My favorite thing about the place, other than its large range of ceramics, is that in the summer the studio will let you have a shot at the potter's wheel and make your own pot. Open: Monday to Saturday from 10 a.m. to 5 p.m., and Sunday from noon to 5 p.m.

✔ **The Scottish Wool Centre,** Aberfoyle, Stirling. (☎ **01877-382-854**). More of an attraction than a shop, this is one store where the kids won't be bored. Besides exhibits that show everything you want to know about Scottish wool and more, the Spinner's Cottage gives you a chance to make your own wool. On weekends, dog lovers and shepherds (seriously) convene here to show off their Border collies and give sheepdog demonstrations. Oh, and the center also has one of the largest selections of woolens and knitwear in the country. In addition to fleeces and jumpers, it carries Scottish gifts and souvenirs. The cost for the exhibits is £3 ($4.35) adults, £2 ($2.90) children, £6 ($8.70) family. Open: Daily, October to March from 10 a.m. to 5 p.m., and April to Sept from 9:30 a.m.–6:30 p.m.

# Doing the Pub Crawl

If you're staying in Stirling or St. Andrews, check out some of these watering holes, which are a notch or two above the norm. Many of the following pubs keep late hours; call for the latest opening and closing times.

✔ **Central Bar,** corner of Market and College streets, St. Andrews. (☎ **01334-478-296**). If you're looking for a quintessential old-fashioned pub, look no further. This fine bar, popular with students, has a good selection on tap, including "guest" ales, and an extensive international wine selection. While you're there, you should try one of the excellent traditional pies or the house specialty, Yorkshire pudding. Despite having one television, the Central Bar fills up when there is a game on, all eyes squinting in one direction. Open: Monday to Saturday from 11 a.m. to 11:45 p.m., and Sunday from 12:30 p.m. to midnight.

✔ **The Jigger Inn,** Old Station Road, St. Andrews. (☎ **01334-474-371**). Next to the Old Course Hotel lies a whitewashed brick building that was constructed as a cottage for the railroad's stationmaster in 1846. Now it's the loveliest little pub in St. Andrews. It's full of comfy seating, golf pictures and memorabilia, and bragging golfers. Out back are those who appreciate an open beer terrace that faces over the famous Old Course. Golfers: No spikes allowed in the pub. Open: Monday to Saturday from 11 a.m. to 11 p.m., and Sunday from noon to 11 p.m.

✔ **Nicky-Tams,** 29 Baker St., Stirling (☎ **01786-472-194**). This fun little pub is a favorite among the locals. It's on one of the main drags of town, but visitors have yet to discover it. It offers good live music (traditional and contemporary) a couple of nights a week and a popular Sunday night pub quiz — although out-of-towners admittedly have a handicap. You can't miss the whitewashed stone façade on an otherwise muted street.

✔ **Settle Inn,** 91 St. Mary's Wynd, corner of Barn Road and Upper Bridge Street, Stirling (☎ **01786-474-609**). Since 1733, patrons have been settling into the booths and cool pints of the oldest alehouse in town. Not just a historical footnote, the pub is a favorite among locals and a good place to meet someone other than the tourists you've seen at all the attractions during the day.

✔ **Victoria,** 4 St. Mary's Place, St. Andrews. (☎ **01334-476-964**). Taking its cue from the Old West, this Scottish "saloon" is a fun place to hear live music or have a pint with the mostly student crowd. Weekends feature bands playing blues or rock, when the bar fills with toe-tappin' fans. It may be difficult to get to the bar's edge during the late happy hour (8–9 p.m.), when pints cost a pound, but it's the best deal in town. Open: Saturday to Wednesday from noon to midnight, and Thursday and Friday from noon to 1 a.m.

✔ **Whistlebinkies,** 73–75 St. Mary's Wynd, Stirling (☎ **01786-451-256**). It sounds like a place for kids, and young patrons are indeed welcome, as evidenced by the kid's menu. But adults will appreciate the comfortable booths and selection of good beers and whiskys. The fireplace and stained-glass windows are nice touches. The building, just down the hill from the Castle, dates to 1595 and originally housed the castle's blacksmith.

# Fast Facts: Fife and the Central Highlands

## Area Code

The area code for Stirling is **01786,** St. Andrews is **01334,** and Aberfoyle and Callander (in the Trossachs) is **01877.** You need to dial the area code only if you are calling from outside the city you want to reach.

## Emergencies

Dial **999** for police, fire, or ambulance.

## Genealogy Resources

**Tay Valley Family History Society,** 179 Princes St., Dundee (☎ 01382-461-845).

## Hospitals

**Stirling Royal Infirmary,** Livilands Road, south of the town center (☎ 01786-434-000). **St. Andrews Memorial Hospital,** Abbey Walk, south of Abbey Street (☎ 01334-472-327).

## Information

Tourist offices include: 41 Dumbarton Rd., **Stirling** (☎ 01786-475-019); 70 Market St., **St. Andrews** (☎ 01334-472-021). Summer offices: Main Street, **Aberfoyle** (☎ 01877-382-352); next to the castle, **Stirling** (☎ 01786-47-9901).

## Internet Access

**CommsPort,** 83 Market St., St. Andrews. (☎ 01334-475-181; Internet: www.comm sport.com). Hours: Mon–Sat 8 a.m.–5:30 p.m., Sun 10:30 a.m.–6 p.m. Cost: £6 ($9) per hour.

## Mail

Post offices are at 127 South St., St. Andrews (☎ 01334-472-321), and 4 Broad St., Stirling (☎ 01786-474-537).

# Chapter 15

# Tayside and Grampian

. . . . . . . . . . . . . . . . . . . . . . . . . . . . . . . . . . . . . . . . . . . . .

## In This Chapter

▶ Finding great places to stay and dine in this vast region

▶ Visiting the top distilleries in Scotland

▶ Skiing — on snow and on dry land

▶ Discovering great castles, famous ships, and top-notch theater

▶ Shopping trail for heather, tweeds, and tartans

▶ Pulling a pint in local pubs

. . . . . . . . . . . . . . . . . . . . . . . . . . . . . . . . . . . . . . . . . . . . .

*T*his chapter is a large one because it covers such a large area of Scotland. Tayside and Grampian are full of excellent attractions, accommodations, and restaurants, but the distances between them can be great. I highlight all the top venues and give you enough options to spend either a day or a week here — it all depends on the amount of time you have. You can either concentrate on the excellent southern towns of Perth and Pitlochry or trek through the eastern Highlands up to the coastal town of Aberdeen. The bottom line is, no matter how much or how little time you give the area, you won't be disappointed. There's plenty to do and see for adults, kids, history buffs, and whisky fans alike.

 I know; it's easy to be overwhelmed. Using the maps to plot a course is important. Take a pencil and mark off the attractions you want to see most. Figure out the best order in which to see them, both coming and going. Then plot your accommodations and dining choices around the attractions you plan to see.

## Orienting Yourself to Tayside and Grampian

The largest town in the region is **Aberdeen.** The first thing you notice about the city is how gray it appears; it seems that all the buildings are the same drab color. It's no coincidence that Aberdeen's nickname is the "Granite City," because much of the town was built from granite mined in Rubislaw. Also known as the oil capital of Europe, Aberdeen is the port that receives oil pumped in the North Sea. It has plenty of bars and restaurants but is short on attractions. The most interesting museum in town, in fact, concentrates on the local oil and fishing industry. The town lies between two rivers, the Dee and the Don, and despite its monotone coloring, the broad streets and elegant buildings give the city a stately feel. In the summer, roses blossom all over town.

**Perth** is a bustling little town between two large open park areas, North and South Inch, about 1,000 yards apart. Both are worth a stroll. This royal burgh beside the River Tay has a couple of decent restaurants and lies near one of Scotland's biggest attractions: Scone Palace. **Pitlochry** is one of the most visited inland resort towns in the country, mainly because of its excellent theater. The city's location — technically at the geographic center of Scotland — makes it an excellent base for day touring in every direction. The River Garry affords lovely views (including sightings of spawning salmon).

## Getting There

Train and bus systems connect many cities in this large area, but they don't serve plenty of the best attractions. Taking the train to Aberdeen from Glasgow or Edinburgh, for example, isn't cheap and leaves you stuck in a town that is long on pubs but short on attractions. If you plan to come this far away from base camp, you'll be happy to have the convenience and flexibility of a car.

- ✔ **By plane:** The **Aberdeen Airport** (☎ 01224-722-331) is 6 miles north of town. Planes connect Aberdeen to Glasgow, Edinburgh, Dundee, and the Shetland and Orkney islands. The **Dundee Airport** (☎ 01382-643-242) is on Riverside Drive; it has service to Aberdeen and Edinburgh.

- ✔ **By ferry:** P&O North Sea ferries (☎ 01224-589-111) run from Aberdeen to Lerwick in the Shetland Islands.

- ✔ **By car:** The A90 stretches from Perth to Aberdeen. The A96 connects Elgin and Aberdeen. Aberdeen to Grantown-on-Spey can be reached from the A944 to A939. Most of the venues and attractions run along one of those major roads.

- ✔ **By train:** ScotRail (☎ 0845-748-4950; Internet: www.scotrail.co.uk) runs to Perth, Dundee, Elgin, and Aberdeen, connecting to Inverness, Glasgow, and Edinburgh.

- ✔ **By bus:** Citylink (☎ 0990-505-050) runs from Inverness, Glasgow, and Edinburgh to Pitlochry, Dundee, Aberdeen, and Perth. The **National Express** (☎ 0990-808-080) runs from London to Dundee. To Aberfeldy, catch **Stagecoach** (☎ 01738-629-339) from Pitlochry and Perth. To Braemar and Elgin, use **Bluebird Buses** (☎ 01224-212-266) from Aberdeen.

*Tayside and Grampian*

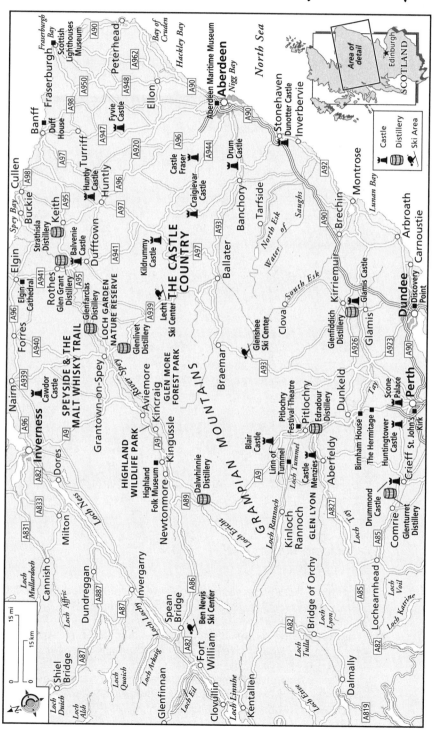

# Knowing Where to Stay

Your best options for accommodations are in or near the three major towns. Like most places in Scotland, the region offers both low- and high-end accommodations. Because it's such a large area, you may want to choose your accommodations around the attractions you decide to visit.

## Atholl Villa Guest House

**$$   Pitlochry**

Flowers are the theme at this pretty, four-star bed-and-breakfast. An Australian couple who had operated a four-star B&B in Edinburgh opened Atholl Villa a couple of years ago, bringing a little sophistication to the tourist trail. The rooms are very comfortable, and the floral theme extends to the interior decoration. The location is convenient, across the street from the tourist board office.

*29 Atholl Rd.* ☎ *01796-473-820. Rack rates: £56 ($81) double. Children half-price. MC, V.*

## Braemar Lodge

**$$   Braemar**

This homey granite country house on the outskirts of town is an unpretentious, comfortable accommodation. The rooms are quite spacious, and most have views of the Cairngorm Mountains. My favorite feature is the oak-paneled bar, where you can sip a whisky nightcap before a log fire — just the thing after skiing on the nearby Glenshee slopes. If the Victorian shooting lodge isn't down-home enough for you, log cabins with kitchens rent by the week.

*6 Glenshee Rd.* ☎ *01339-741-627. E-mail:* info@braemarlodge.co.uk. *Internet:* www.braemarlodge.co.uk. *Rack rates: £40–£100 ($58–$145) double. MC, V.*

## Caledonian Thistle Hotel

**$$$   Aberdeen**

Though not outstanding in any one way, this hotel has a lot going for it. It's in a good location, the staff is efficient and pleasant, and the rooms are comfortable to luxurious. The Victorian front and lobby are lovely, as are the sitting rooms. It's like staying at a Hilton — upscale but not luxe. The hotel does a fine job accommodating foreign guests.

*10–14 Union Terrace, off Union Street, facing Union Terrace Gardens.* ☎ *01224-640-233. Fax: 01224-641-627. E-mail:* aberdeen.caledonian@thistle.co.uk. *Rack rates: £70–£120 ($102–$174) double. AE, DC, MC, V.*

*Aberdeen*

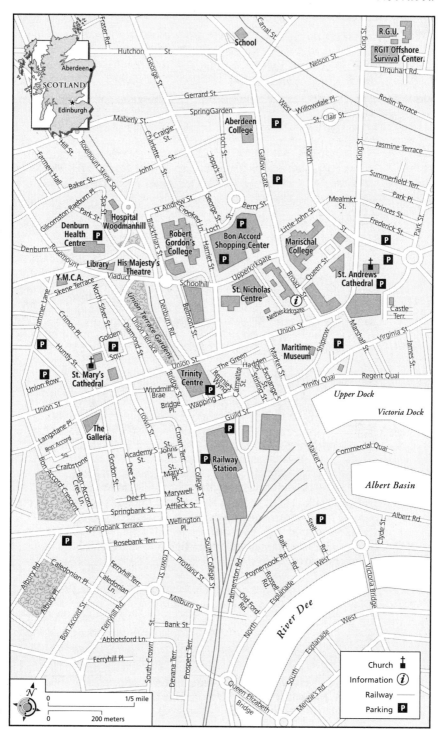

### Farleyer House Hotel
$$$ **Weem, Aberfeldy**

Not far off the beaten path is this luxurious 15th-century country house on a 30-acre estate in the beautiful Tay Valley. If your huge room doesn't provide enough room for maxin' your relaxin', try one of the lovely lounges or drawing rooms full of books, games, and a self-serve bar. Kids will enjoy running around the grounds and choosing from the good selection of movies available to watch in the room. Salmon fishers, take note: The Farleyer's grounds offer some of the best salmon fishing on the River Tay.

*2 miles from Aberfeldy, on the B846 over Tummel Bridge.* ☎ *01887-820-332. Fax: 01887-829-430. Rack rates: £150–£170 ($218–$247) double. AE, DC, MC, V.*

### Fasganeoin Hotel
$$ **Pitlochry**

Just off the main drag, this house hotel is a few minutes' walk from the city or a river walk. The rooms are comfy and cute, featuring a flower and antique motif. Some rooms have a cozy sunken floor, giving the feeling of having your own pad. The peaceful grounds offer a lovely respite. The breakfast is quite yummy. The knowledgeable owners are eager to assist guests. For the price, you can't beat Fasganeoin (pronounced "faze-gannon"; it means "place for the birds" in Gaelic).

*Perth Road, opposite the Blair Atholl Distillary.* ☎ *01796-472-387. Fax: 01796-474-285. E-mail:* sabrina@fasganeoin.freeserve.co.uk. *Rack rates: £60–£64 ($87–$93) double. AE, DC, MC, V.*

### Invercauld Arms Hotel
$$ **Braemar**

This old stone building is comfortable and convenient. With plush sofas and velvet chairs in the front rooms, and big beds in the nicely decorated rooms, the tranquil Invercauld Arms is a welcome retreat after a day of sightseeing or skiing. A log fire in one of the sitting rooms is a lovely place to veg out. The staff is very friendly and helpful, and the hotel recently reduced its prices.

*On the A93 on the north side of town.* ☎ *01339-741-605. Fax: 01339-741-428. Rack rates: £55–£98.50 ($80–$143) double. AE, DC, MC, V.*

### The Lodge Guesthouse
$–$$ **Elgin**

This large, lovely four-star guesthouse is your best bet for a night's stay in Elgin. It books many return visits by business travelers, and it's easy to see why: The rooms are simple and comfortable, the owners are on top of the best places to dine in town, and the overstuffed chairs in the main lounge make it a lovely spot for a cup o' tay or relaxed television watching. The breakfasts are better than mom used to make, and the icing on the cake is that the price is unbeatable. Insider tip: Rooms on the first floor have bigger ceilings and baths, if that's your pleasure. Nonsmokers will rejoice at the Lodge's strict nonsmoking policy.

*20 Duff Avenue.* ☎ *01343-549-981. Fax: 01343-540-527. E-mail:* thelodgeguest house@talk21.com. *Internet:* www.beeandbee.com. *Rack rates: £40–£52 ($58–$74) double. AE, DC, MC, V.*

### MacDonald's Guest House & Restaurant
**$$   Pitlochry**

This popular guesthouse and restaurant has a loyal following. Don't even think about trying to get a room here at the start of the Pitlochry theater season. The rooms are nicely decorated and the hospitality enormous, but the best thing about the place is undoubtedly the food. Don't worry about getting to breakfast on time; it's served all day. And you can't beat the price.

*140 Atholl Rd.* ☎ *01796-472-170. Fax: 01796-474-221. E-mail:* macdonalds. pitlochry@usa.net. *Internet:* www.SmoothHound.co.uk/hotels/ macdonal.html. *Rack rates: £56 ($81) double. AE, MC, V.*

### Mansion House Hotel
**$$$   Elgin**

Literally a mansion, this luxury hotel is without a doubt the nicest and most elegant accommodation you'll find around Elgin. Once the home of a Scottish baron, it has a castlelike tower and views of the River Lossie. The lodgings are pure comfort. The individually decorated rooms have four-poster beds and fine views, and the hotel has a sauna, Jacuzzi, pool, gym, and a Turkish bath. Yes, you heard right, a Turkish bath.

*The Haugh, Elgin. From A96, take Alexandra Road to Haugh Road, behind Lady Hill.* ☎ *01343-548-811. Fax: 01343-547-916. E-mail:* reception@mhelgin.co.uk. *Internet:* www.mansionhousehotel.co.uk. *Rack rates: £110–£160 ($160–$232) double. AE, DC, MC, V.*

### Marcliffe at Pitfodels
**$$$   Aberdeen**

The best place to stay in Aberdeen, the small luxury hotel walks a thin line between high-class accommodation and intimate attention. The family-run, three-story hotel sits among trees and has a country feel despite its proximity to Aberdeen. All the individually decorated rooms are comfortable and spacious, the beds huge, and the antique furniture in good taste. There's evening maid service, 24-hour room service, and other little perks such as bathrobes, fresh fruit, mini-bars, and newspaper and magazine delivery. Mikhail Gorbachev officially opened the place as a guest in 1993, and if it's good enough for the father of *glasnost,* it's good enough for you.

*North Deeside Road, off A92.* ☎ *01224-861-000. Fax: 01224-868-860. Rack rates: £125–£175 ($181–$254) double. AE, DC, MC, V.*

### Parklands Hotel
$$–$$$　**Perth**

This luxury accommodation occupies a stylish Georgian town house once owned by a lord provost (mayor). The hotel overlooks the woods of South Inch parkland and is near the railroad station, a peaceful oasis in a bustling little town. The rooms are wonderfully decorated and very spacious, and the Victorian conservatory makes a lovely spot for high tea. The most remarkable thing about this fine hotel is how little it costs to stay here. Because the Parklands caters to many business travelers, rooms are cheaper on the weekends.

*2 St. Leonard's Bank.* ☎ *01738-622-451. Fax: 01738-622-046. E-mail:* parklands. perth@virgin.net. *Rack rates: £99–£115 ($144–$167) double. AE, DC, MC, V.*

### Salutation Hotel
$$　**Perth**

It's right on the main street, but the Salutation is a quiet haven of big beds and friendly service. After you've walked all over town and had your dinner, relax in the huge overstuffed couches by the fire in the lobby over a nightcap. The Salutation is also a historical footnote — the building was once a meeting place for Bonnie Prince Charlie and his troops. It's no wonder the staff has its act together — the spot has been welcoming guests since 1699. The Adam Restaurant is worth a look-see even if you don't eat here; check out its original barrel-vaulted ceiling. One downside: no private parking.

*34 South St., near the River Tay.* ☎ *01738-630-066. Web: E-mail:* salessalutation@ strathmorehotels.com. *Internet:* www.strathmorehotels.com. *Rack rates: £80–£93 ($116–$135) double. AE, DC, MC, V.*

### Seafield Hotel
$$　**Cullen**

While traveling along the northern coast, you may be struck by the beauty of one small town with viaduct bridges and a stunning coastline: Cullen. Should you choose to spend an evening here, stay at the Seafield. The whitewashed hotel has a three-star rating, but the rooms are definitely five-star, with big tartan-clad beds, large bathrooms, and quality furniture. On the premises are a couple of lovely lounges and a dining room that serves the best dinner in town. When your room is as lovely as the town view, it's difficult to decide where to spend your time. And that's the kind of problem you *want* on your holiday. Parents with kids: An adjoining room with bunk beds holds two children and costs only £10 ($14.50) more. And they can watch movies in the TV room if they're not interested in strolling along the beach.

*Seafield Street (the A96), in the heart of Cullen.* ☎ *01542-840-791. Fax: 01542-840-736. E-mail:* info@theseafieldhotel.com. *Internet:* www.theseafieldhotel.com. *Rack rates: £75 ($109) double. AE, DC, MC, V.*

# Dining in Tayside and Grampian

This chapter covers a large geographical area full of mediocre dining options. Thank goodness you have this guide! I've discovered plenty of great choices in my travels, and I'm happy to pass my selections on to you. A few are a little out of the way, but most are in the major towns of the region.

### Abbey Court Restaurant
$$–$$$   **Elgin   International**

The cuisine of this nice little restaurant in the heart of town is hard to pin down. The menu covers traditional Scottish entrees such as venison, pleasing seafood dishes such as salmon, and vegetarian picks such as homemade pasta. The dining area abounds with fake plants, and the wait staff is pleasant enough. The biggest selling point is the price of a decent meal. The wine list is remarkably extensive, though, and the restaurant's specialty is ice-cream desserts, which are worth more than just a look. Be sure to save room.

*15 Greyfriars St.* ☎ *01343-542-849. Reservations not required. Main courses: £5.90–£16.95 ($8.60–$25). AE, DC, MC, V. Open: Mon–Sat noon to 2 p.m. and 6:30–9:30 p.m.*

### Beiderbeckes
$$$   **Perth   International**

Set in an old brick building, this fine-dining bistro with vintage table settings has a rustic feel. But there's nothing rough about the contemporary menu. It includes veggie-heavy pasta Rondo, Mexican sombrero steak, and savory "swamp pot" sausages. Be sure to indulge in an excellent dessert, like "Cool Jazz" raspberry mouse on a bourbon biscuit.

*10 N. Port, just off Charlotte Street, by the North Inch.* ☎ *01738-451-774. Reservations accepted. Main courses: £7.45–£15.95 ($11–$23). AE, DC, MC, V. Open: Tues–Sat 5:30–11 p.m.*

### The Cross

$$$$ **Kingussie** **Scottish**

This restaurant and the hotel of the same name are in an old tweed mill, but don't confuse its humble blue-collar beginnings with its high-class blue-blood status now. You'd be foolish not to partake of the carefully chosen wine and cheese lists before digging into a mouth-watering entrée. If you're not sure what to get, stick to favorite dishes such as Highland lamb, wild pigeon, or venison Francatelli. Ask for a seat on the terrace overlooking the lovely grounds if the weather is agreeable.

*Off Main Street, Tweed Mill Brae, Ardbroilach.* ☎ *01540-661-166. Reservations required. Fixed price: £35 ($51) for 5 courses. AE, DC, MC, V. Open: Mar–Nov Wed–Mon 7–9 p.m. Closed Dec–Feb.*

### Estaminet

$ **Aberdeen** **Mediterranean**

Estaminet offers plenty to wet your whistle and fill your tummy, but don't miss this college-crowd restaurant and bar's excellent tapas. The "mussels with beer" specials let you enjoy a half pint of ale with excellent mussels. Meals range from made-to-order pizzas and burgers to nachos and a large selection of upscale pub grub. You have the option of sitting upstairs or relaxing in the more casual downstairs area, lighted by a large sunroof and dotted with stuffed couches and a warming fireplace. Estaminet (Flemish for "eating out") has a nonsmoking section and a foosball table.

*8 Littlejohn St., between Broad and W. North streets.* ☎ *01224-622-657. Reservations not accepted. Main courses: £2.95–£5.50 ($4.35–$8). AE, MC, V. Open: Daily 8 a.m. to midnight.*

### La Cloche

$ **Aberdeen** **French**

This little red-walled lunch cafe next to the St. Nicholas Church graveyard is just waiting to be discovered (read: It's not crowded . . . yet). It offers excellent French baguette pizzas and panini breads, as well as superb, imaginative salads such as feta cheese and tomato, and hot grilled goat cheese. So go, but be quiet about it, and make sure no one is following you down the alley along the churchyard.

*9 Correction Wynd.* ☎ *01224-644-166. Reservations not accepted. Main courses: £2.50–£4.50 ($3.65–$6.55). MC, V. Open: 11 a.m.–4 p.m.*

### Let's Eat

$$–$$$ **Perth** **Scottish/Seafood**

Yeah, let's! This popular, tasteful, tasty restaurant used to be a theater. Decorated with lots of plants, it has an upscale feel, sans attitude. The international menu includes filet of sea bass with gazpacho broth, blackened Uist salmon, and other fresh fish dishes and game. The desserts are to die for, and the wine list is impressive.

*77/79 Kinnoull St., at the corner of Atholl, near the North Inch.* ☎ *01738-643-377. Reservations accepted. Main courses: £8.50–£10.50 ($12–$15). AE, DC, MC, V. Open: Tues–Sat noon to 2 p.m. and 6:30–9:45 p.m.*

### The Old Armoury

$$–$$$  Pitlochry  Scottish/Seafood

This cottage-turned-restaurant near the woods is a fine treat. Inside the ivy-covered stone building, you'll find a large fireplace and candlelit tables. If the weather is nice, you may want to dine out on the terrace surrounded by perennials and the sounds of the nearby Pitlochry dam. The eclectic menu features tasty morsels such as excellent Thai green curry, breast of Highland pheasant, and a Cajun filet of salmon caught right here in the River Tay.

*Armoury Road, a 3-minute walk from the town center on the little road to the dam and salmon ladder.* ☎ *01796-47-4281. Reservations recommended on weekends. Main courses: £8.95–£15.95 ($13–$23). AE, DC, MC, V. Open: Daily noon to 2:30 p.m. and 5:30 p.m.–11 p.m.*

### Old Smithy

$$–$$$  Pitlochry  Mediterranean

The lovely old black-and-white cottage with a well outside is a nice place for a great meal. Eat in the formal dining area or in the captain's chairs at the round tables in the cozy tearoom. Either way, you'll be feasting on Mediterranean-inspired dishes made with great care, such as venison with Madeira and wild mushroom sauce, or savory crispy duck. The restaurant serves a pre-theater dinner between 5 and 7 p.m.

*154 Atholl Rd. at Cloichard Place, at the north end of town.* ☎ *01796-472-356. Reservations recommended for dinner. Main courses: £7.50–£12.50 ($12–$20). AE, DC, MC, V. Open: Apr–Oct daily 10 a.m.–9 p.m.; Nov–Mar Mon–Thurs 10 a.m.– 6 p.m., Fri–Sat 10 a.m.–9 p.m.*

### Paco's

$$–$$$  Perth  Mexican-American

This largish restaurant may look and feel like a Scottish version of Bennigan's, but the food is consistently delish and the service, even at a busy time, extremely attentive. The inside is TGI Friday's kitsch, but a nice terrace allows outdoor eating on a nice day. The food will be familiar to American and Canadian palates: pizza, steak, salads, burgers, and enchiladas. Better-than-average choices include black bean enchiladas, blackened chicken, and the pork and apple burger. You can even get a bottle of Dos Equis beer. For dessert, go for the artery-hardening Xangos (pronounced "chang-go"), fried cheesecake with ice cream.

*3 Mill St., next to Marks and Spencer.* ☎ *01738-62-2290. Reservations not required. Main courses: £5.95–£12.25 ($8.65–$18). AE, MC, V. Open: Mon–Sat noon to 11 p.m., Sun 5–11 p.m.*

### Prince of India
#### $$   Pitlochry   Indian

You can find excellent Indian food a mere six time zones away from the mother country. The Prince of India offers many, many options, but you may want to direct your attention to the chef's chili garlic chicken or the tandoori king prawns. Vegetarians won't go hungry, either. The comfortable booths and lovely furnishings are straight out of the how-to-decorate-an-Indian-restaurant handbook.

*5–7 Station Rd.* ☎ *01796-472-275. Reservations not required. Main courses: £5.50–£12.95 ($8–$19). AE, MC, V. Open: Daily noon to 2 p.m.; Sun–Wed 5–11:30 p.m., Thurs–Sat 5 p.m. to midnight.*

### The Shore Inn
#### $$–$$$   Portsoy   Scottish

This snug little spot offers a warm welcome, local character, and excellent food, favoring fresh offerings from the water just beyond its doors. Bits of the area's history, including sailing charts, naval memorabilia, antique guns, and the requisite clutter of smoky old bottles, cover the walls. By the door is an old collection box for the "Shipwrecked Mariner's Society" for the widows left by the "sorrow on the sea." As soon as you find a seat at one of the comfortable wood tables, the bartender will likely sit down next to you to talk you through your order. Then the chef will leave his drink at the bar and make a meal to your liking. Roast salmon stuffed with bulgur wheat and balsamic vinegar is a treat, and roast beef with Yorkshire pudding is just like your mom would make (if she was Scottish). Stroll the harbor's edge when you're done and watch the fishermen bring in their catch.

*The Old Harbour, Church Street.* ☎ *01261-842-831. Reservations not required. Main courses: £6.25–£12.95 ($9.10–$19). AE, DC, MC, V. Open: Daily noon to 9 p.m.*

### Silver Darling
#### $$$–$$$$   Aberdeen   Seafood

Getting to this restaurant at the water's edge is a bit of an odyssey, but it's worth it. Silver Darling sits next to an old converted lighthouse with a modern top. At your table in the conservatory dining room overlooking the River Dee, you'll enjoy succulent dishes such as grilled marinated tuna and swordfish, filet of trout poached in red wine and herbs, and turbot steamed on a bed of seaweed with scallop mousse. And those aren't even the specials. It may be pricey, but from the rooftop views overlooking the sea and harbor mouth to the highest-quality food this side of the Highlands, the Silver Darling is worth the extra dough. Vegetarians may go hungry. Book ahead.

*Pocra Quay, Footdee. Follow the road from Aberdeen harbor along the water until you reach the beach, then make a right. ☎ 01224-576-229. Reservations required. Main courses: £13.90–£19.50 ($20–$28). AE, MC, V. Open: Year-round Mon–Fri noon to 2 p.m., Mon–Sat 7–9:30 p.m.; May–Sept Sun 7–9:30 p.m.*

### Strathearn
**$$$$    Auchterarder    Scottish**

At the Gleneagles Hotel in the Perthshire countryside, this restaurant offers great views overlooking Glen Devon. Impressive standards on the menu include cutlet and loin of lamb with parsnips and apple compote, and medallion of venison. Everything is locally grown and fresh. Live piano music complements the view and the award-winning food. Bob Hope ate here once and was said to have been "moved to tears" when the house pianist played "Thanks for the Memories" upon his entrance. Not surprisingly, Guinness is on tap — the Irish brewery owns the restaurant.

*In the Gleneagles Hotel, southwest of Auchterarder. ☎ 01764-662-231. Reservations recommended. Fixed menu: £41 ($60) for 3 courses. AE, DC, MC, V. Open: Daily 7–9 p.m.*

### The Wild Boar
**$–$$    Aberdeen    Scottish**

This nice cafe is a popular place for all tastes. The menu offers Scottish dishes such as steak and ale pie or Aberdeen haddock, plus great juicy burgers, stuffed potatoes, salads, and more. The mushroom stroganoff pilaf is fantastic, and so are the desserts, made in-house. Whether you want dinner or just coffee and pastry, you'll be happy here. The bar has good specials (buy two glasses of wine, keep the rest of the bottle free), and the downstairs dining area has satellite television that usually shows movies.

*19 Belmont St. ☎ 01224-625-357. Reservations not required. Main courses: £1.60–£7.50 ($2.30–$11). AE, DC, MC, V. Open: Daily noon to 9 p.m.*

# Exploring the Area

The Tayside and Grampian region is home to Scotland's best distilleries and some of its top castles and palatial houses. The only way to see the best of the best is to spend a week or longer visiting the area. It is the mandate of this guide to present only the top options and not bog you down with too many superfluous choices. The problem is, there are simply too many good things to see in Tayside and Grampian. My suggestion? Go through the list now and cross off the things you won't mind missing, and do your best with the rest. And then start planning another trip to Tayside and Grampian.

### Aberdeen Maritime Museum
**Aberdeen**

When you go inside, look up; you'll have the whale's-eye view of a scale model of an offshore oil rig. This ⅓₃-scale, £1 million detailed model is the highlight of this three-story museum devoted to the seafaring history of Aberdeen — a city sustained by North Sea oil drilling. The museum has many interesting sea "treasures," models and old pictures of antiquated submarines and diving equipment, and more. Many exhibits, devoted to oil, shipbuilding, and fishing, have touch-screen computers for your exploration. One part of this large, informative museum is in the 1593 house of seaman and Aberdeen provost (mayor) Ross. A good way to see the building is to start at the top and work your way down.

*Shiprow. ☎ 01224-337-700. Admission: Free. Open: Mon–Sat 10 a.m.–5 p.m., Sun noon to 3 p.m. Time: 2 hours.*

### Auchingarrich Wildlife Centre
**Comrie, Perthshire**

The little ones will enjoy this up-close-and-personal encounter with furry animals. The headliner of the place is the Highland cow, a shaggy, horned variation of the common dairy cow. You can hold baby sheep and marvel at rarer beasts such as the meerkat and emu. Other friends from the animal kingdom who live in the 100-acre wildlife park include wallabies, raccoons, otters, chipmunks, hedgehogs, deer, porcupines, waterfowl, and reptiles. From Easter through October, there are hatchings every day. Parents, be prepared to give a birds-and-bees speech — things are a little liberal down on the farm. Some trivia: A herd of cows is actually called a "fold," and of all the breeds of Highland cow, the black cows are the oldest breed in Scotland.

*Three miles from the main street in Comrie; turn at the bridge. ☎ 01764-679-469. Admission: £4 ($5.80) adults, £3.25 ($4.70) seniors and students, £2 ($2.90) children under 16. Open: Daily 10 a.m. to dusk. Time: 3 hours.*

### Balmoral Estate
**Ballater**

Welcome to the vacation home of the royal family. Because this is a working residence for the Queen and her family, commoners like yourself are only allowed into one room of the castle, the Ballroom. On display are pictures of rooms, as well as clothing and gifts belonging to the family.

More interesting than the Ballroom is the museum in the coach house (read: horse stable). Pictures of the royal family from the last 150 years include shots from official visits, such as the time Czar Nicholas II and his family came to Balmoral. You are free to walk the extensive grounds and gardens, and two-hour pony treks are available for £20 ($29). Because the castle is closed when the Queen is in town, it's a good idea to call or e-mail ahead to make sure you'll be able to get in.

*Balmoral, Ballater, off the A93, 8 miles from Banchory.* ☎ *01339-742-334. E-mail:* info@balmoral-castle.co.uk. *Internet:* www.balmoral-castle.co.uk. *Admission: £4 ($5.80) adults, £3 ($4.35) seniors and students, £1 ($1.45) children under 16. Open: Daily mid-Apr–July 10 a.m.–5 p.m. Closed Aug–mid-Apr. Time: 90 min.*

## Balvenie Castle
### Dufftown

When you visit the popular Glenfiddich Distillery, walk over to the other side of the parking lot, where the ruins of an old castle belonging to the 4th Earl of Atholl lie. The castle is intact enough for you to walk a couple stories up into the bedroom where Mary Queen of Scots once stayed, but otherwise the informational plaques will encourage you to use your imagination.

*Next to Glenfiddich Distillery, on the A941 just outside of town toward Craigellachie.* ☎ *0131-668-8600. Admission: £1.20 ($1.75) adults, £.90 ($1.30) seniors and students, £.50 (70¢) children under 16. Open: Apr–Sept daily 9:30 a.m.–6:30 p.m.; Closed Oct–Mar. Time: 1 hour.*

## Barrie's Birthplace
### Kirriemuir

J. M. Barrie, the author of a little story titled *Peter Pan,* was born here in 1860, the 9th of 10 children. The exhibit memorializing his birthplace is excellent and quite imaginative. Life-size figures, miniature stage sets, dioramas, and stage costumes illustrate the writer's life. A little fast-moving light around the room represents everyone's favorite sprite, Tinkerbell. The museum also contains manuscripts and artifacts from Barrie's life. Don't miss the washhouse; it was Barrie's first theater and the inspiration for the Wendy House.

*9 Brechin Rd.* ☎ *01575-572-646. Admission: £1.80 ($2.60) adults; £1.20 ($1.75) seniors, students, and children under 16; £4.80 ($7) family. Open: Apr–Oct Sat–Wed noon to 5 p.m. Closed Nov–Mar. Time: 2 hours.*

## Blair Castle
### Blair Atholl

There is just too much to see in this fine fairy-tale-white castle chockfull o' interesting items: art, armor, flags, and other items not on the typical furniture-and-portrait castle tour. Between the 30 rooms and the lovely grounds (including a walled garden), the castle has something for everyone. The most common theme in the Duke of Atholl's decorating is hunting. Deer antlers decorate the long hallway and ballroom, and the weaponry collection spans hundreds of years. You'd be hard pressed to find so many guns and swords in one place anywhere else. Blair Castle's long history includes a couple of Jacobite sieges and a sleepover by Queen Victoria. As a thank-you gift, Victoria presented the Duke of Atholl with official colors for his men, and today the Atholl Highlanders are the only remaining private army in Europe. (Although Duncan Atholl was the king murdered in Shakespeare's *Macbeth*, the real Duncan did not live in this castle.)

*Blair Atholl, off the A9, 6 miles west of Pitlochry.* ☎ *01796-481-207. E-mail:* manager@blair-castle.co.uk. *Internet:* www.blair-castle.co.uk. *Admission: £6.50 ($9.45) adults, £5.50 ($8) seniors, £4 ($5.80) children under 16, £16.75 ($24) family. Open: Daily 9:30 a.m.–6 p.m. Time: 3 hours.*

## Braemar Highland Gathering
**Braemar**

The average population of Braemar is around 500 people. But when it holds the Highland games every September, the population jumps an additional 20,000 or more. Make that 20,001: Queen Elizabeth usually attends. Of all the Highland games, Braemar's is the biggest and best. This purely Scottish experience of traditional dance, costumes, and feats of strength is a lot of fun for outsiders, as well. Plenty of crafts and delicious food accompany it. The history of the gatherings predates Scotland as a country, when kings had their best warriors compete to see who were the toughest.

*Gathering: Princess Royal and Duke of Fife Memorial Park. The Highland Gathering Heritage Center: The Mews, Mar Road, Braemar.* ☎ *01339-741-944 or 01339-755-377. Admission: Heritage Center: free. Field admission: £6 ($8.70) adults, £2 ($2.90) children under 16. Open: Gathering: First Sat in Sept. Heritage Center: Daily 9 a.m.–5 p.m. Time: Gathering: 5 hours.*

## Castle Menzies
**Weem Aberfeldy**

This 16th-century home of the Clan Menzies chiefs is on a spectacular ridge in the Tay Valley. The castle doesn't house a huge collection (it's mostly clan memorabilia), but that's true to how the building was furnished hundreds of years ago. History buffs will note that Bonnie Prince Charlie and his troops spent the night here on the way to the Battle of Culloden, and architecture students may be interested in one of the best surviving examples of a Z-plan fortified tower house. The grounds are skippable.

*On the B846, 1 mile west of Aberfeldy.* ☎ *01887-820-982. Admission: £2.50 ($3.65). Open: Apr–mid-Oct Mon–Sat 10:30 a.m.–5 p.m., Sun 2–5 p.m. Closed mid-Oct–Mar. Time: 90 minutes.*

## Dalwhinnie Distillery

**Dalwhinnie**

Although its distinction as the "highest distillery" in Scotland is hardly reason enough to visit, the location among flowing fields of heather truly is. The heather pollen floating into the distillery gives this excellent whisky its special flavor. The tour is informative, and, best of all, you get a dram of whisky at the end. Film buffs may recognize this as the setting for the outdoor scene in *Trainspotting.*

*12 miles south of Newtonmore.* ☎ *01528-522-208. Admission: £3 ($4.35) adults. Open: July–Aug Mon–Sat 9:30 a.m.–4:30 p.m., Sun 12:30–4:30 p.m.; June, Sept–Oct Mon–Sat 9:30 a.m.–4:30 p.m.; Mar–May, Nov–Dec Mon–Fri 9:30 a.m.–4:30 p.m. Closed Jan–Feb. Time: 90 min.*

## Discovery Point

**Dundee**

This port is home to the famous RRS *Discovery,* the scientific ship Captain Robert Scott took into Antarctica. One of the last of the wooden three-masted ships, it set sail in 1901 and lived a long life of polar adventure. You can tour the ship and get all the details of its construction and of Scott's historic trip. The coolest part (literally) is the Polarama, a hands-on exhibit on life in the Arctic that includes a whiff of polar air. By the way, RRS stands for "Royal Research Ship."

*Discovery Quay.* ☎ *01382-201-245. Admission: Free. Open: Apr–Oct Mon–Sat 10 a.m.–5 p.m., Sun 11 a.m.–5 p.m.; Nov–Mar Mon–Sat 10 a.m.–4 p.m., Sun 11 a.m.– 4 p.m. Time: 2 hours.*

## Drum Castle and Gardens

**Banchory**

This lovely little castle is the oldest intact building in the care of the National Trust. It's full of beautiful antique furniture and lovely rooms staffed by knowledgeable guides. Nothing in particular in the Irvine family collection is remarkable, but you'll enjoy the walk through the house which includes a nice collection of early-20th-century toys and an impressive vaulted library. Don't miss the castle grounds, which hold a restored 16th-century chapel, a holly grove, roses, and a walled garden.

*Drumoak, Banchory. Follow signs on the A93, 10 miles from Aberdeen.* ☎ *01330-81-204. E-mail:* drum@nts.org.uk. *Internet:* www.drum-castle.org.uk. *Admission: £7 ($10) adults; £5.25 ($7.60) seniors, students, and children under 16; £19 ($28) family. Open: July–Aug daily 10 a.m.–6 p.m.; Apr–June, Sept–Oct daily noon to 5 p.m. Closed Nov–Mar. Time: 2 hours.*

## Duff House
**Banff**

This fine country house and sprawling wooded estate make a great way to stroll away an afternoon. First tour the house, one of the finest examples of baroque architecture in Scotland, and then move on to the grounds. Duff House's tour rivals many castle tours; it features a fine collection of Chippendale furniture and portraits by top artists such as El Greco. Among the grounds' attractions are a Victorian glasshouse vinery, playground, mausoleum, distillery, and the Duff House Royal Golf Course.

*Banff. ☎ 01261-81-8181. Internet:* www.duffhouse.org.uk. *Admission: £3.50 ($5.10) adults, £2.50 ($3.65) seniors, students, and children under 16, £8.50 ($12) family. Grounds: Free. Open: Apr–Oct daily 11 a.m.–5 p.m.; Nov–Mar Thurs–Sun 11 a.m.–4 p.m. Time: 2 hours.*

## Dunotter Castle
**Near Stonehaven**

Known for its breathtaking views, this clifftop castle is most famous for having secretly housed the Scottish Honors (crown jewels) for four years. You can make a treasure hunt of finding the poorly marked site of the burial. Much of the structure still stands, but there is no inside tour of the castle, and the signs are scant. The tragic history of the place includes a siege by William "Braveheart" Wallace, who set the castle on fire, roasting the soldiers inside. Four centuries later, British troops held 167 men, women, and children captive here until the prisoners starved and suffocated in the deep dungeons. Conanters who swore to keep their Catholic faith were tortured here. Also, Mary Queen of Scots spent the night, but that's not too uncommon. Film buffs may remember Dunotter from the Mel Gibson version of *Hamlet*. If you're feeling adventurous, take the cliff walk from Stonehaven, a 30-minute trek in the misty sea air with a view of the castle ruins looking as if they're floating on a cloud. Either way, don't leave your camera behind.

*Off the A92. ☎ 01569-762-173. Admission: £3.50 ($5.10) adults, £1 ($1.45) children under 16. Open: Apr–Oct Mon–Sat 9 a.m.–6 p.m., Sun 2–5 p.m.; Nov–Mar Mon–Fri 9 a.m. to sunset. Time: 2 hours, 30 minutes.*

## Edradour Distillery
**Pitlochry**

You'll get a good primer on the whisky-making process at this mini-distillery. Edradour holds the cute distinction of being the smallest distillery in Scotland. It's a cute site, too, with little whitewashed buildings with red doors and a stream bubbling through. The friendly staff of six or seven puts out a whopping 12 casks a week and uses the smallest size spirit stills that the law allows. Of course, it's quality, not quantity, that counts. The tours and dram of whisky are free.

*Off the A924, just outside Pitlochry.* ☎ *01796-472-095. Internet:* www.edradour. co.uk. *Admission: Free. Open: Mar–Oct. Mon–Sat 9:30 a.m.–5 p.m.; Nov–Feb Mon–Sat 10 a.m.–4 p.m. Time: 90 min.*

## Elgin Cathedral
### Elgin

The ruins of what was once Scotland's finest cathedral occupy a beautiful spot on the edge of town in a meadow by the river. The ruins are a bit scattered around the old graveyard, so you're better off taking the excellent, informative tour than tackling it alone. A nefarious man named Alexander Stewart, the Wolf of Badenoch, the illegitimate son of King David II, destroyed the cathedral in 1390. It was repaired but, like many Catholic churches in Scotland, fell into disrepair following the Protestant Reformation. Don't leave the site without visiting the biblical garden, full of plants mentioned in the Bible.

*Cooper Park.* ☎ *0131-668-8800. Admission: £2.80 ($4.10) adults, £2 ($2.90) seniors and students, £1 ($1.45) children under 16. Open: Apr–Oct daily 9:30 a.m.–6:30 p.m.; Nov–Mar Mon–Sat 9:30 a.m.–4:30 p.m., Thurs 9:30 a.m. to noon, Sun 2–4:30 p.m. Time: 1 hour.*

## Glamis Castle
### Glamis

Glamis is notable for being the childhood home of the late Queen Mother and of Queen Elizabeth II, as well as the birthplace of the late Princess Margaret. A royal residence since 1372, it is more famous for being the (historically inaccurate) setting for Shakespeare's *Macbeth*. The castle contains excellent collections of china, tapestries, and furniture, and has two interesting exhibits on the Queen and the Coach House. The grounds contain a two-acre Italian garden and impressive Douglas firs.

*On the A494 off the A929, 12 miles north of Dundee and 5 miles west of Forfar.* ☎ *01307-840-393. Admission: £5.20 ($7.55) adults, £2.70 ($3.90) children under 16. Open: Daily Apr–June, Sept–Oct 10:30 a.m.–5:30 p.m.; July–Aug 10 a.m.–5:30 p.m. Closed Nov–Mar. Time: 2 hours.*

## Glenfiddich Distillery
### Dufftown

Fans of this hugely popular whisky will need no introduction or further reason to visit the fine family-owned distillery in the lovely Valley of the Deer (in Gaelic: "Glenfiddich"). Because it attracts huge crowds, it has an entertaining visitor center with a movie (think 10-minute commercial) and outstanding young, knowledgeable, and bilingual (they speak Spanish, French, German, and Italian) hosts. This is also the only distillery where you can see the Scotch being bottled on the premises. Amazingly, the tour is free and still includes a dram of the good stuff.

*On the A941, south of Elgin.* ☎ *01340-820-373. Admission: Free. Open: Apr–mid-Oct Mon–Fri 9:30 a.m.–4:30 p.m., Sun noon to 4:30 p.m.; mid-Oct–Mar Mon–Fri 9:30 a.m.–4:30 p.m. Time: 1 hour, 30 minutes.*

### Glen Grant Distillery
**Rothes**

The Grant brothers founded their small whisky dynasty in 1840, making it one of the first in the Highlands. The tour of the distillery is typical — except that it includes an untypical funny little film shown in a picture frame. Afterward, you can take in the excellent gardens on the grounds, a feature usually reserved for castles and house estates. The restored Victorian garden features a small orchard, a lily pond, and plants from around the world. Another nice touch is that you may enjoy your tasting in the "study" or out on the lovely Dram Pavilion.

*On the A941, between Elgin and Perth, 10 miles south of Elgin.* ☎ *01542-783-318. E-mail:* caroline.mitchell@chivas.com. *Admission: £3 ($4.35) adults, free for children under 18; children under 8 not admitted. Open: Apr–Oct Mon–Sat 10 a.m.–4 p.m., Sun 12:30 p.m.–4 p.m. Closed Nov–Mar. Time: 1 hour.*

### Glenlivet Distillery
**North of Tomintoul**

This very popular single malt makes for a big attraction for visitors. It's especially popular among Americans and reputedly was a favorite of King George IV's. The distillery has an interestingly turbulent history. After fighting off whisky smugglers for many years, Glenlivet finally succumbed in 1978 — to Seagrams. The tour is very good and the reception area quite nice. You'll know why this is such a popular brand after your tasting.

*Ballindalloch. Ten miles north of Tomintoul, on the B9008, off the A95.* ☎ *01542-783-220. Internet:* www.theglenlivet.com. *Admission: £3 ($4.35) adults, free for children under 18; children under 8 not admitted. Open: Apr–Oct Mon–Sat 10 a.m.–4 p.m., Sun 12:30–4 p.m. Closed Nov–Mar. Time: 90 minutes.*

### Glen Lyon
**Near Aberfeldy**

After Glen Coe, this is the most interesting glen in Scotland. But don't trust me — listen to William Wordsworth and Alfred Lord Tennyson, both of whom lauded this picturesque spot where the River Lyon runs through magnificent *munros* (hills favored by hikers). Eagles soar above, fish swim below, and if you make your way to the head of the loch, you'll get to an impressive dam. Near the church and hotel in Fortingall is a tree purported to be the oldest in Europe. Legend has it that Pontius Pilate was born by the tree, which is possible, because his father was serving as a Roman legionnaire in Scotland at the time.

*A827 to Fearnan, then north to Fortingall. Admission: Free. Time: 2–3 hours.*

## The Glenturret Distillery
### Crieff

It may be hard to prove, but this quaint distillery is probably the oldest in Scotland. The tours and the visitor center's audiovisual presentations are excellent, and so is the whisky. If you're not familiar with it, Glenturret has a smoky or roasted aroma and taste, attributed to the local water and other conditions. The shop has the complete collection of whiskys, liqueurs, and gifts. At the tasting bar, you can drink your way through the full range of blended and single malts. A treat at the end of the distillery tour is a dram of the good stuff. If you can't get enough, the nice little restaurant serves whisky-infused food, including Glenturret ice cream.

*On the A85 to Comrie, 1 mile outside Crieff.* ☎ *01764-656-565. Admission: £3.50 ($5.10) adults, £2.40 ($3.50) seniors and children under 16. Open: Feb–Dec Mon–Sat 9:30 a.m.–6 p.m., Sun noon to 6 p.m. Closed Jan. Time: 1 hour, 30 minutes.*

## Highland Folk Museum
### Kingussie

This fascinating museum covering the last 400 years of Highland life occupies a re-creation of an old peat building and crofters' (small farmers') home, painstakingly built by craftspeople using only period tools and technology. The collection of everyday objects, furniture, machines, and more is enormous. Particular items of interest include a 1772 fiddle, bagpipes played at the Battle of Waterloo, a 19th-century harp, and an excellent video presentation, "A Way of Life No More." In the summer, craftsmen in period costume demonstrate Highland skills, and tours run regularly throughout the day, according to demand.

*Duke Street. On the A86, off the A9.* ☎ *01540-661-307. Admission: £3.50 ($5.10) adults, £2.50 ($3.65) seniors and children under 16, £7 ($10) family. Open: May–Aug Mon–Fri 10:30 a.m.–5:30 p.m., Sat–Sun 1–5 p.m.; Apr, Sept–Oct Mon–Fri 10:30 a.m.–4:30 p.m.; Nov–Mar Sat–Sun tours at 11 a.m. and 1 p.m. Time: 2 hours.*

## HMS Unicorn
### Dundee

Dundee's other permanently docked attraction (the first is RRS *Discovery;* see listing earlier in this chapter) is a fine war vessel built for the Royal Navy in 1824. Back then, Britain was a superpower, and the crown ruled the waters. It's the oldest British warship still afloat (partly because it never saw battle). The worthwhile tour gives a good feel for what life was like aboard this lean, mean fighting machine. Exhibits on board cover the history of the *Unicorn* and include an overview of the British Royal Navy.

*Victoria Dock, east of the Tay Bridge.* ☎ *01382-200-900. Admission: £3 ($4.35) adults, £2 ($2.90) seniors and children under 16, £8 ($12) family. Open: Daily mid-Mar–Oct 10 a.m.–5 p.m., Nov–mid-Mar 10 a.m.–4 p.m. Time: 90 minutes.*

## Huntly Castle
**Huntly**

This fun little castle holds a spot that has been housing royals for five centuries. Robert the Bruce laid his head here, but Mary Queen of Scots refused her invitation (wisely — a kidnapping was in the works). The nicest features are the heraldic friezes on the building constructed by past Earls of Huntly and now protected from the elements. You'll also see Catholic images; the castle held fast to its religion during the Reformation, which saw its end. Don't leave without visiting the pretty river.

*On the A96.* ☎ *01466-793-191. Admission: £3 ($4.35) adults, £2.20 ($3.20) seniors and students, £1 ($1.45) children under 16, £3 ($4.35) family. Open: Apr–Sept daily 9:30 a.m.–6:30 p.m.; Oct–Mar Mon–Sat 9:30 a.m.–4:30 p.m, Sun 2–4:30 p.m. Time: 1 hour.*

## Macbeth Experience
**Bankfoot**

You're no doubt weary of roadside attractions inside visitor centers, as you well should be, but the Macbeth Experience is an interesting one-room attraction. In an attempt to distinguish the real Macbeth from the Shakespearean version, this audiovisual production makes the argument that the famous Thane of Cawdor was really a good and just king, not the bloodthirsty usurper of old English propaganda. Interestingly, Macbeth's son Malcolm was raised in London and became a puppet to the crown when he was ruler of Scotland, so Macbeth was arguably the last king of a truly independent country. Warning for small kids: The dark theater and pyrotechnics can be a little frightening.

*Perthshire Visitor Centre. Just off the A9 between Perth and Pitlochry.* ☎ *01738-787-696. E-mail:* wilson@macbeth.co.uk. *Admission: £2 ($2.90) adults, £1.50 ($2.20) seniors and students, £1 ($1.45) children under 16, £5 ($7.25) family. Open: Daily Apr–Sept 9 a.m.–8 p.m., Oct–Mar 9 a.m.–7 p.m. Time: 1 hour.*

## Pitlochry Festival Theatre
**Pitlochry**

This big theater on the south side of the River Tummel is the jewel of the town. The theater recently went through a major overhaul, although it certainly didn't need to improve on its popularity with visitors and locals alike. Scots come from all over to see new and classic professional performances here, usually six a season and running simultaneously. Besides plays, the Pitlochry also schedules concerts, films, and literary and culinary events. Be sure to book in advance.

*Across the river from Main Street.* ☎ *01796-484-626. E-mail:* boxoffice@ pitlochry.org.uk. *Internet:* www.pitlochry.org.uk. *Tickets: £14–£16 ($20–$23). Open: May–Oct.*

### Pitlochry Fish Ladder and Dam
**Pitlochry**

Take the footbridge over the hydroelectric dam and see this small but interesting attraction — spawning fish. The glass-paneled viewing chamber gives a rare look at the salmon ladder built to assist the salmon, which would otherwise not be able to reach the man-made loch. Viewing the ladder is free; the interesting CD and video exhibit isn't.

*Below Main Street, along the river.* ☎ *01796-473-152. Admission: £2 ($2.90) adults, £1.20 ($1.75) seniors and students, £1 ($1.45) children under 16, £4 ($5.80) family. Open: Daily Apr–Oct 10 a.m.–5:30 p.m. Closed Nov–Mar. Time: 1 hour.*

### St. John's Kirk
**Perth**

Although the present building dates back a mere 500 years (construction began before Columbus sailed to America), this spot has held a church since Scotland's first king, David I, founded it in 1126. Protestant reformer John Knox gave a fiery speech or two from the pulpit. Its shrines and architecture are unremarkable, but St. John's is the center of the town. The local community still uses the church, which offers tours on Saturday at 2 and 4 p.m.

*St. John's Street, south of the visitor center.* ☎ *01738-626-159. Admission: Free; £1 ($1.45) requested. Open: Mon–Sat 10 a.m. to noon and 2–4 p.m.*

### Scone Palace
**Near Perth**

This is the hallowed ground where many of the greatest Scottish kings were crowned. Until about 700 years ago, Scone (pronounced "scoon") Palace was the home of the Stone of Destiny, and important rulers such as David I, Macbeth, and Robert the Bruce began their reigns while standing before the legendary rock. Edward I stole the stone in 1296. It returned to Scotland in 1996 and now rests in Edinburgh Castle.

The castellated palace, built in the 1580s and enlarged in 1803, is full of fine furniture, ivories, clocks, needlework, and other interesting pieces from the clan Murray. The clan has held this castle since it was bequeathed to Sir David Murray after he saved the life of King James XI of Scotland (later James I of England). Of particular note is the renowned porcelain collection. Scone Palace also has a hall dedicated to the coronation of kings. Reading material is available, but if you have any questions, ask the expert guides posted throughout the palace. The grounds are also quite nice, but you must contend with the shrieking peacocks that live there. A replica commemorates the spot of the Stone of Destiny outside the palace on Moot Hill, just in front of the little chapel. Out to the left of the chapel is a playground area with huge tire swings, slides, and even a zipwire, which kids (and I) love best about this place.

*Braemar Road. On the A93.* ☎ *01738-552-300. E-mail:* visits@scone-palace. co.uk. *Internet:* www.scone-palace.co.uk. *Admission: Palace and grounds: £6.20 ($9) adults, £5.30 ($7.70) seniors and students, £3.60 ($5.20) children under 16, £20 ($29) family. Grounds only: £3.10 ($4.50) adults, £2.50 ($3.50) seniors and students, £1.70 ($2.50) children under 16. Open: Daily Apr–Oct 9:30 a.m.–5:15 p.m. Closed Nov–Mar. Time: 2–3 hours.*

### Scottish Lighthouses Museum
**Fraserburgh**

This stop is a must for lighthouse enthusiasts and is recommended if you have any interest in the towers of all shapes and sizes that have kept sailors safe at sea for more than 200 years. Knowledgeable salty guides take you on a tour of an unusual lighthouse built atop a castle once home to the powerful and wealthy Fraser clan. The father of the lighthouse, Thomas Smith, sent the first beam out to sea here, and his stepson, Robert Stevenson, improved upon the idea and started a family whose members have been responsible for most of the major lighthouse innovations over the years. The family was so engineering-inclined that some of them were subcontractors on the Brooklyn Bridge and the Golden Gate Bridge. (One of their relatives, Robert Louis Stevenson, was known for a few other accomplishments, like *Treasure Island*.) If you come in winter, you'll have sympathy for the keepers who once lived here (all lighthouses in Scotland are now automated). With nothing between it and the arctic ice, Kinnaird Head is the spot where the fastest sustained wind in the world was clocked just a few years ago.

*Kinnaird Head, on the A98.* ☎ *01346-511-022. Internet:* www.lighthousemuseum. co.uk. *Admission: £3.90 ($5.70) adults, £3.25 ($4.70) seniors, students, and children under 16. Open: Apr–Oct Mon–Sat 10 a.m.–6 p.m, Sun noon to 6 p.m.; Nov–Mar Mon–Sat 10 a.m.–4 p.m, Sun noon to 4 p.m. Time: 1 hour.*

### Speyside Cooperage
**Craigellachie**

What's a cooperage? It's a barrel factory, and here in Whisky Country, that's a very important job. Speyside is more than a factory; it's a museum about the history and process of the craft, which I learned is one of the oldest in the world. It's more interesting than it sounds. This Victorian-style cooperage contains exhibits tracing the development of the industry using an excellent film, life-size models, and an observation area from which to watch skilled coopers and their apprentices working on oak whisky casks. Outside, everyone can get a close-up view of wooly Highland cattle, and those over 18 get a free whisky tasting.

## Skiing Scotland

This region has two decent ski resorts, Glenshee and Lecht. In quality and size, they are by no means the Alps or even the U.S. East Coast, but if you ski, you may enjoy the novelty of skiing in Scotland. Glenshee is the largest ski resort in the U.K. (which isn't saying much). It lies atop Britain's highest road pass and offers more lifts (26 if you count the bunny slopes) than any other resort in the U.K. Lecht is smaller and has snow machines when the temperature is right but the weather won't cooperate. It has only 12 lifts, but a couple are open year-round for dry skiing (no snowboarding allowed). If you're visiting in the summer and have never tried a dry slope, this is your big chance. Glenshee: Braemar. ☎ **01339-741-320**; Internet: www.ski-glenshee.co.uk. Full-day lift tickets: £19.50 ($28) adults, £11 ($16) children; rentals: £15 ($22) adults, £7.50 ($11) children. Lecht: On the A939, Tomintoul, near Ballater. ☎ **01975-651-440.** Lift ticket prices vary; call for information about rentals. Time: 4 hours.

*Dufftown Road.* ☎ *01340-871-108. Admission: £2.95 ($4.30) adults, £2.45 ($3.55) seniors and students, £1.75 ($2.55) children under 16, £7.95 ($12) family. Open: Daily 9:30 a.m.–4:30 p.m. Time: 1 hour.*

### Strathisla Distillery
**Keith**

You may not have heard of the single malt label, but you may know that Strathisla whisky is the main ingredient of Chivas Regal, one of the most popular blended whiskys in the world. The tour through one of the Highlands' oldest distilleries is self-guided: You can get up close and touch the equipment, and workers are on hand to answer questions. Note the mill wheel that turns on the distillery's run-off. What you don't want to miss is the very informative "nosing," followed by a tasting of the single malt or Chivas. When master whisky blenders create blends, they use only their noses — tasting diminishes the ability to discern flavor (in fact, blenders use blue-tinted drinking glasses so that they won't be influenced by color). In your guided "nosing," you will smell different types of whiskys from various regions of Scotland.

*Seafield Avenue. On the A96 between Huntly and Elgin.* ☎ *01542-783-044. Internet: www.chivas.com. Admission: £4 ($5.80) adults, free for children under 18; children under 8 not admitted. Open: Apr–Oct Mon–Sat 10 a.m.–4 p.m., Sun 12:30– 4 p.m. Closed Nov–Mar. Time: 1 hour.*

# Shopping in Tayside and Grampian

While none of the towns in this chapter, including Aberdeen, has a major shopping district or top-notch mall, the region does have several unique shopping experiences. Each is worth the wee side trip.

✔ **Baxter's Highland Village,** Fochabers, 9 miles east of Elgin (☎ 01343-82-0666; Internet: www.baxters.com). More than just a place to pick up some of Scotland's best jams and soups, the Baxter complex has an old-fashioned general store, a film devoted to all things Baxter, daily cooking demonstrations, and a great tearoom with outdoor seating. Besides the food shop, there is also a great store for modern kitchen and housewares. If you want a real treat, order a pancake in the tearoom and smother it with all the free Baxter jam you want. There's no charge to see displays and the audiovisual presentation. Open: Daily April 2 through December 24 from 9 a.m. to 5:30 p.m., December 27 to 30 from 10 a.m. to 4 p.m., and January 13 to April 1 from 10 a.m. to 5 p.m.

✔ **Caithness Glass Factory,** on the A9, Inveralmond, Perth (☎ 01738-492-320). This is a great opportunity to see skilled glassmakers in action and to buy a nice piece of glass from the well-stocked factory shop. Viewing galleries in the glasshouse and an exhibition on the glass give excellent context. The shop charges factory prices for all the goods — not just glass, but also crystal, paperweights, ceramics, and jewelry. The unique and often colorful designs are popular with many visitors. Open: Monday to Saturday from 9 a.m. to 5 p.m., and Sunday from 10 a.m. to 5 p.m.

✔ **Countrywear,** 15, 24, and 35 Bridge St., Braemar (☎ 01339-755-453). Three shops carry nearly everything you'll need. Quality items for Highland living include fishing and hunting gear, body warmers, tweed, cashmere, kids' clothes, hand-knits, tartans, woolens, and more. From shear to gear, you'll get it all on Bridge Street. Call for hours.

✔ **Dunkeld Antiques,** Tay Terrace, Dunkeld (☎ 01350-728-832). Looking over the River Tay, this wonderful old antiques store is a pleasure. If you love browsing around and looking for that special something, you'll probably find it here. The shop sells jewelry, books, prints, clocks, ceramics, hunting items, and a plethora of upscale bric-a-brac (if that isn't a contradiction in terms). Open: Monday to Saturday from 10 a.m. to 5 p.m., and Sunday from noon to 5:30 p.m.

✔ **Johnstons of Elgin,** Newmill, near the Cathedral (☎ 01343-542-849). This factory shop (read: factory prices) has one of the largest selections of cashmere, tweed, knits, and camel hair in the country. The jumpers (sweaters) are world famous. Interested in learning how your new wooly garment was made? Take one of the weekday tours of the factory; it's more interesting than you'd think. Open: Monday to Saturday from 9 a.m. to 5:30 p.m.

✔ **Le Chocolatier,** 29 Scott St., Perth (☎ 01738-620-039; Internet: www.lechocolatier.co.uk). Look for the green awning and all the sweets you can imagine in this downtown chocolate shop, or just let your nose lead you there. The handmade sweets range from butter fudges to diabetic chocolates, and the shop also carries jelly beans, if you need a fix. Open: Monday to Saturday from 9 a.m. to 5 p.m.

✔ **Macnaughtons of Pitlochry,** Station Road (stretching to Athol Road), Pitlochry (☎ 01796-472-722). This big complex made up of several storefronts on Station Road sells the highest-quality clothes. The range of apparel includes kilts, cashmere, tartans, and tweed, as well as other Scottish related gifts.

✔ **McEwan Gallery,** on A939, 1 mile west of Ballater, Tomintoul, Ballater, Deeside (☎ 01339-755-429). From prints to books and many paintings in between, McEwen's stocks an excellent collection of 19th- and 20th-century art and literature. Many of the items are Scotland- or golf-related, and make good high-end souvenirs. The cottage house is an unusual architectural gem, worth seeing even if you don't buy anything. Open: Monday to Saturday from 10 a.m. to 6 p.m., and Sunday from 2 to 6 p.m.

✔ **Speyside Heather Garden and Visitor Centre,** Dulnain Bridge, Skye of Curr, Grantown-on-Spey (☎ 01479-851-359). Without resorting to stealing it off the side of the road (which I don't recommend), this is your best opportunity to buy the national flower, heather. This garden center grows more than 300 varieties of the pretty purple flower in its large greenhouse, and will even mail seeds or plants to you overseas. It also sells antiques, Scottish gifts, and crafts made from heather. Open daily March through October; call for winter hours.

# Doing the Pub Crawl

Of the towns in the region, only the largest, Aberdeen, has a good range of fine bars and nightlife options. If you make it to Aberdeen, enjoy the pub crawl. Perth has a couple of decent bars, but everywhere else you'll have to settle for the local pub or the bar in your hotel. Many of the following pubs keep late-night hours; call for the latest opening and closing times.

✔ **Booth's,** Back Wynd, Aberdeen (☎ 01224-646-475). This polished pub has an interesting history, involving local characters and a bunch of owners with different visions for the place. Luckily for you, the current owner settled on a fine watering hole filled with one of the best selections of whisky in town. The amiable crowd tends to cross generations.

✔ **The Grill Bar,** Flesher's Vennell, South Street, Perth (☎ 01738-622-704). It may not be much to look at, but don't judge a bar by its paint job. This is a fun little pub with friendly service, a pool table, and the best jukebox (everything cool, from Lou Reed to Dave Matthews) I've come across in Scotland. There are drink specials and a huge screen for sports broadcasts.

✔ **The Lemon Tree,** 5 W. North St. at Queen Street, Aberdeen (☎ 01224-642-230; Internet: www.lemontree.org). This eclectic place is understandably popular. By day, it's a whole-foods shop and popular lunchroom. By night, it's a theater and music venue. The schedule is mercurial but offers jazz, pop, folk, cabaret, comedy, and plays. The spacious bar has fast, efficient service, and a recent refurbishment gave the place a nice sparkle. No complaints here.

✔ **Old Blackfriars,** 52 Castlegate, at the top end of Union St., Aberdeen (☎ 01224-581-922). You can read a bit of the place's history on the back of the menu, but this isn't a tourist attraction. It's an excellent pub, full of yummy, under-carbonated, local hand-pumped brews that you should not miss. The friendly place is cozy yet big enough for milling. And the yummy food (venison burgers, vegetarian chili) is served in a nonsmoking area separate from the bar.

✔ **O'Neill's,** 9 Black Wynd, Aberdeen (☎ 01224-621-456). The lengths to which this Irish pub goes to show that it's Irish would be comical on the Emerald Isle — ad posters for Irish products and bric-a-brac no doubt purchased at the Shannon Airport gift shop. The Guinness, Caffreys, and Murphy's (my personal favorite) are the real deal, however. So slip into one of the snugs and drink your stout — and if you dare, play the giant-size Jenga, a game of wooden bricks and finesse.

✔ **Prince of Wales,** 7 St. Nicholas Lane, down an alley off Union Street at George Street, Aberdeen (☎ 01224-640-597). Arguably the best place to grab a pint in Aberdeen, this is your average old-fashioned pub with private booths, wood furniture, stone floors, and an excellent spectrum of ales (I prefer the Orkney Dark Island and Old Peculiar). If you're a little hungry, try the Guinness pie. Only problem? It can get crowded, but that's the price of popularity.

✔ **Royal Hotel Bar,** Comrie (☎ 01764-67-9200). The pub is behind the stylish Royal Hotel, which lies right on Comrie's central square. The folks who run the place also own Cloisters and the Bow Bar in Edinburgh and have brought a city ambience to the countryside. On tap are several great Scottish beers, such as Earthquake Ale made by Caledonian Brewery. There's live music and a lovely beer garden, as well.

✔ **Scaramouch,** 103 South St., across from the Tesco, Perth (☎ 01738-637-479). This large pub on the main drag has lots of seating area and standing room, which is good when the place fills up with crowds who come to hear the live traditional music (Thursday through Saturday nights). The place is comfortable and doesn't get too smoky. It also has a very good selection of beer and daily drink specials.

✔ **Slains Castle,** 14/18 Belmont St., Aberdeen (☎ 01224-631-877). This large Gothic bar is full of eerie nooks and crannies where you can sip the potions and brews from the bar while you contemplate the dark side of life. Actually, the stained glass and chandeliers are more kitschy and fun than scary. The food menu is a scream, as well; try a "sadistic sandwich" or a "feast of the underworld." The place is a bit dark, except for the occasional camera flash as visitors capture a moment. Local ghouls have also been known to do a little dancing here.

✔ **The Snuggery,** 13–15 Market St., Aberdeen (☎ **01224-583-370**). It doesn't have a disco ball for nothin'. This place is often crowded with locals dancing the day and night away, sometimes to DJs and sometimes to keyboard-playing singers. It's not a young crowd, so the hits tend to be '80s and older. But the fun is intoxicating, and so is the beer. The only word of caution: It's a bit too loud to hold any sort of conversation when the music is going.

# Fast Facts: Tayside and Grampian

### Area Code

The area codes for this region are: Perth **01738**, Aberfeldy **01887**, Pitlochry **01796**, Dundee **01382**, Aberdeen **01224**, Braemar **01339**, and Elgin **01343**. You need to dial the area code only if you are calling from outside the city you want to reach.

### Emergencies

Dial **999** for police, fire, or ambulance.

### Genealogy Resources

**Family History Society,** 164 King St., Aberdeen (☎ 01224-646-323).

### Hospitals

**Aberdeen Royal Infirmary,** Foresterhill, on the west end of Union Street (☎ 01224-681-818). **Perth Royal Infirmary** (☎ 01738-623-311), Taymount Terrace, on the west side of town. **Aberfeldy's** cottage hospital (☎ 01887-820-3140) is on Old Crieff Road. **Dundee Royal Infirmary** (☎ 01382-434-664) is on Barrack Road.

### Information

Tourist offices include: The Square, **Aberfeldy** (☎ 01887-820-276); 22 Atholl Rd., **Pitlochry** (☎ 01796-472-215); 4 City Sq., **Dundee** (☎ 01382-434-664; Internet:

www.angusanddundee.co.uk); The Mews, Mars Rd., **Braemar** (☎ 01339-741-600); Lower City Mills, West Mill Street, **Perth** (☎ 01738-627-958; E-mail: perth touristb@perthshire.co.uk; Internet: www.perthshire.co.uk); **Elgin** (☎ 01343-542-666); and St. Nicholas House, **Aberdeen** (☎ 01224-288-828).

### Internet Access

**Comms Port,** 31–33 Loch St., Aberdeen (☎ 01224-626-468; E-mail: abadmin@ commsport.com; Internet: www.comm sport.com). Open: Mon–Wed 8 a.m.–6 p.m., Thurs 8 a.m.–7 p.m., Fri–Sat 8 a.m.–6 p.m., Sun 10 a.m.–5 p.m. Cost: £3 ($4.35) per hour.

### Mail

Post offices are at 371 George St., Aberdeen (☎ 01224-632-904); 3 Main St., Perth (☎ 01738-624-637); and 92 Atholl Rd., Pitlochry (☎ 01796-472-965).

### Police

Grampian Headquarters, Queen Street, Aberdeen (☎ 01224-632-727). North Division Police Headquarters, Moray Street, Elgin (☎ 01343-543-101).

# Chapter 16

# West Highlands

● ● ● ● ● ● ● ● ● ● ● ● ● ● ● ● ● ● ● ● ● ● ● ● ● ● ● ● ● ● ● ● ● ● ● ● ● ● ●

## In This Chapter

▶ Finding a bed for the night on and off the beaten path

▶ Eating fresh and tasty meals in the Highlands

▶ Hunting for the Loch Ness Monster

▶ Skiing and hiking the highest mountains in the country

▶ Shopping for kilts and kitsch

▶ Pulling a West Highlands pint

● ● ● ● ● ● ● ● ● ● ● ● ● ● ● ● ● ● ● ● ● ● ● ● ● ● ● ● ● ● ● ● ● ● ● ● ● ● ●

*A*fter Edinburgh and Glasgow, the West Highland region is the most visited area in Scotland. Many of the attractions are along or near the famous and much-hyped Loch Ness. The tourist trail runs between the towns of Fort William and Inverness along the shores of the dark, deep lake that keeps 'em coming, monster or no monster. Along the way you'll find a combination of unforgettable attractions, top-quality restaurants, and wonderful accommodations, perfectly suited for the out-of-towner.

## Orienting Yourself to the West Highlands

**Inverness** is the capital of the Highlands and the region's largest city, but it's an easy place to get around on foot. The town's name means "narrow place," referring to the fact that this was the narrowest crossing area for trade routes getting around Loch Ness. The lovely River Ness runs through the town, which has a nice castle and museum but few other attractions. Inverness has enough shops, restaurants, bars, and accommodations to fill a couple of days. Its proximity to Loch Ness, which lies southwest of town, makes it a great base from which to explore the Highlands.

**Fort William** lies at the foot of Ben Nevis (the highest mountain in Scotland), at the far end of Loch Ness and the smaller Loch Lochy. Its central location and proximity to Nevis and the Glenfinnan monument make Fort William a magnet for tourists. Several good restaurants and accommodations have thrived as a result.

While Loch Ness attractions, tours, and scenery can easily fill a full day, some great attractions lie off the Fort William–to–Inverness tourist trail. West Coast spots to see include **Eilean Donan, Glenfinnan,** and the lovely fishing town of **Mallaig.** North of Inverness and the Black Isle are **Clanland, Dunrobin Castle,** and the nice little towns of **Tain** and **Dornoch** (the latter is where Madonna got hitched).

Let me also save you a lot of time. Don't bother with the large northern-most region of mainland Scotland; the few attractions aren't worth the hours and hours it takes to get to relatively insignificant towns such as Wick, Thurso, and Durness. Most of the interior area between the coast and Loch Ness lacks worthwhile stops, as well. Stick to the many attractions and venues listed in this chapter, and you'll have plenty to occupy days of serious and substantial traveling.

# Getting There and Getting Around

Although it lies so far north, Inverness is well served by bus and train. If you're making the big leap from Aberdeen, Glasgow, or Edinburgh, you may want to consider taking public transportation to reach the capital of the Highlands. After you arrive, if you haven't driven, you should rent a car for a day or so to see Loch Ness and other area attractions.

  ✔ **By car:** The A82 runs nearly the entire length between Inverness and Fort William and along the west bank of Loch Ness and through Drumnadrochit. The A830 connects Fort William to Mallaig through Glenfinnan. The A9 connects Inverness to Dornoch through Tain. The A835 runs from the A9 to Ullapool.

  ✔ **By train: West Highland trains** (☎ 08457-48-4950) connect Nairn, Fort William, Aviemore, and Inverness to Aberdeen.

  ✔ **By bus: Citylink** (☎ 0990-505-050) connects Aviemore, Inverness, Drumnadrochit, Dornoch, Fort William, Ullapool, and Glencoe to Glasgow, Edinburgh, and other cities outside the region.

  ✔ **By plane: Inverness/Dalcross Airport** (☎ 01463-23-2471) is at Dalcross, 8 miles east of Inverness. It handles flights to Glasgow and Edinburgh.

*The West Highlands*

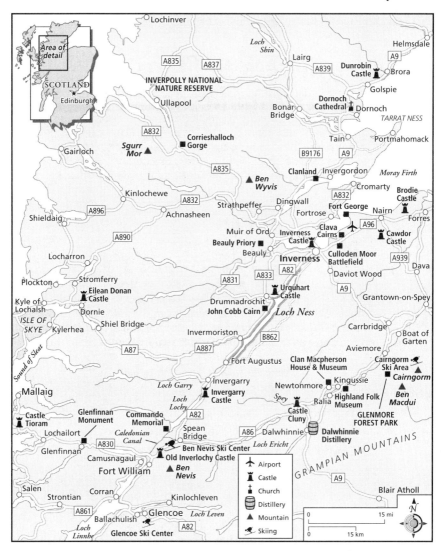

✔ **By ferry: Caledonian MacBrayne (☎ 01475-650-100; fax: 01475-637-607; reservations: ☎ 08705-650-000;** reservations fax: 01475-635-235; www.calmac.co.uk) routes in this region include Mallaig (**☎ 01687-462-403;** fax: 01687-462-281) to Skye, and Ullapool to the Isle of Lewis.

When you're in the region, especially in the Inverness area, a couple of taxi services can help you get around: **Culloden Taxis** (☎ **01463-79-0000**) and **Tartan Taxis** (☎ **01463-23-3033**).

# Knowing Where to Stay in the West Highlands

You may want to stay in tourist-friendly Inverness or Fort William, but the Highlands hills hide some real treats. They're close enough to Loch Ness and other attractions that they create a vacation within a vacation. For an explanation of the Scottish Tourist Board's star rating system, see Chapter 8.

### Alexandra Milton Hotel
**$$–$$$   Fort William**

Part of a fine chain of medium luxury hotels, the Alexandra has long catered to the needs of out-of-towners. Located in the town center at one end of the pedestrian High Street, it's convenient to local shopping and restaurants—and across the street from the railway station. The stately building houses a very efficient hotel with nearly 100 cozy rooms. The lounge and cocktail bar offer traditional live entertainment most nights.

*The Parade, across from railway and bus stations at the end of High Street.* ☎ *01397-702-241; 44-1786-469-469 outside the U.K. Fax: 01397-705-554. E-mail:* sales@miltonhotels.com. *Internet:* www.miltonhotels.com. *Rack rates: £89–£109 ($129–$158) double. AE, MC, V.*

### Ballifeary House Hotel
**$$   Inverness**

You won't find a closer accommodation to town—without hearing car horns and pedestrians—than this hotel. It's in a quiet residential area within easy walking distance of Inverness center and along the River Ness. The Edwardian villa has lovely sitting rooms and immaculate guest rooms that exude comfort. The hotel is entirely nonsmoking. The large free parking area is nice for a central location, as well. If you're traveling with kids, take note: The minimum age is 15.

*10 Ballifeary Road.* ☎ *01463-235-572. Fax: 01463-717-583. E-mail:* info@ ballifearyhousehotel.co.uk. *Internet:* www.ballifearyhousehotel. co.uk. *Rack rates: £68–£78 ($99–$113) double. MC, V.*

*Inverness*

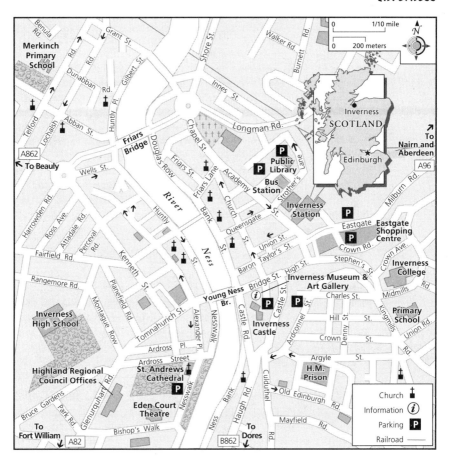

## Clifton House

### $$$–$$$  **Nairn**

There's nothing boring about this exquisite seaside accommodation. J. Gordon McIntyre, who has lived here his entire life, runs the small ivy-covered Victorian house. From the moment you walk in, you will be overwhelmed with hospitality, paintings, and flowers. The best part about staying at Clifton House is the hotel's tradition of staging a series of plays, concerts, and recitals from September through April. Be sure to have dinner here, as well; it's more theater than dining. Book ahead.

*Viewfield Street. Off A96.* ☎ *01667-453-119. Fax: 01667-452-836. E-mail:* macintyre@ clifton-hotel.co.uk. *Internet:* clifton-hotel.co.uk. *Rack rates: £85–£107 ($123–$155) double. AE, DC, MC, V. Closed Dec–Jan.*

## Corriechoille Lodge Guest House

### $ Near Spean Bridge

Normally I wouldn't send you too far off the beaten path, but this is an exception, a couple of miles from the town of Spean Bridge. This little oasis of a guesthouse has a backyard view of the Nevis Range mountains. Justin and Lucy Swabey have turned an old stone farmhouse by the woods into a four-star (bordering on five, no doubt) accommodation with all the trimmings. The beds guarantee a great night's sleep, the baths have bubbles, and the coffee and local jam and bread at breakfast are unforgettably delicious. The decor is modern Scottish with a bit of *feng shui* (Chinese lampshades, for example). If you give notice, the Swabeys will also cook a fabulous three-course candlelit dinner (except on Wednesday). FYI, the unpronounceable name, a Gaelic word for "forest of the glen," honors the former owner, the famous Highland cattle drover John "Corriechoille" Cameron. New to the grounds are luxury turf-roofed log cabins for self-catering.

*Just off the A82, 2 miles east of Spean Bridge. From Fort William, take the first right and a quick left just as you enter the town, and follow the forest-lined road all the way to the end.* ☎ *01397-712-002. E-mail:* enquiry@corriechoille.com. *Internet:* www.corriechoille.com. *Rack rates: £46–£56 ($67–$81) double per night; £285–£330 ($413–$479) cabin per week. MC, V.*

## Dornoch Castle Hotel

### $$ Dornoch

Popular with golfers for its proximity to the Royal Dornoch Golf Course, this 16th-century castle hotel is designed for anyone in need of a little pampering. Formerly a bishop's palace, the hotel now features florally decorated pastel rooms (some with views of the Dornoch Firth). The newest wing of the hotel was built in 1974, and its rooms overlook the garden. Dinner in the dungeon is worth a try, if only to experience the intensity of the huge Gothic fireplace.

*Castle Street, on the town square, opposite the cathedral.* ☎ *01862-810-216. Fax: 01862-810-981. E-mail:* enquiries@dornochcastlehotel.com. *Internet:* www.dornochcastlehotel.com. *Rack rates: £50–£100 ($73–$145) double. AE, MC, V.*

## Dunain Park Hotel

### $$$ Dunain

In a tourist-strategic position between Loch Ness and Inverness, this is a wonderful old Georgian country house surrounded by woods and gardens. Some of the well-dressed rooms have four-poster beds, and some are in separate quaint cottages. You can sip from more than 200 whiskys at the house bar and enjoy your downtime by an open fire. The indoor heated swimming pool and sauna are nice, as well. With only 13 rooms, booking ahead is wise.

*Fort William Road. On the A82, 2 miles south of Inverness on the road to Loch Ness.* ☎ *01463-230-512. Fax: 01463-224-532. E-mail:* Dunainparkhotel@btinternet. com. *Internet:* www.Dunainparkhotel.co.uk. *Rack rates: £138–£198 ($200–$287) double. AE, MC, V.*

### Glen Mhor Hotel
**$$–$$$**   **Inverness**

This cozy Victorian hotel sits on the River Ness just below the city's castle. The lobbies and bar (see the "Dining in the West Highlands" section, later in this chapter) are lovely spots with overstuffed chairs, tartan upholstery, and oak paneling. The rooms are large and the beds perfectly firm. Just be sure to ask for a river view (it's not extra) and the friendly staff will oblige, as they do with most requests.

*9–12 Ness Bank.* ☎ *01463-234-308. Fax: 01463-713-170. E-mail:* glenmhor@uk online.co.uk. *Internet:* www.glen-mhor.com. *Rack rates: £88–£120 ($128–$174) double. AE, MC, V.*

### Glengarry Castle Hotel
**$$–$$$**   **Invergarry**

You'd be hard pressed to find a prettier spot for a country house hotel with its own castle ruins (the real Glengarry Castle). The Victorian mansion is on extensive wooded grounds with nice views of Loch Oich. The hotel is less than ten minutes from Loch Ness. It has tennis courts and rowboats for your use. Some of the warmly decorated rooms have four-poster beds, and all are beam-roofed and spacious. The hotel may seem highbrow, but the staff is friendly and personable—and the price is a bargain for all that.

*Invergarry, where the A87 and A82 meet.* ☎ *01809-501-254. Fax: 01809-501-207. E-mail:* castle@glengarry.net. *Internet:* www.glengarry.net. *Rack rates: £90–£110 ($131–$160) double. MC, V.*

### Hilton Coylumbridge Resort Hotel
**$$$**   **Coylumbridge**

This excellent hotel is perfect for skiers and kids, but it has the luxury and comfort to attract everyone else. Located in the woods in the Cairngorm mountain countryside, the hotel enjoys views as lovely as the rooms. But it is the special extras that make the place stand out. If you ski, you'll appreciate being able to rent downhill or cross-country equipment. Kids will enjoy the in-house tenpin bowling alley, mini-golf course, and films, as well as ongoing special programs to keep them entertained. The hotel also has specially priced family rooms.

*Coylumbridge.* ☎ *01479-811-811. Fax: 01479-811-309. Internet:* www.stakis.co. uk/coylumbridge. *Rack rates: £120–£145 ($174–$210) double. AE, MC, V.*

### Inverlochy Castle
$$$$ **Fort William**

Beautifully situated between Ben Nevis and the water, the castle is an experience fit for a king. Or, rather, a queen. Queen Victoria stayed here for a week in 1873 and wrote in her diary, "I never saw a lovelier or more romantic spot." It's still true today. The sitting rooms and dining area are breathtaking—immaculately decorated and illuminated by chandeliers. The attention to fine detail and maximum comfort extends to the guest rooms, as well. No room in this five-star accommodation has a bad view. The food is gourmet, and after you've had your fill of rich food and posh surroundings, you can tour the 500-acre grounds overlooking Ben Nevis and a private loch. You can even do a little sketching of the area, as Victoria did when she visited. Note that the castle is not wheelchair accessible.

*Torlundy, 3 miles north of Fort William, on the A82.* ☎ *01397-702-177; toll-free from the U.S.: 888-424-0106. Fax: 01397-702-953. E-mail:* info@inverlochy.co.uk. *Internet:* www.inverlochy.co.uk. *Rack rates: £250–£380 ($363–$551) double. AE, MC, V. Closed Jan–Feb.*

### Loch Ness Lodge
$$ **Drumnadrochit**

I think it's fair to say that you won't meet any locals here—unless they work here. This hotel is full of tourists year-round. Look out your window and you're likely to see a plastic reproduction of the "monster" and the Loch Ness Exhibition Centre. That said, the rooms are quite comfortable and rather large, the staff is used to accommodating out-of-towners, and this is a prime location for exploring all the Loch Ness sights. The Lodge, which dates to 1740, also hosts traditional music and dance *ceilidhs*.

*Drumnadrochit, Loch Ness. On the A82, midway between Inverness (13 miles north) and Fort Augustus.* ☎ *01456-450-342. Fax: 01456-450-429. E-mail:* info@lochness-hotel.com. *Internet:* www.lochness-hotel.com. *Rack rates: £80 ($116) double. AE, DC, MC, V.*

### Lodge on the Loch
$$$–$$$$ **Onich**

A stay at the Lodge on the Loch will leave an indelible memory of your visit to the Highlands, not because the building or rooms are spectacular but because of the location. With some of the finest vistas in the country, this serene family-run retreat is a vacationer's vacation. From many of the nicely decorated guest rooms and the peaceful sitting rooms, you look out over the Bay of Onich and the Hills of Morvern. I suggest a walk on the grounds down to the shore or through the gardens. The house was built in 1870 as the country home for Lord and Lady McPherson, and now it can be your country home away from home.

On A82 on the edge of Luss, 5 miles north of Glencoe and 10 miles south of Fort William. ☎ *01855-821-582*. Fax: 01855-821-463. E-mail: reservations@freedom glen.co.uk. Internet: www.freedomglen.co.uk. Rack rates: £146–£210 ($212–$305) double. MC, V.

## The Lovat Arms Hotel
$$   **Fort Augustus**

The Lovat Arms is the newest and best accommodation in the adorable little town of Fort Augustus. As you enter you will find a welcoming bar on your left, a dining room with beautiful views on your right, and straight ahead the welcoming hosts, Bernard and May Greaves. The wonderful old building, in the middle of town, dates to 1859, and the new owners have invested a good deal of planning and money to give you the finest stay in town. The well-sized rooms, with overstuffed beds and large tubs, are reason enough to drop your bags here, but the hotel is more than the sum of its parts; taken as a whole it is as welcoming, friendly, and fun as you hope for in all your accommodation choices, but find only rarely. Also, don't bother looking in town for dinner; the hotel has an award-winning chef and a candlelit dining room.

On the A82, near the Caledonian locks. ☎ *01320-366-366*. Fax: 01320-366-677. E-mail: lovatarms@ipw.com. Internet: http://ipw.com/lovatarms. Rack rates: £80 ($116) double. AE, MC, V.

## Marine Hotel
$$   **Mallaig**

This family-run hotel in a bustling little fishing town is adorable, reminiscent of the set of the film *Popeye*. The staff is memorably accommodating, and the house is lovely. Some rooms have views of the sea and port; all are comfortable and modestly decorated. With the wind and rain in this part of the country, you'll probably appreciate the central heating more than any other amenity.

On the right from A830, adjacent to railway station. ☎ *01687-462-217*. Fax: 01687-462-821. E-mail: Marinehotel@btinternet.com. Internet: www.road-to-the-isles.org.uk/marine-hotel.html. Rack rates: £52–£72 ($75–$104) double. MC, V.

## The Moorings Hotel
$$–$$$   **Fort William**

On a quiet residential stretch outside Fort William's center, this labyrinthine hotel is bigger than it looks. The large, comfortable rooms stretch back to the Caledonian Locks; some units have views of the canal and the boats going through. The service is helpful, the beds are comfortable, and all rooms have satellite television. Superior rooms have Internet access. The location is ideal for a several-day stay while you explore the beautiful Glens areas.

*On the B8004 just off the A830 toward Mallaig, next to Neptune's Staircase.*
☎ *01397-772-797. Fax: 01397-772-441. E-mail:* `reservations@moorings-fortwilliam.co.uk`. *Internet:* `www.moorings-fortwilliam.co.uk`.
*Rack rates: £72–£124 ($104–$180) double. AE, MC, V.*

### Moyness House Hotel
**$$ Inverness**

This is arguably the finest B&B in town (the other contender is Ballifeary House; see review earlier in this section), and it's in a quiet residential location in easy strolling distance of Inverness center. The gracious hosts, Jenny and Richard Jones, have perfectly restored and improved their whitewashed 1880 Victorian villa. Each room is individually and comfortably done up; the whole place is nonsmoking. The five-star guesthouse has a free parking lot and plenty of tourist material if you don't feel like crossing the bridge into the town's tourist office.

*6 Bruce Gardens, just off A82, south side of the River Ness.* ☎ *01463-233-836. E-mail:* `stay@moyness.co.uk`. *Internet:* `www.moyness.co.uk`. *Rack rates: £66–£74 ($96–$107) double. AE, DC, MC, V.*

### The Newton Hotel
**$$$ Nairn**

Just before you enter the little coastal town of Nairn from the west, you'll spot this magnificent castlelike hotel. It's just the thing you need after a busy day of sightseeing. The staff will attend to your every need, and the rooms are quite large. The comfortable public rooms are decorated with antique furniture. In addition to the usual room facilities, other nice touches include a morning paper, cable TV, and heated bathroom floors. In the morning, you have the win-win choice of breakfast in your room or in the lovely glass-enclosed atrium dining area. As a guest at this four-star hotel, you have free use of the gym, pool, sauna, and steam room of its nearby sister hotel, the Golf View.

*Newton Gate, off Academy Street (A96).* ☎ *01667-453-144. Fax: 01667-455-267. E-mail:* `info@morton-hotels.com`. *Internet:* `www.morton-hotels.com`. *Rack rates: £108–£185 ($157–$268) double. AE, DC, MC, V.*

### Polmaily House Hotel
**$$ Drumnadrochit**

For an Edwardian country house, Polmaily sure knows how to provide modern luxury accommodations. The high-ceilinged bedrooms are large and elegant, and the hosts take pleasure in covering all your needs. Perfect for romantic couples as well as families, the hotel features a heated indoor pool, movies for the telly, an Internet room, horse stables (you can even get lessons!), tennis courts, sailing, and fishing. Parents will appreciate the baby-sitting service, organized children's activities, indoor and outdoor play areas, and family-size suites. Adults get posh, kids get loads of fun: Everyone wins.

On the A831 toward Cannish. ☎ **01456-450-343**. Fax: 01456-450-813. E-mail: polmaily@btinternet.com. Internet: www.polmaily.co.uk. Rack rates: £55–£72 ($80–$104) double. MC, V.

### Royal Highland Hotel

$$$ **Inverness**

Everything about Inverness's *other* castle is impressive. The huge hotel overlooks the River Ness and has views of the valley. When you walk in, you see a grand staircase reminiscent of the one on the *Titanic* and a tartan-clad bar with marble columns. Then there are the rooms. Each is as immaculate as it is elegant, decorated with fine antiques, linens, and fresh flowers. The Royal Highland has been a favorite retreat since it opened in 1859 as the Station Hotel (it's adjacent to the train station) and has gone through numerous renovations and modernizations to keep pace with newer luxury hotels.

Academy Street. ☎ **01463-231-926**. Fax: 01463-710-705. E-mail: info@royal highlandhotel.co.uk. Internet: www.royalhighlandhotel.com. Rack rates: £110–£132 ($160–$191) double. AE, DC, MC, V.

### Royal Hotel

$$ **Fortrose**

You'll be treated like royalty at this friendly, family-run hotel overlooking the Fortrose Cathedral ruins. The 14 rooms are uniquely decorated, and two larger units are designed for families. If you get a room with a view over the Moray Firth, you may even see dolphins from your window. If not, the lovely sunroom has the best view. The traditional black-and-white building is quintessentially Scottish, and so are the excellent food and ale served downstairs. A private garden is for guests only.

Union Street, at High Street, next to Fortrose Cathedral. On the main road to Cromarty. Turn east off the A9 at Tore and drive 6 miles along the Moray Firth coast. ☎ **01381-620-236**. E-mail: RoyalFortrose@cali.co.uk. Rack rates: £50–£80 ($73–$116) double. MC, V.

# Dining in the West Highlands

From traditional Scottish to classic Indian, from "gruel" to gourmet, the Highlands serve up an excellent variety of dining options.

### Café 1

$$–$$$ **Inverness** **International**

The small, well-chosen menu never fails to delight, especially when it includes such finely prepared items as wild mushroom risotto, prime Angus beef, and melt-in-your-mouth smoked haddock. The decor is simple and modern, despite the stone exterior, and you'll find the service polite and professional. There is always something for vegetarians (like the Friday night Italian night), and the desserts are to die for.

*75 Castle St.* ☎ *01463-226-200. Reservations accepted. Main courses: £7.50–£12.50 ($11–$18). AE, DC, MC, V. Open: Mon–Sat noon to 2:30 p.m. and 6–10 p.m.*

### Crannog
**$$–$$$    Fort William    Seafood**

This renowned seafood restaurant sits on stilts out over the water. The food is so fresh, you'll swear the staff went out and caught it right there in Loch Linnhe *after* you ordered. And you wouldn't be far off—the restaurant has its own boat fleet and smokehouse. Enjoy a fine meal in the nautically themed dining room to the sound of water gently lapping on the wooden structure, which was once a bait store. Everything is good; the plate of langoustine with hot garlic butter is highly touted. *Crannog* is the Gaelic word for an artificial island on the banks of a loch. How appropriate.

*The Pier.* ☎ *01397-705-589. Reservations recommended for dinner. Main courses: £9–£14 ($13–$20). MC, V. Open: Daily noon to 2:30 p.m. and 6–9:30 p.m.*

### Dickens
**$$–$$$    Inverness    International**

One of the finest dining experiences in Inverness, Dickens has something for everyone. At last count, the menu listed 181 items. The culinary influences are mainly Cantonese and French, and Scottish dishes are also available. If you feel a little daring, try the "carpet bagger," a delicious steak filet stuffed with oysters and mushrooms, or "drunken monkfish," cooked in garlic and Chinese wine. Low lighting gives the place a feeling of intimacy, and the dining room is in the style of the famed Scottish architect Charles Rennie Mackintosh. The one and only down side is the cheesy elevator music playing in the background. Reservations are required on weekends.

*77–79 Church St.* ☎ *01463-713-111. Reservations required on weekends. Main courses: £6.30–£13.20 ($9–$19). AE, DC, MC, V. Open: Daily noon to 2 p.m. and 5:30–11 p.m.*

### Grog and Gruel
**$$    Fort William    Tex-Mex/Scottish**

You may be tempted by the great bar downstairs, but skip the grog and follow the old-fashioned adverts—what the locals call advertisements—upstairs to the gruel. The friendly young staff complements the hip, relaxed atmosphere. As for the food, I suggest you try as much on the menu as you can handle. You'll do well to start with Hog's Breath Chili and then either a bulging burrito or a Cajun-style dish such as salmon or blackened steak. The pizzas and pasta are made to order, and the Scottish steak and ale pie is hearty. And don't forget to order grog with your meal. The newest is the surprisingly tasty organic microbrew Kelpie, a seaweed stout! The restaurant has the largest selection of cask-conditioned ales in the area, as well as a long list of good wines and whiskys.

*66 High St.* ☎ *01397-705-078. E-mail:* greatbeer@grogandgruel.co.uk. *Internet:* www.grogandgruel.co.uk. *Reservations accepted. Main courses: £5.95–£11.95 ($8.65–$17). MC, V. Open: Daily noon to 9 p.m.*

### McTavish's Kitchen
**$–$$$  Fort William  Scottish**

Abundant local publicity makes this restaurant a popular place for tourists. Yes, it does have live Scottish dancing and music, but that's where the attraction ends. The food, heavy on seafood and traditional Scottish dishes, is rather dull, and the crowds of customers tend to overextend the wait staff. Only children won't mind the wait—coloring and bagpipes distract them. Unless you don't mind the cheese and a load of other tourists, you may want to shy away from McTavish's.

*West End High Street.* ☎ *01397-702-406. E-mail:* fortwilliam@mctavishs. com. *Internet:* www.mctavishs.com. *Reservations recommended. Main courses: £7.35–£14.75 ($11–$21). Show: £1.75 ($2.55) adults, £1 ($1.45) children if you dine during show hours. MC, V. Open: Daily noon to 2 p.m. and 6–10 p.m. Show: May–Sept daily 8:30–10 p.m.*

### Nico's Bistro
**$$–$$$  Inverness  Scottish**

This upscale restaurant is very laid-back, considering the quality of food and service it dishes out. Happy patrons have included Prince Charles and Princess Anne. You can't go wrong with one of the catches of the day, such as sea scallops sautéed in olive oil or fried whole langoustines. The chef is proud of his "prize-winning" haggis, and the excellent veggie options include a yummy compote of woodland mushrooms. The lounge is perfect for a pre-dinner beer or an after-dinner cocktail, and outdoor seating is available.

*Glen Mhor Hotel, Ness Bank.* ☎ *01463-234-308. Reservations accepted. Main courses: £5.90–£17.90 ($8.60–$26). AE, DC, MC, V. Open: Daily 11:30 a.m.–10 p.m.*

### Rajah Indian Restaurant
**$$$–$$$$  Inverness  Indian**

This basement restaurant is a hidden treasure. The beautifully decorated and immaculately kept dining area, with plush seating and pleasing Indian art, is the backdrop to a wonderful dining experience. The staff is friendly, and the superb food is rich and flavorful. The chef's specialties include sour Bengal lamb and hot and spicy garlic chili *massalah*. You can't fail with one of the unique wok-served Balti dishes. The inexpensive (\$4.95/\$7.20) lunch special is served Monday to Saturday from noon to 2:30 p.m. And remember: Don't stop eating 'til you see the elephant!

*2 Post Office Ave.* ☎ *01463-237-190 or 01463-711-525. Reservations accepted. Main courses: £10.50–£20.50 ($15–$30). MC, V. Open: Daily noon to 11 p.m.*

### Riva's
**$$–$$$  Inverness  Italian**

Bella! Primo! Fine wine, excellent Italian, and good service on the river— could you ask for more? The intimate bistro-style seating is nice and lively. The subtly flavored meals turn staples such as baked filet of sole or tagliatelle with red peppers into something extraordinary. You'll find a perfect complement to the dinner in the smartly planned wine selection. Oh, and save room for dessert—you'll see why.

*4–6 Ness Walk, by the Ness Bridge.* ☎ *01463-226-686. Reservations not required. Main courses: £6.95–£14.95 ($10–$22). AE, MC, V. Open: Tues–Sat noon to 2 p.m. and 6–9:30 p.m.; Sun 5–9:30 p.m.*

### The River Café
**$  Inverness  Scottish**

This small, comfortable restaurant by the water is a favorite among locals for its good eats at even better prices. It offers several filled croissants, stuffed baked potatoes, and specialty dishes such as filet of Scottish salmon and chili con carne, all at take-away prices. Not bad for a sit-down place by the river.

*10 Bank St.* ☎ *01463-714-884. Reservations recommended. Main courses: £3.95–£5.95 ($5.75–$8.65). MC, V. Open: Tues–Sat 10 a.m.–9:30 p.m.; Sun–Mon 10 a.m.–8:30 p.m.*

# Exploring the West Highlands

You'll find plenty of memorable attractions between Inverness and Ben Nevis. But don't confine yourself to Loch Ness hot spots. You'll have your choice of fine museums, ancient stones, historic monuments, natural areas to hike through, and a good number of excellent castles throughout the region.

### Ben Nevis
**Near Fort William**

At 4,418 feet, the tallest mountain in Scotland is impressive only by U.K. standards. Set next to two other mountains, Ben Nevis doesn't particularly stand out in the landscape, nor does it come to a dramatic peak. It may not take the best picture, but it is a popular climb among locals and hearty visitors. The round-trip climb is 10 miles and takes about eight hours. You will need to wear good boots and plenty of warm-weather gear, because the temperature and weather can fluctuate unpredictably at certain heights. Also, don't attempt to climb after dusk. The tourist office in Fort William has trail maps if you're planning to make the big climb. At the top, you can see about 100 of Scotland's other *munros*. In 2000, a family-owned estate turned the mountain over to the John Muir Foundation.

*Path leaves from Glen Nevis Road just outside Fort William. Time: 8 hours.*

### Ben Nevis Range Gondola and Skiing
**Torlundy**

Snow or no snow, this is a treat year-round. Whether you plan to ski or simply soak in the beautiful mountain scenery, the Nevis gondola, the only one in Scotland, is a wonderful excursion. The trip takes you halfway up the summit of Aonach Mor, a panoramic 2,000-foot spot that houses a restaurant, bar, and shops. You can hike paths around the area before returning down in the gondola, or ski or snowboard to the bottom in the winter. You'll find plenty of mountain bike trails around the base, and bike rentals are available. The mountaintop Snowgoose Restaurant offers home-cooked meals and plenty of outdoor seating. Skiing is even available in July and August! Skiing the artificial slope on the Alpha Tow costs £19 ($28) for adults and £15 ($22) for kids and includes use of the gondola, lift, and ski rental. The gondola easily carries wheelchairs.

If you plan to ride more than just up and down, the all-day tickets are the best bargain.

*Torlundy, 6 miles north of Fort William. Follow the signs for A82 from Inverness and follow signs to lifts from Torlundy.* ☎ *01397-705-825 or 01397-70-5854. E-mail:* nevisrange@sol.co.uk. *Internet:* www.nevis-range.co.uk. *Gondola: £7 ($10) adults, £6.30 ($9.15) seniors, £4.40 ($6.40) children under 16, £18.75–£21.75 ($27–$32) family. All-day ticket: £22 ($33) adults, £12.25 ($18) children. Open: Sept–June daily 10 a.m.–5 p.m.; July–Aug Sat–Wed 9:30 a.m.–6 p.m., Thurs–Fri 9:30 a.m.–9 p.m. Closed Nov 12–Dec 20. Time: 3–6 hours.*

### Brodie Castle
**Brodie**

Although it's a bit austere—one may even say gloomy—the castle has a good deal to explore. It's worth a stop if you're passing by. Staff members are on hand if you have questions about the furniture and items on display—but don't expect them to have all the answers. This is a particularly good stop for art fans; the collection of paintings is large, as is the volume of books. The rugs are a bit faded, and the ceiling has a few cracks. Several unexplained Buddha statues appear here and there.

*Off the A96, 7 miles east of Nairn. (Bus: Stagecoach Bluebird, ☎ 01343-54-422.)*
*☎ 01309-641-371. Admission: £5 ($7.25) adults; £3.75 ($5.45) seniors, students, and*
*children under 16; £13.50 ($20) family. Open: Castle: Apr–Sept Thurs–Mon 11 a.m.–*
*5 p.m. Grounds: Year-round daily 9:30 a.m. to sunset. Time: 2 hours.*

## Cawdor Castle
### Cawdor

This is my favorite of all the castles, mainly because the room-by-room
explanations are so well written and funny. It's easy to get bored reading
long lists of who painted what and the history of furniture. But Clan
Campbell has added welcome candor and personal details to the self-
guided tour of this huge castle. It's full of treasures from around the
world, and the drawbridge and medieval tower are intact. The gardens
are wonderful, with huge, eye-pleasing arrangements of wildflowers, lots
of fountains, and a maze of holly bushes.

Legend has it that a king determined the location of the castle by giving
instructions to build it wherever his donkey decided to rest. The animal
stopped in the shade of a tree, and deep within the castle, the tree stands
today. Although Macbeth was the Thane of Cawdor, the Scottish king
never resided here.

The gift shop is the best I've seen in any castle, and the separate wool
shop has some unique items. Again, don't miss a bit of the writing by
those clever Campbells.

*On the B9090, off the A96 between Inverness and Nairn. ☎ 01667-404-615. E-mail:*
cawdor.castle@btinternet.com. *Admission: £6.10 ($8.85) adults, £5.10*
*($7.40) seniors and students, £3.30 ($4.80) children under 16. Open: Daily May–Sept*
*10 a.m.–5:30 p.m. Closed Oct–Apr. Time: 3 hours.*

## Clanland (Storehouse of Foulis)
### Evanton

Suppress the urge to groan or laugh—this is not as bad as it sounds. I'm
not sure why they call it Clanland, because the exhibit mentions only one
clan. Clanland occupies an old refurbished renthouse (where the locals
would come to pay their rent, usually with crops or livestock), and life-
size figures demonstrate what it was like to work here. The interactive
displays focus on local music, food, topography, and history. The video
is a tribute to the powerful Highland Clan Munro. The Munros are proud
of their heritage, which includes their loyalty to the Jacobites. (Their
castle, Foulis, is not open to the public.) Famous Munros include one of
my least favorite American presidents, James Monroe, and one of my
favorite short-story writers, H. H. Munro (also known as Saki). A small
display concentrates on the seals who frequent the nearby beaches. Next
to the parking lot is a seal-watching area.

*Foulis Ferry Point, Easter Ross, Evanton, 20 minutes north of Inverness on the A9.* ☎ *01349-83-0038. E-mail:* admin@storehouseoffoulis.co.uk. *Internet:* www.storehouseoffoulis.co.uk. *Admission: £3 ($4.35) adults, £2.25 ($3.30) seniors and students, £1.50 ($2.20) children under 16. Open: Daily Apr–Oct 9 a.m.– 6 p.m., Nov–Mar 10 a.m.–4 p.m. Time: 90 minutes.*

## Clava Cairns
**Culloden**

Basically a 4,000-year-old graveyard, the Clava Cairns are significant because they are the most intact Bronze Age tombs in ancient Scotland. You'll find little more to see than large circular pits and a few standing stones in a grove of trees, but you can walk into the ring and passage cairns. It's a slightly eerie place, with a sort of extraterrestrial feel. Take a look when you're visiting nearby Culloden battlefield.

*Take the B9006 from Inverness, beyond the Culloden battlefield, go right on B851, and stay straight through the crossroads.* ☎ *01667-460-232. Admission: Free. Open: Year-round, 24 hours. Time: 1 hour.*

## Culloden Moor Battlefield
**Culloden Moor**

This marshy field is a must-see for anyone interested in the history of Scotland. Bonnie Prince Charlie's Jacobite uprising met its defeat here in 1746 at the hands of the king's troops, led by Charlie's cousin, the Duke of Cumberland. The bloody battle was over in about an hour, and Charlie was among the few men who got away unharmed. The visitor center is long on interesting details; in it you'll find a museum and an excellent film about the battle. Take the time to walk through the battlefield, which has clan stones and cairns in memory of those who lost their lives. In fact, the road to the visitor center goes right over part of the battlefield. The terrain is just as it was during the battle, when the boggy conditions played a role in the Jacobites' defeat. This battle marks the beginning of the end of Highland life; the crown banned tartans and bagpipes after its victory here. Guided tours are available for an extra £3 ($4.35) for adults and £2 ($2.90) for children.

*Culloden Moor, 5 miles east of Inverness on the B9006, which runs parallel to the A96. (Bus: No. 12 on the Highland County Bus,* ☎ *01463-71-0555, from Inverness. Tour bus by Guide Friday,* ☎ *01463-22-4000.)* ☎ *01463-79-0607. Admission: £5 ($7.25) adults; £3.75 ($5.45) seniors, students, and children under 16; £13.50 ($20) family. Open: Daily Apr–Oct 9 a.m.–6 p.m.; Feb–Mar, Nov–Dec 10 a.m.–4 p.m. Closed Jan. Time: 2 hours, 30 minutes.*

## Dornoch Cathedral
**Dornoch**

Before the end of the year 2000, the most interesting thing that happened inside these walls was in 1722, when the last witch to be burned in

Scotland lost her life. Now Dornoch is on the map as the spot where Madonna married film director Guy Ritchie. Never mind the fine stonework and stained-glass windows dedicated to Andrew Carnegie—Gwyneth Paltrow and Sting actually stood here!

*On the main square. No phone. Admission: Free. Open: Daily 9 a.m. to dusk. Time: 1 hour.*

### Dunrobin Castle
**Golspie**

This fine castle belonged to the earls and dukes of Sutherland and holds an excellent collection of tapestries and Louis XV–period furniture. The pieces are all amazingly intricate, and the family heirlooms on display are in good shape. This is the largest home in the Highlands, so it'll take you a little time to get through the tour. There is even a steam-powered fire engine on the grounds. My favorite part of Dunrobin is the perfectly manicured gardens and fountains between the castle and the sea; the estate gardens are some of the finest in Scotland. Good maps are available for long forest walks from the castle to area cairns and monuments. Another crowd-pleaser is the daily afternoon falconry display.

*Just north of town, on the A9.* ☎ *01408-633-177. Admission: £5.50 ($8) adults, £4 ($5.80) seniors and children under 16, £16 ($23) family. Open: June–Sept Mon–Sat 10:30 a.m.–4:30 p.m., Sun 12:30–5:30 p.m.; Apr–May, Oct Mon–Sat 10:30 a.m.–4:30 p.m. Closed Nov–Mar. Time: 3 hours.*

### Eilean Donan Castle
**Dornie**

Grab your camera—Eilean Donan is the quintessential castle. On an islet in Loch Duich, the restored 12th-century castle (which lay in ruins from 1719–1912) is accessible by a lovely bridge that makes a good picture. Alexander II originally built the castle, which underwent restoration following serious destruction at the hands of Jacobite troops and an English man o' war. Inside are a piper gallery, Jacobite relics, and military objects, as well as a war memorial to Clan MacRae, which held the castle on behalf of another clan, MacKenzie. If you catch the BBC in your hotel and see a network promo shot of a hot-air balloon passing over a castle, that's Eilean Donan; it's probably the most photographed castle in Scotland. B-movie fans will be excited by the fact that *Highlander* was filmed here.

*Dornie, Kyle of Lochalsh, on the A87.* ☎ *01599-555-202. Internet:* www.eilean donancastle.com. *Admission: £4 ($5.80) adults; £3.20 ($4.65) seniors, students, and children under 16; £9.50 ($14) family. Open: Mar–Nov 10 a.m.–3:30 p.m. Closed Dec–Feb. Time: 2 hours.*

## The Flora MacDonald Statue
### Inverness

This life-size statue honors the woman who saved the life of Bonnie Prince Charlie after the defeat of his Jacobite struggle against the crown. Flora seems to be looking for something (like the view) through all the mist, or maybe she's just shooing away the birds that like to perch on her head.

*In front of Inverness Castle.*

## Fort George
### Ardersier

Although it still functions as a working army barracks, Fort George is open to visitors, who may walk through the entire complex. Highlights include the magazine room, stocked with old muskets and uniforms from the Napoleonic War; a museum filled with trophies and medals; and a drawbridge. You can walk atop the wall (nearly a mile all the way around) and enjoy a fine view of the Moray Firth and, if you're lucky, a few dolphins. Other interesting items include a dog cemetery, the chapel, barracks, and the Queen's Own Highlander Regimental Museum. King George II had the impressive fort built following the crown's victory over the Jacobite army at Culloden to discourage any future Scottish armies from attempting to take over the country. It seems to have succeeded, even without a shot ever being fired in battle here. This is the largest artillery fortification in the U.K., and its 18th-century bastioned defenses and garrisons are intact and open for you to roam.

*Just off the A96 on the B9006, 11 miles northeast of Inverness and 6 miles west of Nairn. (Bus: Highland Bus and Coach Co., ☎ 01667-462-7777, no. 11, from the Queensgate Post Office.) ☎ 01667-46-2777. Admission: £5 ($7.25) adults, £3.50 ($5.10) seniors and students, £1.50 ($2.20) children under 16. Open: Daily Apr–Sept 9:30 a.m.–6:30 p.m.; Oct–Mar 9:30 a.m.–4:30 p.m. Time: 3 hours.*

## Glencoe
### Glencoe

It's hard to believe that such a beautiful spot has such a bloody history. This is the site of the Massacre of 1692, when Campbell of Glen Lyon and his men brutally murdered 40 members of the MacDonald and the Maclan clans—including women and children who had all been guests of the Campbells. The lovely glen runs 7½ miles to the shores of Loch Leven. Up in one of the hills (Aonach Dubh) is Ossian's Cave, which you can reach via Ossian's Ladder, a moderate-to-difficult rock climb. Ossian was a third-century Gaelic bard, and legend says he was born in the cave. Ranger-led walks take place throughout the summer; the visitor center also has trail maps of the area and excellent new audiovisual presentations that explain local geography and the clan slayings. There is also a monument to the massacre in Carnoch.

## Scotland's Hatfields and McCoys

You may think that after 300-plus years, the rivalry between the clans Campbell and MacDonald (the former murdered some of the latter in 1692 at Glencoe) would be a thing of the past, but old hatreds die hard. Seems the local MacDonalds are unhappy about the 2002 appointment of a Campbell to head the Glencoe Visitor Centre. The MacDonalds may find the move insensitive, but everyone agrees that the real draw of Glencoe is the surrounding beauty.

*Glencoe Visitor Centre, Glencoe, Ballachulish.* ☎ *01855-811-307. E-mail:* dwarner@ nts.org.uk. *Admission: £3.50 ($5.10) adults; £2.60 ($3.80) seniors, students, and children under 16; £9.50 ($14) family. Open: Daily 10 a.m.–5 p.m. Time: 2 hours.*

### Glenfinnan Monument
**Glenfinnan**

This monument marks the zealous, hopeful start of the Jacobite Rising, led by Bonnie Prince Charlie, who was trying to reclaim the English and Scottish crowns through his Stuart family lineage. Be sure to take your camera; this monument and sacred historical ground amid Highland scenery is a great spot for pictures, especially if you're lucky enough to see the steam train cross the aqueduct bridge behind the visitor center. The Jacobites left from this spot to successfully push all the way to northern England before turning back and ultimately finding defeat at Culloden Moor Battlefield (see listing earlier in this section). The Jacobite Rising has captured the Scots' collective imagination, and the museum's visitor center provides a good primer on the Jacobites and Prince Charlie. *Note:* The staff will warn you to mind your head as you crawl through the top hatch of the monument. I managed to hit mine anyway.

*On A830, next to Loch Shiel. 18 miles west of Fort William.* ☎ *01397-72-2250. Admission: £2 ($2.90) adults; £1 ($1.45) seniors, students, and children under 16; £5 ($7.25) family. Open: Daily mid-May–Aug 9:30 a.m.–6 p.m.; Apr–mid-May, Sept–Oct 10 a.m.–5 p.m. Closed Nov–Mar. Time: 2 hours.*

### Glenmore Forest Park
**Kincraig**

This park is not simply stunning scenery full of Scottish flora and fauna. The attractions within the attraction include Wolf Territory and the Brightwater Burn otters. You can drive through the main reserve and walk through to the other attractions, and you'll find all of it scenic and interesting. Kids will enjoy seeing the animals, but with everything else going on, parents won't be bored. The most popular parts of the park are the Watersports Centre, for canoeing and sailing, and the Cairngorm Reindeer Centre, where you can feed Santa's favorite animal.

*On the B9152 off A9 at King Ussie.* ☎ *01540-651-270 or 01540-861-220. E-mail:* wildlife@rzss.org.uk. *Internet:* www.kingraig.com/wildlife. *Watersports Centre:* ☎ *01540-861-221. Cairngorm Reindeer Centre:* ☎ *01540-861-228. Park admission: Free. Reindeer Centre admission: £4 ($5.80) adults, £3 ($4.35) children under 16. Reindeer Centre Open: 10 a.m.–5 p.m. No feedings Nov–Dec. Time: 3–5 hours.*

## Hugh Miller's Cottage
### Cromarty

Who, you may ask, is Hugh Miller? He was an extraordinary man who worked as a stonemason, accountant, geologist, church reformer, journalist, and folklore author. You'll learn his story, which provides an interesting perspective on the times in which he lived here in his birthplace—an authentic thatched-roof building constructed in 1711. Miller's personal belongings are on display, including his geological tools and fossil collection. The audiovisual presentation is interesting.

*Church Street, on the Black Isle, 25 miles northeast of Inverness.* ☎ *01381-600-245. Admission: £2 ($2.90) adults, £1.30 ($1.90) children under 16, £4.80 ($7) family. Open: May–Sept Mon–Sat 11 a.m.–1 p.m. and 2–4 p.m. Time: 1 hour, 30 minutes.*

## Inverness Museum and Art Gallery
### Inverness

This museum's permanent collection is substantial and interesting. It includes period dress, many old bagpipes, a cast of the death mask of Bonnie Prince Charlie, prehistoric stones, the history of the city, and lots and lots of taxidermied animals. The collection of Highland silver is the largest of its kind. The two-story building also holds an innovative art museum with rotating exhibits. Definitely worth a look-see; you can't argue with the price.

*Castle Wynd, off Bridge Street.* ☎ *01463-23-7114. Admission: Free. Open: Mon–Sat 9 a.m.–5 p.m. Time: 1 hour, 30 minutes.*

## The Jacobite Steam Train
### Fort William and Mallaig railway stations

The 42-mile train ride between Fort William and the port town of Mallaig is one of the most picturesque journeys you'll find. The trip lasts only a couple of hours each way; you can take it round-trip or, more practically, one-way to the Isle of Skye via the ferry in Mallaig. Either way, keep your camera handy. As you chug along past mountains, over lochs, and by the sea, you'll pass the Glenfinnan Monument and miles and miles of dramatic, unspoiled scenery. It's hard to believe that the train wasn't built for the delight of visitors; rather, it was created for fisherman who once used it to bring their catch inland. In Fort William is a small train museum and a cafe in an old train car.

*Fort William and Mallaig railway stations.* ☎ *01463-239-026. Internet:* www.steam train.info. *Tickets: £23 ($33) round-trip or £17.50 ($25) one-way adults; £13 ($19) round-trip or £9 ($13) one-way children under 16. Open: Mid-June to Sept. One round-trip daily Mon–Fri, from Fort William at 10:20 a.m., from Mallaig at 2:10 p.m. One round-trip Sun July 30–Sept 3, from Fort William at 12:45 p.m., from Mallaig at 5:05 p.m. Closed Oct–mid-June. Time: 5 hours round-trip.*

### John Cobb Cairn
**Loch Ness**

Many locals and visitors from around the world make the pilgrimage to this memorial for the man who was once the fastest in the world. John Cobb lost his life on Loch Ness in 1952 while making a second attempt at the world water speed record. He had already broken the record, going 206 mph (28 mph faster than the American world record), but he had to do it twice to make the record books. On his second run, his speedboat *Crusader* broke apart and killed him. At the time of his death, he held the world's land speed record.

*On the west bank, between Drumnadrochit and Invermoiston.*

### Loch Ness

This is it, the dark, deep (700 ft.), mysterious, legendary Loch Ness. In addition to looking for the elusive Nessie, you can seek out other area attractions, such as Urquhart Castle and the John Cobb Cairn (see separate listings in this section). Loch Ness is the largest freshwater deposit in the U.K., containing more fresh water than all of England and Wales combined. As you drive along the loch, you'll see many explanatory plaques giving information and the history of the area. The best way to see the loch is by boat (see "Touring the West Highlands," later in this chapter).

As for the monster, whose scientific name is *Nessetarus Rumpeteras,* little is known for sure. Although no one can say if it exists, it's against the law to kill it. Is it out there? While the dark waters of Loch Ness may not be terribly conducive to photosynthesis, thereby stunting the food chain, it offers plenty of room for a large beast to hide. No one can say definitively, so keep the camera ready!

### Loch Ness 2000 Exhibition
**Drumnadrochit**

Visiting this attraction is like reading *Loch Ness For Dummies* (if there were such a book). In other words, it covers all the bases without burying you in details. Focusing mainly on monster myths and the technology of scientific monster hunting, it's a fun walking tour through a series of impressive light and video displays. The exhibition is a little cavernous and kitschy, but who doesn't like a good laser show? And while the kids marvel at the smoke and mirrors, you'll actually learn a couple things about the long history of sightings, research, and theories on the monster.

*Drumnadrochit, Loch Ness, on the A82.* ☎ *01456-450-573. E-mail:* info@loch-ness-scotland.com. *Internet:* www.loch-ness-scotland.com. *Admission: £5.95 ($8.60) adults, £4.50 ($6.50) seniors and students, £3.50 ($5) children under 16, £14.95 ($22) family. Open: Daily 9 a.m.–8 p.m. Time: 1 hour.*

### Mallaig Marine World
**Mallaig**

This small aquarium is a good place to pass some time with the kids while you're waiting for the ferry to Skye. Located on the harbor, the attraction provides some perspective on the interesting and diverse sea life of the area. In addition to the maze of tanks, it has models, photographs, and a video about the town's fishing tradition, all most appreciated by the 12-and-under crowd. Guided tours and talks are available.

*The Harbour.* ☎ *01687-462-292. Internet:* www.road-to-the-isles.org.uk/marine-world. *Admission: £2.75 ($4) adults, £2 ($2.90) seniors and students, £1.50 ($2.20) children under 16, £7.50 ($11) family. Open: Apr–Oct Mon–Sat 9 a.m.–7 p.m., Sun 10 a.m.–6 p.m.; Nov–Mar Mon–Sat 9 a.m.–7 p.m. Time: 1 hour.*

### The Official Loch Ness Exhibition Centre
**Drumnadrochit**

This is the other Loch Ness exhibit, the older and cheaper one, and the one that requires a little more reading than its flashier competition (the Loch Ness 2000 Exhibition; see the preceding listing). Okay, so the entrance is, sadly, inside the mammoth gift shop, but what I like about this exhibit is its focus: not so much on the Loch Ness monster as it is on the lake itself, which has a very interesting history. The film covers the history of Nessie sightings and explains how many are actually of something else, such as sea otters. The exhibition around the theater is full of pictures, including other freak beast lore and a series on John Cobb's fatal attempt to beat the world's water speed record (see the John Cobb Cairn entry, earlier in this section).

*On the A82.* ☎ *01456-450-342. E-mail:* info@lochness-centre.com. *Internet:* www.lochness-centre.com. *Admission: £5 ($7.25) adults, £3.50 ($5.10) seniors, £3.75 ($5.45) students, £3 ($4.35) children under 16. Open: Mar–June, Sept–Oct 9:30 a.m.–5:30 p.m.; July–Aug 9 a.m.–7:30 p.m.; Nov–Feb 10 a.m.–3 p.m. Time: 1 hour, 30 minutes.*

### Sands of Morar
**Near Mallaig**

Bonnie Prince Charlie roamed these beautiful strawberry-blonde beaches 250 years ago while fleeing his oppressors. Set against postcard-pretty Loch Morar, it's a popular locale for filmmakers intent on capturing the quintessential Scottish backdrop—*Highlander* and *Local Hero* were filmed here. The sands get rather crowded with sun-loving locals in the summer.

### Skiing the West Highlands
**Glencoe/Cairngorm**

Outside of Ben Nevis (see listing earlier in this section), this region has two other legitimate ski resorts. Arguably the best ski area in Scotland, **Glencoe** has the most challenging black diamonds, great views, and a cute ski and mountaineering museum at the base (open off-season). **Cairngorm** has unpredictable weather, but when the snow base is good, the whole family can enjoy skiing and other non-ski activities.

*Glencoe Ski Centre: Kingshouse, Glencoe, on the A82.* ☎ *01855-851-226. Cairngorm: Aviemore.* ☎ *01479-861-261. Admission: Lift tickets, rentals, and packages vary. Open: Glencoe: Daily 9 a.m.–5 p.m. year-round. Cairngorm: Daily 8:30 a.m.–4:30 p.m. year-round.*

### Tain Through Time
**Tain**

A combination museum, medieval church, audiovisual presentation, and self-guided tour, this eager little attraction covers the last millennium in the development of Tain and the region. Tain Through Time is a surprisingly interesting look at local archaeology and the religious history of this ancient burgh, with plenty of activities and displays geared to kids.

*Tower Street.* ☎ *01862-894-089. E-mail:* info@tainmuseum.demon.co.uk. *Internet:* www.tainmuseum.demon.co.uk. *Admission: £3.50 ($5.10) adults, £2 ($2.90) seniors and children under 16, £10 ($15) family. Open: Daily Apr–Oct 10 a.m.–6 p.m.; other times by appointment only. Time: 1 hour.*

### Urquhart Castle
**Drumnadrochit**

The impressive ruins of this large and significant castle have no particular clan association. Because this spot on Loch Ness was such an important location for trade routes into the Highlands, the castle has changed hands many times since it was built in the 13th century. The last group to occupy the castle before the tourists invaded was Cromwell's army in the 1650s; it was even blown up in 1692 to prevent it from being occupied by the Jacobites. It's no wonder that Urquhart today is one of the most photographed castles in the United Kingdom—the tower and ruins stand on a beautiful spot right on the water. During the summer months, there is usually a bagpiper playing in the castle, a nice soundtrack as you tour the place and grounds. A recent addition is an awesome A/V display of views and history that plays before you see the real thing.

*Near Drumnadrochit., on the A82.* ☎ *01456-450-551. Admission: £5 ($7.25) adults, £3.75 ($5.45) seniors and students, £1.20 ($1.75) children under 16. Open: Daily July–Aug 9:30 a.m.–8:30 p.m.; Apr–June, Sept 9:30 a.m.–6:30 p.m.; Oct–Mar 9:30 a.m.–4:30 p.m. Time: 2 hours.*

# Touring the West Highlands

The West Highlands lends itself nicely to smartly operated theme tours, whether relating to the area's rich historic heritage or unique natural history. Here are some tours I consider the best in the region.

✔ **Dolphin Ecosse** (☎ **01381-600-323**; E-mail: info@dolphinecosse.co.uk; Internet: www.dolphinecosse.co.uk): The Cromarty bottle-nosed dolphins are the only known group living in the North Sea. The tour takes you out to see the dolphins in action. As many as 130 dolphins live in the area, and they are generally friendly and unafraid to approach the boat. The tour also covers other local coastal attractions, such as seals, natural rocks and caves, and gun emplacements that were used to guard the Royal Navy during World War I. Audiotapes (included in the price) are available, and the knowledgeable crew is happy to answer questions. Coffee and biscuits are handed out, as well. Tours depart from Cromarty Harbor (on the A832 at the junction of Bank Street and High Street) at 7:45 a.m., 10:45 a.m., 1:45 p.m., and 5:45 p.m. daily, year-round. Tickets cost £15 ($22) per person, free for children under 3. Time: 2 hours, 45 minutes.

✔ **Guide Friday** (☎ **01463-224-000**; E-mail: inverness@guidefriday.com; Internet: guidefriday.com): Like most Guide Friday tours, this double-decker sightseeing bus and its informative guides provide a good primer to the area. The theme here is the history of Inverness and the Culloden Battlefield. The tour is a treat, with a little humor and trivia thrown in. It's also a good way to see the whole town of Inverness at one time, with the option of getting on and off where you like. In addition, the side trip to Culloden is a convenient way to see the big out-of-town attraction. Tours run all over Inverness. You can hop on at any point, including outside the visitor center and at the railway station. Buses run May through October from 10 a.m. to 4:45 p.m. The new Loch Ness trip includes a 30-minute boat trip. It runs daily June through September at 10:30 a.m. and 2:30 p.m. Office: Guide Friday Station Square Academy Street. Tickets for the sightseeing tour cost £7.50 ($11) adults, £6 ($8.70) seniors and students, £2.50 ($3.65) children. The Loch Ness tour costs £14.50 ($22) adults, £11.50 ($17) seniors and students, £6.50 ($9.60) children. Time: The entire sightseeing circuit takes 90 minutes. The Loch Ness trip takes 3 hours.

✔ **The Inverness Terror Tour** (Call Mr. Black, ☎ **07730-831-069**; http://drink.to/davytheghost.com): Murder, witchcraft, torture, and hangings are the staples of this macabre tour through the darker history of Inverness. Your tour guide is an 18th-century ghost, and quite funny despite the subject matter. It's not scary, so kids will be fine, but they won't be able to partake of the free drink at the end of the tour. The tour leaves from the Inverness tourist information center daily at 7 p.m. (in summer the company may add a tour at 9 p.m.). Tickets cost £6 ($8.70) adults, £5.50 ($8) students, £4 ($5.80) children, £16 ($23) family. Time: 1 hour, 15 minutes.

✔ **Jacobite Cruises** (☎ **01463-233-999**; E-mail: bookings@jacobite cruises.co.uk; Internet: www.jacobitecruises.co.uk): The views along pretty Loch Ness are the same no matter which boat tour you take, but Jacobite Cruises is perhaps the most efficient and best organized. The boats are large, which means less rocking and rolling. There is also a bar on board. The trip leaves from Tomnahurich Bridge near Inverness, winds down through Dochgarroch Lock, to famed Urquhart Castle, and back. The company offers combination tickets in case you want to get off at Urquhart and tour the castle or visit the monster exhibits in Drumnadrochit. Boats leave from Tomnahurich Bridge, Glenurquhart Road, Inverness. Stay on the same road as the Ness Bridge in Inverness, which eventually becomes Tomnahurich Bridge. Trips run from April through October. Tickets cost £10.50 ($15) adults, £8.50 ($12) seniors, students, and children, £35 ($51) family. Time: 3 hours, 30 minutes.

✔ **Loch Ness Cruises** (☎ **01456-450-395**; E-mail: cruises@lochness-cruises.com; Internet: www.lochness-cruises.com): These monster-centric cruises on the "Nessie Hunter" may be the most touristy, but they are perhaps the most fun. The boats have underwater video cameras and monster-searching sonar equipment. Skippers George Edwards and Dick Raynor have been bona fide monster hunters for decades and provide the commentary. In fact, Skipper George discovered the deepest part of the lake, "Edwards Deep." The tour covers other attractions, but Loch Ness monster hunting is the real draw. Tickets are for sale at the Official Loch Ness Monster Visitor Centre in Drumnadrochit. Boats leave from April through October daily at 9:30, 10:30, and 11:30 a.m., and 12:30, 2, 3, 4, 5, and 6 p.m. Evening cruises are available by arrangement. Tickets cost £8 ($12) adults, £5 ($7.25) children, £24 ($35) family. Time: 1 hour.

✔ **Loch Ness Shuttle** (☎ **01456-450-168** or 07778-837-588; E-mail: shuttle@loch-ness.org; Internet: www.loch-ness.org/files/shuttle.html): What sets this erudite bus tour of Loch Ness apart is its host, local historian Tony Harmsworth. The tour includes the natural and national history of the area and stops at the Loch Ness centers and Urquhart Castle. Nothing is dumbed down for younger ears, either, so this may not be the best tour for young children. Harmsworth wrote the script for the Macbeth Experience (featured in Chapter 15) and other attractions. The shuttle departs from Inverness Tourist Board daily at 10:30 a.m. Because the tour is canceled from time to time, it's best to book ahead through the Web site. Tickets cost £7.50 ($11) adults, £6.50 ($9.45) seniors and students. Time: 4 hours.

# Shopping in the West Highlands

The only shopping center worth noting is the **Eastgate Shopping Centre,** 11 Eastgate, off High Street, Inverness (☎ **01463-226-457**). More than 50 shops in one spot is a big deal for the Highlands. This American-style mall doesn't necessarily cater to tourists, but there are plenty of bargains for discerning shoppers. While you're on your shopping spree, make sure to take a gander at the fascinating ornamental clock that kicks into high gear at the top of every hour.

✔ **Brodie Country,** just off A96, near Brodie Castle, Brodie. (☎ **01309-641-555**). Okay, you haven't picked up a single souvenir for the friends and family yet. Don't panic. Brodie Country is a one-stop shop for everything under the sun—from touristy pap to high-end stuff. You'll find organic chutney in the deli, designer clothes in the boutique area, and more tartan-clad items than you can shake a stick at. The only thing you won't find is a great bargain. Open: Friday to Wednesday from 11 a.m. to 5:30 p.m., and Thursday from 11 a.m. to 7 p.m.

✔ **Chisholms Highland Dress,** 47–51 Castle St., below Inverness Castle, Inverness (☎ **01463-234-599;** Internet: www.kilts.co.uk; E-mail: kilts@chisholms.dial.netmedia.co.uk; Internet: www.kilts.co.uk). This renowned maker of kilts and Highland dress can make any clan tartan, providing the highest-quality tweeds and leather goods. While some kiltmakers have grown too big for their britches, Chisholms takes great pride in its personal supervision of the tailoring process. The shop also has an exhibit on old Highland weaponry. Call for hours.

✔ **Edinburgh Woollen Mills,** 13 High St., Fort William (☎ **01397-703-064**), and 60 High St., at Monzie Square, Fort William (☎ **01397-704-737**). Typical of woolen mill shops, these sister shops offer plenty of variety in finely crafted woolen and tweed apparel. What's great about them are their excellent bargains. Regardless of when you go, there will always be a sale. Call for hours.

✔ **Hector Russell,** 4–9 Huntly St., on the west bank of the River Ness by the Town Centre Bridge, Inverness (☎ **01463-222-781;** E-mail: kilts@russellh.win-uk.net; Internet: www.hector-russell.com). Not just a shop, this kilt store considers itself an attraction, with information and a film about the history, culture, and production of the kilt. You can also see a demonstration of a kilt being sewn and a large tartan display. The shop has a beautiful selection of jewelry, kilts, skirts, sweaters, and accessories. Russell is a renowned kiltmaker, and his wares are of the highest quality and craft. Open Monday to Saturday from 9 a.m. to 10 p.m., and Sunday from 10 a.m. to 10 p.m.

✔ **Highland Stoneware Pottery,** North Road, Ullapool (☎ **01854-612-980;** E-mail: potters@highlandstoneware.co.uk; Internet: www.highlandstoneware.co.uk), and Lochinver, north of Ullapool on the coast road (☎ **01571-844-376**). In just under three decades, Highland Stoneware has gained an international following. Visitors and orders for its unique freehand-decorated pottery come to the two shops from all over the world. In both shops, you can watch craftsmen at work at the pottery wheels and decorating the pieces. The impressive array of tableware, cookware, tile panels, and one-of-a-kind collectibles makes a visit any time of year worth the stop. Look for the white buildings with the gray roofs. Open: Monday to Friday from 9 a.m. to 6 p.m., and Saturday from 9 a.m. to 5 p.m.

✔ **Leaky's Bookshop,** Greyfriars Hall, Church Street, Inverness (☎ **01463-239-975**). This multistory bookshop inside an old (1792) Gaelic church is the second-largest used bookshop in Scotland, but perhaps the most fun to explore. It has more than 100,000 books, maps, plays, and prints, and lots of great, cheap finds. I discovered a copy of the screenplay to the film *Trainspotting* for £2.50 ($3.65). Open: Monday to Saturday from 10 a.m. to 5:30 p.m.

✔ **Moniack Castle Wines,** Beauly Road, on the A862, 7 miles from Inverness (☎ **01463-831-283**). This popular winery and gourmet food shop makes six wines and three liqueurs in the castle's laundry room and stables. You can also purchase top-quality marmalades, sauces, jams, and chutneys, made here, like the wine, from local ingredients. A guided tour visits the fermenting room, maturing vats, cellars, and bottling room, and the kitchen where preserves and sauces are cooked. Open: Monday to Saturday from 10 a.m. to 5 p.m.

✔ **The Music Shop,** 27 Church St., Inverness (☎ **01463-233-374;** E-mail: themusicshop@lineone.net). This wonderful shop is full of instruments and sheet music. You can purchase bagpipes, whistles, *bodhrans* (Celtic drums), and more. If you don't know how to play, teaching materials are available. Call for hours.

✔ **Riverside Gallery,** 11 Bank St., Inverness (☎ **01463-224-781**). This funky little gallery on the east side of the River Ness has a wide range of traditional and contemporary pieces by Scottish artists. The prints, paintings, engravings, and photographs make unique souvenirs. If you're looking for something in particular, make sure to ask the staff; they may have it in the back. Open: Monday to Friday from 9 a.m. to 5:30 p.m., and Saturday from 9 a.m. to 4:30 p.m.

✔ **Treasures of the Earth,** Corpach, on the A830 (☎ **01397-772-283**). Part attraction, part gift shop, this establishment in a converted church is interesting enough to visit even if you're not looking to purchase jewelry, ornaments, fossils, or crystals. Among the unique gifts are clocks and watches. It's all eye-catching and perfect for one-of-a-kind souvenirs. Open: Monday to Saturday, July to September, from 9:30 a.m. to 7 p.m.; October to December, and February to June, from 10 a.m. to 5 p.m.; January by appointment only.

✔ **The Whisky Shop,** Drumnadrochit, next to Loch Ness 2000 exhibit (☎ **01456-450-321**). This small chain of gourmet shops skips the key chains and postcards for high-quality Scottish items. Excellent whisky products are obviously the main trade; you'll also find an impressive collection of china, silver, glassware, and gourmet jams and sweets, all 100 percent Scottish made. Call for hours.

# Doing the Pub Crawl

The West Highlands have a good number of atmospheric, quintessentially Scottish pubs where you can relax and enjoy a bit of pub grub. Here are some of my favorites. Many of the following pubs keep late-night hours; call for the latest opening and closing times.

✔ **Ben Nevis Pub,** 103–109 High St., Fort William (☎ **01397-702-295**). GOOD FOOD, GOOD BEER, GOOD COMPANY, reads the motto along the roof beams of this old pub. True on all accounts. The bar service is fast and competent, as well. The stucco walls, stained wood tables, and overstuffed leather seating give the place character, and it's roomy enough to handle weekend crowds. The fireplace and pool table are nice distractions, and so is the live music on Thursday and Friday nights.

✔ **Chili Palmer's,** 73 Queensgate, Inverness (☎ **01463-715-075**). This stylish bar in the heart of Inverness is a hip place to have a beer. The purple walls, industrial chairs, and plush couches in a single large room are purposefully anti-pub. It can get a bit smoky, but the music is good and not pretentious in the least. During the day, you'll find sports on the telly, and at night, the Deco furniture is sometimes moved for dancing. Elmore Leonard fans will recognize the bar's namesake as the main character in his novel *Get Shorty*.

✔ **Claichaig Inn,** Glencoe. Follow the sign from the A82 or walk across a footbridge from the visitor center (☎ **01855-811-252**). This rustic pub in the heart of the glen is one of my favorite things about visiting Glencoe. A wood-burning stove and the staff's sunny disposition warm the woody lounge and bar. The views are excellent, too. Climbers, tourists, and locals come for a wee rest stop and excellent ales on tap. Everyone is welcome except HAWKERS AND CAMPBELLS, as a sign inside reads—this was the site of the Glencoe massacre, after all (see the "Glencoe" listing earlier in this chapter). The pub frequently features live folk music. If you love the place, consider staying overnight; there's a nice B&B. In the winter (either February or March), the inn hosts a beerfest that's worth sticking around for. Open Sunday to Thursday from 11 a.m. to 11 p.m., Friday from 11 a.m. to midnight, and Saturday from 11 a.m. to 11:30 p.m.

✔ **The Crofter,** High Street, Fort William. (☎ **01397-709-931**). This place doesn't know if it wants to be a restaurant or a bar, but most patrons are there for the pints and the excellent selection of fine whiskys. It also leans toward the pub end, thanks to a newly installed satellite and big-screen TV, making this the best place in the area to get your fill of sports action. A little whisky and water, a little knowledge of football (read: soccer), and you'll fit right in.

✔ **Johnny Foxes,** Bank Street, Inverness (☎ **01463-236-577**; www. johnnyfoxes.co.uk). This popular cookie-cutter pub is clean and big enough to accommodate the crowds who come for the music, the Guinness, and maybe a bite to eat. Its eclectic menu offers Thai, French, and Scottish dishes that are decent for the price. In addition to the world's most famous stout, Foxes has a good selection of Scottish cask-conditioned ales and a whopping 48 malt whiskys. There is live music every night, usually of the toe-tapping traditional Irish and Scottish variety.

✔ **Mr. G's Nightclub,** 9 Castle St., Inverness (☎ **01463-233-322**). This is the best place for dancing in Inverness. Flanked by two bars and some big booths, the dance floor is center stage and augmented by a huge video screen on the wall above and a high-tech light show. Get down and get upstairs to Mr. G's.

✔ **The Saint,** 2 Tower St., Tain (☎ **01862-894-007**). If you're in Tain, drop by the bar in the Saint Duthus Hotel. It's a nice little pub with a well-stocked bar and outdoor seating. Inside, friendly locals who frequent the place are likely to chat you up. Outside the traditional pub area is a more modern dining area.

# Fast Facts: The West Highlands

## Area Code

The area code for Aviemore is **01479;** Drumnadrochit **01456;** Inverness **01463;** Nairn **01667;** Dornoch **01862;** Glencoe **01855;** and Fort William **01397.** You need to dial the area code only if you are calling from outside the city you want to reach.

## Emergencies

Dial **999** for police, fire, or ambulance.

## Genealogy Resources

**Highland Family History Society,** Farraline Park, Inverness (☎ 01463-236-463).

## Hospitals

**Raigmore Hospital,** Inshes Road, Inverness (☎ 01463-704-000).

## Information

**Highlands Information Centre,** Grampian Road, Aviemore (☎ 01479-810-363; Internet: www.highlandfreedom.com). Other tourist offices include: Castle Wynd, just off Bridge Street, **Inverness** (☎ 01463-23-4353); Cameron Square, about halfway down the High Street, **Fort William** (☎ 01397-703-781). Summer offices: 62 King St., **Nairn** (☎ 01667-452-763); and 6 Argyle St., **Ullapool** (☎ **01854-612-135**).

## Internet Access

The **Electric Post Office,** 93 High St., Nairn (☎ 01667-451-617). Open: Daily 10 a.m.–10 p.m. Cost: £4 ($6) per hour.

## Mail

A post office is at 2 Greig St., Inverness (☎ 01463-233-610).

# Chapter 17

# Hebridean Islands

*W*hen the Vikings came to the Western Isles at the end of the eighth century, they dubbed the area *Innse Gall,* or "Islands of the Foreigners." The allure of the Hebridean (Heb-ri-*de*-an) Islands is not hard to understand. The history, culture, and beauty of the landscape are unique — and the islands remain largely unspoiled by the tourist grind.

Getting there is half the fun, and when you arrive, you can expect a peaceful retreat from the mainland. But because the islands get fewer visitors than other places in Scotland, many businesses, including attractions and hotels, close in the off-season. And Sundays render smaller villages virtual ghost towns. The Hebridean Islands also get some of the worst weather in Scotland. Even in summer, the rain can be horizontal and freezing.

Many islands make up the Hebrides (*Heb*-ri-deez). This chapter covers the major islands but skips smaller and uninhabited ones. Island hopping through the Hebrideans can be fun, but it is also time-consuming and expensive.

## Orienting Yourself to the Hebridean Islands

The best and biggest island is the **Isle of Skye.** You can drive onto it, and it offers stunning landscapes, stellar attractions, and plenty of accommodation and dining options. The runner-up is **Mull,** with a side trip to its little sister island **Iona.** Easily accessible Mull is home to a quaint fishing town and two great castles. The joined islands of **Harris** (famous for its tweed) and **Lewis** require a bit of driving from attraction to attraction. **North** and **South Uist** (pronounced "oo-ist") are largely rural with only a few sights to see. The rest — **Barra, Colonsay, Rhum, Eigg, Muck,** and **Coll** among them — are small and mostly devoid of attractions.

The Isle of Skye, 50 miles long and 23 miles wide, is a treat to drive across. Between the sea and the Cuillin Hills, the landscape is beautiful. Keep your camera handy as you make your way, and be sure to brake for the sheep. **Portree,** the capital of the island, is a small, quaint town on the water and is a good base to explore all the Skye attractions.

Mull is the wettest of the Hebridean Islands, so you may want to pack an umbrella. After you arrive in **Craignure** (which has little to offer other than the nearby castles of Duart and Torosay), you can either head north to the fishing village of **Tobermory** or west toward **Fionnphort** to catch the ferry to the island of Iona. Give yourself an hour either way — the roads turn into single lanes in both directions. If you want the best views from Mull, I suggest taking the white-knuckle single-lane scenic route (B8035) between the A849 and Salen, where the cliff views are breathtaking and the sheep get up close and personal. Tobermory, the largest town on Mull, is worth a visit. Brightly colored houses and storefronts painted blue, red, and yellow give Tobermory the look of a little Copenhagen and the feel of an Italian fishing village. Small craft shops, a few pubs, and forest walks to the waterfalls make it a nice place to spend an afternoon. The small neighboring island of Iona is where St. Columba landed in 563 A.D. to convert the locals to Christianity. The monastery built there defended the monks against a Viking invasion; the first Celtic king of Scotland, Kenneth MacAlpine, is buried here. The abbey and all the hotels are in walking distance of each other, but bring good shoes if you want to explore further.

In Lewis and Harris, you arrive at the ferry terminal in Tarbert. Head south to the Church of St. Clement on the southern tip before driving north to Lewis. The southern coastal drive is an attraction in itself — the rocky moonscape soon transforms into a Gulf Stream miracle of beaches and blue waters. Harris is the home of Harris tweed (Canada and the U.S. alone import 3 to 4 million yards a year). You can't call it Harris tweed unless it's made here, and if you're going to buy tweed, you should buy it here. Harris comes from the Norse word for "a hundred," referring to a common division of land. The Isle of Lewis not only adjoins Harris; it's basically the same island. Lewis is larger and has more attractions than its southern cousin, and its town of **Stornoway** is the largest on the dual islands. The roadside views on Lewis and Harris include another uniquely Scottish attraction: peat bogs. Tiny blocks of the partially decomposed soil are carved from the fields and used as a fine source for heat; look for the stacks of peat bricks outside the homes.

## The Hebridean Islands

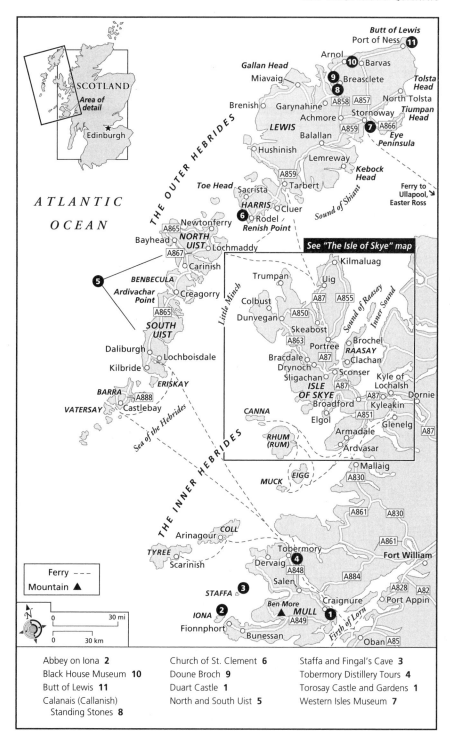

SCOTLAND
Area of detail
★ Edinburgh

Butt of Lewis
Port of Ness **11**
Arnol
**10** Barvas
Miavaig
Gallan Head
**9** Breasclete
**8**
*Tolsta Head*
Brenish
Garynahine A858 A857 North Tolsta
Achmore A859 Stornoway *Tiumpan Head*
**LEWIS** Balallan A866 **7**
Hushinish *Eye Peninsula*
Lemreway
*Kebock Head*
A859
*Toe Head* Sacrista Tarbert Ferry to Ullapool, Easter Ross
**HARRIS** Cluer *Sound of Shiant*
**6** Rodel
Newtonferry *Renish Point*
A865 **NORTH UIST** See "The Isle of Skye" map
Bayhead Lochmaddy
A867
Carinish Kilmaluag
Trumpan Uig
**5** **BENBECULA** A87 A855
*Ardivachar Point* Creagorry Colbust *Sound of Raasay*
Dunvegan A850
A865 Skeabost Brochel
**SOUTH UIST** A863 Portree **RAASAY** *Inner Sound*
Daliburgh Bracdale Clachan
A87
Kilbride Lochboisdale Drynoch
Sligachan Sconser Kyle of Lochalsh
**BARRA** **ERISKAY** **ISLE** A87 Dornie
**VATERSAY** A888 Castlebay **OF SKYE** Broadford Kyleakin
**CANNA** Elgol A851 Glenelg
A87
Armadale
**RHUM (RUM)** Ardvasar
Mallaig
*Sea of the Hebrides* **EIGG** A830
**MUCK**

ATLANTIC OCEAN

THE OUTER HEBRIDES
*Little Minch*
THE INNER HEBRIDES

A861 A830
A861 Fort William

**COLL**
Arinagour Tobermory
**TYREE** Dervaig **4**
Scarinish A848
Salen A884 A828 A82
**STAFFA** **3** Craignure Port Appin
Ben More
**IONA** **2** **MULL** **1**
Fionnphort A849
Bunessan *Firth of Lorn* Oban A85

Ferry – – –
Mountain ▲

0 ———— 30 mi
0 ———— 30 km

| | | |
|---|---|---|
| Abbey on Iona **2** | Church of St. Clement **6** | Staffa and Fingal's Cave **3** |
| Black House Museum **10** | Doune Broch **9** | Tobermory Distillery Tours **4** |
| Butt of Lewis **11** | Duart Castle **1** | Torosay Castle and Gardens **1** |
| Calanais (Callanish) | North and South Uist **5** | Western Isles Museum **7** |
|   Standing Stones **8** | | |

---

# The power of peat

What, exactly, is peat? Peat is a fuel used for heating and cooking, especially in the Highlands and the Hebridean Islands. It's basically soil, cut straight out of the ground—dirt that burns. Well, it's more than dirt. A boggy environment combined with rocky ground creates a waterlog that prevents dead plants from rotting completely. The conditions trap fossil fuels in the soil that burn when you light it.

---

# Getting to the Islands

One of the best things about island hopping is enjoying the ferry rides. A network of ferries links the Outer and Inner Hebrides to the mainland and, in some cases, to one another. Provided it's not raining, you get some great views from the ferry, as well. Whether you reach the Hebrideans by plane, bus, train, car, or ferry, you'll want to have a car after you arrive in order to fully explore the islands.

- ✔ **By ferry:** Caledonian MacBrayne (☎ **01475-650-100;** fax: 01475-637-607; reservations: 08705-650-000; reservations fax: 01475-635-235; E-mail: reservations@calmac.co.uk; Internet: www.calmac.co.uk) offices in this region include Armadale, Skye (☎ **01471-844-248;** fax: 01471-844-212); Castlebay, Barra (☎ **01871-810-306;** fax: 01871-810-627); Craignure, Mull (☎ **01680-812-343;** fax: 01680-812-433); Fionnphort, Mull (☎ **01681-700-559**); Lochboisdale, South Uist (☎ **01878-700-288;** fax: 01878-700-635); Lochmaddy, North Uist (☎ **01876-500-337;** fax: 01876-500-412); Portree, Skye (☎ **01478-612-075;** fax: 01478-613-090); Stornoway, Lewis (☎ **01851-702-361;** fax: 01851-705-523); Tarbert, Harris (☎ **01859-502-444;** fax: 01859-502-017); and Tobermory, Mull (☎ **01688-302-017;** fax: 01688-302-660). Mainland ports connecting to the Hebridean Isles are Ullapool (to Stornoway) (☎ **01854-612-358;** fax: 01854-612-433), Mallaig (to Armadale) (☎ **01687-462-403;** fax: 01687-462-281), and Oban (to Craignure) (☎ **01631-566-688**).

- ✔ **By car:** You can drive onto Skye over the bridge at Kyle of Lochalsh, on the A87. The ferry costs £5.40 ($7.85) to cross. You will need to take car ferries to the other islands.

- ✔ **By plane:** The airport in Stornoway (☎ **0345-222-111**) on Lewis is 4 miles east of town.

- ✔ **By train:** Regular passenger trains do not run on the islands. The only mainland port town with rail service is Oban, which **ScotRail** (☎ **0845-748-4950**) connects to Glasgow.

- ✔ **By bus:** Citylink (☎ **0990-505-050**) connects Inverness to Oban (the port for Mull); **Sheil Buses** (☎ **01967-431-272**) connect Fort William to Mallaig (the port for Skye).

*The Isle of Skye*

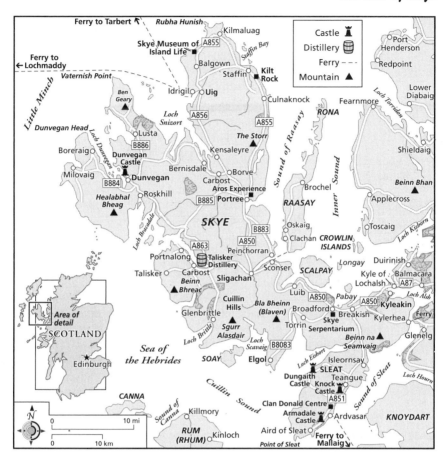

# *Getting Around the Islands*

Public transportation in the Hebrideans is weak, to say the least. Believe me, the last thing you want to do on your island vacation is stand at a rural bus stop in the pouring rain with all of your luggage. You can reach the Isle of Skye (the largest of the islands) by ferry or by driving over a bridge, but no matter how you get there, you'll need a car to truly see the sights. The same is true for Harris, Lewis, and Uist islands — sit back and enjoy the ferry, but rely on the car after you're there. If you simply don't want to drive, opt for a guided tour to both well-traveled and remote areas with a company such as Caledonian MacBrayne (☎ **01475-650-100**).

> ✔ **By car:** Your best bet for getting around the islands is to take car ferries and drive around. If you want to rent a car on an island, contact **Lewis Car Rentals,** 52 Bayhead St., Stornoway,

Lewis (☎ 01851-703-760); **Skye Car Rental,** Broadford (☎ 01471-822-225); **Laing Motors,** Lochboisdale, South Uist (☎ 01878-700-267); or **Mull Car Hire Pierhead,** Craignure, Mull (☎ 01680-812-487).

✔ **By taxi: A1 Cabs,** The Harbour, Portree, Skye (☎ 01478-61-1112 or 01478-61-2851; E-mail: taxi@a1-cabs.com). **Alda's Taxis,** 1 Kersavagh, Lochmaddy, North Uist (☎ 01851-706-900).

✔ **By bus: Citylink** (☎ 0990-505-050) runs through Skye. Mull, Lewis, and the Uists have their own buses, which run infrequently. **Harris** (☎ 01859-502-441) coaches run between Lewis and Harris. **Essbee Coach Hire** (☎ 01631-566-999) operates in Mull.

✔ **By foot:** With infrequent bus service, hitchhiking is your best option if you don't have a car and want to travel from town to town. Every town on the islands is small enough to walk. Iona and other small islands are entirely walkable.

# Knowing Where to Stay

Because the islands have limited dining and drinking options, I've chosen the accommodations listed in this section not only for their high quality and good deals, but for their great food and pubs, as well. The best options are on the larger islands; you can contact local tourist offices if you want to spend the night on a smaller island.

### Ardvasar Hotel

$$   **Ardvasar, Skye**

This lovely hotel, pub, and restaurant is your best bet for a stay in the southern part of Skye. Within stone-skipping distance and Armadale Castle and the ferry to Mallaig and smaller islands, the Ardvasar Hotel sits on the edge of the Sound of Sleat. Rooms are sizable and comfortable, with lovely views of the water and rugged landscape just across the street. The food is as good as it gets anywhere in the area, and the pub bustles with grinning locals. The personable Mr. Richard Jeffrey recently took the place over and has done a great job of getting it up to speed and making everyone feel at home.

*Just off the A851 before the ferry terminal, Ardvasar.* ☎ *01471-844-223. Fax: 01471-844-495. E-mail:* richard@ardvasar-hotel.demon.co.uk. *Internet:* www.ardvasarhotel.com. *Rack rates: £80 ($116); £125 ($181) with dinner. MC, V.*

### Ardvourlie Castle Guest House

$$$   **Aird Amhulaidh, Harris**

When you come to the Ardvourlie, the greeting includes freshly brewed tea and scones. And you'll be waited on hand and foot from that moment till you bid a sad goodbye to the best place to stay on Harris or Lewis.

*Portree*

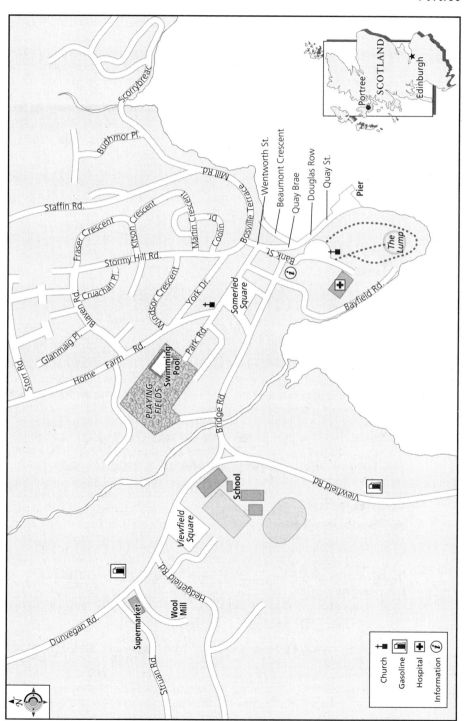

The castle sits on a remote spot near the Lewis-Harris border, along the main road connecting the two. The name means, appropriately, "the headland below the high peak" — nearby hills rise up behind the castle, which overlooks Loch Seaforth. It was built in 1863 for the Earl of Dunmore, and has been restored with period furnishings and linens. The dining room has real gas lighting, and the Victorian motif extends to the well-designed guest rooms and the wood paneling and brass faucets in the huge bathrooms. The sculptured lawns, with 7,000 trees, are worth a stroll. With only four rooms available, booking in advance is a must. I could go on and on about the gourmet meals, but the room rate includes dinner (and breakfast, as at most other Scottish hotels), so you'll see for yourself. Payment is in cash or traveler's checks only.

*Just south of the Harris-Lewis border on the A859, Aird Amhulaidh.* ☎ **01859-502-307.** *Fax: 01859-502-348. Rack rates: £190 ($276) double. Children under 12 half-price. Rate includes dinner. No credit cards.*

### Argyll Hotel
#### $$   Iona

This environmentally friendly hotel, built in 1868 as the village inn, perfectly complements the spiritual nature of Iona. The outstanding and obliging hospitality makes up for what may seem to be lacking in the sparse, smallish rooms. Besides, why hang out in your room when you can spend time in the sitting rooms or the garden room, all of which face the water? A special package includes dinner — I highly recommend it, because this hotel's restaurant has the best food on the island. Much of it grows in the organic garden, and the excellent menu is very accommodating to vegetarians and vegans.

*200 yards from the harbor.* ☎ *01499-302-460. Fax: 01499-302-389. E-mail:* reception@the-argyll-hotel.co.uk. *Internet:* www.the-argyll-hotel.co.uk. *Rack rates: £86 ($125) double. MC, V. Closed Oct–Mar.*

### Cabarfeidh Hotel
#### $$   Stornoway, Lewis

The finest accommodation on Lewis sits in the middle of an eight-acre garden just outside of Stornoway. Best Western bought the place and renovated it over a decade ago, and it hasn't aged a day since. The rooms are large and well upholstered, and the staff is top-notch. Make sure to visit the bar; it's shaped like a Viking ship. The Manor Restaurant specializes in local seafood and game and is worth a visit.

*Manor Park, between Laxdale and Newmarket, Stornoway.* ☎ *01851-702-740. Fax: 01851-705-572. E-mail:* cabarfeidh@calahotels.com. *Internet:* www.calahotels.com. *Rack rates: £96 ($139) double. AE, DC, MC, V.*

### Cuillin Hills Hotel

$$–$$$   Portree, Skye

This 19th-century hunting lodge features large grounds and amazing views of Portree Bay and the Cuillin Hills. This mansion is popular with hikers, birders, and sportsmen alike — the comfort and friendliness appeal to everyone. The conservatory is a great place to relax, and the rooms are full of quality furniture and have large bathrooms. On a historical note, the lodge was built for the Macdonald clan that once ruled the island. The restaurant regularly earns praise for its seafood and traditional Scottish dishes. The breakfast was one of the best I've had in the country, with lovely views of the bay.

*Off the main road, just north of town, Portree.* ☎ **01478-612-003.** *Fax: 01478-613-092. E-mail:* office@cuillinhills.demon.co.uk. *Internet:* www.cuillinhills.demon.co.uk. *Rack rates: £90–£130 ($131–$189) double. AE, MC, V.*

### Dunollie Hotel

$$   Broadford, Skye

The Dunollie Hotel overlooks the old harbor wall in Broadford, with magnificent views across the sea to Loch Kishorn and the Applecross hills. Refurbished a few years ago, the hotel is a friendly and welcoming holiday base from which to explore the magical Isle of Skye. The Dunollie offers a combination of Skye charm and modern-day comforts; it's Skye's largest hotel, and its friendly, trained staff will ensure that your stay on the "Misty Isle" is an enjoyable one.

*On the A87, Broadford, Skye.* ☎ **01471-822-253.** *Fax: 01471-822-060. E-mail:* dunollie@british-trust-hotels.com. *Internet:* www.british-trust-hotels.com. *Rack rates: £50–£70 ($73–$102) double. MC, V.*

### Eilean Iarmain Hotel

$$   Isle Ornsay, Skye

The award-winning Eilean Iarmain offers up quintessential Highland hospitality combined with tranquillity and beautiful surroundings. Many of the century-old building's original antiques are intact, and each of the 12 rooms contains period furniture. The finest room is the *Te Bheag,* or "Whisky One," which contains a canopy bed that once resided in Armadale Castle. The views of the Isle Ornsay harbor from the country house hotel are picture-postcard, especially at sunset. The owners, Sir Ian and Lady Noble, maintain the highest standards for their staff. Another plus: The hotel is open year-round, and in the winter, log fires burn and musicians play.

*Isle Ornsay, Sleat, Isle of Skye.* ☎ **01471-833-332.** *Fax: 01471-833-275. Internet:* www . eileaniarmain.co.uk. *Rack rates: £75–£90 ($109–$131) double. AE, MC, V.*

### Harris Hotel

$$ **Tarbert, Harris**

You can't find a more convenient location in Harris than this Queen Anne–style hotel near the ferry terminal. The pretty, whitewashed building has '70s-era décor, a comfortable selection of rooms (including two family units), a large garden, and a wonderful sun lounge. One famous guest, *Peter Pan* author J.M. Barrie, mischievously etched his initials in a dining-room window. If you're hankering for a nightcap, the bar has one of the largest selections of malt whiskys in the islands.

*Tarbert, Harris.* ☎ **01859-502-154.** *Fax: 01859-502-281. Rack rates: £59–£73 ($86–$106) double. MC, V.*

### The Rosedale

$$–$$$ **Portree, Skye**

This nice white brick building on the water used to house local fishermen. Fully fumigated and warmly decorated, the small, snug hotel has a B&B feel. The Rosedale consists of two buildings on the quay. The main house has rooms with typical hotel furniture, the dining room, and the bar. The rooms in the separate Beaumont House are individually decorated in wonderful style. Most of the guest rooms in both buildings overlook the water.

*On the harbor, Beaumont Crescent, Quay Brae, Portree.* ☎ **01478-613-131.** *Fax: 01478-612-531. Rack rates: £72–£102 ($104–$148) double. AE, MC, V. Closed Oct–mid-May.*

### The Royal Hotel

$$ **Portree, Skye**

In a great spot between the pier and town, the Royal is a fine hotel offering a great stay in a central location. The rooms aren't fancy but are quite comfortable, and for a mere £5 ($7.25) extra you can have one of the "superior" rooms with nicer views. Another treat for this part of the world is the hotel's gym and steam room. They also have room service. Traditional entertainment is brought in most nights in the summer. A historical aside: The hotel is located on the spot of the old MacNab Tavern, where none other than Bonnie Prince Charlie enjoyed a few drinks.

*Bank Street, Portree.* ☎ **01478-612-525.** *Fax: 01478-613-198. Rack rates: £88–£93 ($128–$135) double. AE, DC, MC, V.*

## St. Columba Hotel
### $$$ Argyle, Iona

Between the sun lounges and the lovely dining area, you won't be at a loss for pretty views of the water even if your room faces the other direction. This more upscale hotel edges out the Argyll Hotel only in its larger and better-furnished rooms. The service is fine and the food quite nice. The hotel is very close to the island's main attraction, the Abbey, and a hotel car will collect you and your bags at the boat jetty. If you love seafood, this is the best dining option on the island.

*Argyle, Iona.* ☎ **01681-700-304.** *Fax: 01681-700-688. Rack rates: £100–£132 ($145–$191) double. MC, V.*

## Seaforth Hotel
### $$ Stornoway, Lewis

The largest hotel in the Western Isles, the Seaforth is also the most modern. The modern-style furnishings and decor don't attempt to conform to traditional designs. Rooms are comfortable and equipped with modern conveniences. La Terrazza Restaurant serves Italian Scottish dishes, and the sitting rooms have snooker if you get bored. Note that not every room has a private bath, so if that's important to you, ask in advance.

*11 James St., Stornoway.* ☎ **01851-702-740.** *Fax: 01851-703-900. E-mail:* seaforth@calahotels.com. *Internet:* www.calahotels.com. *Rack rates: £55–£72 ($80–$104) double. AE, MC, V.*

## Sligachan Hotel
### $$ Sligachan, Skye

This fun little hotel books live music and has plenty to occupy the wee ones, such as video games, a playroom, outdoor rec equipment, and a playground. Popular among adult guests are the extensive trails and climbs nearby; fishermen can even obtain permits at the hotel. The hotel was built in the 1830s and retains much of its original stonework, a classic look that complements the stunning location at the head of a sea loch and the foot of the Cuillin Hills. Most of the rooms have a view (you must choose between the loch and the hills), and cots are available for young kids. Located in the middle of Skye, the Sligachan is ideal for visiting both sides of the island. The popular Seumas' Bar serves meals for young kids, too.

*Sligachan, 9 miles south of Portree on the A87.* ☎ **01478-650-204.** *Fax: 01478-650-207. E-mail:* reservations@sligachan.co.uk. *Internet:* www.sligachan.co.uk. *Rack rates: £70–£80 ($102–$116) double. MC, V.*

### Tobermory Hotel
$$ **Tobermory, Mull**

A stay here is like a visit with a favorite grandmother, if said grandmother lives in a pretty fisherman's cottage on the waterfront of a lovely harbor town on the northern end of a Hebridean Island. With comfy beds, excellent home cooking, and a smile to greet you at the door, it's like coming home. The hotel offers extra cots, as well as a toy box, games, and books for the kids, who stay at a discounted cost. The dining room is happy to cater to special diets.

*53 Main St., Tobermory.* ☎ **01688-302-091.** *Fax: 01688-302-254. E-mail:* `tobhotel@thetobermoryhotel.com`. *Internet:* `www.thetobermory hotel.com`. *Rack rates: £62–£90 ($90–$131) double. MC, V.*

### Western Isles Hotel
$$ **Tobermory, Mull**

This Victorian stone-front hotel overlooking the small fishing port of Tobermory exudes charm and hospitality. The staff is cheery and helpful, and the rooms are nicely furnished, many with a tartan or floral theme and canopy beds. The hotel occupies a beautiful spot, and most rooms have views of the harbor and bay. Still, the best view in the house is from the lovely refurbished conservatory. The intimacy of the other sitting rooms encourages conversation.

*Main Street, Tobermory.* ☎ **01688-302-012.** *Fax: 01688-302-297. E-mail:* `wihotel@aol.com`. *Internet:* `www.mullhotel.com`. *Rack rates: £84–£96 ($122–$139) double. AE, MC, V. Closed Jan.*

# Dining in the Hebridean Islands

Because few restaurants in the islands can thrive independent of a hotel, your dining options are limited. Aside from the dining spots mentioned in the accommodations section, several restaurants stand out.

### Balti House
$–$$ **Stornoway, Lewis   Indian**

This restaurant sits in a great location on the main quay, across from the Stornoway ferry terminal. I'm convinced that the dishes are across-the-board delicious, and I can vouch for spicy *rogan josh* (sauce of tomatoes, peppers, and onions), and clay-oven-cooked *shashlik* (barbecued meat) — but you'll have to choose your own favorite variation. The dishes are large and filling, and the staff is very polite and efficient. Worried you'll miss your ferry? Let them know and they'll do their best to speed things up; they're used to it. Balti House also keeps late hours, in case you get into town after normal dinnertime.

*24 South Beach St., Stornoway.* ☎ **01851-706-116.** *Reservations not required. Main courses: £4.10–£8.95 ($5.95–$13). AE, MC, V. Open: Daily noon to 2 p.m., Sat–Wed 5–11:30 p.m., Thurs–Fri 5 p.m. to midnight.*

### Chandlery

$$$   **Portree, Skye   French**

The Chandlery occupies a lovely setting on the cliff overlooking Portree harbor. With minimalist décor in the dining area, the place has an airy feel. The staff is efficient and professional, serving up such gourmet treats as a starter of carved Gaelic rose of melon. Seafood specialties include monkfish and a steamed lobster that would make a Maine native blush with pleasure. If you're staying at the hotel, breakfasts are excellent, as well.

*In the Bosville Hotel, Bosville Terrace, Portree.* ☎ **01478-612-846.** *Reservations recommended. Main courses: £12.95–£15.95 ($19–$23). AE, MC, V. Open: Daily Jan–Mar 8 a.m.–9:30 p.m.; Apr–Dec 8 a.m.–10 p.m.*

### Creelers

$$–$$$   **Broadford, Skye   Seafood/Mediterranean**

Don't be put off by the size of this tiny, simply decorated restaurant. It may look like carryout or a sub shop, but the food is outstanding. The owners are committed to bringing excellent Cajun and Mediterranean-influenced food and superb wine to a part of the country that rarely gets it. You also find traditional dishes such as haggis with neeps and tatties (turnips and potatoes), scrumptious mushroom and broccoli pie, and plenty of local seafood. The pride of the menu is the "authentic" seafood gumbo made with local fish and shellfish. This kind of cuisine is what you'd expect in any cosmopolitan city, and the prices are fair when you consider that a lot of the ingredients must come in by ferry. What is a creel, you ask? It's a basket for carrying peat or fish.

*Broadford.* ☎ **01471-822-281.** *Reservations not accepted. Main courses: £6–£13.50 ($8.70–$20). AE, MC, V. Open: Daily noon to 2 p.m. and 5–10 p.m.*

### Gannet's

$–$$   **Tobermory, Mull   Scottish**

Don't let the plastic tablecloths and generally cheesy decor put you off; Gannet's has friendly service and excellent Scottish cuisine. If you haven't tried haggis yet, here's your chance. Or go for something more familiar, such as Tobermory smoked trout or homemade pork in cider and cream. If you tire of looking at the fake flowers and '70s-era wallpaper, stare out the window instead; the restaurant is right on the main street overlooking the harbor. Can't beat the prices, either.

*25 Main St., Tobermory.* ☎ **01688-30-2203**. *Reservations not accepted. Main courses: £4.10–£9.95 ($5.95–$14). MC, V. Open: Daily Apr–Oct 10 a.m.–10 p.m., Nov–Mar 10 a.m.–3:30 p.m.*

### The Isles Inn

$–$$    **Portree, Skye    Scottish/American**

It's no surprise to see half the bar waiting for dinner on one side of the place while the lucky patrons already have their delicious and economical dinners before them. Not your everyday pub grub: The excellent concoctions include steaks, burgers, lasagna, and mussels. Many meals come with salads and the most delicious fries on the island. The servers never balk at small additions and substitutions, and your food comes fast. Be prepared to wait for a table — good thing this is the best pub in these parts, as well (see "Doing the Pub Crawl," later in this chapter).

*Somerled Sq., Portree.* ☎ **01478-612-129**. *E-mail:* islesinn@hotmail.com. *Internet:* www.theislesinn.co.uk. *Reservations not accepted. Main courses £4.50–£8.50 ($6.55–$12). MC, V. Open: Daily noon to 8 p.m.*

### Thai Café

$–$$    **Stornoway, Lewis    Thai**

Yes, Stornoway is an odd place for Thai, but this spot is very popular and very good — you'll want to call for a reservation even on a summer weekday. On a rather inactive part of Church Street, decorated in typical Asian style, it doesn't have the most attentive service — the real draw is the savory, excellently priced food. The menu is full of the usual suspects, with plenty of options for vegetarians. The adventurous can choose from a few special selections, such as Jungle Curry, a sizzling meat dish on bamboo shoots. Another plus: The restaurant doesn't have a full liquor license, so you can bring in your own wine from the local store. Get there before the corking fee kicks in (at 6:30).

*27 Church St., Stornoway.* ☎ **01851-701-811**. *Reservations not required. Main courses: £4–£6.50 ($5.80–$9.45). AE, DC, MC, V. Open: Daily noon to 2:30 p.m. and 5–11 p.m.*

### Three Chimneys Restaurant

$$$$    **Colbost, Skye    Scottish**

It's not difficult to understand why this shore-side restaurant is probably the most popular on Skye. Serving superb Scottish cuisine with produce from the island, the stone house (with three chimneys) offers the highest-quality seafood and Highland game dishes, such as venison and wild hare, along with homemade soups, breads, and puddings. Cozy twin fireplaces warm the dining area. The menu changes seasonally; in the summer, try one of the organically grown salads with herbs and veggies. The knowledgeable chef can accommodate vegans and gluten-free or nut-free diets. Reservations are required.

*Colbost, 4 miles from Dunvegan on the B884 road to Glendale.* ☎ **01470-511-258.** *E-mail:* eatandstay@threechimneys.co.uk. *Reservations required. Fixed price: £21 ($31) for 3-course lunch; £55 ($80) for 4-course dinner. MC, V. Open: Mon–Sat noon to 2 p.m. and 7–9 p.m. Closed Nov–Mar.*

# Exploring the Area

From the spiritual mecca of Iona to the tourist kitsch of the Aros Experience to the many ancient and royal attractions in between, the islands have it all, with no shortage of natural beauty to boot. Indeed, the islands are attractions in themselves, but you'll find plenty to see besides the scenery.

## Abbey on Iona
**Iona**

This spiritual landmark is a significant shrine to the beginnings of Christianity in Scotland. This is the abbey of St. Columba, the Irish missionary who single-handedly brought religion to a pagan region, starting in Iona. The abbey is a very large building and in very good shape, having undergone several restorations since the 13th century. Crosses laid into the abbey floor mark the graves of several monks buried under the monastery, and three impressive crosses stand on the grounds. Forty-minute guided tours run every day on the hour from 10 a.m. to 4 p.m. Give yourself extra time to explore the grounds.

*Iona.* ☎ **01681-700-512.** *E-mail:* ionacomm@iona.org.uk. *Admission: Free. Tour: £2 ($2.90) contribution requested. Open: Year-round, 24 hours. Time: 1 hour, 30 minutes.*

## Armadale Castle Gardens & Museum of the Isles
**Armadale, Skye**

The Armadale estate covers more than 20,000 acres, traditionally belonging to the clan Donald or Macdonald, known as the Lords of Isles. The old castle is in ruins now but occupies a magnificent spot with 19th-century woodland gardens, nature trails, and sea views. It isn't difficult to understand the allure of this place. In a restored section of Armadale Castle is a museum full of information about and artifacts of the Macdonalds. The museum will be of interest to non-Macdonalds, and those who share the common surname may want to visit the library and study center, which assists with genealogical research. The castle grounds are home to a large variety of different trees and plants, all flourishing thanks to the Gulf Stream breezes. The gardener gives occasional tours through his award-winning grounds.

*Armadale Rd., Sleat, Skye. Just north of the pier on the A851, on the left.* ☎ **01471-844-305.** *E-mail:* office@cland.demon.co.uk. *Internet:* www.highlandconnection.org/clandonaldcentre.htm. *Admission: £4 ($5.80) adults, £3 ($4.35) seniors, students, and children under 16, £12 ($18) family. Open: Mar–Oct daily 9 a.m.–5:30 p.m. Closed Nov–Feb. Time: 2 hours.*

## Aros Experience
### Portree, Skye

This guide focuses on the places you *should* visit, but because this attraction gets a lot of PR in Portree, it's worth a warning. A more touristy road-side attraction has not been built on Scottish soil. There is a cafe and huge gift shop, but the main draw of the Aros Experience is a walking history tour through the last 300 years of Skye. That sounds harmless enough, but the life-size historical mannequins look ridiculous, and the personal audio system is full of jarring static that screeches every time you turn away from the infrared boxes feeding the soundtrack. Only the kids will appreciate such kitsch and forgive the lack of sophistication. So, unless you're entertaining the under-12 crowd, ignore the hype and don't feel as if you've missed a worthwhile "experience." Occasional worthwhile shows demonstrate Gaelic arts such as step-dancing and theater, so call ahead for the schedule.

*Viewfield Road, just south of town on the A87.* ☎ **01478-613-649.** *E-mail:* aros@aros.co.uk. *Internet:* www.aros.co.uk. *Admission: £3 ($4.35) adults; £2 ($2.90) seniors, students, and children under 16; £7 ($10) family. Open: Daily 9 a.m.–11 p.m. summer, 9 a.m.–6 p.m. off-season. Time: 1 hour.*

## Black House Museum
### Arnol, Lewis

Step back a couple of hundred years in island living by exploring this restored traditional Hebridean thatched house. A black house is a structure that serves as both a home and a barn. This one is as quaint as can be. You are free to poke around the house and visit the information center for more on this old way of life. It's the only authentically maintained traditional black house, built in 1885 and occupied until 1964. The unique museum doesn't paint a pretty picture of the rather rough living.

The burning peat fire can fill the house with smoke, but that's the cost of authenticity.

*Just west of Barvas off the A858.* ☎ **01851-710-395.** *Admission: £1.80 ($2.60) adults, £1.30 ($1.90) seniors and students, £.75 ($1.10) children under 16. Open: Apr–Sept Mon–Sat 9:30 a.m.–6:30 p.m.; Oct–Mar Mon–Thurs, Sat 9:30 a.m.–4:30 p.m. Time: 1 hour 30 minutes.*

## Butt of Lewis
**Lewis**

These beautiful high cliffs over the ocean are worth the drive to the tip of Lewis. You'll see seabirds, seals, and spectacular windblown waves crashing against the rocks. The only building on the Butt is a magnificent lighthouse, adding even more grandeur to the scene. Look for the large hole in the ground near the parking area; legend has it that the Vikings cut the hole in an attempt to drag the island back to Norway with them.

*Time: 1 hour.*

## Calanais (Callanish) Standing Stones
**Lewis**

Known as the Scottish Stonehenge, this mysterious ancient formation of large stones is the most significant archaeological find of its kind in the country. There's no charge to see the 5,000-year-old stones, but you don't want to miss the Story of the Stones exhibition, which gives context to the site. The exhibit explores theories on the stones' function and shows what life would have been like at the time they were erected. If it's been raining (and it probably has), don't wear shoes you mind getting a little muddy. And if you're here during the summer solstice, you'll find tents pitched near the monoliths — this is a popular spot for New Agers to come and celebrate the sun.

*Off the A858. Take the Tarbert road and make a left in Leurbost.* ☎ **01851-621-422.** *Fax: 01851-62-1446. Admission: Stones: Free. Exhibition: £1.75 ($2.55) adults, £1.25 ($1.80) seniors and students, £.75 ($1.10) children under 16. Open: Apr–Sept daily 10 a.m.–7 p.m.; Oct–Mar Wed–Sat 10 a.m.–4 p.m. Time: 2 hours.*

## Church of St. Clement
**Rodel, Harris**

You may wonder if it's worth the drive to the southern tip of Harris to see this far-flung attraction. It is. At the end of the wonderful drive on the amazing coastal route, full of white beaches and aqua-blue waters, you will arrive at the small but well-preserved 16th-century church, named after a saint who is popular in Norway. The nicest feature inside the cruciform church is the carved tomb of Alexander MacLeod of Dunvegan, who built the church. Panels include apostle effigies and other religious symbols.

*Rodel, Harris. Admission: Free. Open: Daily dawn to dusk. Time: 1 hour.*

## Cuillin Hills
**Skye**

These dark and massive hills are a point of pride for the residents of Skye. Considered some of the best climbing and walking real estate in Scotland, the 3,000-foot peaks lie along the southern part of the island. You may want to consider spending the afternoon hiking the hills, but if you're not an experienced walker, you may want to enquire about professional guides in the tourist office.

### Doune Broch
**Carloway, Lewis**

This interesting home from the Iron Age is in remarkably good enough shape for you to walk through and on. A broch is a stone tower used for defensive purposes and as a home. The ruins give insight into a life long ago, a life that seems oddly comfortable. In fact, despite the time of year you visit, it will likely be cold and windy, but stepping into the broch provides instant protection from the chill. For a better idea of what life was like in the broch, the center has a somewhat cheesy but informative "Interpretative Chamber" that you walk through and see and hear scenes from the Iron Age house.

*On the A858, west side of Lewis.* ☎ **01851-643-338**. *Admission: Free. Open: Broch: Year-round, 24 hours. Center: Apr–Oct Mon–Sat 10 a.m.–5 p.m. Time: 90 minutes.*

### Duart Castle
**South of Craignure, Mull**

A great variety of items are on display in this fine castle overlooking the Sound of Mull. Make your way through and keep going to the top, where you may walk outside on the parapet. Duart Castle, ancestral home of the clan Maclean, is most famous for the legend of Lady's Rock. At low tide, you can see the exposed rock where Lachlan Maclean abandoned his wife Catherine Campbell after she failed to produce a male heir. Local fishermen saved her, and the clan Campbell later killed Lachlan in revenge. More recently, the 13th-century castle has been the set of several films, including *Entrapment* (1998) and the Anthony Hopkins vehicle *When Eight Bells Toll*. There are no special gardens, but the grounds are free of charge.

*Off the A849, 3 miles south of Craignure.* ☎ **01680-812-309**. *Internet:* www. duartcastle.com. *Admission: £3.50 ($5.10) adults, £3 ($4.35) seniors and students, £1.75 ($2.55) children under 16. Open: Daily Apr 11 a.m.–4 p.m., May–mid-Oct 10:30 a.m.–6 p.m. Closed mid-Oct–Mar. Time: 90 minutes.*

### Dunvegan Castle
**Dunvegan, Skye**

The seat of the Macleod chiefs, Dunvegan is the oldest castle in continual ownership by the same family, going on 800 years now. This home was also the location of a grim scene in 1552, when 11 Campbells of Argyll were guests at a banquet where each was seated between two Macleods. When the feast was over, the Campbells were killed. Things are much safer these days. In addition to antiques, oil paintings, rare books, and clan heirlooms — some dating well into the Middle Ages — the castle is home to the legendary Fairy Flag, thought to bring "miraculous powers" to the clan Macleod. Also here are personal items belonging to Bonnie Prince Charlie, and a bona fide creepy dungeon. Mementos from visits by Queen Elizabeth, Sir Walter Scott, and Dr. Samuel Johnson are on display. Don't miss the stunning gardens, mainly planted with azaleas and rhododendrons. Particularly impressive is the Walled Garden, a perfectly manicured display of unique flora, statues, and tranquil fountains and pools. After you take in the castle, and especially if you have kids with you or you like wildlife, take a short seal boat ride. You'll get up close and personal with the seals who live on the tiny islands in the bay below the castle.

*Duirinish Peninsula, Isle of Skye. On the 850, on the west side of the island.* ☎ *01470-521-206. E-mail:* info@dunvegancastle.com. *Internet:* www.dunvegancastle.com. *Admission: £6 ($8.70) adults, £5.50 ($8) seniors and students, £3.50 ($5.10) children under 16. Seal tour: £4 ($5.80) adults, £2.50 ($3.65) children 5–15, free for children under 5. Open: Daily Apr–Oct 10 a.m.–5:30 p.m., Nov–Mar 11 a.m.–4 p.m. Time: 2 hours.*

### North and South Uist

Although no single attraction on these islands stands out, they are worth a visit if you have a full day to cross the mostly rural landscape and take in the sights, scenery, and landmarks. Several top spots lie along the main road, A865. At the Balranald Nature Reserve, you can spot waders and seabirds. A 125-foot statue of the Virgin Mary, "Our Lady of the Isles," is 5 miles south of Benbecula. The ruins of Flora MacDonald's birthplace are near Milton. And the Kildonan Museum and Heritage Centre covers local culture, history, and archaeological finds. You can drive through the Uists, but buses also run the length of the islands.

*Lochmaddy tourist office:* ☎ *01876-500-321. Lochboisdale tourist office:* ☎ *01878-700-286. Tourist offices open: Apr–mid-Oct daily 9 a.m.–5 p.m. Time: 5–9 hours. The Balranald Nature Reserve:* ☎ *01876-510-730. Kildonan Museum and Heritage Centre:* ☎ *01878-710-343. Hebridean Coaches (*☎ *01870-620-345) and Macdonald Coaches (*☎ *01870-620-288) make two daily runs Mon–Sat from Lochmaddy, Langass, Clachan na Luib, Benbecula, and Lochboisdale.*

### Skye Museum of Island Life and Flora MacDonald's Grave
**Kilmuir, Skye**

This interesting museum consists of seven thatched cottages, each showing how people lived on Skye a century ago. The re-created crofter (farm) homes contain antique domestic items, agricultural tools, and photographs of island life from days gone by. If you follow the path from the museum up to Kilmuir Cemetery, you can see the grave of the legendary Flora MacDonald, the woman credited with saving Prince Charlie's hide.

Bonnie Prince Charlie lived in hiding on Skye and escaped as MacDonald's maid. She was later arrested and held in the Tower of London for eight months, then moved to North Carolina during the Revolutionary War and back to Skye before she died. This lovely little museum, full of old pictures and documents, tells her story and the island's.

*On the A855, north from Portree.* ☎ **01470-552-206.** *Admission: £2 ($2.90) adults; £1.50 ($2.20) seniors, students, and children under 16. Open: Apr–Oct, Mon–Sat 9 a.m.–5:30 p.m. Closed Nov–Mar. Time: 1 hour.*

### Skye Scene Highland Ceilidh
**Portree, Skye**

No trip to the Highlands is complete without going to a *ceilidh* (a Gaelic word referring to an informal social get-together, usually with music and singing). This is some great fun — a couple hours of excellent music and song, and a great introduction to the Isle of Skye. You'll laugh, you'll clap, you won't forget it. And while you'll get to hear the pipers in rare form, don't expect "Scotland the Brave" or "Amazing Grace." This is the authentic experience, real Highland music and beautiful Gaelic song with all the charm of *Waiting for Guffman.*

*Portree community center, Park Road, 1 block from Somerled Square.* ☎ **01470-542-228.** *Internet:* www.skyescene.co.uk. *Admission: £6 ($8.70) adults, £5 ($7.25) seniors and students, £4 ($5.80) children under 16. Tickets available at the door. Performances: 8 p.m., June Mon and Wed, July–mid-Sept Mon–Wed. Time: 2 hours.*

### Skye Serpentarium
**Broadford, Skye**

This little reptile house is a treat for kids of any age. The staff is mad for the slithering, scaly creatures who make their homes here, many of which enter the country illegally. Customs seizes them and turns them over to the serpentarium for care. Don't even think about leaving without handling one of the snakes — the owners want to foster awareness of these magnificent animals, and they believe that contact with them will inspire concern for the environmental and man-made threats they face. Say hi to Kiko for me.

*The Old Mill, Harrapool, on the main A850 road, 9 miles from the Skye Bridge.* ☎ **01471-822-209.** *E-mail:* nik@snakebite.com. *Admission: £2.50 ($3.65) adults, £1.50 ($2.20) seniors and children under 16, £7 ($10) family. Open: July–Aug daily 10 a.m.–5 p.m.; Sept–June Mon–Sat 10 a.m.–5 p.m. Time: 1 hour.*

### Staffa and Fingal's Cave
**Iona and Fionnphort, Mull**

The boat trip to the uninhabited island of Staffa is an attraction you shouldn't pass up if you're in the Mull-Iona area. You'll have a good time watching the sea crash against the multicolored rocks and visiting the cathedral-like columns of Fingal's Cave. The natural cave is one of the wonders of the world and is famous for being the inspiration for Mendelssohn's *Hebridean Overture*. Birders, take note: Staffa is also home to a large puffin colony.

*Iona and Fionnphort, Mull.* ☎ *01681-700-358. E-mail:* dk@staffatrips. f9.co.uk. *Tickets: £12.50 ($18) adults, £5 ($7.25) children under 16. Departures: From Iona harbor at 9:45 a.m. and 1:45 p.m. daily and from Fionnphort at 10 a.m. and 2 p.m. daily. Time: 3 hours.*

## Talisker Distillery Visitor Centre
**Carbost, Skye**

As tours go, Talisker's is tops. Enthusiastic expert tour guides walk you through the distillery, expounding on the virtues of their single malt whisky and its unique production process. About 90 percent of the nearly 2 million liters of whisky made at Talisker annually goes into blends such as Dewar's and Johnnie Walker. At the end of the tour, do a tasting and note the smoky peat taste of the whisky, characteristic of whiskys made on the islands.

*On the B8009, just off the A863, which joins the A87 at Sligachan.* ☎ *01478-640-314. Admission: £4 ($5.80). Open: Apr–Oct Mon–Sat 9:30 a.m.–5 p.m.; Nov–Mar Mon–Fri 2–5 p.m. Time: 1 hour.*

## Tobermory Distillery Tours
**Tobermory, Mull**

This is the best distillery on Mull. It's the only one on Mull, actually. Your half-hour tour of the 1798 facilities is mildly interesting and short, but after you see the inside workings of the distillery, you'll be treated by a rather large dram of the whisky. Tobermory makes a fine single malt with unpeated malted barley that is not typical of island whisky. The shop offers some good gift options.

*The Harbor.* ☎ *01688-302-645. Admission: £2.50 ($3.65) adults, £1 ($1.45) seniors. Tours: Mon–Fri 10:30 a.m.–4 p.m., every 30 minutes. Shop: Mon–Fri 10 a.m.–5 p.m. Time: 1 hour.*

## Torosay Castle and Gardens
**Craignure, Mull**

Unlike the tour of its sister castle, Duart, there is not much to the self-guided tour of this Victorian home, most of which is private. You'll slip in and out of the rooms in less than a half hour and see little historically important or unique in the collection. But that's okay, because the gardens are the real attraction. The 12 acres of well-manicured grounds abound with fine and unique flora, Romanesque statues, and ivy-covered walls. You are welcome to explore the greenhouse and are encouraged to stop and smell the roses. This stop is a treat for anyone with a green thumb; camera buffs will appreciate the views of the Sound of Mull and background mountains.

*Off the A849. ☎ 01680-812-421. Admission: Castle and gardens: £4.50 ($6.55) adults, £3.50 ($5.10) seniors and students, £1.50 ($2.20) children under 16, £10 ($15) family. Gardens only: £3.50 ($5.10) adults, £2.75 ($4) seniors and students, £1 ($1.45) children, £8 ($12) family. Open: Apr–mid-Oct 10:30 a.m.–5:30 p.m. Time: 90 minutes.*

### Western Isles Museum (Museum nan Eilean)
**Stornoway, Lewis**

This museum is home to excellent exhibits on aspects of island life. Although the museum has no permanent collection, the displays, usually borrowed from other museums and collections around the islands and the Scottish mainland, are of excellent quality and significant historical importance. It's definitely worth a visit — and you can't beat the price.

*Francis Street. ☎ 01851-70-3773 x226. Admission: Free. Open: Apr–Sept Mon–Sat 10 a.m.–5:30 p.m.; Oct–Mar Tues–Fri 10 a.m.–5 p.m., Sat 10 a.m.–1 p.m. Time: 1 hour, 30 minutes.*

# Shopping the Hebridean Islands

Despite their remoteness, the Hebridean Islands are home to a fair number of excellent craft and specialty shops.

✔ **Craft Encounters,** Post Office Building, Broadford, Skye (☎ 01471-822-754). This interesting and eclectic shop has one of the strangest collections of crafts in the region, from paintings and ties to glassware, linens, and Scottish music CDs. The only thing consistent about the goods is the high quality of the craftsmanship. You'll find something for everyone here. It's adjacent to Main Road, on the left-hand side as you leave Broadford heading north. Call for hours.

✔ **Edinbane Pottery,** on the A850, between Portree and Dunvegan, Edinbane, Skye (☎ 01470-582-234; E-mail: stuart@edinbane-pottery.co.uk; Internet: www.edinbane-pottery.co.uk). This wonderful little showroom and workshop has an excellent selection of unique items. The glazed landscape design on the glassware and ceramics gives the items a style you won't find anywhere else. Edinbane is famous on the island for its pottery and ships its wares around the world. Open: Daily from 9 a.m. to 7 p.m.

✔ **Isle of Mull Silver Co.,** Main Street, Tobermory, Mull (☎ 01688-302-345). Part manufacturer, part retail shop, this little jewelry store makes pieces in-house and has an impressive selection from other suppliers throughout Scotland. It's as if the Silver Co. had cased the country's jewelry stores, so you don't have to. The owners are very knowledgeable about their craft and happy to answer questions and help you find what you're looking for. Open: Monday to Saturday from 9:30 a.m. to 1 p.m. and 2 p.m. to 5 p.m. Hours may be extended in the summer.

✔ **Isle of Mull Weavers,** Craignure, Mull (☎ **01680-812-381**). This wee shop has none of the jackets and kilts you normally find in weavers' stores. This is the genuine article — bundled Shetland wool yarn and tweed by the meter. If you fancy knitting or want to have your tailor make you something from the finest local material, this is your place. The shop is 1 mile from Craignure on the A849; turn off on the driveway to Torosay Castle. Open: April to October, daily from 9 a.m. to 5 p.m.; November to March, Monday to Saturday from 9 a.m. to 5 p.m.

✔ **Kells Gold & Silversmiths Gallery and Workshop,** Craignure, Mull. One mile from Craignure on the A849, turning off on the driveway to Torosay Castle (☎ **01680-812-526**; E-mail: kells@mull.com; Internet: www.kells.mull.com). Using local material such as Iona and Skye marble, this workshop produces a dazzling selection of perfectly crafted Celtic and Pictish gold, pewter, and silver jewelry. It also gives jewelry-making demonstrations, and the experts behind the counter will have the answer to your every query. The shop is 1 mile from Craignure on the A849, in the same cul-de-sac as Isle of Mull Weavers; turn off on the driveway to Torosay Castle. Open: Daily from 9 a.m. to 6 p.m.

✔ **Lewis Loom Centre,** 3 Bayhead, above Cromwell Street, Stornoway, Lewis (☎ **01851-704-500**; E-mail: lewisloomcentre@madasafish.com; Internet: www.lewisloomcentre.co.uk). The condition of this eclectic tweed store says more about the function of a working shop than the quality of clothes. The amiable owner will give a half-hour guided tour and demonstration of his shop for a small sum, but most people visit for the best traditional tweed and knitwear anywhere around. It offers some deals, as well, because you're eliminating the middleman of a regular shop. Open: Monday to Saturday from 9 a.m. to 6 p.m.

✔ **Luskentyre Harris Tweed Company,** 4 Plockropool, Harris (☎ **01859-511-217**). Anybody can go to a woolen shop and buy a tweed jacket. Heck, why even go to Scotland when you can buy tweed in your local mall? This place is the reason you made the pilgrimage to the home of tweed. The weaver Donald Jon and his wife run this little shop and loom inside a shed down a rocky road. You'll find warm hats, scarves, socks, and other clothes. You can see demonstrations of warping, bobbin winding, and wool plying, and even find out what those things are. Take a left at the Golden Road, south of Harris from the A859, and follow it to the small village of Plockropool. Call for hours.

✔ **Over the Rainbow,** On the road heading down to the water, Quay Brae, Portree, Skye (☎ **01478-612-555**; E-mail: SkyeKnitwear@FSBDial.co.uk; Internet: www.skye-knitwear. com). The colorful (as you could guess) knitwear in this tiny shop is of the finest quality. The clothes, blankets, and rugs are all made using local material and techniques passed down through decades of the business. The shop also has excellent designer jewelry and watches. If you don't see exactly what you want, the tailor will size the garment for you and mail it to you at home (which is one less thing you'll have to carry). Open: Daily from 9 a.m. to 9 p.m. summer, from 9 a.m. to 6 p.m. off-season.

✔ **Ragamuffin,** Armadale Pier (where the Mallaig-Skye ferries dock), Sleat, Skye (☎ **01471-844-217**). This excellent independent shop has fashionable clothes, as well as items to shield you from the wet weather. The designer knitwear and original apparel are popular with visitors not just for the innovative design but for the long-lasting quality. Besides every jumper (sweater) you can think of, the cavernous shop also has plenty of other gift items, such as silks, gloves, scarves, soaps, and cards. Don't be surprised if a staff member offers you a cup of coffee while you browse. Call for hours.

✔ **Skye Batiks,** The Green, just off Somerled Square, Portree, Skye (☎ **01478-613-331**); near the ferry terminal, Armadale, Skye (☎ **01471-844-396;** E-mail: info@skyebatiks.com; Internet: www.skyebatiks.com). Designed and hand-loomed on the Isle of Skye, the colorfully designed and comfortable cotton clothes here are uniquely Celtic in design. Don't be afraid to ask questions; after offering you a complimentary cup of coffee, the staff will be more than happy to explain the meaning of the symbols and designs on the gifts and apparel. The remote business gained popularity after being featured on the BBC and now has a second shop. Both offer the same selection. Call for hours.

✔ **Tobermory Handmade Chocolate,** Main Street, Tobermory, Mull (☎ **01688-302-526**). More than a specialty shop, this local chocolatier is famous on the island for its unique handmade confections. The downstairs factory makes the mouth-watering stuff, so if the smells don't entice you to buy, nothing will. It's just off the main road, a block before the ferry terminal and tourist office. Open: March to October, Monday to Saturday from 9:30 a.m. to 5 p.m., plus Sunday from 11 a.m. to 4 p.m. in July and August.

# Doing the Pub Crawl

The region doesn't boast many standout pubs, with a few notable exceptions. Call for the latest opening and closing times.

✔ **Isles Inn,** Somerled Square, Portree, Skye (☎ **01478-612-129;** E-mail: islesinn@hotmail.com; Internet: www.theislesinn. co.uk). This cozy, friendly pub in the center of Portree is a popular joint featuring traditional music most nights, especially in the summer. The fireplace and the thatched-roofed bar add a bit of warmth and kitsch to a clean and amiable drinking experience.

✔ **MacGochan's,** Tobermory, Mull (☎ **01688-302-821;** E-mail: macgochans@aol.com; Internet: www.macgochans.co.uk). Located next to the distillery, this bar occasionally fills up with tourists from the tour buses parked out front. But the place is big enough to accommodate everybody, and it's the only place in Tobermory where you can sit outside and enjoy your beer. Every Friday and Saturday night, Scottish dance bands play (admission $6/$8.70). MacGochan's has a big selection on tap, and the eats are cheap but nothing special. I recommend taking the waterfall path next to the pub if you want to work up a thirst or just walk off your meal.

✔ **Mishnish,** Main Street, Tobermory, Mull (☎ **01688-302-009**). The curious name is Gaelic for "me now." This quayside bar is rather big for such a wee town. The nautically themed pub full of barnacle-encrusted sea glass has two main areas, comfortable red velvet booths, and a warming fireplace. Small back rooms allow a little privacy or a game of snooker. The little stage is for live local and traditional music, usually Wednesday through Sunday night.

# Fast Facts: The Hebridean Islands

### Area Code

The area code for Portree, Skye, is **01478,** for Iona **01681,** Stornoway, Lewis **01851,** and Tarbert, Harris **01859.** You need to dial the area code only if you are calling from outside the city you want to reach.

### Emergencies

Dial **999** for police, fire, or ambulance.

### Genealogy Resources

**"Co Leis Thue?"** (a resource for all the Hebrideans), The Old Schoolhouse, Northton, Harris (☎ 01859-520-258). For Macdonalds, Armadale Castle (see "Exploring the Area," earlier in this chapter).

### Hospitals

Gesto Hospital, Lower Edinbane, Portree. Skye (☎ 01470-582-262). Another hospital is in Salen, Mull (☎ 01680-300-392).

### Information

**Western Isles Tourist Board,** 26 Cromwell St., Stornoway, Lewis (☎ 01851-703-088; Fax: ″ Other tourist offices include: Bayfield House, just off Somerled Square, Portree, **Skye** (☎ 01478-612-137); Pier Road, Tarbert, **Harris** (☎ 01859-502-011); Pier Road, Lochmaddy, **North Uist** (☎ 01876-50-0321); Pier Road, Lochboisdale, **South Uist** (☎ 01878-700-286); Main Street, Castlebay, **Harris** (☎ 01871-810-336); in the Caledonian MacBrayne ticket office at the far northern end of the harbor, Tobermory, **Mull** (☎ 01648-302-182); and opposite the quay, Craignure, **Mull** (☎ 01680-812-377).

### Mail

Post offices are at Gladstone Buildings, Quay Brae, Portree, Skye (☎ 01478-612-533), and 36 Main St., Tobermory, Mull (☎ 01688-302-058).

# Chapter 18

# Shetland and Orkney Islands

## In This Chapter

▶ Finding a bed and a meal for your island stay

▶ Discovering ancient sites from the Bronze Age, Iron Age, and Norse settlements

▶ Shopping for island crafts

Making the long ferry trip or paying to fly to the far northern islands of Shetland and Orkney may seem like time and money ill spent. That's certainly not true, but if you plan to visit the area, know that getting here takes some extra effort.

After you arrive, however, you won't be sorry. The beautiful islands abound with grand views, old ruins, and interesting history. You won't suffer a shortage of things to do and see, either. On the downside, the islands can get quite cold, year-round, with winters often bringing snow. In fact, the location is so far north that in midsummer it gets no darker than twilight. (The islanders call it *simmer dim.*)

You'll also find that your dining, accommodation, shopping, and drinking options are limited at best — and some never rise above mediocre. The exceptions, of course, appear in this chapter. Off-season, the quiet gets even quieter. So, keep in mind that while the Shetland and Orkney islands offer an escape from the crowds, in many ways you are escaping conveniences, too.

 The Shetlands or Orkneys have no "must-visit" pubs, nor any that are of particular historic or musical importance. Of course, you can always get a pint at the local hotel bar or with dinner.

## Shetland and Orkney Islands Orientation

About half of the 49 **Orkney** islands are inhabited — mostly by farmers — with the top sights on the main Orkney Isle. Attraction for attraction, Orkney has more going on than the Shetlands. The island has spectacular cliff scenery and seascapes and plenty of unspoiled nature. The quaint town of **Stromness** has been a natural harbor since Viking days, and **Kirkwall** is a lovely town near most of the major attractions.

Of the 117 islands that make up the **Shetlands,** only about 20 are inhabited. The Norse passed the island chain to Scotland through a marriage dowry in 1469, and the long Scandinavian history shows in the faces of the locals and the architecture of the main town, **Lerwick.** The scenery is beautiful, and nature abounds, from Shetland ponies that roam free to seals and porpoises that live and play along the coasts. If you have only a couple of days to spare in the islands, try at least to make a day-trip to the Shetlands.

# Getting There and Getting Around

For many people, the simplest way to see the islands is to take part in a tour that covers the major sights. You can leave from the mainland or hook up after you get there. If you prefer to drive around the islands on your own, the fastest way is to fly into Kirkwall in the Orkneys (rather than taking the long ferry from Aberdeen to Stromness), and then renting a car. You can take the ferry to the Shetlands from Stromness if you wish. The cheaper but slower alternative is to drive to the tip of the mainland to catch a shorter ferry from John O'Groats to Burwick in the Orkneys. The islands have hundreds of miles of roadway to explore, and frequent ferry service connects them. Both main islands have airports, and flying is not much more expensive than taking a ferry.

- ✔ **By plane: Kirkwall Airport** on Orkney (☎ **01856-872-421**) is 3 miles from the center of Kirkwall. **Sumburgh Airport** (☎ **01950-460-654**) is 25 miles south of Lerwick, Shetland. British Airways serves both airports from several cities in the U.K., including Edinburgh, Glasgow, and London; flights may connect in Aberdeen. Flights link the two islands in the summer.

- ✔ **By ferry: NorthLink Ferries** (www.northlinkferries.co.uk; info@northlinkferries.co.uk) operates service from the mainland to the Orkneys on the following routes: John O'Groats to Burwick, Gills Bay to St. Margaret's Hope, and Aberdeen and Scrabster to Stromness. You can't get to the Shetlands by ferry without going through Stromness first.

- ✔ **By car:** On Orkney, you can rent a car at **Peace's Coach and Car Hire,** Junction Road, Kirkwall, (☎ **01856-872-866**) or at **Scarth Hire,** Great Western Road, Kirkwall (☎ **0186-872-125**). On Shetland, try **Bolts Car Hire** (☎ **01950-460-666**), at the airport, or **Star Rent a Car** (☎ **01595-692-075**), 22 Commercial St., Lerwick, across from the bus station.

## The Shetland Islands

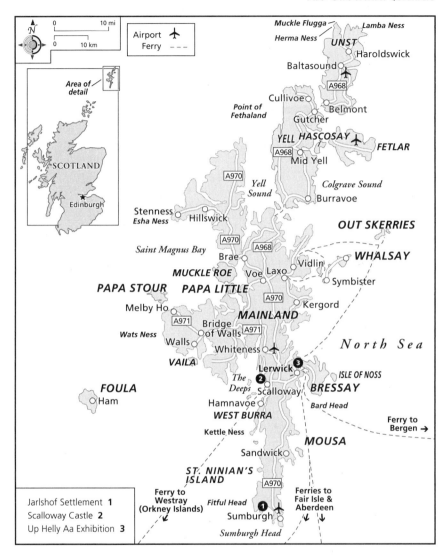

Jarlshof Settlement **1**
Scalloway Castle **2**
Up Helly Aa Exhibition **3**

✔ **By taxi: Cragies** in Kirkwall, Orkney (☎ **01856-878-787**). Taxi service is available at both airports.

✔ **By bus:** On Orkney, **JD Peace** buses (☎ **01856-872-866**) run between Stromness and Kirkwall. For Shetland bus service information, call ☎ **01595-694-100.** As of this writing, bus service was not available from the airports.

**TIP**

You can make arrangements with many car-rental agencies for free vehicle pick-up and delivery at ferry landings and airports.

# Knowing Where to Stay

Your best hotel options are on Orkney, and each of these top picks serves excellent meals — a good thing, because outstanding restaurants can be hard to find in the islands.

### Ayre Hotel

**$$ Kirkwall, Orkney**

This renovated 18th-century town house has plenty of room and hospitality for everyone. Besides the cozy, simply decorated rooms and the friendly service you'd expect from a family-run hotel, the Ayre has two popular bars and live entertainment a couple nights a week, making this one of the liveliest accommodations you'll find. The whitewashed building is near the town center and by the water. Ask for a room with a view of the sea.

*Ayre Road.* ☎ **01856-873-001.** *Fax: 01856-876-289. E-mail:* ayrehotel@btconnect. com. *Internet:* www.ayrehotel.co.uk. *Rack rates: £90–£100 ($131–$145) double. AE, MC, V.*

### Ferry Inn

**$ Stromness, Orkney**

This intimate inn is one of two top choices for an overnight in Stromness (besides the Stromness Hotel, listed later in this section). Located conveniently by the ferry terminal, the pretty little inn is simply decorated; you won't miss all the fancy linens and old furniture — and if you do, stay at the Stromness Hotel. The very friendly staff members go out of their way to make sure you have everything you need. The renovated three-story building makes for a nice warm night in a chilly part of the country. The restaurant serves excellent dishes using local ingredients.

*John Street.* ☎ **01856-850-280.** *Fax: 01856-851-332. Rack rates: £40–£50 ($58–$73) double. AE, MC, V.*

### Foveran Hotel

**$$ Near Kirkwall, Orkney**

On 34 acres of beautiful grounds overlooking the waters of Scapa Flow, this lovely little hotel with a fireplace and IKEA-like furniture is a popular spot for visitors. The architecture and decor are Scandinavian, and the attitude of the staff is friendly and informal. If you decide to eat in-house, you'll have excellent Scottish grub, renowned in its own right. Most rooms have a sea view.

*On the A964/Orphir Road, St. Ola, just outside Kirkwall, Orkney.* ☎ **01856-872-389.** *Fax: 01856-876-430. Rack rates: £70 ($102) double. MC, V. Closed Jan.*

## The Orkney Islands

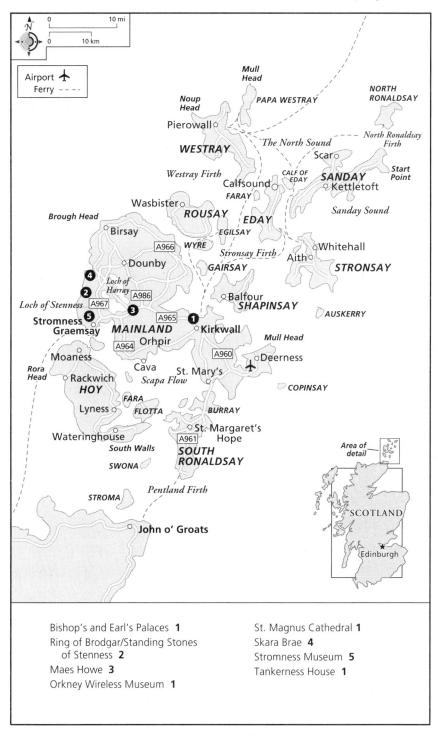

0       10 mi
0       10 km

Airport ✈
Ferry - - - -

Mull
Head

Noup
Head

PAPA WESTRAY

NORTH
RONALDSAY

Pierowall○

The North Sound

North Ronaldsay
Firth

WESTRAY

Scar○

Start
Point

Westray Firth

CALF OF
EDAY

SANDAY

Calfsound○

○Kettletoft

FARAY

Wasbister○

ROUSAY

Sanday Sound

Brough Head

EDAY

Birsay○

EGILSAY

○Dounby

A966

WYRE

Stronsay Firth

Aith○

○Whitehall

GAIRSAY

STRONSAY

**④**

Loch of
Harray

**②**

A967

A986

○Balfour

AUSKERRY

SHAPINSAY

Loch of Stenness

**⑤**

**③**

A965

**①**

Stromness○

MAINLAND

○Kirkwall

Graemsay○

Orphir

Mull Head

A964

A960

Moaness○

Cava

St. Mary's

○Deerness

Rora
Head

○Rackwich

Scapa Flow

COPINSAY

HOY

FARA

Lyness○

FLOTTA

BURRAY

Wateringhouse○

○St. Margaret's
Hope

A961

South Walls

SOUTH
RONALDSAY

SWONA

STROMA

Pentland Firth

○John o' Groats

Area of
detail

SCOTLAND

★
Edinburgh

Bishop's and Earl's Palaces  **1**
Ring of Brodgar/Standing Stones
 of Stenness  **2**
Maes Howe  **3**
Orkney Wireless Museum  **1**

St. Magnus Cathedral  **1**
Skara Brae  **4**
Stromness Museum  **5**
Tankerness House  **1**

### Grand Hotel
$$   **Lerwick, Shetland**

If you want to spend the night in the Shetlands, this is your place. Located in the middle of the capital, Lerwick, this old-fashioned structure is quite grand. The building has an impressive castellated design with gables and turrets, and it's only a block from the water. The service is top-notch, and the rooms are as fancy as the building. The digs may look old, but the facilities are quite modern. In addition to the bar and coffee shop, the hotel has its own beauty salon and even a nightclub, the only one in the Shetlands.

*149 Commercial St.* ☎ **01595-692-826.** *Fax: 01595-694-048. Rack rates: £67–£95 ($97–$138) double. MC, V.*

### Stromness Hotel
$$   **Stromness, Orkney**

The largest hotel on Orkney is well worth a stay. The central location is picturesque, and the hotel underwent a major refurbishment five years ago. Many of the rooms in this traditional stone building with bay windows overlook the harbor and Scapa Flow. The furniture may be a bit old-fashioned, but the staff is committed to modern standards. One of the best features of the hotel is the live traditional music shows it hosts for its guests.

*The Pierhead, Victoria Terrace.* ☎ **01856-850-298.** *Fax: 01856-850-610. E-mail:* info@stromnesshotel.com. *Internet:* www.stromnesshotel.com. *Rack rates: £60–£80 ($87–$116) double. MC, V.*

# Dining in the Shetland and Orkney Islands

Fresh fish, meat, and game dominate local menus. Look for fresh and smoked salmon, trout, and shellfish. Don't forget that many of the hotels and inns mentioned in the preceding section have good dining options on the premises.

### Burrastow House
$$–$$$$   **Near Walls, Shetland   Scottish**

If there is better food on the Shetlands, I can't find it. This is the one standout restaurant that's worth the drive. If you're going to spend the evening on the island, book a dinner reservation here. The meals are heavy on fish and game (sorry, vegetarians), wonderfully prepared and garnished with local produce. While sheep graze on the grass outside, you'll be grazing on mussel stew, lamb, monkfish, homemade soups and breads, and more. It's delicious, traditional food served in a traditional-looking oak-paneled dining area.

*Three miles from Walls.* ☎ **01595-809-307.** *Reservations required for dinner. Main courses: £9–£18.25 ($13–$27). MC, V. Open: Apr–Sept daily 12:30–2 p.m.; Tues–Sat 7:30–9 p.m.*

### Creel Restaurant

$$$ **St. Margaret's Hope, South Ronaldsay, Orkney**
**Scottish/Seafood**

You may think that you'd have to settle for a mediocre meal way out here in the northern isles. Not so at the friendly Creel, arguably the best eats on Orkney. Everything is so fresh and the service is so good, you won't doubt for a second that it's worth the time and price. Meat and fish dishes dominate the menu, but you shouldn't pass on the puddings or local cheeses. If you want a safe bet, get the Orcadian fish stew — salmon, hake, and turbot in a fresh vegetable and basil stew. The Creel is very popular among locals, so it's wise to book ahead. The restaurant also operates a cozy B&B that serves a good breakfast, too.

*Front Road, St. Margaret's Hope, South Ronaldsay, 20 minutes south of Kirkwall.* ☎ **01856-831-311.** *Reservations recommended. Main courses: £10–£16 ($15–$23). MC, V. Open: Apr–Sept daily 7–9 p.m.*

# Exploring the Area

The Shetland and Orkney islands have a good number of major attractions, as well as a lot of minor monuments, archeological sites, memorials, and even small islands you may want to visit. Be sure to stop at the tourist offices on the main islands and pick up the handy maps showing both large and small attractions. You'll find enough to do and see to occupy a few days.

If you plan to stop at all the major and minor Orkney attractions, you can purchase a joint ticket that includes **Maes Howe, Skara Brae,** and other smaller sights. The cost is £9 ($13) adults, £7 ($10) children.

### Bishop's and Earl's Palaces
**Kirkwall, Orkney**

These impressive ruins, built in the 12th century for Bishop William of Old, consisted of a long hall and tower house, an old Norwegian palace design. It is believed that King Haakon of Norway returned here to die. Patrick Stuart built the Earl's Palace next door to the Bishop's Palace in the 1600s. Stuart, a former Earl of Orkney and the illegitimate nephew of

Mary Queen of Scots, was later executed for treason. In its day, the Earl's Palace was considered the finest example of French Renaissance architecture in Scotland — before the money ran out and Stuart's vision fell into disrepair. Illustrated plaques in the Earl's Palace show what life may have looked like when the palace was inhabited.

*Broad Street, across Palace Road from Magnus Cathedral.* ☎ **01856-875-461.** *Admission: £1.80 ($2.60) adults, £1 ($1.45) seniors and students, £.75 ($1.10) children under 16. Open: Apr–Sept Mon–Sat 9:30 a.m.–6 p.m., Sun 2–6 p.m. Closed Oct–Mar. Time: 2 hours.*

## *Jarlshof Settlement*
### Shetland

A storm in 1897 unearthed more than three acres of prehistoric and Norse remains spanning 3,000 years, from the Bronze Age on. Further archaeological digs have uncovered settlements and remarkable artifacts from the different civilizations that have existed here over the years. Sites include an oval Bronze Age house, an Iron Age *broch* (stone house and fortification) and wheelhouses, a medieval farmstead, and a relatively modern 16th-century farmer's house. Sir Walter Scott, who set his novel *The Pirate* around this area, invented the Norse-sounding name of the ancient monument.

*Sumburgh Head, on the southern end of Shetland Island, near the airport.* ☎ **01950-460-112.** *Admission: £2.30 ($3.35) adults, £1.50 ($2.20) seniors and students, £1 ($1.45) children under 16. Open: Apr–Sept Mon–Sat 9:30 a.m.–6:30 p.m., Sun 2–6:30 p.m. Closed Oct–Mar. Time: 2 hours.*

## *Maes Howe*
### Orkney

Dating to 2750 B.C., this burial cairn is the finest megalithic tomb in the U.K. The large mound covers a stone-built passage, a burial chamber, and smaller cells. Look for the inscriptions along the walls written by Vikings who pillaged the tomb's treasures in the 12th century. Crawling through the tomb will bring out the Indiana Jones in you.

*On the A965, 1 mile beyond the Ring of Brodgar.* ☎ **01856-761-606.** *Admission: £2.30 ($3.35) adults, £1 ($1.45) children under 16. Open: Apr–Sept daily 9:30 a.m.–6 p.m.; Oct–Mar Mon–Wed, Sat 9:30 a.m.–4 p.m., Thurs 9:30 a.m.–1 p.m., Sun 2–4 p.m. Time: 90 minutes.*

## *Orkney Wireless Museum*
### Kirkwall, Orkney

During both World Wars, thousands of servicemen were stationed on the Orkney Islands at the Scapa Flow naval base. The museum houses the equipment that the soldiers used and details their wartime history. Items on display include '30s wireless radios and items built by Italian prisoners of war. Anyone who has ever had a ham radio set, likes to tinker in the garage, or is interested in the naval history of the area will enjoy this museum.

*Kiln Corner, Junction Road.* ☎ **01856-874-272.** *Admission: £2 ($2.90) adults, £1 ($1.45) children under 16. Open: Apr–Sept Mon–Sat 10 a.m.–4:30 p.m., Sun 2:30–4:30 p.m. Closed Oct–Mar. Time: 1 hour, 30 minutes.*

### Ring of Brodgar /Standing Stones of Stenness
**Orkney**

These two stone circles, mini-Stonehenges of the north, are as old as the third millennium B.C. The impressive ceremonial sites are amazing and imposing to walk through. The tallest stone of the Stenness group is a whopping 16 feet high. The two circles lie within walking distance of each other — 27 of the 60 stones in the Ring of Brodgar remain standing; only 4 of 12 at Stenness are still upright. When the fog rolls in, it's quite a sight. The origin of the stones is not certain, but they are believed to have been used for some kind of ancient ceremony.

*Between the lochs of Harray and Stenness, Orkney, on the B9055. Five miles north of Stromness, on the A965.* ☎ **01856-841-815.** *Admission: Free. Open: Year-round, 24 hours. Time: 2 hours.*

### St. Magnus Cathedral
**Kirkwall, Orkney**

Dominating the town of Kirkwall, this famous red and yellow sandstone cathedral honors the patron saint of the islands. Back in the 12th century, Magnus Erlendson and his cousin were the co-Earls of Orkney — that is, until the cousin had Magnus murdered. According to legend, a heavenly light shone upon Magnus's grave; soon thereafter he gained a cult following as a healing force. Magnus's nephew (who became St. Rognvald) began construction on the cathedral in 1137. It retains all its grand features, from the narrow naves to the huge sandstone columns to the beautiful stained glass. The relics of both saints lie in the cathedral, surrounded by a mix of Norman, Romanesque, and Gothic architecture. The cathedral also holds a memorial to HMS *Royal Oak,* which a German sub torpedoed and sank off the coast during World War II, killing 833 crew members. On a calm day, on the road south from Kirkwall over Scapa Flow, you can see the underwater outline of the *Royal Oak,* now a National War Grave.

*Broad Street.* ☎ **01856-841-815.** *Admission: Free. Open: Apr–Sept Mon–Sat 9 a.m.–6 p.m., Sun 2–6 p.m.; Oct–Mar Mon–Sat 9 a.m.–1 p.m. and 2–5 p.m. Time: 1 hour.*

### Scalloway Castle
**Scalloway, Shetland**

These amazing ruins dominate the town of Scalloway, dating back to the time when the town served as the capital of Shetland. Earl Patrick Stuart — not a popular figure in these parts — built Scalloway Castle in 1600. In fact, he used forced labor to build it. After he was executed, the medieval building fell into disrepair. The ruins make for good photographs, so bring your camera. If the front door is locked, you can get the key at the Shetland Woolen Co. next door.

*Scalloway center, on the A970.* ☎ **01466-793-191.** *Admission: Free. Open: Apr–Sept Mon–Sat 9 a.m.–5 p.m.; Oct–Mar Mon–Fri 9 a.m.–5 p.m. Time: 1 hour.*

### Skara Brae
**Orkney**

This 4,500-year-old Neolithic village was once home to a few Stone Age families. Buried by a sandstorm thousands of years ago, it was uncovered by another storm in 1850. This Pompeii-like site is one of the best-preserved groups of ancient houses in Europe. You can walk through the half-dozen rooms through covered passage tunnels and see preserved beds and fireplaces. The visitor center contains a replica house that lets you experience what life may have been like when Skara Brae was someone's home. The walk along the shoreline is a windy adventure.

*Bay of Skaill, 7 miles north of Stromness off the A967. From Kirkwall, take the A965 west to the A967 via Finstown.* ☎ **01856-841-815.** *Admission: £4 ($5.80) adults, £1.80 ($2.60) seniors and students, £1.20 ($1.75) children under 16. Open: Apr–Sept daily 9:30 a.m.–6 p.m.; Oct–Mar Mon–Sat 9:30 a.m.–4 p.m., Sun 2–4 p.m. Time: 2 hours.*

### Stromness Museum
**Stromness, Orkney**

This local museum may not be large or full of impressive artifacts, but the exhibitions cover a good range of interesting topics. You'll learn about the German fleet that once roamed the Scapa Flow and the local presence of the Hudson Bay Company (one of the biggest employers in town), and you'll see displays on the area's whaling and fishing industries. One exhibit concentrates on the life and adventures of the explorer and Orkney native John Rae, and a natural-history section covers local birds and insect life. Using artifacts and old photographs, it re-creates local sea life.

*52 Alfred St.* ☎ **01856-850-025.** *Admission: £2 ($2.90) adults, £.50 (85¢) children under 14, £4.50 ($7.45) family. Open: May–Sept 10 a.m.–5 p.m. daily; Oct–Apr Mon–Sat 10 a.m.–5 p.m. Time: 2 hours.*

### Tankerness House
**Kirkwall, Orkney**

This interesting little museum covers every aspect of Orcadian life in the last 5,000 years in engaging and informative ways. The building dates to 1574, when it was a residence for church officials. Exhibits and archaeological finds show the history of Orkney, and a collection of paintings by the native artist Stanley Cursiter presents the landscape of the island chain. The museum also exhibits prehistoric bones, ancient farming materials, Neolithic pottery, and local jewelry and utensils.

*Broad Street, next to St. Magnus Cathedral.* ☎ **01856-873-191.** *Admission: £2 ($2.90) adults, seniors, and students; free for children under 16. Open: Year-round Mon–Sat 10:30 a.m.–12:30 p.m. and 1:30–5 p.m., plus Sun 2–5 p.m. May–Sept. Time: 90 minutes.*

### Up Helly Aa Exhibition
**Lerwick, Shetland**

If you're on Shetland on the last Tuesday in January, you'll want to be in Lerwick for its famous Up Helly Aa fire festival. A huge galley burns at the King George V Jubilee Park (on Kink Erik Street), and nearly 1,000 processioners in Viking costume walk through the town preceding a grand fireworks display. If you aren't visiting then, stop by the Up Helly Aa Exhibition and check out the replica Viking ship used in the parade, as well as costumes, shields, paintings, and photographs. Also here are videos of past festivals, but none of it comes close to the real thing.

*St. Sunniva Street. Admission: £2.50 ($3.65) adults, free for children under 16. Open: Mid-May–mid-Sept Tues, Sat 2–4 p.m.; Tues, Fri 7–9 p.m. Closed mid-Sept–mid-May. Time: 90 minutes.*

# Seeing the Shetlands and Orkneys by guided tour

A guided tour is a smart, convenient way to get around and see the sights on the islands. Here are a couple of the best tours:

- ✔ **Wildabout Orkney Tours** (☎ **01856-851-011** or 07776-378-966; E-mail: wildabout@orkney.com; Internet: www.orknet.co. uk/wildabout). Because you probably won't have a car on Orkney, taking a great bus tour such as Wildabout makes sense. It offers excursions covering slightly different aspects of the island with all the highlights, history, and nature you'd want, including Skara Brae, Maes Howe, and the Stones of Stenness. Your guide will provide commentary on the archaeological, historic, and scenic points of interest. A special tour of wildlife and the night sky takes place in the winter.

You can pick up the bus in Kirkwall at Palace Road next to the cathedral, or in Stromness outside the ferry terminal. Tours run Tuesday through Sunday at 10:05 a.m. (Stromness) and 9:30 a.m. (Kirkwall). A full-day tour costs £16 to £20 ($23–$29). For information, contact Michael Hartley, 5 Clouston Corner, Stenness, Orkney. Time: 4 to 9 hours.

✔ **John O'Groats Ferries** (☎ **01955-611-353** or 01955-611-342). If you're coming from the town of John O'Groats in Caithness on the northern tip of mainland Scotland, and you want the best tour and ferry trip to Orkney, take this one. It offers three tours of Orkney — a "Maxi" bus tour that covers all the sights, a "Highlights" day tour, and a "Wildlife" cruise. You'd be hard pressed to see everything the Maxi tour covers by yourself. Sights include the Ring of Brodgar, the Stones of Stenness, Scapa Flow, and the towns of Stromness and Kirkwall. Another tour runs from Inverness to John O'Groats. Buy your tickets at the John O'Groats Ferry Office on the pier.

Tours operate daily. The Maxi tour leaves at 9 a.m. from May through Sept. The Highlights tour leaves at 10:30 a.m. from June to September 10. The Wildlife cruise departs at 2:30 p.m. from mid-June through August. The Inverness coach leaves from the Inverness bus station at 7:30 a.m. Price: Maxi: £32 ($46) adults, £16 ($23) children; Highlights: £29 ($42) adults, £9 ($13) children; Wildlife: £12 ($17) adults, £6 ($8.70) children, £30 ($44) family; and Inverness to Orkney: £43 ($62) adults, £21.50 ($31) children. Time: Maxi tour 11 hours; Highlights 7 hours, 30 minutes; Wildlife 90 minutes; Inverness 13 hours, 30 minutes.

## Shopping in the Shetlands and Orkneys

The islands are home to many native artisans and craftspeople. They fashion lovely original items, from handmade pottery to jewelry to hand-knitted woolens, the raw materials of which come from the local herds of sheep and cashmere goats.

✔ **Judith Glue Knits,** 25 Broad St., across from the cathedral, Kirkwall, Orkney (☎ **01856-873-536**). The designs on the wool items in this well-known shop derive from traditional ancient patterns and images. In addition to the popular jumpers (sweaters) — just the thing this far north — you'll find stoneware, clocks, jewelry, and yummy preserves. All make for great gifts. Judith Glue's sister, Jane, is a painter, and her landscapes are on sale here, as well. Open: Daily from 9 a.m. to 6 p.m.

✔ **Longship,** 11 Broad St., Kirkwall, Orkney (☎ **01856-873-251**). The high-class, carefully handcrafted jewelry by local designer Ola Gorie bears purely Scottish designs. You'll find Macintosh-style patterns and Viking brooches among the Celtic- and Norse-themed jewelry. Ola brings the Orkney landscape and history into her designs: One of the most popular items is a dragon piece fashioned after the one on the burial chamber at Maes Howe. Open: Daily from 9 a.m. to 5 p.m. (5:30 p.m. in summer).

✔ **Orkak,** 10 Albert St., Kirkwall, Orkney (☎ **01856-873-536**). Since 1967, Orkak has been one of the country's leading designers of gold and silver jewelry. The locally made jewelry at the Orkak Visitor Centre and Shop is excellent, much of it styled with a Celtic theme. The shop has lots of other unique gift items, including crystal, crafts, and pottery. Everything is high quality and made on Orkney. Open: Year-round Monday to Friday from 9 a.m. to 1 p.m. and 2 to 5 p.m., and weekends in the summer, according to demand.

# Fast Facts: Shetland and the Orkney Islands

## Area Code

The area code for Kirkwall and Stromness is **01856,** Lerwick **01595.** You need to dial the area code only if you are calling from outside the city you want to reach.

## Emergencies

Dial **999** for police, fire, or ambulance.

## Hospitals

**Balfour Hospital (☎** 01856-873-166), New Scapa Road, Kirkwall, Orkney. **Gilbert Bain Hospital (☎** 01595-743-300), Scalloway Road, Lerwick, Shetland.

## Information

**Orkney Islands Tourist Board,** 6 Broad St., Kirkwall, Orkney (☎ 01856-872-856; E-mail: info@otb.ossian.net; Internet: www.visitorkney.com). **Shetland Islands Tourist Board,** Market Cross, Lerwick, Shetland (☎ 01595-693-434; Internet: www.shetland-tourism.co.uk).

## Mail

Post offices are at 15 Junction Rd., Kirkwall, Orkney (☎ 01856-872-974), and 46 Commercial St., Lerwick, Shetland (☎ 01595-693-201).

## Police

Lerwick (☎ 01595-692-110). Kirkwall (☎ 01856-872-241).

# Part V
# The Part of Tens

**The 5th Wave**                    By Rich Tennant

Okay, we got one cherry lager with bitters and a pineapple slice, and one honey malt ale with cinnamon and an orange twist. You want these in pints, or parfait glasses?"

# In this part . . .

*I*n this part, I offer my favorite Scottish golf courses, historic sites, pubs, distilleries, nature spots—and maybe you'll find, after you visit these locales, that they become your favorites, too.

# Chapter 19

# Ten (or So) Scottish Golf Courses

• • • • • • • • • • • • • • • • • • • • • • • • • • • • • • • • • • • • •

## In This Chapter

▶ Rubbing shoulders with the golf elite on the Old Course

▶ Sending a ball soaring over the Atlantic

▶ Doing the duffer's dance on the heather

• • • • • • • • • • • • • • • • • • • • • • • • • • • • • • • • • • • • •

*E*ighteen is so much more appropriate than a mere ten don't you think? So this chapter offers 18 picks for where to play golf in Scotland.

I can't say definitively that these are the 18 best courses in Scotland or that they are properly ordered from best to worst. In fact, you can find far more top-notch courses in Scotland than you'll have time to play. The bottom line is that every course has its own unique quality and attractions. Some are more famous than others; some are more difficult than others. This chapter simply gives you my picks for the best of the bunch, listed in order of their greatness.

For every course, call ahead for information about tee times and requirements to play (if any).

## *The Old Course*

The Old Course is arguably the most famous golf course in the world. All the greats have played here, including Mary Queen of Scots. It offers two famously difficult holes: the "Sea" hole (11th) and the "Road" hole (17th) — the only hole I know where you must play the hole off the road.

Corner of Golf Place and the Links Road, St. Andrews; ☎ 01334-475-757. Par: 72.

# Gleneagles Kings

One of the most exhilarating places in the world to play, Gleneagles is world famous for testing the skills of the best players. Much effort went into the course's creation and layout, and the spot is as beautiful as it is challenging.

Auchterarder; ☎ **01764-694-469.** Par: 71.

# Machrihanish

The conditions here are unmatched. Huge greens and unique fairways make this a challenge for high and low handicappers alike. The first hole is famously known for offering an opportunity — when the tide is in — to drive out over the Atlantic Ocean.

Campbeltown; ☎ **01856-810-213.** Par: 70.

# Royal Troon

Despite popular belief, nonmembers can play this famous and fabulous course — provided they have the proper documentation, apply months in advance, and are male. The course has played host to the British Open, and each unique hole provides challenges you've probably not encountered. The 8th hole, or Postage Stamp, is the shortest in Open history.

Troon; ☎ **01292-311-555.** Par: 71.

# Dunbar Course

This stunning natural links course follows the contours of the shoreline and offers unforgettable views across the sea. The most challenging holes are around the turn — the 9th to the 12th — with no let-up on the closing stretch, because even a mild slice will end up on the beach.

East Links, Dunbar; ☎ **01368-862-317.** Par: 71.

# Gullane #1 Course

This is the best course near Edinburgh (only 20 minutes away), and it's regularly a qualifying course for the British Open. Course #1 is the best and most challenging; if your handicap isn't low enough, you can play one of the other two courses.

Muirfield; ☎ **01620-842-255.** Par: 71.

# Carnoustie Championship Course

Although golfers have been playing here since 1560, Carnoustie is an increasingly popular course, in part because it has been the site of several recent British Opens. The course has one of the toughest and longest finishes in the country.

Carnoustie, east of Dundee; ☎ **01241-853-789.** Par: 72.

# Western Gailes

With its unique layout of greens tucked away in hollows, the course requires finesse, accuracy, and precision. This natural course is one of the best in Scotland and easily the best in the Glasgow area.

Irvine; ☎ **01294-311-649.** Par: 72.

# Crail Balcomie Links Course

This excellent course follows a magnificent coastline, with every hole in sight of the water. The clubhouse offers panoramic views of the North Sea. With continual improvements and modifications, the course is gaining a great reputation for being one of the most challenging in the country.

Fifeness, Crail, 11 miles southeast of St. Andrews; ☎ **01333-450-960.** Par: 69.

# Ailsa Course

Ailsa is home to a good amount of Open drama; greats such as Jack Nicklaus, Tom Watson, and Greg Norman have competed for the top prize. The most unforgettable hole is the 9th, Bruce's Castle, where you drive toward a grand lighthouse.

Turnberry; ☎ **01655-331-000.** Par: 72.

# Royal Dornoch Course

This course doesn't have a single bad hole, and its only downside is its location in the far north. You'll have plenty of room off the tee, but placing your drive depends greatly upon the wind and the pin positions. The course is challenging but accessible to nearly everyone.

Dornoch; ☎ **01862-810-219.** Par: 70.

# Elie Golf House Course

From the famed periscope by the first tee to the rock shoreline challenges on the back half, this is an excellent course. James Braid credits this course with teaching him the skills that won him five British Open championships.

Elie, Fife; ☎ **01333-330-301.** Par: 70.

# Glasgow Gailes

A compact, demanding, and well-groomed course, Glasgow Gailes can be fierce, especially if you're trying to drive in a southwest wind. The flanking heather at nearly every hole makes for a uniquely Scottish (and wonderfully fragrant) hazard.

Off the A78, Irvine; ☎ **01294-311-347.** Par: 71.

# Murcar Course

Amid towering sand dunes and sea views, this fine course has a fairly challenging layout that requires more accuracy than strength. The whole course is worth the spectacular 7th hole.

Aberdeen; ☎ **01224-704-354.** Par: 71.

# Prestwick Old Course

The original home of the British Open, this course remains a monument to the early days of golf. It has bumpy fairways, deep bunkers, and many blind shots. This old-school course is well worth the time and challenge.

Prestwick; ☎ **01292-477-404.** Par: 71.

# West Links

Less than a half-hour from Edinburgh, this seaside course offers a great deal of charm and tradition, plus proximity to the capital. The course has a natural layout and several blind shots. Two holes — "Perfection" (the 14th) and "Redan" (the 15th) — are so excellent that golf architects worldwide have imitated them.

North Berwick; ☎ **01620-892-135.** Par: 71.

# Gairloch Golf Club

It may be only nine holes, but this course is a challenging and tricky one. Combine this challenge with a location along a golden beach and overlooking Skye and the Outer Hebrides, and you have a great course for all players. Prince Andrew, the Duke of York, played here when he was in the Royal Navy.

Gairloch; ☎ **01445-712-407.** Par: 71.

# Loch Ness Golf Course

If you're visiting this popular tourist area, this is your spot for a little golf. The parkland course is typical, but the views are amazing. The floodlit driving range is a plus, too.

Castle Heather, Inverness; ☎ **01463-713-335.** Par: 72.

# Chapter 20

# Ten Castles and Other Places That Bring Scottish History to Life

● ● ● ● ● ● ● ● ● ● ● ● ● ● ● ● ● ● ● ● ● ● ● ● ● ● ● ● ● ● ● ● ● ● ● ● ● ● ● ● ● ● ● ●

*In This Chapter*

▶ Knowing where to find the crown jewels

▶ Getting hot on the trail of Bonnie Prince Charlie

▶ Taking tours of the homes of the rich and the royal

● ● ● ● ● ● ● ● ● ● ● ● ● ● ● ● ● ● ● ● ● ● ● ● ● ● ● ● ● ● ● ● ● ● ● ● ● ● ● ● ● ● ● ●

*I*f you're a history buff or get a special charge out of walking in the footsteps of history's giants, put these ten attractions and locations on your must-see list. I list them in preferential order.

## Edinburgh Castle

The country's number-one attraction (see Chapter 10) holds the historic Stone of Destiny and Scotland's crown jewels. When Mary Queen of Scots resided here, she gave birth to the future James VI of England. The excellent CD tour documents a long history of violence and sieges.

Castlehill, Edinburgh; ☎ 0131-225-9846.

## Scone Palace

David I, Macbeth, and Robert the Bruce were among the kings of Scotland crowned on these hallowed grounds, once home to the Stone of Destiny. The Palace alone (see Chapter 15) is an excellent museum.

Braemar Road; near Perth; ☎ 01738-552-300.

# Bannockburn

King Robert the Bruce beat the English troops of Edward II here in a decisive win that secured Scottish independence in the wake of William "Braveheart" Wallace's struggle for Scottish freedom. See Chapter 14 for more on this historic area.

Heritage Centre: Glasgow Road, Stirling; ☎ **01786-812-664.**

# Culloden Moor Battlefield

The English defeated Bonnie Prince Charlie's Jacobite troops here in 1746, ending a valiant but ultimately unsuccessful movement for Scottish independence. (See Chapter 16.) No other military movement followed Charlie after his loss here.

Culloden Moor, 5 miles east of Inverness; ☎ **01463-79-0607.**

# Holyrood Palace

Scotland's first king, David I, built an abbey here after a near-death experience (see Chapter 10). The palace was built for Charles II. A gruesome footnote in history is the murder of Mary Queen of Scots' secretary by her jealous husband in the Palace.

Royal Mile, Canongate, Edinburgh; ☎ **0131-556-1761.**

# Dunvegan Castle

Clan Macleod still owns this fine castle (see Chapter 17), but the massacre of the Campbells of Argyll is what Scots will remember long after the family leaves. The Campbells were invited as guests to a banquet and then murdered. Queen Elizabeth, Sir Walter Scott, and Dr. Samuel Johnson have all been guests here; their thank-you letters (on display) show they had a much nicer time than did the Campbells.

Dunvegan, Duirinish Peninsula, Isle of Skye; ☎ **01470-521-206.**

# Falkland Palace

Eight (and counting) Stuart monarchs have called Falkland their home away from home (see Chapter 14). Mary Queen of Scots lived here as a young girl; her father, James V, died here. The current queen stills pops in from time to time.

High Street, Falkland; ☎ **01337-857-397.**

# Calanais Standing Stones

The "Scottish Stonehenge" is one of the most significant ancient sites in the United Kingdom (see Chapter 17). Much mystery surrounds the purpose and origin of the 5,000-year-old stones, which remain an attraction to pilgrims who camp out here during the summer solstice.

Lewis; ☎ **01851-621-422.**

# Holy Rude Church

Bullet holes both in the walls of this historic church (see Chapter 14) and on grave markers date to the 1651 invasion of Cromwell's troops. John Knox preached the Reformation here, and other events surrounding the succession of kings and queens who once called Stirling home took place at the church.

St. John Street, Stirling; ☎ **01786-47-5275.**

# Glamis Castle

Glamis (see Chapter 15) was the childhood home of Queen Elizabeth II and the birthplace of Princess Margaret. But English majors will recognize the name as the setting for Shakespeare's *Macbeth* — even though the Thane of Cawdor never actually lived here.

Glamis; ☎ **01307-840-393.**

# Chapter 21

# Ten Top Scotland Distilleries

*In This Chapter*

▶ Capturing the bottling process up close

▶ "Nosing" about for a taste of the good stuff

▶ Soaking up the view with a dram in hand

**S**cotland has many distilleries, but not all distilleries are created equal. This chapter gives you my ten favorites, in order of their greatness. For the majority of these distilleries, see Chapter 15 for more information on the surrounding areas; for a few, other chapter references are given.

One disclaimer, however: Not everyone has the same palate or the same opinions, so you'll have to do your own taste tests. Poor you.

## Glenfiddich

If you haven't heard of Glenfiddich, you have little business looking at this list. In addition to being hugely popular, this is the only distillery where you can see the Scotch being bottled on the premises.

Dufftown; ☎ 01340-820-373.

## Talisker

The tour at this distillery is one of the best in the country and produces the quintessential island flavor of peaty whisky. You'll find Talisker in popular blends like Dewar's and Johnnie Walker. See Chapter 17 for additional information about this region.

Carbost, Skye; ☎ 01478-640-314.

# Strathisla

This fine single malt is better known for being the main ingredient in Chivas Regal, one of the most popular blended whiskys in the world. The distillery tour ends with an informative and unique "nosing" of different whiskys from the various regions of Scotland.

Seafield Avenue, Keith; ☎ **01542-783-044.**

# Glenlivet

The whisky is popular, the tour is quite good, and the reception area is a joy to relax in while you sip your dram of yummy Highland Scotch.

Ten miles north of Tomintoul; ☎ **01542-783-220.**

# Dalwhinnie

The "highest distillery" in Scotland is in a beautiful valley of heather, which adds to the whisky's flavor. The tour of this distillery is good, too.

Dalwhinnie; ☎ **01528-522-208.**

# The Glenturret

It's one of the oldest distilleries in the country, and the tours and audiovisual presentation make this one unforgettable. Glenturret's smoky or roasted aroma is unique to the region.

Crieff; ☎ **01764-656-565.**

# Glen Grant

The beautiful gardens on the grounds are a highlight of this fine family-run distillery. After the decent tour, take your dram of whisky out to the Dram Pavilion to soak in the view.

Rothes; ☎ **01542-783-318.**

# Edradour

Edradour is the smallest distillery in Scotland, putting out only 12 casks a week. The picturesque buildings and grounds are unforgettable.

Between Edradour and Pitlochry; ☎ **01796-472-095.**

# Laphroaig

The taste of this unique whisky takes on the local peat and sea air (see Chapter 13). For such a fine distillery tour, it's odd that you have to make an appointment.

Port Ellen; ☎ **01496-302-418.**

# Tobermory

The tour is short, but the tasting is tall. Tobermory is on the waters of its picturesque namesake town (see Chapter 17), and it's one of the best things going on there.

On the harbor in Tobermory, Mull; ☎ **01688-302-645.**

# Chapter 22

# Ten Great Scottish Pubs

*W*hat, exactly, makes the perfect pub or bar? The answer lies in a combination of good service, excellent whisky and stout, and a welcoming interior. For different reasons and many shared ones, the pubs listed in this chapter are the best in a country full of fine watering holes. I'm sure I've missed some hidden gems, but after plenty of "research," here's what I've uncovered, listed in preferential order.

## Claichaig Inn

This traditional pub is as woody and sheltering inside as it is outside. It's in the heart of Glencoe (see Chapter 16), with excellent views. The place is popular with hikers, tourists, and locals alike.

Glencoe; ☎ **01855-811-252.**

## Brunswick Cellar

This hip underground bar with candlelight and wood furniture has more atmosphere than you can shake a stick at. The staff and the drinks on tap are top-shelf, and the music is cool but not loud. See Chapter 11.

239 Sauchiehall St., Glasgow; ☎ **0141-353-0131.**

# Bannerman's

Located in an old brick building and decorated with posters and old couches, this is the kind of spot you'd like to see in your own neighborhood so that you could be a regular. Great music gets the patrons on their feet, as well. Chapter 10 has more on the area.

212 Cowgate, Edinburgh; ☎ **0131-556-3254.**

# Prince of Wales

This old-fashioned pub — with private booths, wood furniture, stone floors, and an excellent spectrum of ales — gets crowded from time to time, but it's worth the wait at the bar. The whisky selection is excellent, and so is the Guinness pie. Take a peek at Chapter 15 for more on the area.

7 St. Nicholas Lane, Aberdeen; ☎ **01224-640-597.**

# Republic Bier Halle

There's nothing Scottish about this subterranean beer hall, but its worldwide beer selection and boisterous crowds sitting along the long, wooden tables make it pure fun. See Chapter 11.

9 Gordon St., Glasgow; ☎ **0141-204-0706.**

# White Hart

Sir Walter Scott, William Wordsworth, and Robert Burns all enjoyed a pint or two here in their day. These days, the clientele is largely students. The drink specials are great, the service is fast, and the live music is good. See Chapter 10 for more on the area.

34 Grassmarket, Edinburgh; ☎ **0131-226-6997.**

# Ben Nevis Pub

"GOOD FOOD, GOOD BEER, GOOD COMPANY" reads the sign along of the roof beams of this old pub. True on all accounts. The fireplace and pool table are nice distractions, as is the music. See Chapter 16 for more on the region.

103–109 High St., Fort William; ☎ **01397-702-295.**

# The Commercial

By day a quiet pub, popular with whisky drinkers; at night the Commercial is the social mecca of the region (discussed in Chapter 13), popular with just about everyone. You'll often find tasty local micro-brews among the beer selection.

Campbeltown; ☎ **01586-553-703.**

# The Ensign Ewart

Just outside Edinburgh Castle (discussed in Chapter 10), this small pub is a popular place for visitors — but in spite of all the tourists, the place is fun, and the beers, jukebox, and pub grub are all great. The only problem is finding a seat.

521 Lawnmarket (Royal Mile), Edinburgh; ☎ **0131-225-7440.**

# Oban Inn

This classic whitewashed pub near the water is popular for serving an excellent range of fine whiskys. The crowds are always friendly, and the service usually comes with a smile. See Chapter 13 for information on the town that bears this inn's name.

Stafford Street, Oban; ☎ **01631-562-484.**

# Chapter 23

# Ten Top Natural Attractions in Scotland

• • • • • • • • • • • • • • • • • • • • • • • • • • • • • • • • • • • • • • • • • • • • • •

### In This Chapter

▶ Climbing every munro

▶ Seeing sea monsters (maybe)

▶ Frolicking with reindeer

▶ Taking the high road to Arthur's Seat

• • • • • • • • • • • • • • • • • • • • • • • • • • • • • • • • • • • • • • • • • • • • • •

**S**cotland is more than just the golf courses, castles, and distilleries discussed in Chapters 19 through 22. The country is also home to some of the prettiest countryside you can imagine. Whether you like to hike, watch birds, or just hunt for perfect photographic backdrops, take in as many of these top nature spots as you can. I list them in preferential order, with my favorites first.

## Ben Nevis

The tallest mountain in Scotland offers a popular climb if you have the stamina and enough warm clothes to reach the top. The climb is a rite of passage among Scots, but it's also a fun bit of exercise. Nevis has a gondola and ski area if you enjoy coming down more than going up.

Fort William (see Chapter 16).

## Glencoe

This lovely glen runs 7½ miles and is beautiful every step of the way — even though it's best known as the site of a bloody massacre. You can climb Ossian's Ladder to a famous cave or take a more moderate ranger-led hike.

Glencoe, Ballachulish (see Chapter 16).

# Loch Ness

Monster hunting aside, this huge lake in the middle of Scotland is a natural wonder. As you drive along the loch, you'll pass a number of plaques containing fascinating information on the largest freshwater deposit in the United Kingdom. But the best way to see the loch is by boat; sign up for one of the excellent tours.

Western Highlands (see Chapter 16).

# Glen Lyon

William Wordsworth and Alfred Lord Tennyson lauded this picturesque spot where the River Lyon runs through the hills. Eagles soar above, fish swim below, and if you make your way to the head of the loch, you can see an impressive dam.

Near Aberfeldy (see Chapter 15).

# Glenmore Forest Park

The whole family will love this park full of Scottish flora and fauna. You may see otters, wolves, and even reindeer. You can canoe and sail at the park's Watersports Centre.

Kincraig (see Chapter 16).

# Loch Lomond

Take the high road to this excellent lake (or loch) near Glasgow. The pretty scenery is best explored on a boat tour, but plenty of spots along Lomond make good picnic stops.

Central Highlands (see Chapter 13).

# Arthur's Seat and the Holyrood Park

It's rare to find a hike of such natural beauty as close to a city as this magnificent cliff in Edinburgh. You can hike to the top or cheat and drive to the park — either way, you'll find plenty to soak in, especially the views.

Edinburgh (see Chapter 10).

# Ring of Brodgar / Standing Stones of Stenness

These two stone circles are impressive and mysterious ceremonial sites. The area is particularly haunting when the fog rolls in, which is often. The area is a bit of a hike, however — the stones and the two circles are rather spread out.

Orkney (see Chapter 18).

# Butt of Lewis

These beautiful high cliffs over the ocean are worth the drive to the tip of Lewis. Grab your camera: You'll encounter seabirds, seals, and heavy winds blowing spectacular waves against the rocks.

Lewis (see Chapter 17).

# Cuillin Hills

These dark, massive hills make a stunning backdrop as you drive through Skye, and you can also get out and hike the area. Some of the trails are easy, but attempt to climb the peaks only if you're a more experienced hiker.

Isle of Skye (see Chapter 17).

# Quick Concierge

## Fast Facts

### American Express

The Amex International offices in Edinburgh, Glasgow, and Aberdeen exchange money and traveler's checks. Cardholders can get emergency replacement cards and have mail held for them. Offices: 130 Princes St., Edinburgh (☎ 0131-225-7881); 115 Hope St., Glasgow (☎ 0141-221-4366); 35 St. Nicholas St., Aberdeen (☎ 01224-63-3119).

### ATMs

In Scotland, ATMs are called *service tills.* They often connect to large bank systems such as Cirrus, Plus, and Access. Most give cash advances on major credit cards.

### Baby-Sitters

Most large hotels offer baby-sitting, with advance notice, and some guesthouses will make arrangements to find a baby sitter. Some hotels have in-house daycare for small children.

### Business Hours

Most **businesses** are open Monday through Saturday from 9 or 9:30 a.m. to 5 or 5:30 p.m., with some exceptions. Many businesses and shops are closed Sunday. Outside Edinburgh and Glasgow, many businesses close for lunch, generally from 12:30 to 1:30 p.m.

**Bank** hours are normally 10 a.m. to 12:30 p.m. and 1:30 to 3 p.m. on weekdays. In larger cities, some main branches remain open during the lunch hour. Banks are good places to exchange currency and get credit card cash advances.

Most branches of the **post office** are open Monday to Friday from 9 a.m. to 5 p.m. and Saturday from 9 a.m. to 12 p.m. Minor branches are open weekdays from 9 a.m. to 1 p.m. and 2:15 to 5:30 p.m. and Saturday from 9 a.m. to 1 p.m.

**Shops, restaurants,** and **pubs** stay open through the lunch hour (1–2 p.m.), but offices and government buildings generally close during that time. Shops customarily stay open until 5:30 or 6 p.m., and sometimes later in larger cities. Pubs are open from 11 a.m. until 11 p.m. Some bars and nightclubs in cities and larger towns have late-night hours, staying open until between 1 and 3 a.m.

### Cameras and Film

Most pharmacies sell photo supplies and have photo-developing services. One-hour film processing is available in larger cities. These services and products are more expensive than in the U.S. If you do have to buy photo supplies or film while you're away, go to a camera shop or department store. Never buy film from a souvenir stand near a tourist attraction, where the mark-up is almost criminal.

It's not a travel myth: **Don't pack your film in the luggage you're checking.** Instead, store it in big, see-through plastic bags so that security people at the airport will pass it around the potentially harmful X-rays (the higher the film speed, the more likely multiple exposures to X-rays will fog the film).

## Currency Exchange

You can change money at any place with the sign BUREAU DE CHANGE. You'll find these at banks, major post office branches, and many hotels and travel agencies. You'll get the best rates in banks. (See Chapter 4.)

## Doctors and Dentists

The Yellow Pages lists doctors under "doctors—general practitioners," dentists under "dental surgeons." Some hotels (but not many) have a house doctor. For medical emergencies, dial ☎ **999.** You can also call ☎ **0800-66-5544** anytime for the nearest doctor. (See Chapter 9.)

## Driving Rules

You'll be driving on the left side of the road in Scotland. (See Chapter 7.)

## Drugs and Firearms

These are strictly prohibited in Scotland. Consult a British consulate before trying to bring any firearm into the country.

## Drugstores

Drugstores are called *pharmacies* or *chemists.* The regulations for over-the-counter and prescription drugs differ from those in the States, so you might not find commercial pharmaceuticals or your preferred medicine. Consider bringing your own from the U.S.

## Electric Current

The electric current in Scotland is 240 volts AC, which is different than the U.S. current, so most small appliances, such as hair dryers and shavers, won't work (and the current could damage the appliance). If you're considering bringing your laptop or iron from home, check the voltage first to see if it has a range between 110v and 240v. You'll still need to buy an outlet adapter, because your prongs won't fit in the Scottish sockets. You can buy one for about $10 at an appliance store or even at the airport. If the voltage doesn't have a range, the only option is to purchase an expensive converter.

## Emergencies

For any emergency, contact the police or ambulance by calling ☎ **999** from any phone.

## Etiquette

This is an important consideration as a tourist. The Scottish are courteous and neither loud nor overly assertive. It's a good idea to make an extra effort to behave in the same manner.

If you find that the locals are making light of your nationality, be good-humored about it. Scots hold no general animosity toward tourists, but they may crack the odd joke. They'll expect you to laugh along and not take it personally or get embarrassed.

One point of etiquette that's in contrast to the States is smoking. Smoking is common, especially in bars and pubs, and smokers are not particularly sensitive to nonsmokers. The only real way to avoid the smoke is to stay outdoors. It's one of the downsides to European travel, so there's little point in making a stink over it.

## Fare Terminology

The terminology for fares is different than that in the States. Tickets for air, train, or ferry are either *single,* meaning one-way, or *return,* meaning round-trip.

## Hospitals

Every city and region chapter lists local hospitals.

## Language

English is the principal language spoken in Scotland, but Gaelic is the official national language. Signs are bilingual, and certain small areas of the country have concentrations of people who still speak the native language.

## Laundry/Dry Cleaning

Many hotels offer laundry and dry cleaning services. It may be cheaper to go to a public laundry, which charges by the load or by weight. Do-it-yourself coin-operated washers and dryers are rare. At most places, you drop off your clothes for pickup either later that day or the next day.

## Liquor Laws

The minimum drinking age in Scotland is 18. Liquor stores, called *Off-Licenses,* sell liquor, beer, and wine, and generally operate during the same hours as pubs (11 a.m.–11 p.m.).

## Mail

Red awnings, signs, and post boxes identify post offices for the Royal Mail. Sending a postcard or a small letter to the U.S. costs 40p (60¢). Mail usually takes less than a week to get to the States. If you're going to mail packages, you can save money by sending them economy, or surface mail. If you need to have mail sent to you while you're on your trip in Scotland, have the sender address the mail with your name, care of the Post Office, Restante Office, and the town name. It'll be held for you to pick up. See Chapter 9.

## Newspapers and Magazines

Many towns have their own small local newspapers. Large British publications such as the *Independent,* the *Daily Telegraph,* and the tabloid *Sun* are everywhere. International publications are available as well. *USA Today, The Wall Street Journal,* and *The International Herald Tribune* are available at a limited number of newsstands and bookstores throughout Scotland.

## Police

For emergencies dial ☎ **999.**

## Radio and Television

The BBC (British Broadcasting Corporation) runs several television and radio stations, each with its own identity (a classical radio station, say, or a news and documentary television station).

The satellite service SKY offers cable and satellite links for more stations. Most radio stations broadcast 24 hours; non-satellite television usually runs between 6 a.m. and midnight.

## Restrooms

Never ones to mince words, the Scots call these *toilets.* Ask for the bathroom and you'll get a funny look. Public toilets, generally found on streets and in shopping malls, may cost 10p (15¢). Toilets are available in most restaurants, museums, pubs, theaters, and gas stations but are generally for customer use only.

## Safety

The occurrence of violent crime and theft is very low in Scotland. Scotland has so few guns on the streets that many police don't even carry them. As a tourist, the most important thing you can do is guard yourself against theft. Pickpockets look for people who seem to have the most money on them and know the least about where they are.

## Tax

The tax is 17.5% and applies to pretty much everything you pay for. It's called VAT (value-added tax), and tourists are entitled to a refund of most of it (see Chapter 4). The only time the VAT is non-refundable is for services such as hotels, meals, and car rentals.

## Telephones

There are two types of pay phones in Scotland, **Card-Phones** and **Coin-Phones.**

Buy small denominations, such as £5 ($7.25), so you don't buy time you won't use in the end. Cards are for sale all over, particularly at post offices and convenience shops. See Chapter 9.

### Time

Scotland follows Greenwich mean time, which is five time zones ahead of the United States. So when it's noon on the East Coast of the U.S., it's 5 p.m. in Scotland. The high latitude blesses the country with long days in the summer, with sunset as late as 10 p.m., but the opposite is true in winter, when the sun sets as early as 4 p.m.

### Tipping

Especially at hotels and finer establishments, the total bill often includes a gratuity, usually a service charge of 10% to 15%. Be sure to check the bill to see if a gratuity has already been added — you don't want to stiff a server if the tip hasn't been added, but you probably don't want to double the tip, either. If the service was exceptional, it's appropriate to give a little more. The standard tips for bellhops are 50p to £1 (75¢–$1.45) per piece of luggage. For taxi drivers or other service providers, tip between 10% and 15%.

In restaurants, you're welcome to tip 20% or more, especially if that's what you normally give, but don't feel obliged to or guilty about giving less than normal. Unlike in the U.S., servers in Scotland earn a pretty decent hourly wage. The same goes for table service at pubs — 10% to 15% is normal. Barkeeps aren't tipped at all, normally. This might feel even more odd, but it's the custom. An exception to this is any barkeep who is familiar with American ways of tipping and expects it. To avoid any discomfort, include the bartender in a round, paying enough extra to buy him or her a drink.

### Water

Scottish water is perfectly safe to drink, but finding bottled water is easy if you prefer it. If you can avoid it, don't drink from bathroom sinks. That water often sits in holding tanks, so it's not as fresh as that from a kitchen sink.

### Yellow Pages

The Yellow Pages functions the same as in the U.S. It might be a bit more difficult to locate correct headings, though (lawyers are called "solicitors," for example, and a podiatrist is called a "chiropodist"). If you can't find a certain heading, **directory assistance** is available by dialing 192 for domestic numbers and 153 for international numbers.

# Toll-Free Numbers & Web Sites

## North American carriers

**Air Canada**
☎ 800-555-1212 (Canada);
☎ 800-776-3000 (U.S.)
www.aircanada.ca

**American Airlines**
☎ 800-433-7300
www.aa.com

**Continental Airlines**
☎ 800-525-0280
www.continental.com

**Delta Airlines**
☎ 800-241-4141
www.delta.com

**Northwest Airlines**
☎ 800-447-4747
www.nwa.com

**United**
☎ 800-241-6522 or 800-538-2929
www.ual.com

# European and U.K. carriers

**Aer Lingus**
☎ 800-IRISH-AIR (U.S.); ☎ 020-
8899-4747 (London); ☎ 0645-737-747
(all other U.K. areas)
www.aerlingus.ie

**British Airways**
☎ 800-247-9297 (U.S. and Canada);
☎ 020-8897-4000 or 034-522-2111 (U.K.)
www.britishairways.com

**British Midland**
☎ 0345-554554
www.britishmidland.co.uk

**KLM UK**
☎ 0990-074-074
www.klmuk.com

**Qantas**
☎ 008-112121
www.qantas.com.au

**Ryanair**
☎ 44-0870-333-1231 (U.K.)
www.ryanair.com

**Virgin Atlantic Airways**
☎ 800-862-8621 (U.S. and Canada);
☎ 01293-616-161 or 01293-747-747 (U.K.)
www.fly.virgin.com

# Major car-rental agencies

**Alamo**
☎ 0131-333-1922; ☎ 800-522-9696 (U.S.)
www.alamo.com

**Avis**
☎ 0131-344-3900; ☎ 800-331-1084 (U.S.)
www.avis.com

**Budget**
☎ 0131-333-1926; ☎ 800-472-3325 (U.S.)
www.budgetrentacar.com

**Europcar/AutoEurope**
☎ 0800-2235-5555; ☎ 800-223-5555
(U.S.); ☎ 800-12-6409 (Australia);
☎ 800-44-0722 (New Zealand)
www.auto-europe.co.uk

**Hertz**
☎ 0990-906-090; ☎ 800-654-3131 (U.S.)
www.hertz.com

**National**
☎ 800-301-401; ☎ 800-227-3876 (U.S.)
www.nationalcar.com

# Where to Get More Information

You've got a question. Who do you call? These resources are good for providing a variety of information that can prep you for your trip.

A good place to start is the **Scottish Tourist Board** (☎ **020-7930-8661;** www.visitscotland.com). The board's Web site is your best resource. From accommodations to attractions to general information, this is the first stop in a long line of helpful clicks. The Web site details special offers and promotions and has a listing of tour operators by country to help you plan your trip to Scotland. You can find itineraries and recommended attractions, as well as listings for hotels, guesthouses, B&Bs,

self-catering lodging, caravan and camping sites, serviced apartments, and hostels. Keep in mind that hotels and restaurants sometimes pay to be included in these listings, so the reviews might be biased.

The following regional offices will also provide information. Outside the U.K., the Scottish Tourist Board falls under the British Tourist Authority.

- ✔ **In the U.S.:** BTA, 551 Fifth Ave., 7th Floor, New York, NY 10176 (☎ **800-462-2748;** E-mail: travelinfo@bta.org.uk).

- ✔ **In Canada:** BTA, 5915 Airport Rd., Suite 120, Mississauga, Ontario L4V 1T1 (☎ **905-405-1840;** toll-free: 888-VISIT-UK; Fax: 905-405-1835; Internet: www.visitbritain.com/ca/).

- ✔ **In Australia:** BTA, Level 16, Gateway, 1 Macquarie Place, Sydney, NSW 2000 (☎ **02-9377-4400;** Fax: 02-9377-4499; E-mail: visit britainaus@bta.org.uk).

- ✔ **In New Zealand:** BTA, 17th Floor, NZI House, 151 Queen St., Auckland (☎ **09-303-1446;** Fax: 09-377-6965; E-mail: bta.nz@bta.org.uk).

- ✔ **In the U.K.:** Scottish Travel Centre, 19 Cockspur St., London SW1 5BL (☎ **0171-930-8661**).

## Getting information on fishing in Scotland

Game and sea fishing are very popular in Scotland. The rivers and streams abound with trout, salmon, pike, and more. The two most popular catches are probably **brown trout** and **salmon.** Brown trout season runs from October to March; salmon season is between February and October.

Unlike in other European countries, Scotland does not require a license to fish. Local permits, required for fishing on private land, are available for about £15 ($22) at bait and tackle shops. Local tourism offices have fishing information. To get specific information before you leave concerning the type of fishing you're interested in, contact one of the following organizations:

- ✔ **Scottish Federation of Sea Anglers:** ☎ 0131-317-7192; Internet: www.sfsa.freeserve.co.uk

- ✔ **The Scottish National Anglers Association:** ☎ 0131-339-8808; Internet: www.sana.org.uk

- ✔ **Scottish Federation for Coarse Angling:** ☎ 01592-64-2242; Internet: www.sfca.co.uk

- ✔ **Salmon and Trout Association:** ☎ 0131-225-2417; Internet: www.salmon-trout.org

The one major fishing touring company, **Fishing Scotland,** leads fly, spin, and bait fishing excursions for individuals, small groups, families, and kids. It covers instruction, coaching, all fishing tackle, and wellie boots. The Web site is also a fly-fishing encyclopedia including fishing guide books for the Highlands and Argyll. Contact: James Coutts, Roy Bridge, Inverness-shire, Scotland PH31 4AG (☎ **01397-712-812;** E-mail: gofishing@fishing-scotland.co.uk; Internet: www.fishing-scotland.co.uk).

# Getting information on outdoor tours

Scotland has no shortage of woodland trails, coastal hikes, and highland climbs. Hiking in Scotland is a popular pastime and a great form of exercise — especially for tourists who sit in a rental car and restaurants for most of the day. This book mentions a few hikes; if you want to know about a good convenient spot, ask the local tourism center wherever you are, and they'll find something that meets your abilities.

The most popular climbing in Scotland is **munro bagging.** Any mountain higher than 3,000 feet is called a *munro,* and many Scots make a hobby of climbing as many munros as they can and keeping a record of each climb. ("Bagging" is a climber term meaning to reach the summit of a mountain.) The name comes from Sir Hugh Munro of Linderlis, the first person to catalog all the major mountains of Scotland.

For beginners and visitors, the most climber-friendly munros are **Ben Lomond** (from Rowardennan at Loch Lomond), **An Teallach** (from Dundonnell), **Ben More** on the island of Mull, and **Blah Bheinn** of the Cuillin range on the Isle of Skye. The highest of the munros is **Ben Nevis** near Fort William, which you shouldn't attempt without a guide. If you want to climb one of these peaks, visit a local tourism center for a trail map, start early in the day so that you're back before sundown, and take water, good hiking boots, and a warm jacket (it gets chilly at the higher elevations).

- ✔ **Scot Trek:** Walking tours throughout Scotland. Contact: 9 Lawrence St., Glasgow G11 5HH (☎ **0141-334-9232**).

- ✔ **C-N-Do Scotland:** Guided walking and mountaineering activities year-round, from day-trips to two-week packages, for all ages and levels of ability. Contact: Unit 32, Stirling Enterprise Park, Stirling FK7 7RP (☎ **01786-445-703;** E-mail: info@cndoscotland.com; Internet: www.cndoscotland.com).

- ✔ **Albannach Guided Walking and Wildlife Holidays:** Low-impact, all-inclusive hiking holidays in the Highlands and islands for small groups, emphasizing wildlife and history; good for older folks. Contact: Sandy Mitchell, 6 Burn Farm, Killen, Avoch, Rosshire IV9 8RG (☎ **01463-811-770;** Fax: 01463-811-555; E-mail: Alban79@aol.com).

✔ **Alfresco Adventure:** Wilderness canoe trips, mountain biking, orienteering, clay-pigeon shooting, fishing, and more. Also, canoes and camping equipment rentals if you prefer to go it alone. Contact: Camus-na-Heiridhe, Onich, Fort William PH33 6SA (☎ **01855-821-248;** E-mail: alfrescoadventure@zetnet.co.uk).

## Surfing favorite Web sites

The following are some of my favorite Web sites for information on Scotland and travel tips in general.

✔ **Currency Converter** (www.xe.net/ucc/): Why do all that math in your head? This currency converter will do it for you.

✔ **Genealogy** (www.genuki.org.uk/big/sct/): The top guide to tracing your Scottish ancestry, broken down by region — encyclopedic, to say the least.

✔ **Famous Scots** (www.geo.ed.ac.uk/home/scotland/greatscots.html): Want to know more about the famous Scots whose names you'll encounter as you travel? Go here.

✔ **Newspapers** (www.start4all.com/newspapers/uk.htm): Want to catch up on local Scottish news before you go? From gossipy tabloids to mainstream papers, this site offers all the online links.

✔ **State Department** (http://travel.state.gov/travel_warnings.html): The site every American should consult before leaving the country. From water warnings to passport information, the user-friendly State Department site is very informative.

✔ **Strange Tales** (www.electricscotland.com/history/strange.htm): This small page contains interesting tales of Scottish lore that make for good reading on the plane or before bed.

✔ **The Universe of Bagpipes** (www.hotpipes.com): Can't get enough of the pipes? Check out Oliver Seeler's site for history, articles, a beginner's guide for players, and more.

✔ **Vegetarian Guide** (www.veggieland.co.uk): Vegetarians can use all the extra tips and help they can get in a meat-and-potatoes country like Scotland. This site is the best reference.

✔ **Weather** (www.weather.com/): Before you leave home, get an accurate forecast for the places you plan to visit.

✔ **Word of the Day** (www2.scotland.net/frontpage/word/word_up.cfm): Scottish phrases, words, and slang decoded for you.

# Making Dollars and Sense of It

| Expense | Daily cost | x | Number of days | = | Total |
|---------|-----------|---|----------------|---|-------|
| Airfare | | | | | |
| Local transportation | | | | | |
| Car rental | | | | | |
| Lodging (with tax) | | | | | |
| Parking | | | | | |
| Breakfast | | | | | |
| Lunch | | | | | |
| Dinner | | | | | |
| Snacks | | | | | |
| Entertainment | | | | | |
| Babysitting | | | | | |
| Attractions | | | | | |
| Gifts & souvenirs | | | | | |
| Tips | | | | | |
| Other | | | | | |
| *Grand Total* | | | | | |

# Fare Game: Choosing an Airline

When looking for the best airfare, you should cover all your bases — 1) consult a trusted travel agent; 2) contact the airline directly, via the airline's toll-free number and/or Web site; 3) check out one of the travel-planning Web sites, such as www.frommers.com.

Travel Agency_____ Phone_____
  Agent's Name_____ Quoted fare_____

Airline 1_____ Quoted fare_____
  Toll-free number/Internet_____

Airline 2_____ Quoted fare_____
  Toll-free number/Internet_____

Web site 1_____ Quoted fare_____

Web site 2_____ Quoted fare_____

## Departure Schedule & Flight Information

Airline_____ Flight #_____ Confirmation #_____

Departs_____ Date_____ Time_____ a.m./p.m.

Arrives_____ Date_____ Time_____ a.m./p.m.

## Connecting Flight (if any)

Amount of time between flights_____ hours/mins

Airline_____ Flight #_____ Confirmation #_____

Departs_____ Date_____ Time_____ a.m./p.m.

Arrives_____ Date_____ Time_____ a.m./p.m.

## Return Trip Schedule & Flight Information

Airline_____ Flight #_____ Confirmation #_____

Departs_____ Date_____ Time_____ a.m./p.m.

Arrives_____ Date_____ Time_____ a.m./p.m.

## Connecting Flight (if any)

Amount of time between flights_____ hours/mins

Airline_____ Flight #_____ Confirmation #_____

Departs_____ Date_____ Time_____ a.m./p.m.

Arrives_____ Date_____ Time_____ a.m./p.m.

# Sweet Dreams: Choosing Your Hotel

Make a list of all the hotels where you'd like to stay and then check online and call the local and toll-free numbers to get the best price. You should also check with a travel agent, who may be able to get you a better rate.

| Hotel & page | Location | Internet | Tel. (local) | Tel. (Toll-free) | Quoted rate |
|---|---|---|---|---|---|
| | | | | | |
| | | | | | |
| | | | | | |
| | | | | | |
| | | | | | |
| | | | | | |
| | | | | | |

## Hotel Checklist

Here's a checklist of things to inquire about when booking your room, depending on your needs and preferences.

- ❏ Smoking/smoke-free room
- ❏ Noise (if you prefer a quiet room, ask about proximity to elevator, bar/restaurant, pool, meeting facilities, renovations, and street)
- ❏ View
- ❏ Facilities for children (crib, roll-away cot, babysitting services)
- ❏ Facilities for travelers with disabilities
- ❏ Number and size of bed(s) (king, queen, double/full-size)
- ❏ Is breakfast included? (buffet, continental, or sit-down?)
- ❏ In-room amenities (hair dryer, iron/board, minibar, etc.)
- ❏ Other_____

## Places to Go, People to See, Things to Do

Enter the attractions you would most like to see and decide how they'll fit into your schedule. Next, use the "Going My Way" worksheets that follow to sketch out your itinerary.

| Attraction/activity | Page | Amount of time you expect to spend there | Best day and time to go |
|---|---|---|---|
| | | | |
| | | | |
| | | | |
| | | | |
| | | | |
| | | | |
| | | | |
| | | | |
| | | | |
| | | | |
| | | | |
| | | | |
| | | | |

## Going "My" Way

### Day 1

Hotel_____ Tel._____

Morning_____

_____

Lunch_____ Tel._____

Afternoon_____

_____

Dinner_____ Tel._____

Evening_____

_____

### Day 2

Hotel_____ Tel._____

Morning_____

_____

Lunch_____ Tel._____

Afternoon_____

_____

Dinner_____ Tel._____

Evening_____

_____

### Day 3

Hotel_____ Tel._____

Morning_____

_____

Lunch_____ Tel._____

Afternoon_____

_____

Dinner_____ Tel._____

Evening_____

_____

## Going "My" Way

**Day 4**

Hotel_____ Tel._____

Morning_____

_____

Lunch_____ Tel._____

Afternoon_____

_____

Dinner_____ Tel._____

Evening_____

_____

**Day 5**

Hotel_____ Tel._____

Morning_____

_____

Lunch_____ Tel._____

Afternoon_____

_____

Dinner_____ Tel._____

Evening_____

_____

**Day 6**

Hotel_____ Tel._____

Morning_____

_____

Lunch_____ Tel._____

Afternoon_____

_____

Dinner_____ Tel._____

Evening_____

_____

# Index

● **Z** ●

## FOR DUMMIES®

**Helping you expand your horizons and realize your potential**

---

## PERSONAL FINANCE & BUSINESS

**Investing**
0-7645-2431-3

**Home Buying**
0-7645-5331-3

**Grant Writing**
0-7645-5307-0

### Also available:

Accounting For Dummies
(0-7645-5314-3)

Business Plans Kit For Dummies
(0-7645-5365-8)

Managing For Dummies
(1-5688-4858-7)

Mutual Funds For Dummies
(0-7645-5329-1)

QuickBooks All-in-One Desk Reference For Dummies
(0-7645-1963-8)

Resumes For Dummies
(0-7645-5471-9)

Small Business Kit For Dummies
(0-7645-5093-4)

Starting an eBay Busine For Dummies
(0-7645-1547-0)

Taxes For Dummies 200
(0-7645-5475-1)

---

## HOME, GARDEN, FOOD & WINE

**Feng Shui**
0-7645-5295-3

**Gardening**
0-7645-5130-2

**Cooking**
0-7645-5250-3

### Also available:

Bartending For Dummies
(0-7645-5051-9)

Christmas Cooking For Dummies
(0-7645-5407-7)

Cookies For Dummies
(0-7645-5390-9)

Diabetes Cookbook For Dummies
(0-7645-5230-9)

Grilling For Dummies
(0-7645-5076-4)

Home Maintenance Fo Dummies
(0-7645-5215-5)

Slow Cookers For Dummies
(0-7645-5240-6)

Wine For Dummies
(0-7645-5114-0)

---

## FITNESS, SPORTS, HOBBIES & PETS

**Fitness**
0-7645-5167-1

**Golf**
0-7645-5146-9

**Guitar**
0-7645-5106-X

### Also available:

Cats For Dummies
(0-7645-5275-9)

Chess For Dummies
(0-7645-5003-9)

Dog Training For Dummies
(0-7645-5286-4)

Labrador Retrievers For Dummies
(0-7645-5281-3)

Martial Arts For Dummies
(0-7645-5358-5)

Piano For Dummies
(0-7645-5105-1)

Pilates For Dummies
(0-7645-5397-6)

Power Yoga For Dummi
(0-7645-5342-9)

Puppies For Dummies
(0-7645-5255-4)

Quilting For Dummies
(0-7645-5118-3)

Rock Guitar For Dummi
(0-7645-5356-9)

Weight Training For Dummies
(0-7645-5168-X)

---

**Available wherever books are sold.**
**Go to www.dummies.com or call 1-877-762-2974 to order direct**

WILE

# FOR DUMMIES®

## A world of resources to help you grow

---

## TRAVEL

 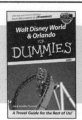

**Italy**
0-7645-5453-0

**Hawaii**
0-7645-5438-7

**Walt Disney World & Orlando**
0-7645-5444-1

### Also available:

America's National Parks For Dummies
(0-7645-6204-5)

Caribbean For Dummies
(0-7645-5445-X)

Cruise Vacations For Dummies 2003
(0-7645-5459-X)

Europe For Dummies
(0-7645-5456-5)

Ireland For Dummies
(0-7645-6199-5)

France For Dummies
(0-7645-6292-4)

Las Vegas For Dummies
(0-7645-5448-4)

London For Dummies
(0-7645-5416-6)

Mexico's Beach Resorts For Dummies
(0-7645-6262-2)

Paris For Dummies
(0-7645-5494-8)

RV Vacations For Dummies
(0-7645-5443-3)

---

## EDUCATION & TEST PREPARATION

 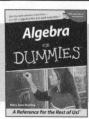 

**Spanish**
0-7645-5194-9

**Algebra**
0-7645-5325-9

**U.S. History**
0-7645-5249-X

### Also available:

The ACT For Dummies
(0-7645-5210-4)

Chemistry For Dummies
(0-7645-5430-1)

English Grammar For Dummies
(0-7645-5322-4)

French For Dummies
(0-7645-5193-0)

GMAT For Dummies
(0-7645-5251-1)

Inglés Para Dummies
(0-7645-5427-1)

Italian For Dummies
(0-7645-5196-5)

Research Papers For Dummies
(0-7645-5426-3)

SAT I For Dummies
(0-7645-5472-7)

U.S. History For Dummies
(0-7645-5249-X)

World History For Dummies
(0-7645-5242-2)

---

## HEALTH, SELF-HELP & SPIRITUALITY

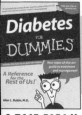  

**Diabetes**
0-7645-5154-X

**Sex**
0-7645-5302-X

**Parenting**
0-7645-5418-2

### Also available:

The Bible For Dummies
(0-7645-5296-1)

Controlling Cholesterol For Dummies
(0-7645-5440-9)

Dating For Dummies
(0-7645-5072-1)

Dieting For Dummies
(0-7645-5126-4)

High Blood Pressure For Dummies
(0-7645-5424-7)

Judaism For Dummies
(0-7645-5299-6)

Menopause For Dummies
(0-7645-5458-1)

Nutrition For Dummies
(0-7645-5180-9)

Potty Training For Dummies
(0-7645-5417-4)

Pregnancy For Dummies
(0-7645-5074-8)

Rekindling Romance For Dummies
(0-7645-5303-8)

Religion For Dummies
(0-7645-5264-3)

---

**Available wherever books are sold. Go to www.dummies.com or call 1-877-762-2974 to order direct**

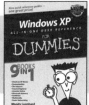

# FOR DUMMIES®

## A world of resources to help you grow

## HOME & BUSINESS COMPUTER BASICS

**0-7645-0838-5**

**0-7645-1663-9**

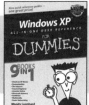

**0-7645-1548-9**

### Also available:

Excel 2002 All-in-One Desk Reference For Dummies
(0-7645-1794-5)

Office XP 9-in-1 Desk Reference For Dummies
(0-7645-0819-9)

PCs All-in-One Desk Reference For Dummies
(0-7645-0791-5)

Troubleshooting Your PC For Dummies
(0-7645-1669-8)

Upgrading & Fixing PCs For Dummies
(0-7645-1665-5)

Windows XP For Dummies
(0-7645-0893-8)

Windows XP For Dummies Quick Reference
(0-7645-0897-0)

Word 2002 For Dummies
(0-7645-0839-3)

## INTERNET & DIGITAL MEDIA

**0-7645-0894-6**

**0-7645-1642-6**

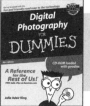

**0-7645-1664-7**

### Also available:

CD and DVD Recording For Dummies
(0-7645-1627-2)

Digital Photography All-in-One Desk Reference For Dummies
(0-7645-1800-3)

eBay For Dummies
(0-7645-1642-6)

Genealogy Online For Dummies
(0-7645-0807-5)

Internet All-in-One Desk Reference For Dummies
(0-7645-1659-0)

Internet For Dummies Quick Reference
(0-7645-1645-0)

Internet Privacy For Dummies
(0-7645-0846-6)

Paint Shop Pro For Dummies
(0-7645-2440-2)

Photo Retouching & Restoration For Dummies
(0-7645-1662-0)

Photoshop Elements For Dummies
(0-7645-1675-2)

Scanners For Dummies
(0-7645-0783-4)

## Get smart! Visit www.dummies.com

- **Find listings of even more Dummies titles**

- **Browse online articles, excerpts, and how-to's**

- **Sign up for daily or weekly e-mail tips**

- **Check out Dummies fitness videos and other products**

- **Order from our online bookstore**

**Available wherever books are sold. Go to www.dummies.com or call 1-877-762-2974 to order direct**

# FOR DUMMIES®

Helping you expand your horizons and realize your potential

## GRAPHICS & WEB SITE DEVELOPMENT

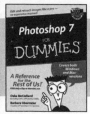

**Photoshop 7**

0-7645-1651-5

**Creating Web Pages**

0-7645-1643-4

**Macromedia Flash MX**

0-7645-0895-4

**Also available:**

Adobe Acrobat 5 PDF For Dummies
(0-7645-1652-3)

ASP.NET For Dummies
(0-7645-0866-0)

ColdFusion MX for Dummies
(0-7645-1672-8)

Dreamweaver MX For Dummies
(0-7645-1630-2)

FrontPage 2002 For Dummies
(0-7645-0821-0)

HTML 4 For Dummies
(0-7645-0723-0)

Illustrator 10 For Dummies
(0-7645-3636-2)

PowerPoint 2002 For Dummies
(0-7645-0817-2)

Web Design For Dummies
(0-7645-0823-7)

## PROGRAMMING & DATABASES

**C++**

0-7645-0746-X

**Visual Studio .NET**

0-7645-1626-4

**XML**

0-7645-1657-4

**Also available:**

Access 2002 For Dummies
(0-7645-0818-0)

Beginning Programming For Dummies
(0-7645-0835-0)

Crystal Reports 9 For Dummies
(0-7645-1641-8)

Java & XML For Dummies
(0-7645-1658-2)

Java 2 For Dummies
(0-7645-0765-6)

JavaScript For Dummies
(0-7645-0633-1)

Oracle9i For Dummies
(0-7645-0880-6)

Perl For Dummies
(0-7645-0776-1)

PHP and MySQL For Dummies
(0-7645-1650-7)

SQL For Dummies
(0-7645-0737-0)

Visual Basic .NET For Dummies
(0-7645-0867-9)

## LINUX, NETWORKING & CERTIFICATION

**Red Hat Linux 7.3**

0-7645-1545-4

**TCP/IP**

0-7645-1760-0

**Networking**

0-7645-0772-9

**Also available:**

A+ Certification For Dummies
(0-7645-0812-1)

CCNP All-in-One Certification For Dummies
(0-7645-1648-5)

Cisco Networking For Dummies
(0-7645-1668-X)

CISSP For Dummies
(0-7645-1670-1)

CIW Foundations For Dummies
(0-7645-1635-3)

Firewalls For Dummies
(0-7645-0884-9)

Home Networking For Dummies
(0-7645-0857-1)

Red Hat Linux All-in-One Desk Reference For Dummies
(0-7645-2442-9)

UNIX For Dummies
(0-7645-0419-3)

vailable wherever books are sold.
o to www.dummies.com or call 1-877-762-2974 to order direct

**WILEY**